MW01200123

A Matter of Complexion

A Matter of Complexion

The Life *and* Fictions *of* Charles W. Chesnutt

TESS CHAKKALAKAL

ST. MARTIN'S PRESS
NEW YORK

First published in the United States by St. Martin's Press, an imprint of St. Martin's Publishing Group

A MATTER OF COMPLEXION. Copyright © 2025 by Tess Chakkalakal. All rights reserved. Printed in the United States of America. For information, address St. Martin's Publishing Group, 120 Broadway, New York, NY 10271.

www.stmartins.com

Designed by Gabriel Guma

Library of Congress Cataloging-in-Publication Data

Names: Chakkalakal, Tess, author.
Title: A matter of complexion : the life and fictions of Charles W. Chesnutt / Tess Chakkalakal.
Description: First edition. | New York : St. Martin's Press, 2025. | Includes bibliographical references and index.
Identifiers: LCCN 2024041788 | ISBN 9781250287632 (hardcover) | ISBN 9781250287649 (ebook)
Subjects: LCSH: Chesnutt, Charles W. (Charles Waddell), 1858–1932. | Novelists, American—19th century—Biography. | African American novelists—Biography. | LCGFT: Biographies.
Classification: LCC PS1292.C6 Z58 2025 | DDC 813/.4—dc23/eng/20240909
LC record available at https://lccn.loc.gov/2024041788

Our books may be purchased in bulk for promotional, educational, or business use. Please contact your local bookseller or the Macmillan Corporate and Premium Sales Department at 1-800-221-7945, extension 5442, or by email at MacmillanSpecialMarkets@macmillan.com.

First Edition: 2025

10 9 8 7 6 5 4 3 2 1

For Fred Flahiff and Leslie Sanders
Teachers ~ Mentors ~ Friends

Contents

PART IV: HOME

PART V: AGE OF PROBLEMS

Distinctions of color are unduly emphasized in the United States.
—Charles W. Chesnutt, c. 1928

Prologue

———— · ————

A Friendship Across the Color Line

Looking back on the meeting that would launch him into the world of book publishing, Charles W. Chesnutt recalled an unusual feeling of freedom. It was September 1897. His train ride from Northampton to Boston had been surprisingly pleasant. The seats were comfortable, and there were no "For Colored" cars to strike him with the usual consternation and dismay. Here, passengers were assigned seats by number, not color. He was fortunate to have a window seat. He looked out at the pretty fall foliage, brooks, and stone fences surrounding golden meadows. This was the New England captured by the great American authors: Hawthorne, Emerson, Longfellow, Melville. But he wasn't thinking of these men. He was thinking of his girls, Ethel and Helen, whom he had just left at Smith College; like most parents leaving college drop-off, he still couldn't believe they were all grown up. When he said goodbye to them at the boardinghouse just a few blocks from campus, his eyes filled with tears. He hoped they would be happy. Helen's joy balanced Ethel's nervousness. He was glad they were starting out together. They were the first "colored girls" to set foot on the green lawns of the pristine campus. At least they would be together. In a few days, they would begin classes at one of the country's most prestigious women's colleges. Helen would study Latin and then go on to teach it at Central High School when she returned home, penning a Latin textbook that would become essential reading for her students. After college, Ethel would marry Edward Christopher Williams, the first professionally trained African American librarian in the United States, who would go on to write literary fiction of his own. Chesnutt loved talking literature with Ed and was thrilled when Ethel and Ed decided to marry after she graduated. What a dashing duo they were, surrounded by books and at the center of Black intellectual circles in Washington, DC. They worked and mingled among members of the literary society her father had taught her to appreciate.

But Chesnutt didn't know what the future would hold for his daughters as he rode to Boston on that autumn day. He wondered what they would study and read. He loved reading to them when they were little girls. They were both the first in the family to go to college as well as the first Black women to attend Smith. Their clothes, including loafers, skirts, and sweaters carefully purchased from Rheinheimer's, their favorite tailor in Cleveland, meticulously packed by their mother, made them appear to fit right in. Chesnutt was sure they would thrive, especially Helen. He glowed just thinking about their life at college, a life he could only imagine.

That feeling of freedom and pride at his daughters' success dissipated by the time he boarded the southbound train in Northampton for Boston. The train pulled up at North Station in Boston, and he made his way to 4 Park Street, the offices of *The Atlantic Monthly*. Now *he* was nervous. He twisted his mustache, smoothed it down, then pulled at it again. He was sweating in his wool coat. The silk buttons, matching vest, and trousers, and his carefully tied Windsor knot, were beginning to wilt. Charles W. Chesnutt, lawyer, stenographer, and writer, was now a fidgety, anxious mess as he sat outside George Harrison Mifflin's corner office. Mifflin, the president of the esteemed Houghton, Mifflin and Company publishing house, held the fate of Chesnutt's career in his hands. Mifflin was going to see right through Chesnutt's carefully assembled attire. Behind the clothes, inside the tie, beneath the silk: Chesnutt feared Mifflin would not see an author but a parochial Southerner, and a Negro, too. These moments reminded Chesnutt that he was an uneducated dropout who had grown up in rural Fayetteville and ended his formal education at the age of thirteen. He knew that forfeiting his own schooling to work as a schoolteacher at the North Carolina State Colored Normal School would hardly impress Mifflin and his new assistant editor, Walter Hines Page. But he waited, wiping his forehead with his white handkerchief, trying to remain calm, until Mifflin opened the door and invited him inside.

Mifflin had gone to the Boston Latin School, graduating the same year Fort Sumter fell to the Confederacy, in 1861. Rather than fighting to defend the Union, as did many of his contemporaries, Mifflin made his way to Harvard College. Mifflin was blessed with affluent pleasures. He spent winters in the family house on the corner of Beacon and Somerset and summers at Nahant, varied by frequent travel abroad. Alongside Mifflin sat Page, a new face at the press who had just been hired as an assistant editor. There was something familiar about Page. He looked serious and formal, with his deep-set eyes, round spectacles, and double-breasted blazer. But as he spoke, Chesnutt could detect a sense of humor, one that matched his own. He had a firm handshake, and Chesnutt accepted the cigar he offered.

Chesnutt had first heard Page's name earlier that year, when he submitted three stories to *The Atlantic*: "The Wife of His Youth," "The March of Progress," and "Lonesome Ben." He knew these were good stories but wasn't sure *The Atlantic* would be interested. It had been almost a decade since one of his stories appeared in the magazine. Chesnutt recalled with pleasure seeing his name appear under the magazine's masthead in August 1887 when the magazine published "The Goophered Grapevine." Less than a year later, they accepted "Po' Sandy." A decade had passed. Surely, no one could accuse him of being a one-hit wonder. But the press had rejected his book proposal for a volume of stories, explaining that "we like your stories—some more than others—but our experience leads us to the conclusion that a writer must have acquired a good deal of vogue through magazine publication before the issue of a collection of his stories in book form is advisable."[1] This letter was not signed by a particular editor, but it reflected the editorial policy of *The Atlantic's* editor at the time. Chesnutt would later bemoan his timing. He was a Black writer who wrote years before the Harlem Renaissance flowered. Years later, he would call himself a "pre-Harlem, postbellum writer," because without the Harlem Renaissance provenance, he could not find a place for his work on the shelves of most bookstores.[2]

Not yet in "vogue," Chesnutt lacked the literary reputation for publication.[3] The trip to help settle his daughters into school in Northampton offered a good opportunity to meet the editors in person. But now he wondered if he'd made a mistake. He wanted to show all of them who he was, a writer with prospects and ideas. Chesnutt was keen to meet them, but also a little nervous. He feared their judgment. He knew too well that he was an outsider, lacking the education and pedigree that seemed essential for entry into the literary world of *The Atlantic*. But since he had received that rejection six years earlier, things had changed at *The Atlantic*. Page was interested in Chesnutt's work; he needed to capitalize on that interest.

From its beginning, *The Atlantic* had been a "miscellaneous" periodical, its concerns—literature, art, science, and politics—were intended to attract a broad, but highly literate, audience. Under William Dean Howells and Thomas Bailey Aldrich, it had become increasingly preoccupied with fiction and criticism. It was under Aldrich's editorship that Chesnutt became an *Atlantic* author, the first "colored" author to publish his fiction in the prestigious monthly. But Aldrich's forced resignation in 1890 marked a shift in the magazine's focus, when Horace Elisha Scudder took over as editor in April. Scudder made it his mission to give more space in *The Atlantic* to articles on contemporary, controversial topics. Chesnutt deliberately avoided controversy in his stories. Scudder solicited articles from those with an insider's perspective on American political life. Scudder wanted stories from men of high birth. Chesnutt was one of those that he would have considered lowly. Scudder was looking for stories about politics and courage, like Roosevelt taming the West. Chesnutt wrote about former slaves and their descendants just trying to make a living. Scudder wanted stories from insiders about insiders. Chesnutt knew he was an outsider, but wanted in. Would his stories be enough? With gatekeepers like Scudder and Howells, Chesnutt knew he didn't stand a chance.

All that changed in 1895, when Scudder tapped Page to be his assistant and possible successor. Unlike Scudder, who had been born and raised among the Boston Brahmins and a graduate of the elite Williams College, Page was "bawn en raise," as Chesnutt put it in a letter to him on May 20, 1898, within sixty miles of Fayetteville, where Page spent his boyhood and early manhood. Like Chesnutt, Page was a Southerner who had made his way to Boston by sheer tenacity. The North Carolina connection was only one of the reasons Page was drawn to his stories. Page thought Chesnutt's stories "illustrated interesting phases of the development of the Negro race" and was eager to publish them "under a common heading" so that they "would produce a better effect than if published separately."[4] Page knew that Chesnutt's stories would be a hard sell among the Boston literati, but that did not deter him from finding space in the magazine for them. Chesnutt was delighted by Page's interest but had no idea that he was also from North Carolina. To Page's left sat Mifflin. Despite a slight discrepancy in power, Chesnutt saw the two men as equals. Page persuaded Mifflin to publish Chesnutt's work—even though he was not well known among those who read. Page wanted Chesnutt to write more. Chesnutt was eager to produce so long as he would be published and paid. That Mifflin promised. *The Atlantic* paid its authors well, better than the magazines and syndicates Chesnutt had written for in the past decade. With Page's encouragement and Mifflin's financial commitment, Chesnutt returned to Cleveland elated, ready to write more, and shared the good news with Susan.

He got home on a Thursday night and reported to his wife what Page had told him, that his stories would come out in the December or January issue of *The Atlantic*. She was less interested in the meeting than she was in Boston. What was the Robert Gould Shaw Memorial like? And was the new public library as grand as she had read about in the papers? And what about Helen and Ethel? What were their rooms like? He answered her questions calmly; he was used to Susan's obsession with the children. Helen, Ethel, Edwin, and Dorothy were her whole world. Susan's devotion to their children was one of the things he loved most about her. Chesnutt decided to wait and think about his meeting with the editors by himself. He lit a cigar after dinner in the comfort of his well-appointed library. It was only there, surrounded by his books, that he could think—and write. Despite his nerves and fear of rejection, he had enjoyed his meeting with Mifflin and Page. But it was Page who would become his friend and ally at *The Atlantic*. With Page on his side, Chesnutt knew his dream of becoming an author was all but guaranteed. So captivated was he by his dream that he neglected to find out much about Page on that sunny day in Boston. It was not until he got back home and returned to his day job as a court reporter and stenographer that he learned who Page really was.

It was quite unusual that Page did not reveal his Southern roots during their first meeting. Chesnutt learned Page's backstory from Mr. Keating, a business associate from New York, a few months after their first meeting.

Chesnutt had "business for several years in connection with a railroad receivership" with Mr. Keating in Cleveland. As Chesnutt explained in his "rather personal" letter to Page on May 20, 1898: "In the course of our conversation the *Atlantic* was referred to whereupon Mr. Keating said that one of his best friends edited the magazine, and mentioned your name, also the fact that you were a North Carolinian by birth and breeding, and a member of the old Virginian family of the same name." Chesnutt blamed his oversight on his own ignorance: "Of course I ought to have known all this before, but when one lives far from literary centers and is not in touch with literary people, there are lots of interesting things one doesn't learn."[5] But the oversight was as much Page's as it was Chesnutt's.

Chesnutt's stories were set explicitly in North Carolina. Why not mention his own familiarity with the place during their conversation? Perhaps Page had good reasons for keeping his past and family connections hidden, not only from the up-and-coming Negro author but also from his colleagues at *The Atlantic*—especially Mifflin, whom he needed to impress. Echoing the resentments displayed by the well-known Basil Ransom, Henry James's controversial Southern hero introduced in his novel *The Bostonians*, Page kept silent about his North Carolina roots. James's novel had been serialized in *The Century* a couple of years before "The Goophered Grapevine" made its appearance in *The Atlantic*. When *The Bostonians* appeared as a novel in 1886, Scudder gave it a long and glowing review in *The Atlantic*. Scudder thought Basil Ransom "was a clever notion."[6] With Ransom, James brought "the antipathetic element from the South" to those readers of *The Atlantic* who had never been in the South. Scudder applauded James's use of Ransom to represent the Southern character: "Suffice it to say that the fact of an extreme Southern birth and breeding count for a great deal in orienting this important character."[7] The same could be said of the real-life Southerner Walter Hines Page, upon whom James might have based his character. Page was not a big fan of James's fiction; he found it to be dull and tiresome, even though he did accept a few of his stories during his time as editor of *The Atlantic*. Perhaps Page saw a little too much of himself in James's Ransom. Or perhaps James's writing revealed that he hadn't spent much time in the South. James, like the other men at *The Atlantic*, was more of a Bostonian than he would have liked to admit. Page was like Ransom: a man of unpredictable temper, diverging in disposition and politics from his Northern, elite colleagues.

Page was born a few years before Chesnutt, in Cary, North Carolina. His parents, Frank and Catherine, hailed from wealthy landowning families who had built the Page-Walker Hotel, but had, like most white Southerners after the war, experienced a major financial setback. Page was eager to leave his family's past behind him and pursue a career in journalism; but leaving the South behind, and making a home among the Northern elite, who despised his kind, proved difficult. After a successful stint at *The Forum*, Page became known for frequent outbursts, perhaps due to the snobbery and prejudices of his Northern colleagues. But his friendship with Chesnutt was set apart by its display of what he frequently called "tar-heel cordiality" in their letters to each other. Though born into very different families, on opposite sides of the color line, Chesnutt and Page shared ideas and a common commitment to reforming—rather than reconstructing—the South.

There has been considerable critical speculation about the Page-Chesnutt relationship. Some, like the editor Joseph R. McElrath, believe that Chesnutt took advantage of Page's generosity and relied too heavily on the talented editor for advice on making his work appeal to publishers and readers. Others, like the critic Robert Stepto, present Page as using Chesnutt to forward his own editorial and political career, imposing his racial views on the less experienced author.[8] After publishing Chesnutt's last novel in 1905, *The Colonel's Dream*, about a former Confederate soldier who moves to New York City after the war, Page moved to England, where he served as the U.S. ambassador to the United Kingdom during World War I. Since much of our knowledge of their relationship is based on their correspondence, what actually transpired between the two men is a matter of interpretation. We do know that Chesnutt and Page met frequently, exchanging ideas, and often engaged in heated conversation about the political currents of the time. Their conversation was especially concerned with the South, a place they knew intimately. Chesnutt visited Page after attending Mark Twain's seventieth birthday party, held at Delmonico's in New York on December 5, 1905, where the most famous literary men and women of the time had gathered to celebrate Twain's life and work. He was the only Black author in attendance. Page did not attend the gala event. So it was up to Chesnutt to tell his editor about all he'd missed—the food, the speeches, the clothes, and, of course, a few tidbits about the other authors who attended. There are no records of their conversations. We also know that Chesnutt valued his friendship with Page deeply and that Page was eager to publish Chesnutt's work. Page was especially drawn toward his work set in North Carolina. He saw it as a way to educate the North about the South, where he, like Chesnutt, had grown up and felt a deep affection, despite its many flaws. However we choose to interpret their relationship, there can be little doubt that they needed each other to tell a new story of the old American dilemma. That these two North Carolinians, living on opposite sides of the color line, found common cause in the pages of *The Atlantic* among the literary elite of Boston is just the beginning of a new story about an old American problem: the problem of racial and regional divisions in the United States. Chesnutt closed his personal letter to Page with a promise:

> I am going to work on the novel I have been speaking of; it is a North Carolina story. With your permission I shall sometime soon write you a note briefly outlining the plot & general movement, and ask you whether there is anything in the subject that would make it unavailable for your house. I am not easily discouraged, and I am going to write some books, and I still cherish the hope that either with my conjuh stories or something else, I may come up to your standard.[9]

It was a promise Chesnutt kept and the beginning of an unlikely literary friendship between two Southerners, one white, one Black, at the turn of the twentieth century in Boston. It is a story that would change the canon of American literature forever. Charles W. Chesnutt would become the first American to write of the American dream from the Black side of the color line. But before we get to the novel that changed American Literature, we must return to the dusty streets of Fayetteville, North Carolina, where his parents met just before moving to Cleveland. This is the story of their firstborn son, Charles Waddell Chesnutt, who would dream of becoming a literary artist in a country divided by race.

PART I

Youth

I

Ancestry

We are under no moral obligation to inflict upon others the history of
our past mistakes, our wayward thoughts, our secret sins, our desperate
hopes, or our heartbreaking disappointments. Still less are we bound to
bring out from this secret chamber the dusty record of our ancestry.

—*The House Behind the Cedars* (1900)

Charles Waddell Chesnutt's father, Andrew Jackson Chesnutt, was one of many Union men who returned to the South after the war, in 1866. Named after the seventh president of the United States, who also hailed from North Carolina, AJ, as he was known among friends and family, was born the free, Black, and illegitimate son of Waddell Cade and Ann Chesnutt of Fayetteville, North Carolina, in 1833. Born out of wedlock, AJ was given his mother's surname; but it was from his father, a prominent landowner in Cumberland County, that he inherited property in Fayetteville, which drew him back to his native state after the war. AJ died in January 1921. He was eighty-eight years old. He lies buried in Brookside, among the Chesnutt clan, in the African American section of Fayetteville's Cross Creek Cemetery, far from the burial place of his white father.

Cross Creek is one of several creeks meandering through Fayetteville from the west as it makes its way to the Cape Fear River east of the town. In the early nineteenth century, when AJ was growing up, about 3,500 people lived in Fayetteville. Fayetteville's population was divided into three categories: white, slaves, and free people of color. It was to this latter group that AJ belonged. "Free persons of color" was simply a label that signaled an individual was free but not considered "white" in a society dominated by an ideology that called for the acceptance of racial categories to justify slave labor. North Carolinians labeled as "free people of color" were assumed to comprise people of African descent, free people of Native ancestry, free persons with heritage in the East Indies, and a variety of individuals with mixed ancestry. Understanding this little-known group, and the lives of the individuals who belonged to it, became central to Chesnutt's life's work, as he became one of the first to write about "The Free Colored People of North Carolina."[1] In this 1902 essay, Chesnutt argued against the popular view "that the entire colored race was set free as a result of the Civil War." By going against "our generalizations upon American history," Chesnutt revealed "a very considerable technical exception in the case of several hundred thousand free people of color, a great many of whom were residents of the Southern States."[2] Constituting a "considerable exception" of "several hundred thousand" made the free people of color more than just an exception; the numbers reveal that free people of color were a part of American history, but a part that had been, until Chesnutt started telling their stories, invisible. To set the historical record straight, Chesnutt provided his readers with a few neglected facts. By simply consulting U.S. census records for the years 1850 and 1860, he found that "between nine and ten percent of the colored population, and about three percent of the total population in each of those years, were free colored people."[3] Prior to the invention of the cotton gin and the consequent great demand for laborers on Southern plantations, the numbers of free people of color had been on the rise. North Carolina was one of the few Southern states in which the free colored population had been growing in the early nineteenth century, and most of them lived in or around Fayetteville, near the Eastern Seaboard, in what, during Chesnutt's lifetime, was called the "black district" of North Carolina.

Fayetteville, during AJ's youth, was a lively town; most of it had been rebuilt and modernized because of a devastating fire that occurred in 1831. Shortly after Fayetteville's fire, news of Nat Turner's rebellion, on a Virginia plantation less than two hundred miles north of Fayetteville, spread throughout town with equal fury. The story of the slave insurrection that resulted in the deaths of at least fifty-five white people and hundreds more Black people sent shock waves throughout the South. Town residents who had previously looked the other way when it came to the relationships of free colored people were now more wary. New laws were made to keep the free colored people from growing or prospering. Amid these singular events, Waddell and Ann developed a relationship. From what we can gather of their relationship, Ann was likely employed by Waddell as a housekeeper. When his legal wife died, he and Ann started a relationship of their own, one that was kept mostly to themselves to avoid gossip and social judgment. They gave their firstborn a stately name, a name that might allow him to put aside the stigma of his illegitimate birth. Elected to the presidency in 1828, Andrew Jackson would come to be known for his commitment to democracy and the common man. It was a convention in early America to name firstborn sons after the sitting president. As either a patriotic gesture or with the hope that their son too would become president of the United States someday, Ann and Waddell christened their first son Andrew Jackson. AJ, as he came to be known, must have felt the irony of being named after a slaveholding president whose policies would help to establish the principles of the Democratic Party. Fayetteville's new Market House was completed shortly after AJ was born. It still stands at the center of town, joining its main streets and forming a crucial link between Fayetteville's past and present. It served multiple purposes during AJ's life: a slave market, town hall, and general meeting place. Its clock tower sits atop a three-bay, double-story block that can be seen from a mile away so that as you make your way into town, it feels as though time rises above the hustle and bustle below, standing perfectly still.

As the illegitimate son of a white man and a free colored woman, AJ was a well-known anomaly in central North Carolina. But unlike the more familiar and scandalous stories of illegitimate children abandoned by their white fathers to be raised by their Black mothers, AJ maintained a close relationship with his father. Waddell's support and love for his son did not seem to matter to a system of marital union based on race. The unconventional relationship between his parents determined just about every move he made; he likely had to endure raised eyebrows and meaningful glances from officious town residents who looked down on free colored people, like AJ and his siblings.

Since 1715, North Carolina law had either discouraged or banned marriage between whites and non-whites. The first law to address marriage

fined any white man or woman who intermarried with "any Negro, Mulatto or Indian Man or Woman" fifty pounds.[4] The general assembly updated this law in 1741 by levying the same fine on any white man or woman
who married "an Indian, negro, mustee, or mulatto man or woman, or any
person of mixed blood to the third generation, bond or free."[5] Neither of
these laws prohibited intermarriage between whites and non-whites; they
simply discouraged such marriages by imposing heavy fines. Both laws also
fined clergy and other officials who married whites to non-whites. These
laws appear to have discouraged the issuances of legal marriage bonds to
mixed couples in Fayetteville and many other parts of the state. It was in
1830, just a few years before AJ was born, that the state decided to crack
down on such relationships. Just around the time Waddell and Ann had
gotten together, the general assembly passed an act making it unlawful
for a "free negro or free person of color" to marry a white person or "to
intermarry or cohabit and live together as man and wife with any slave."
This new law was enforced by a few methods. First, any town clerks who
knowingly issued a marriage license "between any free negro or free person
of color and a white person" would be found guilty of a misdemeanor, and
fined or imprisoned. Second, those "free negroes or free people of color"
who are convicted of intermarrying or cohabiting with either a white person or a slave "shall be fined and imprisoned or whipt at the discretion of
the court; the whipping not to exceed thirty-nine lashes."[6]

Fortunately for AJ's parents, this new law did not apply to them. The
law included a provision that it "shall not extend to any case where an intermarriage or cohabiting or living together took place before the passing
of this act." While AJ's parents were relatively safe from the law, he was
not. As a free person of color, AJ's private life was regulated by the state,
so he was restricted from forming intimate relationships with the majority
of people living in Fayetteville: white people and slaves. It is no wonder he
was eager to leave. What did it mean to be free if you were told that you
could not form relationships with people outside of the tiny community
into which you were born? And if the man who was your father was legally
barred from acknowledging you as his son? To be free and colored was
not just an oxymoron in nineteenth-century North Carolina—the whole
concept was a lie made up to keep slaves bound to slave owners. Realizing

the precarity of his position, AJ did what some, particularly adventerous free people of color of his generation did: he left the South.

The migration of free people of color from the South to the North in the mid-nineteenth century has not received much attention from historians. Unlike the later Great Migration of the early twentieth century, when approximately six million Black people moved from the South to Northern, midwestern, and western states, radically altering the constitution of the United States, the migration that AJ was part of was relatively minor. Many of those, like AJ, who left the South before the Civil War, in the mid-1850s, returned a decade later, after the war, with the hope of living freely once the laws governing slave society, laws that dictated who you could and couldn't marry, had been abolished. But AJ could not have known that slavery would end when he decided to leave. He, like other migrants who decide to leave their homes in search of greater freedom, believed he was leaving Fayetteville forever. Having said his goodbyes to his parents and siblings, he joined a group of men and women like himself, those branded by the state as "free people of color," who threatened the very foundation of the slave society.

Perhaps AJ's father, Waddell Cade, had seen the war and the abolition of slavery coming. Why else would he have given his son property right in the center of town as a gift before AJ lit out for the North? Waddell Cade was a property owner who met and had several children with Ann Chesnutt, his free colored housekeeper. Was this relationship based on love, infatuation, or economic expedience?

Though Waddell may have owned slaves, he did not own Ann, who was already free when they met. Most free women of color like Ann, of mixed ancestry, who had white partners chose men of wealth and property. Ann, like most free women of mixed ancestry, likely chose Waddell with the hope of securing economic stability for her family. In this regard, Ann and Waddell's relationship was not unlike most nineteenth-century legal marriages that were based on property and a contract binding a husband and wife together for life. The difference was that there was no legal document binding Waddell to Ann and their children. How Waddell decided to live and have children with Ann, a free Black woman forty years his junior, sometime around 1830, remains a mystery. There are no records of their union; there are no letters written by them or others, evincing their love for each other. All we know is that they were living together, with two of their three children, in 1860, before the war. By the time of the 1860 census, AJ had already left home. Waddell's occupation is listed as "Farmer" and their daughter, Mary, is listed as a "Seamstress." No occupation is listed for either Ann or their youngest child, Dallas. This information strongly suggests that Waddell Cade supported and lived with his "free colored" family until his death. And this family was, according to the law of the state of North Carolina, not just illegitimate but expressly prohibited. Those engaging in such prohibited relationships could be fined, imprisoned, or "whipt." Since there were so many reasons why Ann and Waddell should *not* be together, we are left to wonder not only why they got together in the first place but why they *stayed* together and why Waddell risked fines and prison to make this relationship public by giving his son land. Lacking legal documents and DNA evidence, all we can do is imagine how Ann Chesnutt and Waddell Cade, Charles Waddell Chesnutt's paternal grandparents, found a way to live together and raise their family, amid the legal and social customs that rendered such a union against the law.

Because the law did not permit unions like that of Chesnutt's grandparents, evidence of its existence has been mostly hidden from family and public history, requiring a bit of sleuth work, or imagination, to understand. It is also the case that some, perhaps even most, people would prefer that these relationships remained hidden, as they might disturb the moral and political commitments of later generations. But not for Chesnutt. The story of his grandparents offered hope and inspiration. Here were people who refused to conform to the arbitrary rules of the state that divided people into racial categories. Though most would sneer at his grandparents and the children they had together, Chesnutt declared his origins with pride. "I know my pedigree for a hundred and fifty years. It would make, I suspect, a somewhat ragged family tree in spots, but at any rate in the legal line of descent it was always free on both sides, as far as my knowledge goes."[7] For Chesnutt, Waddell and Ann offered up an example of mutual affection and personal interest triumphing over state-sanctioned racism. They chose to live together despite being told, ordered even, that they shouldn't. But what of the children produced out of this union? How would they live in a society so opposed to where they came from? When AJ left home, he was seeking not only freedom but legitimacy, a way of belonging to a society that rejected who he was and limited who he might become. AJ may have found greater freedom in the North, but it was Ann Maria Sampson, Chesnutt's mother, with whom he found the legitimacy he needed to live freely.

When Ann Maria Sampson was born in 1835 in Fayetteville, her father, Henry E. Sampson, was thirty-five and her mother, Chloe Sampson, was twenty-five. Little is known about her father, but the fact that they shared the same last name suggests that he was married to Ann Maria's mother; little more is known about him. Most of what we know about the Sampsons is based on oral history, stories told from one generation to the next. Ann Maria died in Fayetteville, in 1871, when Chesnutt was thirteen. He does not mention her death in his journal. He does reveal in a letter being told that his "mother surreptitiously taught slaves, which was against the law."[8] We learn much more about Ann Maria from Chesnutt's daughter Helen, whose biography of her father, published two decades after his death, included stories about her grandmother that she recalled her father telling. But Helen may have embellished much of what her father told her to create a family history that she and her siblings could celebrate. Perhaps the most important bit of family history we learn from Helen, in the opening pages of the biography, is how AJ met Ann Maria, fell in love, and got married. As Helen tells it, the two met as part of a group of free Blacks who had joined together to leave North Carolina, a slave state, to escape its social conventions and laws limiting their mobility and interactions. In Helen's words:

> The journey was long and tedious. Discouragement and fear and bitter hardship cast their blight over the spirits of the group. At times they ran into positive danger, and often it seemed the wiser course to abandon their hopes and return to North Carolina. But Ann Maria browbeat them, railed at them, cajoled them and laughed at them, poured out her charm, her indomitable courage, and sparkling wit to lift their spirits and lead them forward. Andrew fell in love with her, and Ann Maria began to dream too.[9]

Eventually, AJ and Ann Maria found themselves in Ohio. And it was there they were married. Signed by Judge Dan R. Dilden and William H. Brown in Cuyahoga County in the state of Ohio, Ann Maria and AJ's marriage certificate, for their firstborn at least, was as much a literary source as it was a legal document. Like the hundreds of books he read and collected over the course of his life, Chesnutt preserved this document meticulously in his personal archive. "This is to certify," the document states, "that by the authority of a License under the Seal of the Probate Court of Cuyahoga County, Mr. A.J. Chesnutt and Miss A.M. Sampson were by me, on the twenty-sixth day of July in the Year of our Lord, One Thousand Eight Hundred and Fifty-seven legaly [sic] united as HUSBAND AND WIFE."[10] Like Frederick Douglass, William Wells Brown, William and Ellen Craft, and other less well-known fugitive slaves, Ann Maria and AJ sealed their freedom in the North with a legal marriage certificate; with this certificate, their marriage received the legal recognition that their parents— Chesnutt's grandparents— had been denied.

The Chesnutts' marriage certificate was a testament not only to their mutual love but also a powerful cultural symbol for their children—and grandchildren—of their legitimacy; a legitimacy that their parents, who had engaged in unconventional intimate unions, were denied. Ann Maria and AJ had made their way to the North, as far as Cleveland, where they began a new free and legitimate family, one that was far from the stigma of being free and Black in the slaveholding South.

Born on June 20, 1858, Charles Waddell, or CW, as AJ called him, was the first of the five children Ann Maria and AJ had together. Though AJ could not legally take his father's name, he did pass on Waddell Cade's legacy to his firstborn. Though he never spoke of him, Charles always kept a place for Waddell between his first and last names. Two more sons would follow Charles, Lewis two years later and then Andrew Jackson Jr. in 1862. AJ and Ann Maria, and their three sons, had begun a new life in free Ohio, and it was one the boys would return to, but first they would need to return to the South, to live among their parents' fellow free people of color, to understand where they came from.

When AJ returned to Fayetteville in 1866, he was filled with grand ideas for rebuilding his hometown and settling the family he planned to raise there after the war. The town of Fayetteville had been key to Union general William T. Sherman's strategy to destroy Confederate resources in his infamous march to the sea. Sherman arrived in Fayetteville not long before AJ did, on March 11, 1865—the same day a shooting took place around the Market House, Fayetteville's town center, between Confederate general Wade Hampton, members of his staff, and a Union cavalry patrol. After the brief skirmish, Hampton fled crossing the Clarendon Bridge over the Cape Fear River, which was later burned. That night, the main body of Sherman's troops marched into Fayetteville, and the mayor formally surrendered the town. Sherman's troops were everywhere. While in Fayetteville, Union forces burned several important structures, including textile mills and the office of the local newspaper, *The Fayetteville Observer*. Confederate forces had already burned stockpiles of cotton and naval stores to deny the Union enemy the spoils of war. Headquartered in Fayetteville for three days, Sherman gave orders for the arsenal to be razed when he left on March 14, 1865; he wanted to destroy the last source of military arms for the Confederacy. For AJ, Sherman's march to the sea marked the beginning of a new era in Fayetteville's history. Fayetteville's reconstruction was a time to rebuild from the ruins left by Sherman's army. While most of Fayetteville's residents denounced Sherman's destructive strategy, AJ likely saw the logic in it: before there could be a reconstruction, destruction was needed. For AJ, Sherman's march to the sea planted the seeds for the South's reconstruction. Now that the Fayetteville of AJ's youth was mostly destroyed, he could begin to imagine a future in which the divisions imposed by slavery—free, slave, Black, white—had been blown up by Sherman's march. With his wife by his side and three young sons in tow, the future, from where Andrew Jackson Chesnutt stood, looked bright.

Unlike his white and enslaved neighbors, who were forbidden from forming relationships with one another, AJ and Ann, and their children, developed a broad social network that included both enslaved people and white people. Of course, the difference in their status shaped these relationships, but their differences did not forbid them from getting to know one another; they, unlike most people living at the time, had the personal freedom to choose their friends, lovers, and enemies. But if race did not determine who they should love and hate, how would they know they were making the right choice?

That Chesnutt's parents were able to escape the stigma of their births to marry lawfully and produce a legitimate family was proof of their personal freedom at a time when most Black people were enslaved. After slavery was abolished throughout the South, they returned home, happily married, with their three sons, ready to start a new life under a more democratic regime. But the end of slavery did little to alter the condition of the formerly free colored people. In the immediate aftermath of the Civil War, former slaves either continued to live and work for their former owners or received federal assistance through the newly established Freedmen's Bureau. Left for the most part on their own, the free colored people were forced to create a separate world for themselves, one that was founded on a long history of interracial relationships in North Carolina.

The record of Waddell Cade deeding land to Andrew Jackson Chesnutt in 1836 marks the beginning of Chesnutt's personal history in the South. This transfer of land was made before emancipation, but this property deed, like the marriage certificate of his parents, helps us to understand Chesnutt's origins. Bucking legal convention and social custom, Cade had ensured that his son, whom the law did not recognize as his son, would inherit land legitimately. By giving a share of his land to AJ, Cade would establish a bond with AJ and *his* sons. Stories of white fathers transferring land to their free Black partners and children were not uncommon in North Carolina at the time. According to state records, Cade decided to pass on land to his son as a real estate property transfer during his lifetime, rather than in the form of a promissory note or will, two methods of passing property posthumously on to illegitimate children whose inheritance rights could be challenged by legal heirs, such as siblings or nieces and nephews. Unlike with wills and promissory notes, Cade could personally prevent challenges to his wishes by guaranteeing that the register of deeds recorded the deed in the county records. Though there is no record of Cade having left a will, and though there are no Cumberland County estate papers in his name, the index of deeds shows that Cade often bought and sold land. He started acquiring land in 1805; twenty-five recorded deeds show that he is the grantee. The earliest date is 1821; in that year, he got a "Lot Russel St. Fay[etteville]" from Thomas D. Burgh. In 1836, Cade deeded to Andrew Jackson Chesnutt a "lot Morgan-Russell Sts. Fayetteville." That land transfer is confirmed by AJ's will, dated June 21, 1920, which mentions a "house & lot on C Street which was given me by my father."[11] With this land, AJ built a home for his family in Fayetteville after the Civil War, a home that he hoped would allow the former slave state where he was born to join the free states where he had, for a short time at least, lived.

Surveying his hometown upon his return in 1866, AJ began to make plans. He now had to decide what to do with the property his father gave him. He started a grocery store on the property, providing his neighbors with things they might need to put food on their tables and rebuild their homes. It was not long after AJ's return that there appeared on the scene "the vanguard of a second army," aptly called the Freedmen's Bureau, "which came to bring light and the fruits of liberty to a land which slavery and the havoc of war had brought to ruin."[12] That most Southerners felt somewhat ambivalent toward this newly established federal bureau of freedom was to be expected. During Chesnutt's time, it was "fashionable to assume that those who undertook the political rehabilitation of the Southern States merely rounded out the ruin that the war had wrought— merely ploughed up the desolate land and sowed it with salt."[13] In our time, the Freedmen's Bureau has come to be viewed as an unprecedented federal agency created in early 1865 to try to provide massive social welfare to millions of Black and white displaced people in the South. Whichever way one looks at the work of the bureau, from the perspective of the South or North, past or present, all sides seem to agree that its presence was needed, even if it was just symbolic, to begin the work of reconstructing the South after the war. While the form that reconstruction should take varied widely among different geographies and the politics of each Southern state, it was in the field of public education that the Freedmen's Bureau made its mark. Although the establishment of schools was an important aspect of improving the lives of the newly freed slaves, there was no organized department concerned with matters of education when the bureau began operations in 1865. The educational activities of the bureau and the organization for supervising these activities grew as the educational needs of the freedmen increased. Perhaps it was the disorganization of the bureau that enabled the former free people of color, Chesnutt's people, to take a leading role in public education, since many of them, like Chesnutt's mother, had experience in teaching slaves before the war. Where previously they had been considered criminals for teaching slaves to read, free people of color were soon inversely viewed as a harbinger of a new era. Those who could read and write might even be paid, or at the very least encouraged by the bureau, to teach those who had been forced to labor without education.

This was no easy task and required skills that only a few possessed. It also required land and a building of some kind—to function as a school—where these former slaves could gather to learn. With three sons of his own to educate, AJ was preoccupied with the two questions that loomed over the minds of most Fayetteville residents: Where would the school be? And who would run it? Already a landowner, AJ knew a thing or two about acquiring land, and the first thing you needed to build a school was land on which to build it. It is not surprising then that AJ became one of seven colored men who, in 1867, raised $136 to purchase two lots on Gillespie Street, not too far from his own property, to build a schoolhouse.[14] On November 29, 1867, AJ became one of seven men who signed the deed that would grant land on Gillespie Street to the Freedmen's Bureau for Fayetteville's first public school. With a little help from the bureau, a building was erected on the site and became known as the Howard School, named after the head of the bureau, former Union general Oliver Otis Howard.

At first, Fayetteville's Howard School was no different from the other schoolhouses built by the bureau that "dotted every hillside" across the South to provide "education for rich and poor, for white and black alike."[15] Chesnutt's memories of the school, which he attended until his mother died, formed some of his happiest recollections. It was here, in this simple clapboard building, with its little school bell jutting out from its shingled roof, that transformed the former slaves and former free colored people of Fayetteville into students. Most of these Freedmen's Schools were run by those known at the time in the South as "Yankee schoolmasters and schoolma'ams."[16] These Northern men and women viewed it as their mission to travel to the South to teach the freedmen, continuing the work of the Union generals and soldiers who had sacrificed so much to clear the land of slavery. Some in the South viewed their presence as a kind of second invasion. After General Sherman's men had left with their guns and bayonets, this new army was equipped with textbooks and chalk, eager to teach where it had once been a crime to teach people to read or write. But in Fayetteville, with its population of free colored people who could *already* read and write, the Yankee presence seemed less necessary. In Fayetteville, free colored people could teach the newly freed, and this made for a Howard School unlike most others; this was a Howard School that sat on land owned by free colored people and was taught by free colored people for the newly freed. With the completion of the Howard School in 1867, Fayetteville's reconstruction had formally begun. Having built his home on his father's land and securing the educational futures of his children with the construction of the Howard School nearby, AJ then turned his attention to the political scene.

The year after Fayetteville's Howard School was completed, AJ became preoccupied with the election of April 1868. This election was the first to be held after the war, and central to its outcome were the issues of reconstruction of the South and suffrage not just for the newly freed slaves but also for the formerly free people of color like AJ, who had for much of his life been denied the right to vote. AJ, like most property owners, believed voting was a right he deserved. Struggles over reconstruction policy had led to military occupation of the South and to the impeachment of President Andrew Johnson. While AJ was busy building his home, his business, and the Howard School, much of the nation seemed to be in chaos. AJ had not followed politics closely during these years; but he knew the importance of civil rights, since he had lived for much of his life without them. And he knew from reading the papers that Republicans like the recently assassinated Abraham Lincoln favored civil rights for people like him, while Democrats opposed the Republican approach to reconstruction and called for the states to decide on political issues such as the franchise. We don't know for sure if AJ voted in that first election after the war, but we do know that the Republicans managed to secure a victory that resulted in AJ becoming one of the first colored men to be elected a justice of the peace in the town of Fayetteville. That election was also marked by the rise of the Republican Party in North Carolina. Shortly after, the Constitution of 1868 was approved by Congress, and North Carolina's senators and representatives, all Republicans except one, took their seats in Washington. The new state legislature met in Raleigh on July 1, 1868, and on July 2 ratified the Fourteenth Amendment. With its passage, AJ's legitimacy as a citizen, son, husband, and father could no longer be questioned. AJ took the Fourteenth Amendment personally. It spoke directly to his experience as a free colored person who had previously been considered illegitimate. "All persons born or naturalized in the United States," it held, "are citizens of the United States and of the State wherein they reside. No State shall make or enforce any law which shall abridge the privileges or immunities of citizens of the United States; nor shall any State deprive any person of life, liberty, or property, without due process of law; nor deny to any person within its jurisdiction the equal protection of the laws." General Edward Canby followed the amendment by a declaration ending military rule. Civil government under Republican auspices had come to North Carolina, and it seemed that AJ's gamble to move back to the South had paid off. He was now a property owner, a husband and father, and, perhaps most remarkably, an elected public official.

AJ's financial and political success, like Republican dominance in North Carolina, was short-lived. In 1870, the Republicans lost control of both houses of the state legislature. And so began a period in North Carolina history of white supremacy during which the formerly free colored people became the target of virulent racist attacks. The Democratic gubernatorial nominee, Zebulon B. Vance, set the tone of the Democrats' campaign when he characterized the Republican Party as "begotten by a scalawag out of a mulatto and born in an outhouse."[17] His remarks were circulated in the pages of Wilmington's *Morning Star* newspaper, the same paper that would later play a crucial role in both the real and Chesnutt's fictional history of the Wilmington massacre of 1898.

For the Chesnutts, the rise of the Democrats in North Carolina resulted in AJ losing his seat as justice of the peace. Soon after the defeat, he lost his business and home but did retain the land given to him by his father. In 1871, Chesnutt's mother died. She had just given birth to her fifth child, Chesnutt's sister Lillian, who survived and whom Chesnutt would help raise. Ann Maria's death marked not only the systematic defeat of the Republican Party at all levels of government in North Carolina but also the end of Chesnutt's boyhood.

Chesnutt would look back on his first five years of his life in the South, before the death of his mother, with some nostalgia. These were the years of Reconstruction when his father's grocery business was thriving, when he attended the school his father had worked so hard to build, and when his father held political office. During this time, they had looked forward to a future of prosperity, peace, and happiness after AJ's long years of struggle. And it was during these years that Chesnutt would form his political outlook, develop his literary imagination, and set his goals. In this regard, Andrew Jackson Chesnutt was not just a devoted father and husband, he also became his son's political role model.

In a speech delivered many years after he had left his family and home in North Carolina for Ohio in 1892, Chesnutt revealed his reasons for his ongoing commitment to the Republican Party.

> I am a Republican because my father was one. A poor argument it may be said. I could not expect this argument to convince anyone else. But as time goes on and I see more clearly the superiority of our party, I thank the old man for saving me the necessity of changing my politics, as I should otherwise have had to do; for, I cannot imagine how I could have remained a Democrat after arriving at years of discretion.[18]

The association Chesnutt drew between his allegiance to the Republican Party and his relationship with his father helps explain the otherwise elusive terms of his political identity. Chesnutt understood himself as belonging to a political party rather than to a race. Of course, he belonged to this party not only because of his father but also because he believed in the principles it espoused. His father, Chesnutt believed, embodied the path to Reconstruction that he associated with the Republican Party. Throughout his life, AJ had sought greater freedom for himself and his family. Like his father before him, AJ had committed his life to changing the policies and conventions of the old South, an institution that kept three million of the poor in bondage and subjugated free men to the competition of unpaid labor. In his speech, Chesnutt positioned his father next to other, more famous, Republican men: "[Abraham] Lincoln the emancipator, the martyr, [Ulysses S.] Grant the hero . . . [Horace] Greeley, [William H.] Seward, [Salmon P.] Chase, [Charles] Sumner, [William T.] Sherman, [Philip] Sheridan."[19] Though Andrew Jackson did not achieve the political fame of these men, he was, as historian Eric Foner terms him, one of "Freedom's Lawmakers."[20] Unlike most Black Republicans, AJ was one of the few to hold public office during Reconstruction, when voting and elective office in the South continued to be restricted to whites. Amid the backlash against former slaves and the free colored people in particular, Andrew Jackson managed to find a way to implement his plan for the future of Fayetteville. Though few remember his contributions in the annals of North Carolinian and American history, his undertakings did not go unnoticed by his son. After leaving home at thirteen, Chesnutt maintained a connection with his father, until AJ's death in January 1921, through letters. None of these have survived. Despite serving as one of the founders of the first institutions of higher learning for former slaves and free colored people, little has been preserved of AJ's contributions to the reconstruction of the South and his political legacy. He was responsible for establishing the first state-run institution of higher learning in Fayetteville and was one of the first colored men to hold public office in the state. Through his hard work and commitment, he helped to educate legions of future Black men and women, chief of whom were the children he raised, infusing them with his political values and enterprising spirit.

The Teacher

Aristotle gave instruction in the form of lectures, which he delivered
while walking in a pleasant grove near Athens, called Academia.
—"Methods of Teaching" (1883)

Chesnutt was ten when he enrolled in the Howard School. When
he arrived in Fayetteville from Cleveland, he was well ahead of his
peers, most of whom were still learning the rudimentary skills of reading,
writing, and arithmetic. As his maternal grandmother, Chloe, recalled,
Chesnutt was a voracious reader at an early age, quipping that had she not
been present at his delivery, she could have believed that he was born with
a book in his hand. In an early photograph of Chesnutt with his brother
Lewis, taken in 1865, in which he is seven and Lewis five, the brothers are
dressed in matching suits, with stiff shirt collars underneath blazers neatly
buttoned. The boys are holding hands, looking like two shy schoolboys,
posing for the camera on picture day. Surely, Chesnutt would have stood
out among the roughly three hundred students enrolled at the Howard
School in 1868. This was a school built to serve the newly freed; funds for
it were raised by those in the community who had some change to spare,
with the assistance of the federal government. It would come as no surprise
that the school's principal, Robert W. Harris, took a special interest in
Chesnutt's talents. Harris, along with his brother Cicero, who was also a
teacher at the school, became Chesnutt's early supporters; but it was the
elder Harris who would become the single most important influence on
Chesnutt's education.

Born in Fayetteville in 1839 of free parents, Harris would grow up to be an austere man, working hard to support his family, avoiding vices such as tobacco and alcohol. In later years, he wore a thick beard that gave him the demeanor of a generous patriarch. He had migrated to Ohio with his family in 1850 at the age of eleven. While living in Cleveland, Harris enjoyed "excellent educational facilities" and supported his widowed mother and younger sisters by working for the railroad, likely laying track for the new Cleveland, Columbus & Cincinnati lines that were stretching across the Midwest at the time. This period of expansion in Ohio came to an end with the financial Panic of 1857, coupled with the outbreak of war a few years later. During the summer of 1864, when Ulysses S. Grant was promoted to the rank of lieutenant general and moved across the Rapidan and Rappahannock Rivers in Virginia, Harris decided to follow in his older brother William's footsteps and applied for a teaching position with the American Missionary Association.

Founded in 1846 to protest the silence of other missionary agencies regarding slavery, the AMA positioned itself as staunchly antislavery. Several of its key members—Lewis Tappan, Gerrit Smith, and Joshua Leavitt— had first joined forces in their common effort to defend the well-known case of the *Amistad* captives in 1839. The Amistad Committee, as they called themselves, managed to secure freedom for thirty-nine Mende African refugees who had been kidnapped and then imprisoned on a slave ship. Following a celebrated U.S. Supreme Court trial, in which former president John Quincy Adams successfully defended the rights of the Africans, the captives sailed home, accompanied by several missionaries who set up missions in and around the former captives' homes. By the time war erupted in the United States, the AMA shifted its direction from legal defense of the enslaved to educating the freemen. Following the war, the AMA went on to establish hundreds of schools for Black Americans in the South, as well as other minority groups, including Appalachian whites.

The central principles and missionary spirit of the association appealed to Harris. Though reluctant to leave his mother and sisters behind, he, like his brother William, who had recently become pastor of the African Methodist Episcopal church in Richmond, Virginia, was beckoned to join the AMA's cause. Along with his letter of application, in which he explained his interest in "assisting in the noble work of elevating and evangelizing our oppressed and long abused race," he also submitted a letter of recommendation from his pastor in the Cleveland branch of the AME, who described Harris as a "model young man . . . with but one great object in view, the glory of God and the prosperity of Mankind."[1] Harris's previous teaching experience was limited to privately teaching slaves in North Carolina. Given the fact that he was only eleven when he left Fayetteville, it is hard to imagine how Harris conducted his lessons. Perhaps Harris, like the young George Shelby in the opening scenes of *Uncle Tom's Cabin*, used the Bible to instruct those slaves eager to learn their letters for the sake of spiritual salvation. Despite his lack of formal teaching experience, the AMA approved his application. They sent him to the front lines in Virginia and then to more familiar territory in Fayetteville. He would become the first principal of the Howard School, when it was established in 1867, and would go on to make it one of the most successful of its kind in the South.

Fayetteville's Howard School was one of the largest that had been erected under the auspices of the Freedmen's Bureau. Harris also managed to solicit support from private foundations, such as the Peabody Fund, which up until that time only funded white schools. Unlike most of the Howard Schools in the South that relied on the bureau for funding and organization, Harris's Howard School found funding from multiple state sources and private foundations to support its students. Perhaps it was the hybrid private-public model that led to its success. Mostly, though, it was Harris's leadership and commitment that helped to develop the school and keep its students engaged in its lofty project of intellectual freedom and economic prosperity.

The pious, studious, and industrious Harris became both a model of virtue and a mentor for Chesnutt. As Harris and his wife, Mary, had no children of their own, they opened their home to students. In his obituary, written when he died on October 24, 1880, Chesnutt compared Harris's role in Fayetteville to that of President George Washington. "It has been beautifully said of Washington: 'Providence left him childless, that his country might call him Father'; so may it be said of the subject of these remarks, that Providence left him childless, that he might bestow the affections and patience of a father upon the work to which his life was devoted."[2]

As a teacher, Harris was devoted to his students, and as Chesnutt was one of the most outstanding, Harris devoted considerable time to him. Based on Aristotle's classic discussion on education, Harris's teaching placed a strong emphasis on the development of character. Play, physical training, music, debate, alongside religious study of the Bible, math, and science, were to all have their place in forming the bodies, minds, and souls of his students.

Diverging from later philosophies of Black education, such as those developed by Booker T. Washington and W. E. B. Du Bois in the early twentieth century, Harris's teaching mission was less about uplifting the race than developing the individual characters of his students, instilling in them a sense of self-reliance derived from reading both sacred and practical texts. He kept a personal library in his home. Shelves were filled with all kinds of books that served Chesnutt's practical desire for knowledge and his love of a good story. Chesnutt spent hours in Harris's home, reading, playing the organ, and talking with his teacher about current events. It was with Harris that he began to dream of going to college, perhaps to Atlanta University, like William Sanders Scarborough, who would become the first Black professor of classics in the United States. Perhaps he would leave the South altogether and attend Harvard College, where Richard Theodore Greener had recently become the first Black student to graduate from the storied Ivy League institution, in 1870. Harris helped Chesnutt believe that excellence in education would ensure success, both spiritual and material.

Chesnutt experienced a rude awakening when his mother died in 1871. AJ needed his oldest son at home to help with his younger siblings or find other ways to support the family. Fortunately, Harris used his influence and standing in the community to intervene. Rather than give up on developing Chesnutt's "remarkable intelligence," Harris recommended him to a North Carolina congressman, Representative Alfred Moore Waddell, who served as a Democrat in the U.S. House of Representatives from 1871 to 1879. Ironically, this was the same Waddell who went on to lead the Wilmington insurrection of 1898, a coup d'état by a white mob, and became the city's mayor, serving in this role until 1906. At Harris's suggestion, Waddell nominated Chesnutt to take the competitive examination for entrance to

Annapolis and West Point to continue his education. Chesnutt was one of the first "colored men" to be considered for entrance into the esteemed United States Naval Academy. Little is known of Representative Waddell's letter to the examination board regarding the avowed white supremacist's support for Chesnutt's application. Addressed simply to "Gentlemen," Waddell wrote: "A colored youth named Chesnutt from Fayetteville has made application to be examined—through a friend—and if he presents himself is entitled to the benefit of my advertisement." It is signed "Respy. A.M. Waddell."[3] It is not clear if Waddell supported other candidates for entrance into the academy. But this letter shows that Representative Waddell was already aware of Chesnutt's talents long before Chesnutt fictionalized Waddell's bloody exploits thirty years later in *The Marrow of Tradition*. It is also not clear whether Chesnutt was aware of Waddell's recommendation, though it seems unlikely that Harris would have kept this detail hidden from his prize pupil.

While supporting very different political ideologies, Harris and Waddell seem to have been on friendly terms. Perhaps they even relied on each other to advance their divergent causes. Harris had in mind the expansion of public education for Blacks, while Waddell was interested in maintaining the distinction between whites and Blacks. The success of Harris's colored school would ensure that the nascent idea of integrating public schools was kept from gaining traction. With Harris's help and Waddell's recommendation, Chesnutt earned a coveted spot before the examination committee, which he passed with flying colors. Despite his high marks and impressive interview, Chesnutt was not selected by the board of examiners for entrance into the academy. Chesnutt never mentioned taking the exam or his disappointment. Perhaps the experience had left him so dispirited he did not want to recall it or share it with others. Still, the experience, as described by others who witnessed it, must have left a significant emotional scar.

Shortly after the examination, on May 29, 1873, G. W. Jewett wrote to Harris "as one of the Board of Examiners at the recent competitive examination of applicants for the Annapolis Cadetship." In his letter, Jewett explained that "the Committee gave him a very high rank among his competitors, and while we unanimously agreed upon the successful candidate as fairly entitled to our choice, your young friend was freely admitted to rank among his most formidable competitors." Despite Chesnutt's "fine mental powers," Jewett went on to explain in his letter that "such talents can find a fitter field than the Navy or Army." Instead, Jewett declared: "Let him be fitted for a teacher of some kind and devote his rare talents to the enlightenment and elevation of the colored people."[4] While Chesnutt's career as a teacher of "the colored people" of the South began at sixteen, his turn to teaching was less of a choice than the result of other doors being closed on him. It was the only position open to a "colored youth" with "remarkable intelligence" at the time. Chesnutt's experience evinces the more general claim by historians who insist that many Black teachers would rather have been lawyers, journalists, businesspeople, or government workers had they not been so restricted by discrimination in the upper echelons of U.S. institutions.[5]

The kind of polite discrimination Jewett revealed in his letter had far-reaching ramifications. Jewett held the mistaken view that "colored men" like Chesnutt were best fitted for teaching. No wonder Chesnutt's relationship to teaching in the South was complex and conflicted. In some respects, Jewett's prejudices would lead Chesnutt, under Harris's guidance, to develop methods of teaching that would prove Jewett and others like him wrong. A talented "colored youth" could achieve great things in any field, even in higher education or public life, if given the opportunity. But the prejudices of men like Jewett boxed him into a career in teaching that he, unlike Harris, did not choose. While he lacked Harris's missionary spirit, he did possess a love of learning, which would have to be enough to sustain him in a career that over the years he found increasingly frustrating.

Chesnutt began his career as a teacher in 1873. He was fifteen years old when he left the sand hills of Fayetteville for the more urban city of Charlotte. He worked for Cicero Harris at the Peabody School. Robert Harris most likely arranged for Chesnutt to work with Cicero so that he might gain necessary teaching experience that granted him a sufficient wage to help support his family. It would also give him time to mourn the loss of his mother without having to perform household chores at home for his father and help take care of his five siblings. At the end of his nine-month apprenticeship with Cicero, Chesnutt was awarded a "First Grade Teachers

Certificate," which entitled him to earn at least forty dollars a month. In 1874, forty dollars would be a little over a thousand dollars today, an amount that would, if he could find an appropriate teaching job, make AJ, and the rest of his family, comfortable. But things didn't go exactly as planned.

Though this certificate entitled Chesnutt to a good wage, finding a position proved difficult. In the journal Chesnutt started during this time, he described his failed attempts to secure a position, amid the scarcity of resources available to public schools in rural North Carolina. An entry from July 6, 1874 reveals much about the conditions of the schools and the difficulties newly minted Black teachers like Chesnutt faced:

> I went up town to look around and see the country folks about a school. Got on the track of one. It was in the same township Mr. Petty was to teach in. Yesterday, Sunday, I went out to Moore's Sanctuary to find of Mr. Petty who the school committee were. I waited until morning service was over, and he told me that he had lost his school, that there was but $89.93 in the treasury for that school, and that they were going to build a school-house with it, and that there was but $20.00 for the school I was on the track of.

Chesnutt recalled conversations between him and members of school committees negotiating employment: from the duties he would perform as a teacher, which included teaching in the Sunday school for which he would not be paid, his daily wages, the cost of room and board, to the number of pupils he would instruct, how often, and the length of the school term. Although there were certain standards established by the all-white, statewide school board, local school committees, in Chesnutt's telling, had a great deal of power determining the quality of a teacher's life.

As he recounted these conversations in his journal, Chesnutt offered a panorama of the diversity of opinion held by members of the community. Some, like "Mr. Ayler, one of the school committee" who "lived about 2 miles from the church" and "was a German," felt "that the colored people ought to have colored and the whites, white teachers." Chesnutt refrained from offering his own view on the subject. He was much more vocal, however, when speaking with parents of potential students who felt that schools for their children were a waste of time and money. After a lengthy conversation with Sam, his wife, and their son, John, about the importance of schooling to the material success of their community, he walked away, frustrated and tired. After trying to persuade the family of the value of going to school, he confronted a resistance impossible to overcome. "'We can't do it,' was all I could get out of them." Despite the many obstacles Chesnutt had to overcome before being able to fulfill his duties as a teacher, he remained surprisingly optimistic about his prospects and work. Ultimately, he found pleasure in teaching students how to read, write, and understand the principles of math and science.

Still, the frustration he felt in response to the members of the school committee who held the purse strings determining his wages and the structure of the school is apparent throughout these early entries. While he used his journal to develop his own philosophy of teaching—"no one need tell me, that a school cannot be governed without the administration of corporal punishment"—he also used it to register the shortcomings of the administration: "The 'committee' said they were going around to see about my board this week, but they 'haint' gone yet." It is unclear if Chesnutt spoke with a Southern drawl, though he does occasionally use Southern speech patterns to record his personal reflections. In entry after entry, Chesnutt celebrated the work of his students while complaining of having to deal with the dreaded school committee. Despite his complaints, these entries show Chesnutt developing close relationships with both his students and members of the committee. We also see Chesnutt's occasional use of Black dialect in the early journal. Words like *haint* and terms like *large-sized time* appear in quotation marks to indicate their distinction from the formal English Chesnutt employs. In the short stories, or what he calls "real attempts at literature," in this first journal, Chesnutt sticks to formal English, with very few exceptions.

By July 1874, Chesnutt has settled into his new life as a teacher. He described his "Adventure in the Capital" city of Raleigh where he attended an "Educational Convention." While here, Chesnutt caught a glimpse of politics for the first time. During his trip, he heard North Carolina's Democratic senator Augustus Summerfield Merrimon deliver a speech on

education. Elected to the Senate in 1872, Merrimon would gain a reputation as one of the bitterest partisan Democrats in Congress. No wonder Chesnutt left the room at "about the middle of this discourse ... and
fell asleep on an old sofa." Chesnutt wrote nothing about the content of
Merrimon's speech, only that he left in the middle of it. A few days after this adventure, Chesnutt found himself in "a right nice little place"
called Rockfish Village on Election Day. It was on this day that North
Carolina residents voted for their representatives to the U.S. Congress. It
would be the first election in the state in which Black men were elected to
hold federal office. As a sixteen-year-old certified schoolteacher, Chesnutt
was invited to act as an election clerk. He concluded his journal entry for
this momentous occasion by noting simply, "The Democrats gained from
5 to 15 votes at Rockfish." The following entry continued the political
theme. On his way home from practicing his organ at Harris's house, he
"met Democratic Delegation from Gray's Creek, for the Grand Democratic Rally." He then offered more of an analysis of the election's results:
"I hear today that Buxton is elected; and Hyman, the colored candidate
for Congress in the eastern part of the state is also elected. This somewhat
weakens the Democratic victory." The Republican Party, Chesnutt's party,
decisively lost the 1874 congressional elections. While historians have generally described this election as the beginning of the end of Reconstruction,
Chesnutt viewed the election more optimistically. Yes, the Democrats had
won a landslide victory, but Chesnutt, characteristically, focused on the
positive: Joseph Potts Buxton, a onetime anti-secessionist candidate to the
1861 state convention and longtime supporter of Negro rights, was re-
elected as a superior court justice, and Representative John Adams Hyman,
a former slave from Warrenton, was elected North Carolina's first Black
representative. Chesnutt's optimism amid what most considered dire to the
project of Southern Reconstruction would become typical of his response
to political events.

Back at school in Charlotte, Chesnutt developed a serious crush on a
girl called Josie. With an unembarrassed frankness, he wrote in his journal
about his feelings for her. When he left Charlotte for Spartanburg, South
Carolina, to teach at a new school, he pined for Josie, believing that "nothing would make me so happy as her presence." This early love led him to

reflect on the power of women over men, musing: "It is a strange thing—a little strange why women have so much influence with men. They are the 'weaker vessel,' yet they often wield the stronger." In his first published novel, *The House Behind the Cedars*, he would develop this theme in the character of Rena Walden whose "beauty and brains" captivated men, inspiring them to broaden their narrow political views. This burgeoning theory of women's power would prove key to the relationships between men and women that he developed in his later fiction.

Chesnutt spent most of 1875 in Charlotte, with a brief foray into Spartanburg, where he managed to land a short-term teaching position. It was during this time that Chesnutt started to study phonography. An entry on March 20 is written entirely in Pitman shorthand. Developed in England by Sir Isaac Pitman earlier in the century, shorthand was a system of writing based entirely on the sounds of words. Most of us would have learned to read through a similar method called *phonics*, in which we sounded out words and letters as we wrote them in our notebooks. Some of us learned to print letters by tracing them in our workbooks. Others learned to read letters by identifying them in books or on flash cards. While Chesnutt taught reading and writing to a broad range of students, he encountered phonography as a form of writing that for many was easier to grasp than the English alphabet. The English alphabet was based on the classical Latin alphabet and divided into upper- and lowercase letters, letters that did not match the sound of spoken language. Phonography was said to be more practical and easier to grasp after a bit of practice. Its purpose, according to its most ardent practitioners, was "to drop one's thoughts upon paper with the rapidity of speech, and with the clearness of unerring certainty to the eye."[6] Chesnutt used shorthand to save time and to write, at least at first, about particularly private experiences in his journals. He wrote about the kinds of experiences that he wouldn't want to share with others. In this way, shorthand functioned as a private language for Chesnutt. Unlike the other languages he studied at the time—French, German, and Latin— shorthand was not a literary language; it was entirely practical. His first entry in shorthand revealed that he was "getting along finely with the girls.

I heard last night that J.J. is back. I do not know whether to believe it or not." He went on in the entry to list all the girls who he believed were in love with him. These adolescent musings end on a political note: "The civil rights bill has passed! Glorious! Hurrah for the 43rd Congress! They were a long time about it, but it has passed at last." This entry marked the beginning of Chesnutt's lifelong commitment to the art of writing short-hand. Practicing it served multiple purposes. Shorthand allowed him to write more quickly; unlike writing in complex poetic forms like the sonnet or ballad, he could write about private matters of the heart in a form that did not require a great deal of thought. Another benefit of studying short-hand was that its alphabet, unlike the Latin or Greek alphabet, was in-tended to be a true representation of spoken sounds that allowed Chesnutt to develop a way of writing the conversations he heard spoken by Black men and women who were mostly illiterate.

Toward the end of Chesnutt's school term, on August 13, 1875, Chesnutt was exhausted from teaching. "I hope I shall be well in a few days, but I cannot shut my eyes to the fact that schoolteaching directly or indirectly, has ruined my health. I don't feel at all like a boy of seventeen should." Additionally, he was worried about money. He concluded his first journal with a tally of his expenses, his earnings, and his debts. After sending money home, paying for his room and board, and various other expenses, including medicine and transportation costs, his accounts were "square," but there was little money left over to spend on luxury items like books and paper.

He took a break from his journal when the regular school term started in September. There is not a single entry for the year 1876. Per-haps Chesnutt, like the rest of the country, was preoccupied with national political events. This year marked the centennial of the founding of the United States of America. It was also a presidential election year. Chesnutt turned eighteen on June 20 of that year and, according to the recently passed Fifteenth Amendment to the Constitution, was now eligible to vote in the presidential election held on Tuesday, November 7, 1876. This was not just any election year. It was the election that would determine the future direction of Southern Reconstruction. In the months that preceded the presidential election that year, the Republican Party seemed to be in disarray. After President Ulysses S. Grant declined to run for a third term, James G. Blaine, representative from Maine and a longtime Speaker of the House, emerged as the front-runner for the Republican nomination.

Chesnutt seemed to approve of Blaine and would extol his policies in later years, particularly regarding trade. Chesnutt believed that "it was by the policy so wisely conceived and so ably executed by the Hon. James G. Blaine, may his fame grow ever brighter, we are able by means of reciprocity to gain the advantages of commercial freedom and at the same time to avoid the evils of absolute free trade."[7] He must have been disappointed when, during the Republican National Convention held in Cincinnati just a few days before his birthday, Blaine lost the nomination to Ohio governor Rutherford B. Hayes. Hayes would go on to win the presidency, following a highly contentious election, in which the newly elected president agreed to withdraw all federal troops from the South. Historians have come to refer to this as the Compromise of 1877 that brought an end to the Reconstruction era. Chesnutt most likely voted for Hayes in the election of 1876. But he was no fan of President Hayes. Speaking to a group of students at the Ohio State Night School decades after the election, he declared "that after the election of Hayes as President the Republican party abandoned the Negro in the South."[8] It was one of the few occasions in his life when he would openly criticize the party to which he belonged.

The end of Reconstruction marked a new era in Chesnutt's life, as well as in the life of the nation. Chesnutt had transitioned from boy to man at a rapid pace. At fifteen, he had quit school to work. He worked long hours teaching an array of students, with classrooms full to the gills, sometimes with upward of fifty scholars. He worked on weekends at Sunday schools. He traveled long distances by horse and carriage and on foot in search of a school or church, where he might earn enough money to cover his living expenses and send a few dollars home to "Daddy." These first years of teaching were filled with worry and constant labor. He wanted to support his family; but he also wanted to spend his time and money on books. He revealed his feelings of love, guilt, homesickness, and self-loathing in his journal.

Those boyish feelings of guilt and despair over his lack of resources would disappear in the fall of 1877 with his return to Fayetteville. Though no longer supported by the Freedmen's Bureau, Harris's Howard School managed to grow and develop in new directions. At the end of the Reconstruction era, Howard Schools marked the beginning of the State Colored Normal Schools in the South. The remarkable success of Harris's Howard School entitled it to become the first State Colored Normal School in North Carolina. Funded now by the state of North Carolina rather than from the coffers of the former federal Freedmen's Bureau, Harris shifted his purpose from teaching the newly freed to training teachers for the colored elementary public schools of North Carolina. With this shift in funding and purpose, Harris invited Chesnutt to join him in his educational mission. As Harris's assistant principal, Chesnutt was tasked with innovating the curriculum to impart to other teachers the central principles of living a good life. And it was in literature that he found the principles he needed to teach—and to write.

Chesnutt's sense of himself had changed during the past year. He was now more organized and ambitious. He developed a new interest in imagination and became committed to the business of writing. The new journal, beginning in fall 1877, is marked by a new intersection between teaching and writing. He opened the journal with a declaration, stating its purpose in the grand scheme of both his personal education and that of his students. "In beginning this journal I have several things in view. I shall keep a record of any noteworthy events that may occur in my knowledge, a record of my performances as recapitulator in the Literary society, facts concerning teaching which are worthy of preservation; criticisms on men and things, on literature and current events. My principal object is to improve myself in the art of composition." Chesnutt seems to have taken his role as Harris's assistant seriously and had wholeheartedly embraced his role as teacher. He also revealed that he was now doing more than just teaching, he had taken on the extracurricular activity of recapitulator of the normal school's newly established literary society. In a remarkable turn away from his previous schoolteaching activities in Charlotte and Spartanburg, in which he struggled to teach students who barely knew how to recognize the letters of the alphabet, Chesnutt's journal shows a marked and steady interest in ancient history, classical literature and language, and rhetoric.

Chesnutt was now feverishly active. He spent the fall semester teaching himself Latin, French, and algebra, focusing on solving difficult problems to develop his mind. He also read history, both ancient and modern. He wrote little during these months, however. His schedule exhausted him. He woke up early to read before classes began and went to bed late. He needed more time, but much of the day was spent in school, teaching. By the end of November 1877, Chesnutt took another long break from his journal. He seemed to be distracted again by current events, but this time, it was not a political affair that distracted him; it was a personal one.

Chesnutt revealed little about his future wife, Susan Perry, in his journal. We know from Helen's biography that Susan's father owned a barbershop in the Fayetteville Hotel and that she taught at the Howard School. But Chesnutt said nothing about their courtship or how they fell in love. His previous experience of young love with Josie seems to have been forgotten. Perhaps this maturer relationship did not summon the verses of longing and despair that Josie inspired. In a later journal entry, penned on Thursday, July 21, 1881, after they had been married for about three years, Chesnutt would offer a somewhat fuller picture of his feelings for Susie. "I have found an old picture of Susie taken several years before she was married. She was not pretty, but she was *good*—the picture shows it. I was lucky in my marriage. If I were on the carpet now, I should not know which way to turn for a woman I could admire and *respect*." This feeling of good fortune and respect characterized the Chesnutts' fifty-four-year marriage.

Chesnutt married Susan on June 6, 1878. He was nineteen and she sixteen. It must have been a very low-key ceremony because there is no mention of a church wedding. Nor were any photographs of their wedding preserved. Their daughter, Ethel, was born shortly after the marriage, on April 12, 1879. Eleven days later, on April 23, Chesnutt reflected on the utility of keeping a diary. "Some think it is a wise thing to keep a diary; others think it very foolish, but, in my opinion, very few try it for a sufficient time to ascertain which of the two views is really correct." He continued, "It seems to me that a record of the most important events in one's own life, and the results to which they have led, together with the reflections which were suggested by them at the time of their occurrence, would be useful and entertaining in after life." Several paragraphs later, in the same entry, he mentioned, in passing, the birth of his first child. "I had the pleasure of a long conversation with Dr. Haigh when he was waiting for the advent of my little Ethel into this 'sinful world.'" That is all he wrote about the birth of his first child. He does not mention when, precisely, his daughter was born or the circumstances of her delivery. Only that he and Dr. Haigh had been engaged in a conversation about his moving north to pursue "more opportunities" because of "less prejudice." April 23 is the first entry for 1879; the previous entry is from Christmas 1878. Born between these two entries, Ethel arrived with little fanfare. Given the circumstances surrounding his quiet and quick marital union, it would be safe to assume that Susan might have been pregnant when Chesnutt married her. Neither a shotgun nor grandiose wedding, the Chesnutts' union was something in between. Susan was several shades darker than Chesnutt, but there is no mention of a difference between them. Their families both hailed from the "free colored" population of North Carolina, so there were no obstacles to the union. At twenty, Chesnutt moved with his new wife and baby into the Perry family home, which Helen recalls vividly: "The Perrys lived in an interesting old colonial house with white columns and open fireplaces, and with a great magnolia tree standing guard at each side of the house." Susan was used to living relatively well; Chesnutt was obliged to find a way to provide not only for himself and his siblings but also for Susan and little Ethel. Chesnutt did not take his familial responsibilities lightly. Nor did his interest in books and reading diminish. In fact, it only grew, just as Ethel did.

Reading Alone

When we turn back, as we can through the medium of books, to the
dawn of history, and follow its course down to our own time, the troubles of any one individual or any one race dwindle into comparative
insignificance; and when we look around us and see the forces of progress in operation on every hand, imagination pictures for us a future for
which the troubles of to-day are but a brief apprenticeship.

—"Literature in Its Relation to Life" (1899)

In the months following his marriage to Susan, Chesnutt started to read
with increased intensity and purpose. Though he had risen in the ranks
of teaching rapidly, Chesnutt's heart was just not in it. He tried to follow
Harris's noble example and was grateful for the salary and respect derived
from teaching, but he was always dissatisfied. He wanted to do something
else, "some literary avocation," and live in a metropolis, like Benjamin
Franklin or Horace Greeley, his heroes at this time.[1] It was to the business
of literature that Chesnutt gave all the time and energy he could salvage
from teaching. Out of the classroom, he became his own pupil.

Chesnutt was intellectually isolated during these early years of marriage and fatherhood, finding true companionship mostly in the books
he read. Chesnutt's second journal kept from 1877 is the lengthiest and
densest of the journals he kept throughout his life. This second journal
is full of quotations from his reading along with personal responses to
books and drafts of essays, stories, and poems. During this active seedtime,
Chesnutt's reading moved in several directions. He started with Homer's

Iliad, translated into English by Alexander Pope, providing pages and pages of notes on the epic, drawing parallels between the ancient Greeks and his contemporary Americans. He read Voltaire's history of Charles XII in its original French, *Histoire de Charles XII* (1731), and then transcribed his favorite passages from the book into his notebook to memorize. He became enamored by Alexandre Dumas and Charles Dickens, the poetry of Henry Wadsworth Longfellow and Robert Burns. He culled phrases, details, facts, metaphors, anecdotes, witticisms, aphorisms, and ideas from almost everything he read. While this intensive reading heightened his feelings of isolation, it also allowed him to develop his own version of Emersonian self-reliance. "As I have been thrown constantly on my own resources in my solitary studies, I have acquired some degree of *self-reliance*. As I have no learned professor or obliging classmate to construe the hard passages, and work the difficult problems, I have '*persevered*' till I solved them myself." Departing slightly from Ralph Waldo Emerson's famous essay on "Self-Reliance" that he composed in 1841, which celebrated a person's relationship to nature in opposition to the laws regulating society, Chesnutt's self-reliance derived from creating an identity for himself born of the books he read. Chesnutt and Emerson were united, however, by their mutual aversion "to badges and names, to large societies and dead institutions."[2]

When he returned to Fayetteville at nineteen, Chesnutt had acquired a good deal of experience and independence. He no longer saw himself as a boy of sixteen lost in the woods but was now a man with considerable responsibility developing his own methods of teaching. In Chesnutt's first months in his new position at the normal school, he found his classes progressing well. Still, he was less interested in teaching his students than in being a student himself. Before and after teaching his classes, he turned his attention to his own learning. He initiated his education with algebra, observing that "the properties of the Equations are not hard to understand; the difficulty is in remembering them." A little later, he turned to the study of ancient history. He concluded that reading history, like doing algebra, is useful, but in a different way. Practicing algebra allowed him to remember difficult things, whereas through history, he gained a general view of the founding of a government, the settlement of a country, the building of a city, and the manners and customs of its people. Chesnutt studied algebra and history by himself. He pursued these subjects because he understood their value and took great pleasure in studying. In this way, Chesnutt's education departed from that of the typical undergraduate at the time who was required to take a set of classes in four years of college to earn an *artium baccalaureus*, or AB, the Latin name given for a degree in the liberal arts. Unable to attend a college or university of his choice, Chesnutt developed a liberal arts curriculum of his own that he recorded in his journal.

Chesnutt's curriculum repudiated formulae and outcomes. He read what he liked, what gave him pleasure, unconcerned about practical application or moral duty. Learning what he fancied offered relief from his teaching posts, where he was told what to do and how to instruct. He was at the center of the universe in this journal; he allowed himself to determine who he was (or would become) simply by what he chose to read and write. He also developed a new sense of himself. He saw himself as a man of the world, no longer a boy who wrote of his crushes on girls and political events with the same enthusiasm. Chesnutt became more analytical, developing his own perspective on current events. Married and expecting a child, his social life was restricted to taking care of his new family. Space in his journal was reserved for important matters and self-improvement: "If a scientific fact is new, or particularly impressive, it shall be deemed worthy of a place in my note-book. As this book is intended only for my own perusal, if I write trash no one will be the worse for it. If I write anything that is worth reading, I, perhaps, shall be the better for it." At nineteen, Chesnutt had grown tired of being told who he was or who he should be. He did not want to be a colored teacher; he wanted to learn new things and go to new places, places where he was either not allowed to enter or more often could not afford the cost of the journey. With the beginning of the new school term in the fall of 1877, Chesnutt was ready to take a new path, one that he paved himself, though he had no idea at the time where it would lead.

On August 13, 1878, just a couple of months after his marriage and twentieth birthday, Chesnutt read Homer's *Iliad*. He read it not in its original ancient Greek (though he would learn Greek later) but in the best

English translation he could find. This was a standard book for most undergraduates at the time. Perhaps it was for this reason, to be the undergraduate that he could not be, that Chesnutt chose to read Homer. His reading of Homer began with the understanding that "although every undergraduate has criticized him, though all his real and imaginary beauties have been pointed out, though mountains of paper and rivers of ink have been sacrificed to his memory, yet there may still remain some reflections on his style, or some criticism on his heroes, some bright spot which has not been overflowed by those rivers of ink, or buried under those mountains of paper." By taking up the *Iliad*, Chesnutt was going to prove to himself that he was as good as any undergraduate, those (mostly young white men) who had the intelligence and good fortune to attend an elite liberal arts college.

Homer gave Chesnutt a solid foundation. He seemed to have read books one through three of the classic epic in a single sitting, copying noteworthy passages, remarking on the characters' virtues or their lack of them. Mostly, he was in awe of Homer as a writer, the breadth of the poet's knowledge, a knowledge acquired from "personal observation" rather than reading books. Comparing Homer's "bookless days" to his own days that were filled, from morning till night, with books, Chesnutt realized the importance of traveling, seeing *his* country as Homer saw ancient Greece. Homer, in Chesnutt's mind "seemed to possess an accurate knowledge of every city, river, and mountain in Greece; to have been familiar with all their local traditions and history." Unable to travel like Homer, Chesnutt relied on books for encouragement and stimulation.

He followed the advice he read in what was then a popular book among students by John Todd called *The Student's Manual: Designed by Specific Directions to Aid in Forming and Strengthening the Intellectual and Moral Character and Habits of the Student.* The book offered several aphorisms in Latin that Chesnutt tried, by writing them in his journal, to commit to memory: *Non omnes omnia possumus.* Everyone is not capable of everything. Be diligent but thorough in your studies. *Ferret taurum qui tulit vitulam.* He who would carry the ox must every day shoulder the calf. Chesnutt was training himself to be a good student—one who studied hard and never gave up. He reread these words to himself when he felt despair toward his condition, when he felt lonely. Repeating these words to himself, Chesnutt believed, would allow him to be the kind of student he desperately wanted to become.

However, reading broadly and intensively seemed only to lead Chesnutt to lament the limitations of his environment. Rather than feeling liberated by reading, by gaining the knowledge that was supposed to set him free from the constraints of his environment, he felt more hemmed in by the smallness of Fayetteville than ever before. He wrote, "I have studied and practiced till I can understand and appreciate good music, but I never hear what little there is to be heard. I have studied German and have no one to converse with but a few Jewish merchants who can talk nothing but business. As to procuring instruction in Latin, French, German, or Music, that is entirely out of the question. First-class teachers would not teach a 'nigger' and I would have no other sort." Chesnutt wanted a "first-class teacher," but such a teacher, he believed, was unavailable to him because of who he was. Chesnutt longed to live in a place where who he was or where he was from did not affect his ability to learn. He came to believe that the only way to get the education he wanted was "to go to the North." There, he imagined, he could take on the prejudice against him and "show to the world that a man may spring from a race of slaves, and yet far excel many of the boasted ruling race." He imagined that in the North he would find people not blinded by race, people who would recognize him for what he could do rather than for who he was. Vowing to avoid those "so blinded by prejudice as not to recognize and honor true merit wherever discovered," he set his sights on leaving Fayetteville.

In the meantime, he continued his study of the classics at home. Homer, Voltaire, Virgil, Goethe, Thackeray. Latin, Greek, French, German. He read closely Hugh Blair's classic *Lectures on Rhetoric* and wrote frequent compositions. Blair provided a lucid, reasonable, widely accepted approach to English style. Blair treated figurative language not as "the invention of schools" but as the natural clothing of the energetic and passionate speech of ordinary people. It was from Blair that he learned that "a writer's chief dependence must be on himself, for no author wishes to be a servile imitator, and good sense, and certainly a cultivated taste will be sufficient to detect the improper use of figures, while a lively imagination is necessary to supply them." With Homer and Blair as his virtual instructors, Chesnutt created for himself a first-class education without having to pay tuition or having to encounter hostile roommates.

Despite Chesnutt's passionate commitment to self-reliance and independence of thought in these journal entries, his literary writing from this period relied heavily on well-worn conventions that were commonplace and dull. He wrote several poems in his journal, mostly in rhyming couplets, imitating the style of English romantic poets.

> It was in the joyful spring-time
> That first I saw the light
> And raised from earth my tiny head
> To greet the sunbeam bright.
> The husbandman had plowed his land
> And sowed the yellow grain
> And left it to the genial sun.
> And the softening spring-time rain.

This poem, untitled, goes on for another fifteen stanzas in much the same way. It is a poem that personifies a kernel of corn that grows into a stalk. The lesson of the poem is for man to care not only for the plant but also for the "little ones" that "may grow on a thousand years." The little ones are the seeds of corn, probably representing future generations. There are more like it, concerning different subjects from love and the evening to Christmas. They are written in different forms but tend to stick closely to classical forms: sonnets, heroic couplets, and ballads.

Midway through the second journal, on March 11, 1880, there was a shift in Chesnutt's writing. At this moment, his journal takes on a new, different purpose from the one with which he started. Chesnutt grew less interested in reading the work of other men. Instead, he wanted to record his own thoughts. His journal became a "mental Phonograph, into which I speak my thoughts by means of the pen; and at any future time I can recall them by simply opening the book. If it could copy my thoughts without the aid or intervention of the pen, it would contain a great many more than it does; for with school and church, with shorthand and music, with correspondence and general reading, my time is so fully occupied that I seldom write in my Journal."

The phonograph had been invented by Thomas Edison a few years earlier in 1877. While Chesnutt had already been studying Pitman's shorthand, Edison's phonograph represented something new. Chesnutt was quick to jump on this new technology, impressed by the practical value of the new machine and by its impact on his own writing. A few months later, on June 28, 1880, he was still musing on the possibilities of the phonograph: "I must write a lecture on phonography—the principles of the art; its uses, and the method of learning it." Interested less in ancient history and more in current events, particularly scientific inventions of the time that were changing the way people communicated and related to one another, Chesnutt was beginning to enter a new era; this era was moving well beyond Reconstruction, an era that was mostly focused on rebuilding old institutions that had been destroyed by war. This new era, what people would come to refer to as the Gilded Age, a name drawn from a recently published novel by Mark Twain and Charles Dudley Warner, was fully focused on the future, creating new systems and machines that would transform the way people lived and thought.

On April 19, 1878, *The Washington Post* reported on Edison's trip to Washington, DC. It was here that Edison introduced to an audience comprised of members of the National Academy of Sciences, congressmen, senators, and President Hayes the possibilities of the phonograph. The phonograph could record voices and play them back to you so that you could *hear* poetry rather than having to read it for yourself. Edison anticipated using sound-recording technology to make books *speak*, rendering a closer relationship between writing dialogue and recording speech.

Chesnutt visited DC about a year after Edison's famous performance, in the summer of 1879. It was his first trip away from home since his marriage. The trip was taken in some distress and haste. He had been working hard at school and spending so much of his spare time reading that he had "worried Susie into a positive dislike of me, and the following week took the train for Washington." It was an odd time to take a solo trip. Ethel would have been no more than three months old; his young wife must have had her hands full with care of the baby and juggling household duties.

Why leave now? Chesnutt saw Washington not only as the nation's capital, a center of politics and culture, but also as a place where colored men like himself enjoyed the privileges and rights denied to him in Fayetteville. He searched for a way to realize the life he could only imagine by reading books and practicing shorthand, void of the drudgery and restrictions he lamented at home. However, he soon learned that there were just as many restrictions in DC as there were in Fayetteville, only of a different kind. He started his journey by train and found the "journey to Washington about as disagreeable as traveling generally is. The dust and dirt of the R.R. cars, the smoke (of which I had the full benefit, as I traveled second class), the tiresome stoppages, the provoking slowness of some of the trains, the rapacity of porters and luggage boys, all combined to make the journey an infliction which is endured simply because it can't be helped." By "second class," Chesnutt referred to his colored status, which mandated him to those areas of the train reserved for colored passengers and for smoking. He described his experience of traveling "second class" in considerable detail in subsequent paragraphs of his journal that he would draw on when writing the train car scenes for *The Marrow of Tradition* years later.

He traveled from Raleigh through Weldon, North Carolina, and arrived in Norfolk, Virginia, by train. At Norfolk, Chesnutt bought a ticket on the steamship *George Leary*, which he described as "a handsome steamer" that was "roomy and comfortable, the water was smooth, the crowd large, and some of the women were handsome. There was a piano in the ladies cabin, and a string band which discoursed quadrilles for the dancers on the lower deck." It seems the ship was not divided into separate class cars, as was the train, and proved to be the most enjoyable part of Chesnutt's journey to the nation's capital. Upon arrival, Chesnutt made his way to a friend's house, whom, for some reason, he did not name. Drawing on the eighteenth-century literary convention of dashes to disguise the names of real people who appear in novelistic fiction, he referred to his "friend W—" living "in a dirty room in the 6th story of a large house right in the business part of the city." Having settled into his friend's room, he embarked on his first tour of the capital. He started his tour of DC at the Capitol Building, which he visited several times during his two-week stay, describing what he observed in considerable detail. Chesnutt found the

Capitol to be "a magnificent structure . . . worthy to be Capitol of a great nation." For the first time, we get a sense of Chesnutt's patriotism, his love of his country, despite its many flaws. From the Capitol, he went on to visit less impressive sites: the Senate Chamber, where he heard Senators Blaine and Vance argue, the post office, the Patent Office, and other department buildings before visiting with relatives of Robert Harris, who took him on a tour of the public schools of the city, which he found "well graded, and generally having efficient teachers."

Chesnutt had hoped that he might find employment as a stenographer in some government agency but learned from Senator Vance that was unlikely. Having succeeded in delivering his letter of introduction to the Democratic senator from North Carolina, he was told that "as far as an office was concerned, there were none to be got; that there were more stenographers in Washington than could obtain employment." Less interested in what he described as Washington's corrupt politics, Chesnutt was captivated by the architecture of the city. "It is large, systematically planned, embellished with broad avenues, parks, handsome public and private buildings." He also visited Howard University, which he admired, at least for its location and architecture. "The buildings are grouped on a hill overlooking the city; a very healthy location, removed from the noise and dust, and quite near enough for the conveniences of the city. A street car line runs by the gate, and the mail is carried out twice a day." He does not comment on the university's academic buildings, students, or professors. Chesnutt was impressed mostly by the city's efficiency; yet he returned home with renewed appreciation for his small town and the people who lived there. "There is too much noise, too little fresh air. The water from the hydrants is good, but I prefer mine from a well. There are so many people, and so many men of wealth and distinction that a man must be very rich or very distinguished to attract any notice." Chesnutt's trip to the capital gave him ideas for distinguishing himself but also allowed him to appreciate those things about life in Fayetteville that he previously ignored or, worse, disparaged as being backward.

Upon his return home, Chesnutt wrote in his journal with a speed and efficiency he hoped mirrored life in the city. Working like a phonograph, he wanted to speed up the rate of his literary production. Chesnutt wrote in a loopy cursive style, painstakingly acquired as Harris's student at the Howard School. This style required time that he did not have. Like so many in the United States at the time, Chesnutt was interested in inventions. Inventions were reported in the papers almost daily. Men like Samuel Morse, Isaac Singer, George Pullman, Alexander Graham Bell, and of course Thomas Edison made fortunes from patenting their inventions and making headlines. These inventions made a difference in the lives of poor Americans, including Chesnutt, his fellow teachers, and their students. Americans across the economic spectrum believed that such inventions would save time, putting an end to the tedious chores that occupied most of their days. Chesnutt wanted to spend time on more pleasurable pursuits, like reading and playing the organ. He even came up with an invention of his own, which he described in his journal as "a contrivance, to be attached to reed organs, by means of which the position of the reeds may be shifted, so as to enable the performer to play in any key without shifting the position of his hands on the key-board." The intended purpose of Chesnutt's invention was to move faster, play faster, and do more with the little time he had between teaching school, attending church, studying, being a father and husband.

Over a decade after the invention of the phonograph, Chesnutt would expound more explicitly on its value in a speech to the Ohio Stenographers' Association in 1889, of which he served as president for two terms. Chesnutt ranked phonography as one of "the great inventions of the nineteenth century; along with the steam engine, the telegraph, the sewing machine, and the telephone." But when he first heard of the phonograph, he saw it as more than just another technological innovation. Edison's phonograph would change the way Chesnutt thought about writing literature. Literature wasn't just about reading books or joining elite society to speak in a coded language that only few could understand. It was also, as he learned from Homer, a living record of a people. Literature could record the conversation and emotions of those who were kept, for one reason or another, apart from the ruling class—unlike those people he observed in Washington, DC, or those who could attend expensive private colleges or ride in first class. Chesnutt wanted to tell the stories of people like himself. The phonograph would become

Chesnutt's ticket into the first-class literary world that seemed until its invention out of his reach.

Chesnutt's newfound interest in the phonograph and other mechanical inventions led him to make a literary discovery: "that a collection of ballads or hymns which the colored people sing with such fervor, might be acceptable, if only as a curiosity to people, literary people at the North." For the first time, Chesnutt was beginning to appreciate his fellow Black North Carolinians. Previously, he had seen these people as illiterate, uneducated, bigoted, superstitious, and hardheaded. Now he viewed them as original and worth writing about. He found their music to be original: "These songs are not of much merit as literary compositions, they have certain elements of originality which make them interesting to a student of literature, who can trace, in a crude and unpolished performance, more of the natural ability or character of the writer than in the more correct production of a cultivated mind." This was not the first time, nor would it be the last, a notable writer would remark on the originality of the ballads sung by Black people in the United States. In fact, these songs, and efforts to collect them, to record them in one way or another, would become the hallmark of what now goes by the name *African American literature*.

Perhaps the first mention of these songs, at least in print, appeared in Frederick Douglass's 1845 autobiography, *Narrative of the Life of Frederick Douglass, an American Slave*. In this influential work, Douglass described with dismay being "utterly astonished" by Northerners "who could speak of the singing, among slaves, as evidence of their contentment and happiness." Setting the record straight, Douglass reprimanded those who made this mistake. He went on to explain the meaning and beauty of these songs in a single unforgettable sentence: "The songs of the slaves represent the sorrow of his heart; and he is relieved by them, only as an aching heart is relieved by its tears." Decades later, in the early twentieth century, W. E. B. Du Bois and James Weldon Johnson, both prominent members of the newly formed National Association for the Advancement of Colored People, would publish books, now classics of African American literature, in which the songs of the colored people, what Du Bois aptly called "Sorrow Songs" in his 1903 book, *The Souls of Black Folk*, constituted the apex of Black culture in the United States. Unlike Du Bois and Johnson, who capitalized on the beauty and originality of the songs in their literary work, Chesnutt did not collect the songs or write about them publicly. Instead, he made literature by recording the voices of the colored people, copying their speech patterns in writing, a practice that he would first develop in his journal.

Chesnutt turned to his journal on March 16, 1880, to confide his mixed feelings of jealousy and admiration for an author he knew only by reputation but who would become a lifelong friend. Next to his entry on Homer's *Iliad*, this is the longest entry of the journal. Of all the authors Chesnutt read as a young man, no author had a greater impact on his future career as a writer than Albion Winegar Tourgée. And this was partly because unlike most of the authors Chesnutt was reading in his early twenties, Tourgée was one of the few who was Chesnutt's *contemporary*, a real, live, American author writing about the lives of North Carolinians like himself. In this journal entry, as in his later letters to him, Chesnutt employed the formal title *Judge* when referring to Tourgée, even though Tourgée had given up his position as a superior court judge in North Carolina upon the publication of his first novel, *Toinette*, in 1874. By the time Chesnutt recorded his thoughts on Tourgée's third, and most popular, novel in his journal in 1880, Tourgée's literary career was in full swing. By this time, Tourgée had given up on his political career in the South, having found writing literature about politics in the South to be far more lucrative. Chesnutt would have first heard Tourgée's name when he was around ten years old, when Tourgée was nominated by North Carolina Republicans for the position of superior court judge of the Seventh Judicial District in 1868.

Originally from Ohio, Tourgée had joined the 105th Volunteer Infantry for the Union army at the outbreak of the Civil War. Like Chesnutt's father, Tourgée decided to relocate to North Carolina after the war, in October 1865. Growing up in Fayetteville, about a hundred miles from where Tourgée had settled with his family in Greensboro, the Chesnutts would have viewed Tourgée as something of a political celebrity. Tourgée was not the only Northerner to rail against the political conventions and ignorance of Southerners, particularly in his newly adopted state of North Carolina. He was part of a Reconstruction literary clique of Northerners that included writers such as John William De Forest, Anna E. Dickinson, and Constance Fenimore Woolson. All were Northerners who had traveled to the South and reported on their experiences in the form of fiction. The purpose of their fiction was to portray their personal interactions with Southerners to help the North develop better relations with their former enemy. Of the members of this emerging literary movement, Tourgée was perhaps the most vocal and certainly the most disliked by those, particularly Southern Democrats, who were eager to reassert Southern values by removing the presence of Northerners. Transplanted Northerners—or carpetbaggers, as they were derisively known at the time—like Tourgée, were a thorn in the side of the South's efforts to reassert its power, or just its dignity, after losing the war.

Tourgée became a key figure for the struggle to protect voting rights for African Americans promised by the passage of the Fifteenth Amendment. Elected as a delegate to the 1868 constitutional convention, he was instrumental in drafting the state's new constitution. That same year, he won election as a superior court judge, serving from 1868 until his defeat in 1874. He made a name for himself as a defender of Black civil rights, introducing "color-blind" justice to a racially segregated U.S. court system.

Chesnutt certainly agreed with Tourgée's radical political positions, especially concerning voting rights. He was less sympathetic with the methods by which Tourgée expressed his views. Tourgée didn't really know the South as Chesnutt did. He had come to the South as an adult, after fighting in the war, to rebuild the region and convert its citizens to the democratic principles espoused by the North. Unlike Chesnutt, who took a more passive approach to political affairs, Tourgée was a radical. He wanted change for the South, and he wanted it now. Though he wrote of Tourgée in his journal with admiration and respect, Chesnutt was also skeptical of Tourgée's popularity as a *literary* author.

The publication of Tourgée's *A Fool's Errand* in 1879 was just as much a political event as it was a literary one. Its New York publisher, Fords, Howard, & Hulbert, released the first edition without naming its author, creating a good deal of speculation about the author's identity. The original title page stated that the novel was written "By One of the Fools" followed by a quotation from one of William Shakespeare's lesser-known plays, *Timon of Athens.* It tells the story of an important political figure who is also a poor judge of character and, after a series of misadventures, departs from society to die in the wilderness. But it is to Shakespeare's fool, a standard character of comic relief found in his plays, that the author of *A Fool's Errand* calls our attention. Drawing on the English tradition of the fool, the novel introduced readers to Colonel Comfort Servosse. The novel's protagonist is based largely on Tourgée's own experiences of living and working in the South as a carpetbagger, first as an owner of a vineyard and then as a lawyer and judge. While the novel is mostly a tragic-comical account of Reconstruction, as seen through the eyes of a carpetbagger who becomes embroiled in local politics, it also introduced Northern readers to several Black characters whom Servosse (or Tourgée) encountered during his time in the South. There is Uncle Jerry, Andy, and Bob Martin, all former slaves who speak in dialect to indicate their lack of education and continued degraded position in the post-emancipation South. Despite their position and limited vocabulary, these men are presented in the novel as intelligent and brave.

No wonder *A Fool's Errand* was viewed as a kind of Reconstruction sequel to Harriet Beecher Stowe's best-selling antislavery novel, *Uncle Tom's Cabin.* The *Raleigh Observer* declared the novel to be "a powerfully written work, and destined, we fear, to do as much harm in the world as 'Uncle Tom's Cabin,' to which it is, indeed, a companion piece." And, like *Uncle Tom's Cabin,* it sold more than 150,000 copies within the first year it appeared on the lists of booksellers, prompting its publisher to put out a second edition the following year, adding a note about its original reception. "The reception accorded to this anonymous book, both by press and public, has been so unusual, and the impression made by the work has been so marked, that these facts are worth recording." The publisher included extracts from some press notices to give readers both a sense of the novel's popularity and influence. They also included an advertisement for other works by Albion W. Tourgée, *Figs and Thistles* and *Toinette.* The first is a thinly veiled biography of his friend and political ally James Abram Garfield, who was inaugurated the twentieth president of the United States on March 4, 1881. Tourgée was devastated, as was much of the country, when Garfield was assassinated four months later, on July 2, 1881, at the

Baltimore and Potomac Railroad Station on his way to attend his college reunion in Williamstown, Massachusetts. Tourgée had written *Figs and Thistles*, an homage to Garfield's early life and political experience, the same year as *a Fool's Errand*. Though the latter novel garnered much more political attention, both books were said to have played a pivotal role in soliciting support for Garfield's presidency.

Judging by press releases and literary reviews, it seemed as though everyone was talking about *A Fool's Errand* in 1880. And Chesnutt was no exception. On March 16, he mused in his journal:

> Judge Tourgee has sold the "Fool's Errand," I understand for $20,000. I suppose he had already received a large royalty on the sale of the first few editions. The work has gained an astonishing degree of popularity, and is to be translated into the French... Judge Tourgee is a Northern man, who has lived at the South since the war, until recently. He knows a great deal about the politics, history, and laws of the South. He is a close observer of men and things, and has exercised this faculty of observation upon the character of the Southern people. Nearly all his stories are more or less about colored people, and this very feature is one source of their popularity.

The publication and popularity of Tourgée's novel signaled a new turn, at least for Chesnutt, in American literature. People in the progressive North, it turned out, were actually interested in reading about the lives and circumstances of colored people in the South. It was not just the amount of money Tourgée was rumored to have earned from the novel that impressed Chesnutt. The novel's popularity revealed to Chesnutt the great demand for books set in the South about the condition of the "colored people" now "struggling for education, for a higher social and moral life, against wealth, intelligence, and race prejudice, which are all united to keep him down." Prior to the novel's publication, Chesnutt saw himself at a great disadvantage. How could he compete with English writers like Charles Dickens and William Makepeace Thackeray, who had first-class educations and whose fictions were set in cosmopolitan London, a world far removed from

Chesnutt's backward, middle-of-nowhere Fayetteville? Tourgée was writing about people and places that Chesnutt knew. Heck, he could have been easily mistaken as one of Tourgée's characters himself. He continued:

> And if Judge Tourgee, with his necessarily limited intercourse with colored people, and with his limited stay in the South, can write such interesting descriptions, such vivid pictures of Southern life and character as to make himself rich and famous, why could not a colored man, who has lived among colored people all his life; who is familiar with their habits, their ruling passions, their prejudices; their whole moral and social condition; and habit;—why could not a colored man who knew all this, and who, besides, had possessed such opportunities for observation and conversation with the better class of white men in the south as to understand their modes of thinking; who was familiar with the political history of the country, and especially with all the phases of the slavery question;—why could not such a man, if he possessed the same ability, write a far better book about the South than Judge Tourgee or Mrs. Stowe has written? Answer who can!

Chesnutt sounds here about as worked up as those former Confederate Southerners, like William Lawrence Royall, who viewed Tourgée's novel "as a wilful, deliberate, and malicious libel upon a noble and generous people." Of course, Royall was writing mostly in defense of *white* Southerners. In 1881, Royall published *A Reply to "A Fool's Errand, by One of the Fools"* to defend Southerners with whom Royall "was born and raised, and in full sympathy."[3] Despite Chesnutt's and Royall's very different points of view, both complain of Tourgée that "much as the writer has seen of the people of that section, he does not know them." Interestingly, Royall also critiqued Tourgée's representation of Black characters: "He has manifestly heard a good deal of the negro dialect; and yet his representation of that dialect is ridiculous to those who have been raised with the negro."[4] Tourgée's characters were not just ridiculous to Chesnutt, they were also offensive. For Chesnutt, the problem with Tourgée's representation of Black characters was less a political issue than it was a literary one. Like Royall,

Chesnutt's objective was to point out Tourgée's ignorance about Southern life. In contrast to Royall, Chesnutt was less interested in the novel's politics than he was in its representation of colored people like himself and those with whom he lived and worked. Tourgée's Black characters were not *real*; they were false, almost cartoonish, in their one-dimensionality. If Tourgée could write a best-selling novel about the people Chesnutt knew intimately, surely, Chesnutt could do the same. Chesnutt's characters would be drawn from life, *his* life, and the people he encountered every day.

Chesnutt wasted little time in pursuing his new goal. With the publication of *A Fool's Errand*, the idea of being a writer became more tangible. He ended his reflections on the novel and its author by making a literary promise to himself.

> I intend to record my impressions of men and things, and such incidents or conversations which take place within my knowledge, with a view to future use in literary work. I shall not record stale negro minstrel jokes, or worn out newspaper squibs on the "man and brother." I shall leave the realm of fiction, where most of this stuff is manufactured, and come down to hard facts.

Unlike his broken promises to write in his journal more frequently, this was a promise Chesnutt kept. Rather than reporting on his reading as he did in the beginning of the journal, he turned to "men and things," and the first conversation he decided to record was one that he'd had that day with a man called "Mr. George H. Haigh, Bookseller."

Haigh came from a prominent white Fayetteville family. His brother, Dr. T. D. Haigh, helped to deliver Chesnutt's daughters and served as chairman of the board of managers of the State Colored Normal School. Though they were white and wealthy, Chesnutt knew the Haighs well. Chesnutt would have dealt with Dr. Haigh frequently as part of his administrative work for the normal school. Upon Chesnutt's resignation from the school, Dr. Haigh provided a reference letter for him, describing him as "a thoroughly reliable man" whose conduct "as a citizen has been such as to merit and incite the approval of all." But it was George who proved to be an important literary source. Born in 1832 in Fayetteville,

George H. Haigh earned his AB from the University of North Carolina in 1852, the same year *Uncle Tom's Cabin* hit bookstands. He would go on to marry the daughter of E. J. Hale, a wealthy landowner who also owned the local newspaper, *The Fayetteville Observer*, that Haigh would eventually inherit. In 1861, Haigh enlisted in the Confederate army as a private, rising to the rank of captain. Upon his return to Fayetteville after the war, he opened a bookstore on the northwest corner of the Market Square, where Chesnutt spent hours discussing current events, books, and magazine articles and getting to know the former Confederate. It was time well spent. It was through these conversations, meticulously recorded in his journals, that he would create the complex antihero Major Philip Carteret, who would play a leading role in *The Marrow of Tradition*, published a couple of decades later.

Chesnutt's conversation with Haigh was just one of several conversations he recorded in his journals. He also recorded conversations he had with the Reverend J. W. Davis, the minister of the African Methodist Episcopal Zion church where Chesnutt worshipped every Sunday. We can already detect in these early recorded conversations Chesnutt's ironic tone, a generous sense of humor and wit that would become characteristic of his literary style. Chesnutt had a great deal of fun recording and commenting on Davis's sermons or what, quoting the minister, he called his "style of preaching." Chesnutt described Elder Davis as "an energetic man" who despite being "uneducated" developed complex sermons that aimed to reach "the three classes of people" who attended his church. Chesnutt recorded Davis's words, as he did Haigh's, verbatim in his journal, with minimal interruption or description. But unlike the political, even antagonistic, tone of his conversation with Haigh, Chesnutt's conversation with Elder Davis sounds more like a story. After recording Davis's disquisition on preaching, Chesnutt provided his own commentary on Davis's description, making his narration sound like that of a novelist more than a diarist. In fact, the conversation with Elder Davis is set off from the date of the journal entry. Chesnutt even gives it the title "A novel Idea in Preaching," using quotation marks to distinguish Davis's speech from his thoughts on it. In remarking on what Davis says, Chesnutt functioned as both narrator and witness. "The effect is truly dramatic. I saw Davis once jump down from the pulpit and run across the altar. A scene ensued, such as I had never witnessed before, and never wish to see again."

Beginning in March 1880, Chesnutt wrote less about what he was reading and more about what he was hearing. Moving away from copying or imitating the style of other authors, Chesnutt used his conversations with people to create stories of his own. He wrote down what he *heard* and created a context for these conversations that was based on his personal experience and reactions. But it was not enough. Chesnutt longed for more "friction of mind upon mind." Instead, he found himself too often alone with his thoughts. By this time, Susan had taken Ethel to Wilmington to visit with friends and relatives. They had been gone for over a month, and Chesnutt was beginning to feel lonely, melancholy, and bored. It was around this time that Chesnutt developed a plan to leave Fayetteville, in search of a place, a *society*, where he might find people to talk to, exchange ideas with, and argue against openly. Having traveled to DC, having become a father and husband, he was now developing his own sense of what he needed to be happy, live a good life—and to write.

> A harmonious, healthy mental development requires the friction of mind upon mind. If men never argued, they could never perceive those weak places in their own opinions, which their adversaries are so quick to see and animadvert upon. Reading stores the mind with knowledge—"maketh the full man;" writing classifies and arranges the results of reading; but only debate, argument, interchange and criticism of opinion can give one that skill and judgement which is necessary to select the valuable and reject the worthless.

Desperate for conversation, Chesnutt was spending his energies on developing the literary society at the normal school. This was an extracurricular activity for the students, but it was, at least for Chesnutt, more important than the classes students were required to take. The literary society was like all "clubs social and political" in which "the American citizen, however humble can cultivate self-reliance, judgement, and can prepare himself to exercise those political rights with wisdom." Of course, books could "partially supply the want of conversation," but books could never *replace* conversation. While Susan and Ethel were away, Chesnutt made another decision: one that would affect not only him; it would also transform the lives of his wife and children. "Hitherto I have devoted my time almost entirely to study during vacations; but this summer I must make some provision for exercise of the body as well as of the mind." Equipped with a "fair knowledge of the classics, a speaking acquaintance with the modern languages, an intimate friendship with literature," Chesnutt decided it was time to take a risk, to see more of the world, to move his family to a more stimulating environment. But above all these other changes, Chesnutt now felt called to write a book. "I am almost afraid to undertake a book so early and with so little experience in composition. But it has been my cherished dream, and I feel an influence that I cannot resist calling me to the task."

There are a million reasons why, at this time, Chesnutt could not have written a book. He was poor, he was Black, he didn't have time, he lacked credentials, education, and experience. But he managed to come up with a few reasons why he *should* write a book. Chesnutt believed that with "seven years experience in the school room, two years of married life, and a habit of studying character" as well as "fifteen years of life in the South, in one of the most eventful eras of its history; among a people whose life is rich in the elements of romance; under conditions calculated to stir one's soul to the very depths," he could write a book that would uplift—or *elevate*, as he put it—not just Black people, as most Black authors were trying to do at the time, but a book that would elevate "the whites,—for I consider the unjust spirit of caste which is so insidious as to pervade a whole nation, and so powerful as to subject a whole race and all connected with it to scorn and social ostracism." With this goal in mind, Chesnutt started to plot his departure. He had to find a way to get himself and his family out of Fayetteville. Perhaps these were the same feelings of restlessness and frustration that moved his father to leave Fayetteville before the war. Unlike AJ, however, there were greater forces holding Chesnutt back than those encouraging him to leave. Ironically, the person holding him back the most was the person who first set him on his path of self-reliance and learning.

On March 14, 1880, Chesnutt reported that "Mr. Harris *is* very sick, and I do not notice any improvement." Robert Harris died seven months later, on October 24, 1880. Though Chesnutt had months to prepare for

Harris's death, it came as a shock. Everyone at the school, indeed all of Fayetteville, seemed to expect that Chesnutt would step into Harris's big shoes. After all, he had been working as Harris's trusted right-hand man for almost three years. He had gained an excellent reputation with the school board, and the students adored him. Why wouldn't Chesnutt want the job? It was one of the most respected positions a colored man could hold in Fayetteville. How could he pass up such an opportunity? Chesnutt knew what was expected of him the moment Harris got sick. He confided to his journal months before Harris's death that he understood that some of Harris's "*friends* have been making calculations about the future management of the Normal School, in case of Mr. H's death; but he is not dead yet, and even if he should, I am afraid his friends' hopes will be dashed." As it turned out, it was Chesnutt's hopes that were dashed and not Harris's so-called friends. Chesnutt did not mention taking on the job of principal of the normal school after Harris's death. Instead, he continued using his journal for his intended purpose: to be a writer. Only then, with Harris gone and most of his time taken up in running the normal school, there was almost no time for him to write. Before concluding his second journal on March 26, 1881, Chesnutt reaffirmed his commitment to write.

> Everytime I read a good novel, I want to write one. It is the dream of my life—to be an author! It is not so much the *monstrari digito* [to be famous] though that has something to do with my aspirations. It is not altogether the money. It is a mixture of motives. I want fame, I want money; I want to raise my children in a different rank of life from that I sprang from.

This was Chesnutt's dream. The only question that remained was how to make it come true.

———— · ————

4

Leaving Fayetteville

Education will open our eyes. Like the magic stone of the Arabian Nights, which revealed to its possessor all the treasure of the earth, it will broaden our views, it will take us out of Fayetteville, out of North Carolina, out of America. It will take us beyond this narrow earth, which to the simple appears so great; and carry us far away to the glittering worlds above us.

—"The Future of the Negro" (1882)

On October 7, 1880, *The Raleigh Signal*, a Republican newspaper published by the Republican State Committee of North Carolina, introduced Chesnutt to the public. Hailing Chesnutt's "rare accomplishments" as "a thorough English scholar" and his ability to speak French and German fluently, the editors also called readers' attention to his mastery "without assistance" of "the Pittman [*sic*] system of phonography." These credentials, according to the paper's editors, qualified Chesnutt to report "*verbatim et literatum*"—word for word and letter for letter—on Frederick Douglass's speech delivered on October 1. Douglass's 1880 speech in support of James A. Garfield's presidential campaign was part of the second annual Industrial Exhibition, organized by a group of North Carolina's most prominent Black businessmen and held at the state capital's Metropolitan Hall. Chesnutt's skills in shorthand had become so well known in the state that he was invited by the organizers to share the podium with the great orator.

Chesnutt would have traveled to Raleigh from Fayetteville by train on the Cape Fear and Yadkin Valley Railway. It was an important trip. This would have been the first time Chesnutt could apply and get paid for the shorthand and literary skills he had been practicing for months. He had already published a couple of short sketches in the school's newspaper and delivered several speeches for the school's literary society. Reporting on Douglass's 1880 speech marked Chesnutt's entry into the public sphere as a literary man. We don't know how much Chesnutt was paid for reporting Douglass's speech or if he was paid at all. Perhaps seeing his name and biography in print, coupled with the name "Fred. Douglass," was sufficient remuneration for his labor. Douglass's speech, like so many the former slave delivered in his lifetime, is a work of literary genius. Entitled "Why Should the South Be Solidly Democratic?" Douglass's speech opened with a quote from, in his words, the "god-like" Daniel Webster:

> The right to canvass the policy of public men and public measures, is a homebred right, a fireside privilege; that it belongs to private life as a right, but it belongs to public life as a duty. Aiming to exercise it calmly and temperately, except when the right itself is questioned, then, said he, I will step to the verge of my right and hurl defiance to any power that would move me from my place. Living, I shall assert it; dying, I shall assert it; and, if I leave no other heritage to my children, it shall be a manly defence of free principles.

Like Webster, speaking publicly was Douglass's way of exercising the "free principles" he championed throughout his life. Printed on the second page of the four-page newspaper, Douglass's speech took up three and a half of its six columns. Chesnutt reported the speech in its entirety, including the moments when the audience broke into "[Applause]" and "[Laughter]." The purpose of the speech was to provide a resounding endorsement of Garfield for president. Douglass claimed that Garfield was "a good man . . . because he is like me . . . a self-made man." Midway through the speech, written almost entirely in standard English, Douglass quoted from "a colored brother of mine." In quoting from this "colored brother," Douglass switched to Black dialect. Chesnutt reported Douglass's words this way:

"Well," said the preacher, "I should like to preach the Gospel to de people here, but I cannot consent to preach on dem terms. Why," said he, "do you know dat one word on dat subject would throw a dampness and coldness over de whole congregation?"

Well known for his antislavery speeches and powerfully written autobiographies, Douglass was not known for his use of Black dialect. He almost never employed it in his writings, and there are few, if any, examples of it in his published speeches. Even in his only published work of literary fiction, *The Heroic Slave*, an 1853 novella that dramatized the life of Madison Washington, a slave who led a successful rebellion on a slave ship in 1841, Douglass presented his hero speaking in a highly literate, even poetic, form of English. But in Chesnutt's report, Douglass can be heard speaking in Black dialect. In doing so, the audience (and readers) of the speech got a better sense of Douglass's literary range and sense of humor. Here was a man who can quote from Webster and an unnamed colored preacher in the same breath, giving both men equal status on the podium.

In reporting on Douglass's speech, Chesnutt absorbed more than just his words. He also absorbed Douglass's literary style, a style that integrated both Black and white voices that spoke to both Black and white audiences. It was a lesson he would not forget. Recalling in vivid detail the experience a couple of years later in one of his speeches to the literary society entitled "Self-Made Men," Chesnutt described how Douglass "held the audience spell-bound for several hours. He had lost none of his old-time power, and the audience were alternately moved to laughter by his wit, or tears by his pathos. My heart swelled with pride and happiness as I saw the veteran abolitionist stand before an audience, half of former slave-holders, in a State where he once would have been hunted by bloodhounds or sold on the auction block." As the nation's preeminent self-made man and Chesnutt's personal role model, Douglass was nothing short of an inspiration for Chesnutt. Chesnutt's 1882 speech would serve as a first take of his only book-length work of nonfiction. Published less than a decade later, Chesnutt would write the first full-length biography of the former slave, orator, and political figure that would set off a revival of Douglass's work in the twentieth century. Though other biographies of Douglass would surpass Chesnutt's in length and popularity, his was the only one written by someone who had seen, heard, and transcribed Douglass's speech as it was being spoken.

But that fall of 1880, when Chesnutt returned from Raleigh, he would not have been thinking of the future. He was preoccupied with the gloomy present. Harris was dying. Once again, Chesnutt was left with little choice about his future. Dr. Haigh and the rest of the dreaded local school board insisted that Chesnutt return to Raleigh. This time, it was not to report on a speech or attend a political convention; instead, it was to apply for the position of principal of the normal school. Members of the board even appealed to the president of the state board of education, Governor Thomas Jordan Jarvis, an adamant supporter of public education in the state, to raise the salary for the position from sixty-two dollars and fifty cents a month to seventy-five dollars per month. Such a substantial raise made it virtually impossible for Chesnutt to decline the position. The raise was granted unanimously by the members of the state board. In November 1880, just a week after Harris's death, twenty-two years old, with a wife and one daughter and another child on the way to support, Chesnutt was appointed principal of Fayetteville's State Colored Normal School. Harris's widow, Mary, took over from Chesnutt the position of first assistant teacher. Though Chesnutt accepted the torch passed to him reluctantly, he carried it with a sense of moral duty and gratitude to the man who had been a teacher, mentor, friend, and second father to him. Harris died on October 24, 1880, of "liver complaint." The funeral was held at the AME church where Elder Davis "paid a glowing tribute to the virtues of the deceased." The schoolhouse was draped in black for thirty days, during which Chesnutt prepared to embark on his new job as principal of one of the most successful colored normal schools in the South.

Harris was forty-one when he died, having served as the first principal of the normal school for just three years. Though his tenure as school principal was brief, he played a foundational role in ensuring the success of its students. Chesnutt was effusive in his praise of his mentor, whose influence he credited with "the temperate habits of the younger colored people" in Fayetteville. "The influence of Mr. Harris," Chesnutt felt, had improved not only his own life but that of all "his scholars."[1] Now that he was gone, it fell to Chesnutt to carry on Harris's legacy. Though Chesnutt had not chosen to become a teacher or to follow in the footsteps of his mentor, he threw himself into the task. Chesnutt had to find a way to continue to shape the character of the school for the new decade, to prove to the state school board, which determined his wages and the school's conditions, that he could continue training *his* scholars to become excellent teachers.

When Chesnutt took over as principal in the middle of the 1880/81 school year, the normal school enrolled 109 students: 63 men and 46 women. One of the first innovations Chesnutt introduced as principal was to publish an annual catalog. The catalog opened with a list of the names of all the school's students, teachers, members of the state board of education, and the members of the local board of managers. As the school's new principal, Chesnutt offered "General Remarks" inviting teachers and friends to visit the school. Like most college catalogs, Chesnutt's included a great deal of information about the school, its history, geography, and curriculum, as well as information about its sources of funding and the cost of tuition.[2] Fayetteville State Colored Normal School was established by the state of North Carolina in 1877 for the training of teachers for the colored schools of the state. It received an annual appropriation for the state of $2,000, and had received, until the year Chesnutt took over as principal, an annual appropriation of $500 from the Peabody Fund. That amount was reduced in 1880 to $220 as the result of North Carolina having opened several additional normal schools. The students who attended the school were mostly members of North Carolina's Black and poor population. So long as they presented "sufficient evidence of good moral character" and passed "a satisfactory examination in Reading, Spelling, Writing, and the Fundamental Rules of Arithmetic," students could enroll in the school without having to pay tuition. Books were made available to all students without charge. And for those students who lived too far to walk to school, board was provided in the homes of local families for $7 or $8 per month. For many, Fayetteville's normal school provided a primary source of income and a good home.

Chesnutt's responsibilities seemed to have quadrupled overnight. By the end of the year, Chesnutt had become principal; his second daughter, Helen, was born on December 6. Soon after her birth and his promotion, he moved his family from the Perry house to a home of their own, promising himself that he would write and read more. Despite the increase in his salary, his new job and baby brought more expenses; he had to travel frequently to Raleigh on his own dime, and his new responsibilities took up more of his time so that by the new year, Chesnutt could no longer afford to continue his French and German lessons with Emil Neufeld. Occupied by his growing family, teaching, and financial matters at the school, he had little time or money to spend on learning new languages. He did, however, find time to "take a thorough course in History and poetry," deciding that despite all his other duties, he still wanted to be a scholar, "and a scholar should be accurate in all he knows." Chesnutt's commitment to scholarship was what distinguished him as a teacher and school principal of the normal school. While Chesnutt was writing reports requested by the Bureau of Education and worrying about Governor Jarvis's latest political statement on the amount of tax dollars to be appropriated for running the school, he was also reading Oliver Goldsmith's *History of Rome*, Charles Merivale's *General History of Rome*, and *The Life and Letters of Lord Macaulay*, as well as Horace Greeley's *The American Conflict: A History of the Great Rebellion in the United States of America* "with the greatest minuteness." Surrounded by deeply partisan newspapers, literature, and conversation, Chesnutt was now in search of good histories—and good friends—that, in his words, were "perfectly impartial." These books provided him with models of good historical and literary writing.

As he settled into his new role as teacher, principal, and chief representative of the normal school, Chesnutt began to make a name for himself. As principal, Chesnutt joined an ever-expanding coterie of teachers committed to improving the lives of former slaves and their descendants. Perhaps it was his bird's-eye view as principal that allowed him to develop his later school stories about Reconstruction-era schoolteachers. The most successful of these was published as "The March of Progress" almost two decades later in New York's *Century Magazine*. Southern teachers—Black and white—would become a mainstay of Chesnutt's fiction and the subject of his first attempt at novelistic fiction. Though *Mandy Oxendine* did not find a publisher in Chesnutt's lifetime, its characters and scenes were drawn from his personal memories of his students and fellow teachers that he painstakingly recorded in the pages of his journal.

Around the time Chesnutt had been appointed principal, and about five hundred miles south of Fayetteville, Booker T. Washington was similarly taking charge of a colored normal school in the town of Tuskegee, Alabama. Like Chesnutt's Fayetteville normal school, Washington's would receive a $2,000 appropriation from its state government with the purpose of training "fit teachers." But that was about the extent of the similarities between the two schools. Washington wanted to teach his students "to study actual things instead of mere books alone" so that they "might return to the plantation districts and show the people there how to put new energy and ideas into farming."[3] Chesnutt's view of the purpose of education differed from Washington's. Education, Chesnutt felt, was important because it made people aware of their rights. "In order to understand our rights we must know how to read and understand the laws. Suppose an election were held to vote for a railroad appropriation or something of the kind? How would a man know whether he should vote for or against unless he could read the arguments? It is true he could follow the politicians; but alas! experience has shown that these are not always safe leaders. A wise man will see and know and act for himself, and only follow the advice of others when he can make it accord with his own convictions."[4] Acquiring these skills required books and instruction. As principal, Chesnutt emphasized the power of books as a way of moving away from the plantation so that students might use their minds rather than just their bodies to earn their living. Ironically, it would be their political differences rather than their similar positions as principals of colored normal schools in the South that would unite Chesnutt and Washington several years later.

For now, Chesnutt enjoyed his newfound celebrity in North Carolina. He made frequent trips to Raleigh and was delighted when he saw his name in the local newspapers. Referred to as "Prof. Chesnutt," he felt some pride in being recognized as a "scholar and gentleman" by the Committee on Education. These new titles appealed to Chesnutt. He preferred being recognized by these professional titles than by the more common method of being identified by the color of his skin or by the racial category attributed to him. He used the legend of Mahomet's coffin being suspended in midair to understand, and ultimately repudiate, the racial classifications of his time. "I occupy here a position similar to that of the Mahomet's Coffin. I am neither fish, flesh, nor fowl—neither 'nigger, poor white', nor 'buckrah.' Too 'stuck-up' for the colored folks, and, of course, not recognized by the whites."

In early 1881, Chesnutt confronted the challenges of living in a culturally divided society. He could either embrace the racial categories and accept the arbitrary divisions that kept him from pursuing his interests and happiness, or leave Fayetteville and go North, where he imagined such divisions were not so entrenched. Chesnutt began recording in his journal conversations with men and women he found engaging and intelligent. One of these men was Robert Hill, whom he described as "a very intelligent man, uses good English, and understands what he talks about. He was once a slave, and was badly treated." Chesnutt recorded a conversation that Hill related to him with "Jno. McLaughlin—a poor white man, and a clerk in Williams's store." This is the first conversation Chesnutt wrote in a third-person voice; it is written as a dialogue between two *characters* Bob and McLaughlin, about our *narrator*, Charles Chesnutt. The two men were presented as having a conversation about our author who commented on their conversation as an objective observer. Looking back on the conversation in his journal, Chesnutt found himself in agreement with Bob, who argued for the "equality of intelligence." He also realized it was futile to argue with men who would never change their minds no matter what men like Bob or Chesnutt did or said. The problem was that McLaughlin's views "embodies the opinion of the South on the 'Negro Question.'" Chesnutt seemed to be at once professionally gratified and personally frustrated by the conversation. Argument would not work on men like McLaughlin; rather, you needed to show him how his way of thinking about people according to their racial categories rather than their abilities was holding himself back and slowing the progress of everyone living in the South.

While Chesnutt found most of his new responsibilities tedious and time-consuming, there was one aspect of the normal school that gave him pleasure and a sense of purpose: the literary society. The society had been organized by Robert Harris when the normal school first opened in 1877. But since Harris had been preoccupied with the work of the abstinence society, Chesnutt ran Fayetteville's literary society. While considered an "auxiliary means of education," it was formalized by a collectively written constitution, though likely penned by Chesnutt, which stated its purpose "for mutual improvement in the arts of composition and debate, and in other literary exercises."[5] Throughout the late nineteenth and early twentieth centuries, virtually all state normal schools had literary societies to which most enrolled students belonged. The focus of these societies was to discuss literature, and it was in this area that they most helped students become conversant with the high culture of the well educated. In many literary societies, and certainly in Fayetteville's, students explored great literature by performing it. Chesnutt recorded his "performances as recapitulator in the Literary society" in his journal.

In the months after he was appointed principal, he wrote and delivered a loosely related group of lectures on self-improvement. He saw self-respect and self-cultivation as essential in forming good relations with others. The "main principle which underlies every social system," he explained to students in his lecture on "Etiquette," "is a proper regard for the tastes and feelings of others." Drawing on a few old proverbs and well-known anecdotes, Chesnutt told his listeners who lacked the tutelage and wealth of "cultivated people" that the "power of money is very great; but however much wealth you may have, there are others as rich as you, and your money will not bring you into their society unless you can render yourself agreeable to them." The way to enter society was to develop good manners. Chesnutt made a sequence of them, beginning with practical matters like "The Etiquette of the Toilet." He concluded his lecture on a more ethereal note with a discussion of the rules of conversation. Setting aside all the rules of correct behavior that he had outlined, he moved to a lengthy discussion of the dos and don'ts of conversation since "it is in conversation that a man most clearly shows what he is."[6]

Chesnutt now had a platform. He had listeners, an eager audience who looked to him for instruction as well as guidance in how they should conduct themselves to be successful and good. With his new position, he had a new purpose. Though he was no preacher or politician, he was extremely interested in the cultivation of individuals as the best method for improving society. He came to believe that conversation was even more important than reading in connecting the individual to the wider society. "Reading stores the mind with knowledge—'maketh the full man,'" he wrote in his journal, "but only debate, argument, interchange and criticism of opinion can give one that skill and judgement which is necessary to select the valuable and reject the worthless." The literary society served the purpose of debate and argument. "This is one great advantage derived from our literary society, our clubs social and political; it is one of the most valuable features of our system of government." Chesnutt shared his view of conversation with Samuel Johnson, Benjamin Franklin, Margaret Fuller, and Frederick Douglass. *"Don't talk shop,"* he instructed his students, "don't talk about yourself or your own affairs. It may be very interesting to you, but very stupid to other people. A preacher should not preach, nor a lawyer plead in the parlor. Talk about things that will interest the whole company." This injunction, to talk about things other than oneself or one's own affairs, was the essence of literature. "It is the love of literature, common to all cultivated minds, that furnishes a market for the works of the great army of poets and historians, novelists, and journalists. I know of no purer intellectual pleasure than that derived from reading the great masterpieces of literature." At a time when Washington was beginning to make a name for himself by denouncing "mere book education" for industrial education, Chesnutt's commitment to reading *for pleasure* and developing the school's literary society distinguished him from other normal school principals.

The literary society met weekly after school hours. Chesnutt was a frequent speaker at the society's meetings. In October 1881, well into the second year of his principalship, he provided its members with a thorough history of the society, illuminating its purpose for all those who "have a general idea that the society is designed for improvement, but have no clear idea just exactly in what respect they are to be improved."[7] Chesnutt's speech was more than a rhetorical exercise. His speech was intended to impress upon students the importance of reading and discussing literature to achieve both material prosperity and happiness. His words must have sounded outlandish to a population struggling to survive. Most members of the society were like Chesnutt; they were trying to earn enough money to clothe and feed themselves as well as their families. How would reading books buy food and clothes, let alone allow them to develop lives filled with prosperity?

Chesnutt's commitment to reading classical works of literature, studying the rules of rhetoric and grammar, was precisely what Washington was dismantling down in Tuskegee. Washington described how the study of literature, particularly the study of foreign and ancient languages, ruined the lives of former slaves and their descendants struggling to move "up from slavery." When he first started teaching in Tuskegee, Washington observed students who had read "big books." He would go on to mock these students openly in his autobiography: "The bigger the book and the longer the name of the subject, the prouder they felt of their accomplishment. Some had studied Latin, and one or two Greek. This they thought entitled them to special distinction." At the same time as Chesnutt was making a case for the "Advantages of a Well-Conducted Literary Society," Washington called out those students who followed Chesnutt's advice as entitled snobs who lived in "filth all around him" while "engaged in studying a French grammar."[8]

Surely, Chesnutt was aware of Washington's different teaching philosophy and his critique of encouraging students at colored normal schools to read classical literature *for pleasure*. Washington was not alone in denouncing literary societies like Chesnutt's while promoting vocational education for the former slaves and their descendants who populated the South, but he was the most vocal and eloquent. And Chesnutt understood and took Washington's complaint seriously. Chesnutt based his defense of the literary society, with its emphasis on political debate and discussing literature, especially classical literature, "as a means of improvement because it furnishes I. Recreation; 2. Instruction in practical business knowledge; 3. Discipline for the mental faculties." He went on to explain what he meant by "mental faculties" by dividing the somewhat vague concept into four more concrete categories: "I. Self-possession; 2. Self-control; 3. Respect for constituted authority; 4. The rule of argument."[9]

In laying out the purpose and benefits of engaging in literary activity so clearly, Chesnutt hoped to quell accusations of it cultivating snobbishness and dilettantism. Spending time reading the great masterpieces of literature for most people struggling to survive would have seemed like something that only people who had the time and money could afford to do. But not Chesnutt. As principal, he insisted that the literary society met a "universal desire" for "recreation or mental amusement." Moreover, the literary society constituted a space in which students were encouraged to build up "our tired energies of body and mind" through "good debate" which was "a source of pleasure to participants and listeners."[10] On and on, Chesnutt expounded on the literary society's benefits, calling on the likes of Demosthenes, Shakespeare, Hugh Blair, Lord Macaulay, and Levi Hedge to support his claims. Without disparaging those, like Washington, who felt otherwise, Chesnutt showed his students how attending the meetings of the literary society and spending time reading for pleasure would teach them how to work more effectively, conduct public meetings, speak eloquently and humbly, and, most importantly, "acquire that graceful self-possession, that absence of fear or awkwardness on the floor which is necessary to enable a man to do his best." In other words, reading literature could teach people like Chesnutt and his students something that most thought only money could buy: self-confidence. Chesnutt's words must have resonated with his students and fellow teachers. The following year, he was invited to present his methods of teaching at the first annual meeting of the North Carolina State Teachers Educational Association (NCTE) in Raleigh.

On November 23, 1882, six months before he submitted his letter of resignation as principal of the State Colored Normal School to its board of managers, Chesnutt delivered one of the first speeches at the newly formed NCTE. The NCTE, a coalition of teachers and administrators formed in 1881, was a new kind of teachers' union and, as principal of Fayetteville's normal school, Chesnutt was among its founding members. The main purpose of the association was to support public education and to ensure that Black schools received an equal amount of tax dollars from the state as white schools. But at its first annual meeting, members gathered to discuss various methods of instructing students and broader systems of education to decide on which might best serve their students and communities. Chesnutt's "Methods of Teaching" is an expanded account of everything he had learned about teaching from the books he read on the subject and his personal experience.[11] His audience in Raleigh had no idea that his speech was not just a lecture on the best methods of teaching, a history of the development of pedagogical principles; for Chesnutt, the speech was also a personal swan song. This was Chesnutt's public farewell address to his fellow teachers, to his students, to Fayetteville, and to the South. It was no longer enough to read and teach literature; Chesnutt felt it was time to write literature of his own. Or, as he put it to himself in his journal, on a Saturday afternoon after having finished reading William Thackeray's masterpiece *Vanity Fair,* "Every time I read a good novel, I want to write one. It is the dream of my life—to be an author!"

While most of Chesnutt's acquaintances and family wrote his wish to be an author off as a pipe dream, there was one man, John Patterson Green, someone Chesnutt considered a close relation, who gave him hope. Though the relation between Green and Chesnutt cannot be precisely traced, he seems to have had a close relationship with Chesnutt's father, AJ, and his aunt, AJ's sister Sophia Carter. He was also well acquainted with the Harris brothers. In his autobiography, Green explained that Fayetteville "was doubly endeared to me by the dual facts that, my dear parents, were married there in 1837 and there were a host of good people, residing there, to whom I was related, by ties of blood."[12] Whether or not Chesnutt was related to Green by "ties of blood," it was certainly the case that the two men had a great deal in common. Green's parents, like Chesnutt's, had moved to Cleveland in 1857. But Green was about twelve when he left his hometown of Newberne, North Carolina, to live in Cleveland. Green's success was almost legendary among the colored people of Fayetteville. Though Green's family did not return to North Carolina after the war like Chesnutt's, Green did return to North Carolina with his wife after studying law at Union Law College. He worked as a lawyer in Wilmington and made frequent visits to Fayetteville, where Chesnutt got to know him better and better, feeling increasingly like he was a close relation. In later years, they would exchange letters about books and politics that conveyed an intimacy and mutual respect. Green returned to Ohio in 1872, where he was, like AJ, elected as a justice of the peace in 1873. Green would continue his career in politics in Ohio, serving in the state house of representatives, setting the stage for his successful bid to the state senate in 1891.

Chesnutt's first mention of Green's name appeared in his journal on July 13, 1880:

John Green has written a book. I have just finished reading a review of it in the Cleveland Herald. The review or resumé rather occupies more than a column. It speaks in very complimentary terms both of the book and the author. The subject is the author's experience in the South. The work is issued anonymously and purports to be written by a "Carpetbagger who was born and bred there." I suppose I must get a copy.

Chesnutt felt that Green's book was "one of those ephemeral productions which have sprung up in the wake of the 'Fool's Errand.'" But unlike *Fool's Errand*, this book was written by someone Chesnutt knew, someone who was like him, someone who came from the same family. As Chesnutt was contemplating writing a book of his own and leaving Fayetteville, he reached out to Green in Cleveland. He visited him during his summer vacation, and the two discussed his prospects. Chesnutt had no interest in running for office like Green; he wanted to be an author. But he needed money first. He had already made a name for himself as a shorthand reporter. With Green's endorsement and his shorthand skills in tow, he would secure a job in a Northern metropolis, and from there, anything was possible. At the very least, Green's success in Cleveland and mild encouragement were enough to counter the naysayers back home.

On May 12, 1883, Chesnutt wrote his letter of resignation. Addressed to the board of managers of the State Colored Normal School, the letter was brief and to the point. His resignation would take effect at the close of the present session, on June 22, 1883. He expressed his gratitude to the board for their cooperation, courteous treatment, and confidence. He then wished the school continued prosperity under the management of the current board. These expressions of regret and thanks were typical of letters of resignation. What was unusual about Chesnutt's letter was the "motive" he revealed in the letter behind his resignation. He wrote, "My motive in resigning the position is to enter into another business which I have long contemplated following," he explained.[13] Curiously, Chesnutt did not name the other business, only that he had long contemplated it. More interesting is how Chesnutt chose the word *business* to describe his dream of becoming an author. Perhaps he used the word to give his dream some credibility, perhaps he feared being mocked by the board, who surely would have thought his decision to resign such a position for becoming an author was ridiculous. How would Chesnutt support his wife, his daughters, especially now with Susie pregnant with their third child? Chesnutt must have agonized over how to frame his motive in his resignation letter for hours, days even. He was not just entering "another business," he was entering the business of literature, a business he hoped would allow him to serve his race and bring personal happiness. He kept at least one draft of the letter, handwritten on plain notepaper, alongside his journals, for the rest of his life.

PART II

Going North

——— · ———

5

Adventure in New York

I had come to New York to seek my fortune. The path over which I was to pursue the fickle goddess was but vaguely defined, at least in regard to details. But I knew what I wanted to do, and that was to practice my profession.

—"Stranger Taken In" (1887)[1]

Writing in his journal on April 23, 1879, just after Ethel was born, Chesnutt vowed to "go to the Metropolis, or some other large city, and like Benjamin Franklin, Horace Greeley and many others" he hoped to "get employment in some literary avocation, or something leading in that direction." Depending principally on his knowledge of stenography, he believed he could "secure a position on the staff of some good newspaper, and then,—work, work, work!" Four years later, in the summer of 1883, Chesnutt made good on his promise. He quit his job as principal of the normal school, said his goodbyes to his pupils and fellow teachers, and headed out for a metropolis. He had already tried and failed to secure stenography work a few years earlier in the nation's capital, so now he turned to that other metropolis: New York City. This was the New York of one of Chesnutt's heroes, Horace Greeley, who had, in 1841, founded the *New-York Tribune*. The offices for the paper were now located in Printing House Square, one of the first to require elevator service so that workers could get to the ninth floor without having to climb stairs. It was one of the tallest buildings in New York City.

The newspaper industry was enjoying a golden age when Chesnutt arrived in 1883. New York was now the capital of the news industry, and as the industry grew, so too did the demand for good stenographers. Newspapers needed people who could record interviews with the Wall Street bankers and brokers who spoke too fast for the average reporter. Chesnutt's experience reporting Frederick Douglass's speech a few years earlier in 1880 had given him a taste of success in stenography. He had been learning and practicing the art of stenography in his off-hours as principal. Now he was able to write two hundred words a minute. And he had made a name for himself as a trusted reporter. He had even been using his knowledge of stenography in Fayetteville to make a little extra cash. Businessmen and organizations were beginning to call on Chesnutt to provide accurate transcriptions of their meetings. "By the by," he wrote in his journal on July 7, 1881, "I wrote a report of the Odd Fellows' celebration today, for which I demanded one dollar." He could see, even from his home in Fayetteville, a lucrative future in stenography. The odds of getting a job in New York were good. But not certain. He did what most would have done in his position. He left behind his pregnant wife and his daughters, Ethel, now four, and Helen, two and a half. Like many looking to make a fortune, he set out for New York city alone. He knew Susan and the girls would be well taken care of by the Perrys, even though moving back in with them was not ideal. But it would be temporary. Once he found a position, they would join him, and then they would start a new life as a family, without race holding them back. The Perrys, like his own father and members of the school board, had discouraged Chesnutt from leaving. Chesnutt managed to refute their opposition. He had convinced himself that he could "serve my race in some more congenial occupation." He also had a more personal reason for leaving Fayetteville. "I shudder to think," he wrote in his journal on March 7, 1882, "of exposing my children to the social and intellectual proscription to which I have been victim. Is not my duty to them paramount?" In response, a year later, he bid farewell to Fayetteville, to teaching, and to AJ. He arrived in New York City looking for work in the summer of 1883.

New York was the desired destination of young Southerners like Chesnutt looking to escape the restrictions and ignorance of the South. "I get more and more tired of the South," Chesnutt wrote a year before his departure. "I pine for civilization, and 'equality.'" But few made it out of the South. Reading his sample copy of *Rumor*, "A Representative Colored American Paper," in the summer of 1881 gave Chesnutt a sense of the possibilities afforded by living in New York. *Rumor* was a New York paper started by Timothy Thomas Fortune in 1880, shortly after he had moved there from Florida in 1879. Fortune was born a couple of years before Chesnutt, to slave parents who worked on a plantation in Marianna, Florida. The two men had much in common. Both of their fathers had been active in state politics during Reconstruction. Fortune's father, Emanuel, had been elected delegate to the constitutional convention of Florida. Fortune pursued higher education at Howard University for just a year; but having run out of funds to continue, he returned to Florida to work as a journalist and teacher. Like Chesnutt, Fortune was dissatisfied with the conditions of the South and went to New York City at twenty-three looking for a change. What he found was a thriving newspaper industry. Though *Rumor* did not last long in the city's highly political and cutthroat newspaper business, Fortune's paper expressed unconventional views for a Black newspaper, which appealed to Chesnutt: "It echoes the popular clamor against the Garfield Administration for its scanty recognition of the claims of the colored office-seekers. *Tempora mutantur!* [Times change!] If the Democrats adopt an equally fair platform, and bid higher for our support, why shouldn't they get it?" Chesnutt and Fortune shared a similar nonpartisan view of politics, though they expressed their views differently. Fortune was making a name for himself as an independent, even radical, thinker who refused to play the game of partisan politics as newspaper editor. To implement his philosophy of political independence, he urged his fellow Black Americans to form their own nonpartisan organization, one in which they could express their personal views without worrying about party loyalty. He would succeed in this venture a few years later with the formation of the National Afro-American League.

By the time Chesnutt arrived in the city, Fortune had already moved on to a second newspaper venture, *The New York Globe*. Coincidentally, shortly before Chesnutt's departure from Fayetteville for New York, on Saturday, January 6, 1883, *The Globe* carried a front-page story entitled "North Carolina Letter" that described Raleigh as developing into an educational center, having recently earned the title of "City of Schools." The story did not include the author's name, only that it was "From our Special Correspondent." Except for letters from different areas of the country, most of *The Globe*'s articles were penned by Fortune. Some of the letters written by correspondents outside New York City have authors' names attached to them, but not the one from North Carolina. There is no evidence to suggest that Chesnutt was Fortune's special correspondent from North Carolina, but there is something about the tone of this article describing the state's senatorial contest, effect of the late elections, and the weekly literary exercises of the city lyceum that echoed in both form and content that of Chesnutt's journal and speeches to the literary society from this period. Whether Chesnutt was the article's author or not, we do know that Chesnutt was keeping up with national and local affairs by reading newspapers, was attending political conventions, and had access to papers published in New York while living in Fayetteville. Chesnutt may have corresponded with Fortune before arriving in New York. More likely, he met Fortune in New York: there were few Southern Blacks who had made their way to the city at this time. They must have been aware of each other. The record of Fortune and Chesnutt's friendship is scant; their correspondence officially begins more than a decade later, in 1898. From this correspondence, we can surmise that they admired each other, read the other's work avidly, and would later ally themselves with Booker T. Washington, disagreeing with him on occasion, but equally committed to protecting the civil rights of Black Americans. But how did they meet? Did Chesnutt enter the offices of *The New York Globe* looking for work? Might Fortune have introduced Chesnutt to his friends in the newspaper industry? Unfortunately, we do not know where or how Fortune and Chesnutt first met, because once he left Fayetteville, he stopped recording his experiences in his journal. Unlike his well-documented years in the South working as a schoolteacher and principal, we have no record of the people he met, the conversations he had, or where he lived in New York City. He was likely too busy looking for work and worrying about his family back in Fayetteville.

Although there are few details about Chesnutt's brief time in New York City, we do know, mostly from his daughter Helen's account, that

Chesnutt "became a reporter for Dow, Jones and Company, a Wall Street News agency, and contributed a daily column of Wall Street gossip to the New York Mail and Express." But since these columns, like many appearing in most New York papers at the time, were published without naming their author, it is almost impossible to attribute Chesnutt's authorship to any of the articles appearing in these papers in 1883. Helen also quotes from an essay Chesnutt wrote many years later entitled "Literary Reminiscences."[2] The essay was likely never published, but it was passed down to Chesnutt's daughter and used by her to offer some details about his time in New York.

Based on Helen's citation, here's what we know about Chesnutt's time in New York: He worked for six months in a Wall Street news agency, in the shadow of the New York Stock Exchange, when Jay Gould and William H. Vanderbilt were the money kings that dominated the financial world. And yet he never saw either of them or sought to have them pointed out to him. He supplied a daily column of Wall Street gossip to the *Mail and Express*, owned at the time by the wealthy entrepreneur Cyrus West Field. The job required him to interview various prominent brokers and occasionally Field himself. One of his principal subjects was Henry W. Clews, even then a much sought-after banker and broker, who had, as Chesnutt put it, "maintained a prominent place in the public eye on a shore which has been strewn with innumerable wrecks." Chesnutt was referring, of course, to the various financial panics of the late nineteenth century that left millionaires paupers and, for those who had the good luck and prudence to speculate, also transformed poor men into wealthy ones. Looking back on his time in New York, Chesnutt mused: "I often wonder, when I read newspaper comments on stock market conditions and prospects, whether any of them were written by green young men from the country, with as little knowledge of finance as I had; and I am always suspicious of the man who foretells the course of the market."

Occupying a position in the shadow of the New York Stock Exchange as a stenographer, Chesnutt would have had a clear view of the inner workings of American finance. Gould and Vanderbilt, both New Yorkers, were commonly known as the robber barons of the Gilded Age for their unscrupulous practices in the railroad business. Such men were inaccessible to Chesnutt, though he was sure to have felt the impact they made when he traveled to New York. Their railroad lines, being laid while Chesnutt was practicing shorthand, would get him to New York. Once he arrived, Chesnutt would find his way to offices occupied by Field and Clews, giving him an insider's view of Wall Street. Clews would publish an interesting account of his experiences on Wall Street in an autobiography/instructive manual called *Twenty-Eight Years in Wall Street* in 1887. Clews began his book with a note to his readers in which he offered a brief description of his style and intention. "In sketching the men and events of Wall Street, I have freely employed the vernacular of the speculative fraternity as being best adapted to a true picture of their characteristics, although probably not most consonant with literary propriety."[3] Of course, Clews did not name any of his readers. But his explanation of the vernacular he employed and his departure from "literary propriety" suggests that he might have had someone like Chesnutt in mind when he wrote the book. Perhaps his conversations with Chesnutt influenced his decision to write a book of his own, just as Chesnutt was trying to break into literature while working on Wall Street. Whether or not Clews was influenced by Chesnutt, we do know that Chesnutt would draw extensively on his interviews with men like Clews and Field to craft stories that defied the literary conventions of the time.

Of the businessmen Chesnutt encountered during his time in New York, Cyrus West Field seems to have made the deepest impression. Field had made a name for himself in the 1850s for his role in laying the first telegraph cable across the Atlantic Ocean. But before founding the Atlantic Telegraph Company on November 6, 1856, Field had made a fortune in the paper trade. When Field entered the paper business, the paper industry was in its infancy. Field had left his home in the small, picturesque New England town of Stockbridge, nestled in the Berkshire Mountains of Massachusetts, for the streets of New York City at fifteen to begin his business career. He left home with eight dollars, a gift from his father, the Reverend David Dudley Field. Unlike his father, who had graduated from Williams and Yale Colleges, Field shunned higher education to learn a trade. Having made his way to New York, Field found a job in the dry goods house of A. T. Stewart and Company, located on Broadway between

Murray and Warren Streets. His first job was as an errand boy, and he later rose to a clerkship. From here, he would rise through the ranks of the paper industry, working first as a bookkeeper for his brother Matthew D. Field, who was part owner of a paper mill in Lee. Later, he became a successful paper salesman, learning the ins and outs of the paper industry, from the grinding of wood into pulp for the manufacture of newsprint to the making of paper for books. By 1842, Field had established his own paper manufacturing firm called Cyrus W. Field & Company. By 1852, at thirty-three, Field had built up a successful business and was worth over a quarter of a million dollars. Unlike the well-known robber barons, Field was known for his methodical habits and his conscientious dealings with customers and associates, though he was known to be dictatorial in the management of his business. His purchase of the *Mail and Express* in 1881 allowed Field to return to the newspaper industry, this time with the aim of giving readers immediate access to financial news and the lives of the businessmen who were shaping the ever-changing world of finance.

Field must have been a man larger than life when Chesnutt met him in New York. Field had taken enormous risks, traveled all around the world making, and losing, millions of dollars. What must it have been like for the young, Southern, Black schoolteacher to talk with one of the wealthiest men in America? Though Chesnutt could not claim authorship of the work he produced for Field's newspaper, he did use the material he gathered about Field and others like him to write stories. These stories were a far cry from the stories of North Carolina's former slaves, Black preachers, and schoolteachers he'd been recording in his journal. The most significant of Chesnutt's new urban stories was a romantic novel about the lives of the men and women working in the tall office buildings that were now a symbol of the city. *A Business Career* was the first of Chesnutt's novels set entirely in a Northern metropolis. The novel is a romance, told mostly from the point of view of a woman stenographer he named Stella Merwin; but its hero was a man, Wendell Truscott, who was drawn from Chesnutt's memories of the real-life Cyrus West Field.

A Business Career was not completed until he left New York. He set the scenes of this early fiction in Groveland, Chesnutt's thinly disguised pseudonym for Cleveland, which he introduced to readers as that "great city of the Middle West" in the novel's opening sentence. Chesnutt's Cleveland was, of course, smaller and more amiable than Chicago, which writers like Theodore Dreiser and Richard Wright would later develop in their novels. Chesnutt's metropolis displayed the culture of wealth and opulence, while his descriptions of the novel's central characters recalled the businessmen and working women of New York City whom he first encountered when he left the South.

Despite having spent less than a year in New York, Chesnutt's experience of the city left a deep impression. New York in 1883 was a bustling metropolis of almost two million. According to census figures taken in 1880, Blacks made up less than 2 percent of the city's population, most of whom lived in an area south and west of Washington Square, where Chesnutt would have likely found a room in a boardinghouse. Chesnutt was not alone in marveling at the wealth of, as he put it, "several families in New York who could buy out the whole colored race and have money to spare."[4] How was their wealth acquired? How did these people live? Chesnutt could only imagine what their lives were like. Unlike contemporary authors, such as Henry James and Edith Wharton, who wrote of the New York elite and their wealth with familiar intimacy and complexity, Chesnutt had no such insider knowledge or experience of what Wharton called "the wealthy tribes of New York City." Compared to James and Wharton, Chesnutt was a country bumpkin—a poor Black Southerner who had been teaching Black students in a one-room schoolhouse how to read and write. What did he have in common with rich New Yorkers?

And yet he found himself, almost by magic, sharing offices with some of the wealthiest men in the country. The incongruity of his New York experience was worth writing about, but it was an experience almost entirely singular. Up until this time, Chesnutt had been immersed in the world of the South, its politics, its fraught relations between whites and Blacks, and, of course, the aftermath of the war. But in New York, such matters vanished in the all-encompassing pursuit of money and power. Most new fiction writers wrote about what they knew; in his first attempt at long fiction, Chesnutt decided to try something new, to write from a different perspective, that of a white female stenographer and her complicated relationship with her wealthy boss, sole proprietor of the Truscott Refining Company. This would not be the last time Chesnutt stepped outside himself to craft a tale about individuals far removed from his personal experience, but it was his only fiction in which the business of stenography, which he relied on to make his living, would be featured so prominently.

As a youthful admirer of Charles Dickens, Chesnutt may have come to identify the literary, as well as the monetary, value of stenography. In *David Copperfield*, one of Chesnutt's favorite books, Dickens launched the novel's action with his hero learning the first principles of stenography by mastering the shorthand alphabet. *David Copperfield* was based on Dickens's own experience as a parliamentary stenographer. Shorthand for Dickens and Chesnutt served a similar purpose: upward mobility. But shorthand was seen by those who already enjoyed positions among the elite as hack work. When Dickens's fellow journalist R. H. Hutton asserted that "in some important intellectual, if not mechanical respects, Mr. Dickens did not cease to be a reporter even after he became an author," the social connotations of "mechanical" must have grated on Dickens, an author who was known to be sensitive to criticism even in the face of his enormous popularity.[5]

Like Dickens and the fictional David Copperfield, Chesnutt owed his professional start to stenography. When Dickens's stenographic hero appeared in 1849, it was a literary sensation. Perhaps Chesnutt could capitalize on Dickens's method in *David Copperfield* by creating a stenographic hero of his own. But by the time Chesnutt decided to mix stenography with literary fiction in the 1880s, stenography had changed. While the ravages of the war were not as visible in New York as they were in Chesnutt's hometown of Fayetteville, its effects could be seen in the makeup of the workforce. For better or worse, the war had removed men from the workforce in the North and South; the commercialization of the typewriter and the invention of the phonograph upped the demand for white-collar labor. These notable social and technological shifts were worth recording. But he would have to make these historical shifts interesting to the average reader, particularly women readers who were most affected by these changes and most interested in buying novels.

A Business Career is an unlikely love story, a romance that brings together a wealthy businessman with a beautiful stenographer. On its surface, the novel avoids political controversies of the time, instead sticking close to the personal and professional lives of its characters. We meet Wendell Truscott, "a gentleman of dark complexion, with coarse dark hair growing slightly grey about the edges" in a "handsomely appointed room on one of the upper floors of a tall office building" in search of his absent stenographer, Mr. Peters. In Peters's absence, Truscott tries and fails to write his business letters himself. His failure leads him to look for a new stenographer, "an experienced male stenographer who does not drink."[6] The opening chapter concludes with Truscott, awaiting the arrival of his new stenographer, reading the morning paper and falling "deep in the financial news." While the wealthy businessman is absorbed in the news, the action shifts to a stenography firm run by Mrs. Paxton, "a short, stout woman, with strongly marked features of the German type." Sitting opposite Mrs. Paxton is Stella Merwin, "a slender girl, whose most salient features at first glance were an oval and somewhat pallid face, very large deep-blue eyes with long lashes, and more than usually abundant light-brown hair." The romance begins when Truscott meets his new stenographer, a woman whose abilities to take dictation and type letters accurately impress the stern boss much more than her physique. As one of the male clerks in the office explains: "Wouldn't need to know whether she was a woman or a man, if he didn't look. *He* talks and *she* writes and that's the end of it."[7] Yet the question concerning the stenographer's womanhood lingers. Surprisingly, much of the novel is preoccupied with developing Stella's character not only as a beautiful woman but also as an exceptional stenographer.

Prior to the invention of the typewriter, men had had a near monopoly on stenographic work. At the end of the nineteenth century, however, women were rapidly making inroads into stenography. First trained as typists, it wasn't long before they began learning shorthand as a complementary skill. It quickly became clear that combining typing ability with stenographic skills was the future of clerical work, and women's incursion into typing and stenography was rapid and pronounced. Chesnutt, unlike many of his fellow male stenographers, welcomed the incursion of women into the ever-expanding field of stenography. Once he left New York, he would work closely with female stenographers and eventually embark on a long and productive partnership with Helen C. Moore, known to be one of the fastest and most accurate typists in Cleveland.

The romance that develops between Truscott and Stella defies all social barriers. She is young, and he is old. He is rich, and she is poor. Stella's mother holds a long and deep grudge against Truscott because she (mistakenly) believes he has robbed her and her family of their rightful inheritance after the death of her husband. Stella must keep her work with Truscott a secret from her mother; once she reveals her secret to her mother, she then must keep her identity a secret from her boss. Mostly, though, the novel reveals how Stella's mother has passed on her prejudices to her. Stella struggles with overcoming her long-held prejudices against the wealthy businessman as she gradually falls in love with him. However implausible the story sounds, what makes Stella's transcendence and romance possible is stenography. When Stella is asked, before she begins working for Truscott, what she will do with stenography after having taken the trouble to learn it, she replies confidently: "I shall find a use for it. I can take notes of lectures that I attend, I can keep my diary in it, I can correspond with [it] and I shall doubtless find it useful in the school-room. Besides, they talk of introducing shorthand into the public schools at Cloverdale, and in that event I shall stand first chance to become the teacher."[8] Stella's explanation sums up why Chesnutt took up stenography while teaching at the normal school. But the novel examined not just the practical application of stenography, it also took up its romantic possibilities. Stenography is the source of Stella's independence and Truscott's happiness. We learn in the very first chapter of the novel that without Stella's stenography, Truscott's business cannot function. This is a love story not just between a man and a woman that ends with marriage, it is also the story of a business partnership in which the businessman and the stenographer collaborate to ensure the success of the firm.

A Business Career was ahead of its time. It wasn't until 1900 when women would come to completely dominate the stenography business. In subsequent years, women characters working as stenographers would show up in fiction, film, newspapers, and magazines—becoming one of the most visible figures in popular culture to link women with literate labor and modern technologies for writing. Stella Merwin is an intelligent, independent, twentysomething who "found time to learn shorthand, and had learned also to manipulate with some degree of speed the little white-keyed machines that have made penmanship almost a lost art." Chesnutt is referring here to the stenotype machine that had been invented in New York City in 1875 and was starting to be used in some offices in the 1880s. Chesnutt appears not to have used the stenotype machine himself, relying instead on shorthand, transcription, and the typewriter in his own stenographic practice. But Stella is a young white woman, who had "advantages of training and study otherwise beyond her means."[9] It is this training that allows Stella to pursue the business career that is the novel's primary subject. Chesnutt's *Business Career* is not that of the Wall Street brokers and bankers that was flashed in the pages of the newspaper and the subject of so much gossip at the time. Chesnutt's novel takes up the business career of a young woman, and it is a career that ends, somewhat surprisingly, in a marriage between Stella and her boss. The marriage, like Stella's stenographic skills, is a sign of the changing times, a time when a rich girl can lose her fortune overnight; but then, through hard work and ingenuity, find herself once again living among the rich and famous.

Viewing the business world through Stella's very large deep-blue eyes with long lashes reveals details about this world that would be unnoticed by men who occupied positions of power or those too busy vying for such a position to notice the stenographers who recorded every word of their business transactions and ambitions. As a particularly observant stenographer, Stella

> saw many things that seemed unjust to her, though perhaps strictly in accordance with the commonly accepted standards of commercial morality. That a small dealer should be driven to the wall because he could not compete with a larger concern, seemed to her like predatory warfare. That a strictly legal advantage should be taken of some unimportant violation of a contract suggested highway robbery. At the same time, she was imaginative enough to recognize in the gradual but resistless growth of the corporation the work of a commanding intellect, which instinctively perceived and promptly grasped every opportunity, even out of apparent failure wresting ultimate success.[10]

Stella was an altogether different kind of woman character than the ones who were dominating fiction of the time. Stella was less interested in the marriage market than in the financial market. "She possessed in larger measure than most women the analytical turn of mind, by which she was enabled to link cause with effect in such a manner to make clear many things which to other women would have been merely Greek." It is her analytical mind, as much as her youth and physical beauty, that not only attracts Wendell Truscott to her but leads him to realize that he cannot run his business without her. That Chesnutt's very modern romance introducing readers to a woman character who is beautiful, independent, and financially astute did not appeal to the mostly male publishers of the time should come as no surprise.

When Chesnutt submitted the novel to Houghton, Mifflin and Company in 1897, he could not have known how much Stella Merwin would offend the sensibilities of their readers. The publisher's reader's report is particularly revealing of how prejudices of the time influenced their decision to reject Chesnutt's novel. "The author's conception of cultivated people," the reader explained, "is a decidedly vulgar one. The heroine herself—the refined and educated type-writer" is the most "striking and unpleasant example of this." The reader continued to imagine that the novel might be interesting and exciting "to a reader of no taste and small intelligence. But there can be no doubt," he concluded, "that it is not a story that H. M. & Co. would care to offer to the public."[11] The novel's early reader took issue with Chesnutt's portrayal of women, not just Stella but also the novel's other women characters, which included Stella's mother, Alice, who, after the death of her husband, finds literary work with a women's journal. There is also Stella's shorthand teacher, Mrs. Paxton, who owns her own shorthand business, and Wendell Truscott's other love interest, the wealthy and beautiful Matilda Wedderburn.

But when Chesnutt was writing about these women in the 1880s and 1890s, they had less cachet. Or perhaps it was the fact of a Black man writing about a white woman's personal and professional life that made *A Business Career* "decidedly vulgar" for the reader at Houghton. Though Chesnutt did not manage to find a suitable publisher for his stenography romance, it is a novel that captured the complexities of the business world during the late nineteenth century and one its reader could not believe was drawn entirely from personal experience. Unfortunately, Houghton's narrow view of the novel kept it hidden from readers until well after Chesnutt's death.

Chesnutt never saw the reader's report for *A Business Career*, nor did he re-submit the novel for publication elsewhere, even though his trusted editor, Walter Hines Page, had encouraged him to do so. Still, the novel reveals much about stenography and the business world that occupied Chesnutt as he embarked on his literary career.

The pointed objections to Chesnutt's portrayal of female characters by Houghton's reader reveals a familiar sentiment against the financial independence of women at the time. Most nineteenth-century American romances, particularly those written by male authors, portrayed women as stuck in the rut of seeking a proper marriage for financial security and personal happiness. Though *A Business Career* concluded with its heroine's marriage to a wealthy businessman, the two enter the relation as equal partners. Indeed, Stella insists on her independence as she accepts Mrs. Paxton's advice by refusing to throw herself "on the mercy of some man, who will crush [her] higher aspirations and degrade [her] to the level of housekeeper." From start to finish, *A Business Career* presents women as being highly educated, successfully engaged in business, and cultured. This was not the kind of romance that would be read and appreciated by Houghton's readers. It was, however, the kind of fiction that women like Stella, her mother, and Mrs. Paxton might enjoy, if they happened to come across it next to the paperbacks published by popular women authors like Laura Jean Libbey and Mary Jane Holmes, who had mastered the conventions of "working girl" fiction selling for fifteen or twenty cents. Though Chesnutt did not find a publisher for his novel about Stella Merwin's *Business Career*, it revealed his growing expertise and confidence in stenography to earn a living and provide his family with the education and culture he was denied.

Chesnutt had now been apart from Susan for six months, the longest they'd been apart in their five years of marriage. Susan was anxious, and so was he, to be together again. Though there are no surviving letters from Chesnutt to Susan sent from New York, a few of hers to him were partially transcribed by their daughter Helen. In one, dated November 20, 1883, Susan is thrilled with the news that Chesnutt "had secured a posi-tion in Cleveland." She went on: "You can't imagine what a load was taken off me when I read it. When I heard you had gone to Cleveland, not only my eyes were open, but my heart, for I saw you were not satisfied in New York, and I was afraid you couldn't get employment in Cleveland right away." Susan had been sick and lonely after the birth of their third child, Edwin Jackson, on September 24, 1883. Chesnutt had not yet met his infant son, but Susan assured him, "Little Edwin is a beauty."[12] She also told him that she needed money. She owed her father fifteen dollars for the six months the family had been living with him; she also needed money for medicine, washing, and a new dress. The dress, of course, was a luxury, but she felt she deserved "*something* since I have given you up for such a long time."[13] Chesnutt would not be reunited with his family until April 1884. In the meantime, he continued to rely on stenography to pay the bills, but he still did not have enough to get a new dress for Susan.

Though we do not have Chesnutt's response to Susan's letter, he would use her letter in which she makes several requests for money while he tries to make a living in New York as the subject for one of his early published stories. In "The Wives," published in 1886 by the newly established S. S. McClure Syndicate, Chesnutt described the experiences of John Mullenix, who lived in a small country town and was married, like Chesnutt, by the time he was twenty-one. At twenty-three, John decides to relocate his family in New York City "at a salary somewhat in advance of that he had formerly earned. But he found that city life was not without its drawbacks. It is true there were theaters and concerts, museums and libraries. But when the very high rent of the very narrow rooms in a very remote part of the city was paid, and the wants of the family of four were supplied, there was very little money left for tickets to theater or concert, or even for car fares to parks or libraries."[14] John dreams while at work that his wife and children suddenly die from illness and he marries a wealthy, beautiful woman with whom he has two disabled children. His new wife eventually leaves him for a wealthier man, and he is left with the care of the children. In the dream, he is just about to put a revolver to his head when he is suddenly awoken by a secretary. The dream leads to a change of heart; the story ends with John giving his wife the money she needs for the dress he had previously withheld. Unlike John's wife in the story, Chesnutt did not have enough money to spare to buy Susan the dress she wanted. But her letters must have made it perfectly clear to him that if he was not earning a considerable salary, she and the children had no desire to relocate to New York. Obviously, Chesnutt was not making enough at the newspaper to make ends meet in New York. He needed more money to take care of Susan and the children, and he needed to find a place where they could live. If Chesnutt had found Washington, DC, to be expensive and extravagant, he must have found the opulent lifestyle of New Yorkers unbearable. After that first trip to DC, he recalled in his journal that he "should like to live just far enough away from a large city to avoid the disagreeable things, and near enough to get a taste of its pleasures." Cleveland seemed ideal. He knew Susan would like Cleveland, too. She would have friends, and the children would have company. There was, of course, Senator John Green and his wife, Annie, whom he already knew and admired. But getting there from New York would require more than just hard work; it would require a little bit of good luck. Fortunately for him, the desire among the well-known railroad barons William Vanderbilt and Jay Gould to monopolize the railroad business gave Chesnutt the ticket he needed to land a job in the city where, twenty-six years earlier, he'd been born.

— · —

6

A Professional Writer Is Born

But literature pays—the successful. There is a fascination about this calling that draws a scribbler irresistibly toward his doom. He knows that the chance of success is hardly one out of a hundred; but he is foolish enough to believe, or sanguine enough to hope, that he will be the successful one.

—Journal entry, Saturday, March 26, 1881

Chesnutt's New York experience was brief but monumental. Having previously reported the sacred sermons of the Reverend J. W. Davis in Fayetteville and Frederick Douglass's stirring political speech in Raleigh, his work reporting Wall Street gossip for the *Mail and Express* in New York City must have felt trivial, though enlightening. Interviewing wealthy and up-and-coming brokers, bankers, entrepreneurs, and even telegraph operators would have introduced him to the lifestyles of the rich and almost famous—and those who overheard their conversations. Their words would help substantiate or put to rest rumors concerning the fluctuations of the market. Sometimes the market was dull, other times it was lively and full of scattered speculations concerning where and when William Vanderbilt and Jay Gould would be laying more track or buying each other out.

The Wall Street gossip columns comprised long, verbatim quotations from men who worked on or near the New York Stock Exchange. While the *Mail and Express* reported on some breaking international and national news stories, it mostly covered the financial news originating in New York City. The district it mainly covered was Wall Street, extending from

Trinity Church to the East River, known then, as it is now, as the financial heart of the country that determined the incomes of millions of Americans and the business of their everyday lives. People relied on the Wall Street gossip to learn what men like Vanderbilt and Gould were thinking. The column relied heavily on long direct quotations from the lips of William K. Vanderbilt, who was, at the time, the wealthiest man in America. In an August column, with the subtitle "Mr. Vanderbilt's Views," which appeared shortly after Chesnutt had begun working for the *Mail and Express*, Vanderbilt was reported saying: "I have always made it a principle to hold on to a good thing when I had it." He was referring to the Lake Shore Limited, recently added to the New York Central Railroad, that he had purchased earlier that year. Vanderbilt's interest in the railroad, also known as the Nickel Plate Road, had been the subject of several stories in the paper that year. With the purchase, Vanderbilt had seemingly single-handedly connected Cleveland to New York City. The Cleveland–New York connection reported by the *Mail and Express* interested Chesnutt. He was looking to make another move. He needed to find a suitable home for his growing family. On October 1, 1883, the new depot of the Nickel Plate at Cleveland, later known as the Broadway depot, was opened to the public. A couple of months after it opened, Chesnutt boarded a train, bid farewell to New York, and started work for the Nickel Plate Road, where he would become one of many young men capitalizing on Vanderbilt's speculation in the ever-expanding railroad business of the mid-1880s. Shortly after he relocated to Cleveland, Susan and the children joined him.

By the end of 1884, Chesnutt had settled the family into a house on Ashland Avenue. "It was a white, one-story house in a wide, well-kept yard with a white picket fence around it," his daughter Helen recalled. Just the kind of home Chesnutt dreamed of living in when he first read the eighteenth-century popular English poet William Cowper's "The Task" back in Fayetteville. Cowper was one of England's most popular poets in the eighteenth century and one, along with Robert Burns, whom Chesnutt read avidly. Cowper is probably best known, if he is known today at all, for his poem "The Negro's Complaint," which has entered the canon of English antislavery literature. But Chesnutt never mentioned Cowper's antislavery poems or sentiments. He was more interested in Cowper's romantic rendering of domestic life in his long blank-verse poem, *The Task: A Poem in*

Six Books, published in 1785. Its six books were divided by different aspects of domestic life: "The Sofa," "The Timepiece," "The Garden," "The Winter Evening," "The Winter Morning Walk," and "The Winter Walk at Noon." Chesnutt referred to the poem repeatedly in his journal. "Cowper's 'Task' is splendid," he wrote in his journal on July 16, 1875. "I will build a castle in the air. Cowper gives me material in his Task. I don't wish my castle to be realized when I am old and worn-out, but I would delight to lead a life like the one he describes in 'The Garden.'" Chesnutt transcribed his favorite section of the poem in his journal:

> "Domestic happiness, thou only bliss
> Of Paradise which has survived the fall"
> Though few now taste thee unimpaired and pure
> Or tasting long enjoy thee! Too infirm
> Or too incautious to preserve thy sweets
> Unmixed with drops of bitter, which neglect
> Or temper sheds within the crystal cup,
> Thou art the nurse of Virtue, in thine arms
> She smiles, appearing, as in truth she in
> Heaven-born and destined to the skies again." &c. &c."

Chesnutt must have committed these words to memory because now, almost a decade later, he was beginning to realize the life he imagined through Cowper's poem.

Once he and the family were settled into their new home in Cleveland, he turned his attention to writing. Chesnutt had seen and met people in New York in the publishing industry, and writing for such magazines no longer felt like a pipe dream. So he started writing stories and sending them out. Many of these were rejected. His first published short story, "Uncle Peter's House," was bought by Samuel Sidney McClure for publication in his newly established newspaper syndicate in December 1885. Chesnutt was paid ten dollars for the story and was invited by McClure to send more stories for publication.[1] "Uncle Peter's House" marked the beginning of Chesnutt's career as a professional writer and the start of what would become a long and fruitful association with McClure's syndicate. Working with McClure's syndicate gave Chesnutt a national audience and allowed him to participate in a new publishing venture that would transform the way literature was read and written in the United States.

At first, McClure believed he could make his fortune by selling work by well-known writers of the time, like William Dean Howells, Henry James, Helen Hunt Jackson, Elizabeth Stuart Phelps, and Sarah Orne Jewett, to newspapers across the country. His idea was to work directly with the authors, to persuade them to sell him a short story for, say, one hundred dollars, to a hundred newspapers at five dollars apiece, earning a profit, after his authors were paid, of roughly four hundred dollars on a single story. He met with authors across the country to convince them of the benefits of his scheme, and he managed to convince several. He even got Walt Whitman on board, considered at the time to be the greatest living American writer. For his scheme to work, to earn the profits he needed to keep the business going, he needed more than just established writers. He needed to find *new*, not-yet-known writers. These writers, like Chesnutt, he might pay less and broaden the scope of his syndicate. To achieve this new purpose, McClure developed literary contests, inviting authors to submit their work to him without having to do the heavy lifting of meeting with individual authors. To entice aspiring authors, McClure offered prize money and the opportunity to have their work published in one—if not more—of the newspapers that belonged to his syndicate. It was through McClure's contest that Chesnutt became one of McClure's go-to authors. Chesnutt entered "Uncle Peter's House" into McClure's literary contest. McClure delivered his bad news in the form of a handwritten note in purple ink on November 14, 1885. It read:

Dear Sir:—

Your story has not taken the prize, but I can use it in my syndicate, and pay you **$10.00** for it, if you are willing. I shall welcome there, and if possible shorter sketches from your pen.

Very truly yours,
S.S. McClure[2]

Chesnutt was elated by McClure's note. He got to work right away on "shorter sketches" that met McClure's literary criteria, which was, as everything McClure did, simple and to the point: "It is possible for me to use an average of one or two stories each month from any one writer if his work is sufficiently varied and interesting."[3] However, as McClure would go on to explain, there was very little money in such publication at present "since these papers pay me $1.00 each." Still, a buck a story might be enough of an incentive for Chesnutt, who was still working full-time as a stenographer in the legal department of the Nickel Plate Road, to enter the highly exclusive and elusive world of literary publishing in the United States.

To say that McClure *discovered* Chesnutt might be something of an overstatement. But he was the first to recognize and value the beauty of Chesnutt's writing. Most critics continue to ignore Chesnutt's early stories for McClure, considering them to be no more than formulaic "hackwork."[4] Yet "Uncle Peter's House" was written in the style for which he would become known—it is a story of Reconstruction, told in the voice of an unnamed third-person narrator, tinged with Chesnutt's characteristic quiet irony. The title—and the story—is a play on the popular story of Harriet Beecher Stowe that captivated the nation a generation earlier. Like *Uncle Tom's Cabin*, "Uncle Peter's House" presented readers with the tragedy that meets a good Christian slave, one who is a wonderful father, husband, and worker but who meets a tragic end because of the cruelties of slavery and its aftermath. But Peter, unlike Tom, lives to experience freedom.

Born in slavery, Uncle Peter is freed when the war finally ends. Chesnutt presented the opposing sides of the dispute that led to a destructive Civil War without judgment, delivering the details of Peter's struggles to survive in the now impoverished and bitter South with almost perfect objectivity. Chesnutt did not, like Stowe, relate the well-known horrors of slavery, blaming the South for supporting such a system and the ignorance upon which it was based. Instead, he presented the whole history of slavery and emancipation from the point of view of an average Black man named Peter, who was born into slavery, freed by the Civil War, and managed, through his labor and faith, to raise a family and build a house of his own. It begins: "Ever since the broad column of Sherman's army swept through Central North Carolina, leaving the whites subjugated and impoverished and the blacks free and destitute, it had been Peter's dearest wish to own a house—a two-story white house, with green blinds."[5] By the time the story begins, slavery is a relic of the past. While the story is set in the aftermath of war and slavery it is less about the trials Peter faced in slavery and freedom than his ability to overcome the obstacles that prevented him from fulfilling his dream. For Peter, owning a home of his own represents independence, freedom, and everything good in the world. Though he does not live to enjoy the fruits of his labor, he does pass down his values to the next generations—his son and his son's children—and, of course, to the readers of the story. Having been a slave, we learn, makes his quest for a house even more poignant and important. Peter understands what it means to own a home and have a family more than most who had never experienced the cruelty of slavery and post-emancipation racism.

Readers witness and admire Peter's resilience and good nature, even if we might pity the suffering he endured, first at the hands of slave owners and then by members of the Ku Klux Klan who destroy the skeleton of his home that delays its completion. But his ability to overcome both, to remain steadfastly committed to his dream until his death, is without parallel. This is a story of one man's triumph over slavery and Jim Crow, one we should admire, perhaps even imitate, because we know that Peter is a good man who works hard and loves his family. Peter leaves slavery behind when he "found work and tasted the first substantial fruits of freedom when his horny hand closed upon a greenback. It was a dirty, foul-smelling bit of paper, but it represented power and made Peter a capitalist."[6] It is the image of Peter as a burgeoning capitalist rather than of Stowe's Christlike Tom dying to save the souls of his cruel and ignorant masters that we remember. His untimely death is the result of an accident:

> In getting everything in readiness for this supreme effort, he climbed to the roof of the house one morning to saw the opening in the top for the chimney. The scaffolding, not having been securely put up, broke under his weight, and he fell to the ground, unfortunately striking on the pile of bricks which had been placed near the house for the use of the masons. His groans brought Aunt Dinah to the door, and with the help of her son Primus, she carried the wounded man into the cabin and laid him on the bed.[7]

Peter never succumbs to the injustices of slavery and racism that he experiences. His death is not the fault of slave owners or racists; his death is the result of an accident he experiences while building his own house, it occurs on the property he owns, and he dies surrounded by his family. Chesnutt transformed Stowe's sentimental antislavery story into a story of freedom that arrives when the former slave embraces capitalist principles of labor and investment. His dying words, delivered in a form of Black dialect that would have been already familiar to readers of the time, are addressed to his wife and children rather than benevolent or cruel slave owners. Rather than forgiving the cruelty and ignorance of slave owners as Uncle Tom does, Peter assures his family that his work on earth will be rewarded in heaven: "I see de angels comin' to carry me home; and on de othe' side of de ribber I see dat hebbenly mansion—a big white mansion, wid green blin's on de winders, and broad piazzas all 'roun'it; and the ribber of life flows by it."[8] Despite his suffering, Peter dies a free man, and the story of his life exemplifies what it means to be free. Rather than wallowing in the tragedy and injustice of slavery, Peter uplifts himself and dies a happy man.

No wonder the great entrepreneur and Irish-born American immigrant S. S. McClure would appreciate such a story.[9] It was one that appealed to his own literary sensibility and one he knew would resonate with a great many new Americans like himself. McClure had arrived in northern Indiana with his widowed mother and three brothers from Ireland amid the Civil War. McClure was nine. Sam, as his friends and family called him, had toiled to overcome the poverty and drudgery that most immigrants experienced upon arrival. With a little luck and a lot of hard work, McClure managed to secure a degree from Knox College in Illinois. It was in college that McClure gained experience in developing what would later become his syndicate. In his senior year, he developed an intercollegiate bulletin in which correspondents from various western colleges would send him news of college activities that he would compile in a weekly bulletin and sell to students as well as other news outlets. This venture led to the organization of the Western College Associated Press, of which McClure was elected president in his senior year. His extracurricular activities in college gave him the cash he needed to travel east, to Boston, where he became editor of a magazine devoted to the interests of bicycling enthusiasts, called *The*

Wheelman. From there, he would make his way to New York City to take advantage of the explosion in magazines that were being produced to meet the demand for cheap, quick, fun reading material. McClure started his newspaper syndicate scheme against terrible odds.

In the American literary world of the mid-1880s, the syndicate was considered uncouth. Nearly every country weekly in the United States printed some sort of syndicated stuff, and it was all mediocre. Most editors of reputable literary magazines like *The Atlantic, The Century,* and *Harper's* viewed syndicates as distasteful, literature written by third- or fourth-rate authors who couldn't get published in the New York or Boston magazines. But McClure believed in the idea of a syndicate despite the odds and the chorus of critical voices who felt such a venture only diminished the quality of American literature.

U ncle Peter's House" departed in many ways from the most popular and critically acclaimed stories on the American literary scene. In 1885, when Chesnutt's first work of literary fiction appeared in the pages of several local newspapers, including Chicago's *Daily Inter Ocean,* the *New Haven Evening Register,* St. Paul's *Daily Pioneer Press,* the *Pittsburgh Chronicle Telegraph,* and Denver's *Rocky Mountain Daily News,* the country's major literary magazines were focused on the work of three American writers: William Dean Howells, Henry James, and Mark Twain. The dominance of these writers over the American literary scene is hard to overstate. In 1885, all the space available for fiction in *The Century,* published out of New York and run by the most influential literary editor in the country, Richard Watson Gilder, was given over to three novels running concurrently— *The Rise of Silas Lapham, The Bostonians,* and *Huckleberry Finn.* Howells had just secured a contract with Harper & Brothers to publish a novel a year under their imprint as well as run a monthly column in the pages of *Harper's Magazine* in which he held forth on current literary trends and determined which authors were worth reading. The author he celebrated most eloquently and vociferously was Henry James Jr., whom he called, again in the pages of *The Century* in 1882, "a metaphysical genius."[10] Not only was it difficult to assert one's voice among this tightly knit trio, who were constantly reaffirming one another's genius and having their collective genius affirmed by the editors of *Harper's*, *The Atlantic*, and *The Century*, but it was nearly impossible for an emerging author like Chesnutt without cultural or monetary capital to break up the monopoly these three writers exerted on the literary market of the 1880s. But all that changed when McClure decided to capitalize on those authors who were not Howells, James, or Twain.

McClure needed volume to keep all his syndicates well fed and contented: a story a week to start, then two, then three, and later, as many as eight or ten a week. To meet his quota, he was obliged to buy inferior stuff, and he knew it; he was the happier, then, to find the occasional well-wrought realistic story from an author no one had ever heard of before. To buy stories from one of the big three did not suit McClure's business model. These stories were either too expensive, too long, or not varied and interesting enough to meet the expectations of his clients, the newspaper editors who had to sell their papers on a daily or weekly basis. Indeed, McClure had received several suggestions from his clients in the first year of his syndicate service that he had to address to save his syndicate from going under. The editor of the *Pittsburgh Chronicle Telegraph*, for instance, put the problem bluntly to McClure and offered him a simple solution: "The new authors excite more interest than the old stand bys. You get more originality with the new writers . . . A reader of a *short* story in a daily newspaper cares very little about literary polish. He only wants to be interested or amused."[11]

Chesnutt's subsequent stories for McClure were all committed to interesting and amusing readers who only had enough time to read *short* stories. Readers of these stories were too busy to spend time reading and reflecting on the complex, realist novels being published serially in the major literary magazines. Chesnutt's early publications, mostly humorous short sketches and anecdotes, poked fun at various social and political conventions, from interactions between Blacks and whites in New York City to the folly of inherited wealth and the changing nature of marital relations amid the rise of women entering the labor force. While the stories are primarily amusing, some even downright funny, they also have embedded within them a covert moral purpose. While the eleven stories Chesnutt sold to McClure for publication vary in form and theme, they all reveal, in one way or another, the negative consequences of valuing the material or superficial aspects of life—wealth, beauty, social position—over a genuine connection between individuals and the desire to treat others, regardless of their social position or economic status, with respect and goodwill. Like his later critics who considered these early stories beneath the dignity of literary criticism, Chesnutt may not have submitted these stories to McClure's syndicate *as literature*; they did not, as he would put it later, necessarily "rise to the dignity of literature."[12] Still, these stories did possess a kernel of what he believed literature should be: "a force directly affecting the conduct of life, present and future."[13]

Though McClure did not pay Chesnutt much—and rarely on time—for his stories, these checks allowed him to take his writing more seriously. McClure valued Chesnutt's stories in ways that no one before had. He did not care, nor seemed to know, anything about Chesnutt's background; he only cared about the stories, whether he could sell them so that he could grow his syndicate business. Over the next few years, Chesnutt sent McClure about a dozen stories, some of which were published and some not. These stories are short, so short that they seem to lack the weight necessary to count as literature. With the exception of the first two stories Chesnutt submitted to McClure—"Uncle Peter's House" and "A Tight Boot"—none of these early stories deal with race or slavery. Instead, the stories are about men and women, husbands and wives, and the fraught relations between them. Though he does not mention the race of his characters explicitly, we assume these characters are all white. The stories are intended to be instructive, to teach young people, particularly young men, how to make the right choice when it comes to marriage and, just as important, how to treat their wives well, to avoid conflict at home, and raise a family. The stories are mostly amusing accounts of men trying to impress women but falling short. It's intriguing that the subject of marriage is presented in these stories almost entirely devoid of romance, as in "A Doubtful Success" and "Cartwright's Mistake," in which male suitors fail to win the hands of the women they love because men value material prosperity and appearance over that of genuine connection.[14]

At first glance, the McClure stories seem to have little to do with Chesnutt's personal experience. Set mostly in urban environments, regarding the lives of middle-class white Americans, the stories seem to have more to do with Chesnutt's observations of those men and women he might have encountered while working at the *Mail and Express* in New York or at the Nickel Plate Road in Cleveland. But these stories also reflect Chesnutt's view of marriage derived from his own experience of being married. Shortly before leaving for New York, back in the summer of 1881, Chesnutt reflected on his marriage, considering current changes between the relations of men and women. Believing himself to have been "lucky in my marriage," he also felt relieved that he married at a time when women, especially the one he married, were respectable. As he put it in his Journal: "If I were on the carpet now, I should not know which way to turn for a woman I could admire and *respect*. They do not seem to understand the first principles of maidenly modesty or even common self-respect. I shall try to raise my daughters on a different plan."

Chesnutt's thoughts on marriage and womanhood were inspired by looking at an old photograph of Susan. The photo Chesnutt describes in this journal entry has, like so much about the intimate details of their marriage, been lost. There is a later photo of Susan in Chesnutt's papers at Fisk University, taken when she was still a young woman, likely by Lewis or Andrew, Chesnutt's younger brothers, who owned a successful portrait studio in Cleveland. It is undated, but Susan appears to be in her twenties. Her black hair is parted in the middle and pulled loosely back. She wears a dark Victorian dress with a high, ruffled collar. Her skin is dark, and her high cheekbones and broad nose suggest that unlike her husband and their children, she could not pass as white. She looks stately and serene, not looking directly at the camera, looking at something or at someone off to the side. It is a beautiful portrait. Looking at this picture, it is no wonder Chesnutt feels lucky in his marriage. Strangely, there is only one surviving photo of the couple together, taken shortly before Chesnutt's death, when receiving the Spingarn Medal in 1928. But this picture is not of *just* the two of them. It is of a group, including the writer James Weldon Johnson, who presented Chesnutt with the award. By the time the photo was taken, Chesnutt and Susan had lost much of the sensuality we see in photos of them in their younger years.

When Chesnutt wrote his reflections on Susan in his journal, he had been married for about three years. A few years later, he would leave his wife and daughters behind to pursue a literary career in New York. During their year apart, they wrote often. Most of these letters have been lost. But Helen includes a few excerpts from Susan's letters to Chesnutt, which she kept among her personal archive and revealed in her biography of her father. Writing to him on January 22, 1884, Susan is melancholy and lonely. She begins: "Your letter has been received. I had been thinking for several days you had forgotten us, as I had waited so long to hear from you." After recounting some local events, she concludes the letter on a higher note:

> How I long to be with you once more. I don't believe I ever looked forward to the coming of warm weather so eagerly before. I have found out since you left what you were to me. You were a companion, and you knew me better even than my father or mother, or at least you were more in sympathy with me than anybody else, and my failings were overlooked. No one can tell, my dearest husband, *how* I miss that companionship.[15]

Companionship was the defining feature of the Chesnutts' marriage. And it became a central feature of Chesnutt's earliest published short stories.

"Marriages," Chesnutt explains in his essay "Advice to Young Men," published in *The Social Circle Journal* in November 1886, "are getting to be such common, every-year affairs in Cleveland, that I think it might be well to lay down a few rules for the guidance of young men who may be contemplating matrimony." *The Social Circle Journal* was "a little four-page pamphlet containing essays, stories, and poems written by members of the Cleveland Social Circle."[16] According to Helen, the club had been organized a few years after the Civil War, in 1869, by "a group of young colored people who wanted to promote social intercourse and cultural activities among the better-educated people of color." Helen recounts her memories of the club's gatherings at the Chesnutt home with rapture. "When the Chesnutts entertained the club for the first time, the children were wild with excitement... There were songs, piano solos, and recitations. The recitations delighted the children, especially 'The Wreck of the Hesperus' and 'The Bells.'" While Helen recounts her memories of Social Circle gatherings, including an annual picnic at Cuyahoga Falls or Silver Lake or Rocky

River, with glee, Chesnutt was more cynical about this "very exclusive organization" that only admitted "business or professional men" and their wives and daughters who "stayed at home and took lessons in music, embroidery, or elocution and helped their mothers with the housework."

For Chesnutt, the Social Circle manifested a society divided strictly by class, race, and gender roles. In his essays and fiction, Chesnutt poked fun at the group's pretensions. Writing under the pseudonym "Uncle Solomon," Chesnutt intended his *Social Circle* essays to be humorous, but they also reveal an underlying critique of the club's members perhaps overlooked by the essay's first readers. Or perhaps the club's members found Chesnutt's essays to be funny and read them in the spirit of good-natured humor in which they were likely written. It isn't clear why he chose the moniker Solomon. Perhaps he was referring to the biblical figure known to have had hundreds of wives and concubines? Or perhaps it was a sly reference to the famous author of *Twelve Years a Slave*, Solomon Northup, the free Black man from New York who had been illegally kidnapped and sold as a slave in Louisiana? Since the Social Circle comprised mostly descendants of free Blacks, like Chesnutt and Susan, the latter seems likelier. It was probably Chesnutt's play on the pretensions of the group, who viewed themselves, as he would explain in his later "Blue Vein" stories, as those Black men and women whose parents and grandparents had been slaves.

In "Advice to Young Men," Chesnutt enumerates the six rules of marriage that, if observed, will allow young men "to avoid mistakes" in the "serious matter" of marriage. Delivering his rules with tongue firmly planted in cheek, Chesnutt follows each rule with a brief explanation. Rule 1: "Marry early and often." Rule 2: "But though early marriages are advisable, it is never too late to marry." Rule 3: "Always marry for money." Rule 4: "Beware of widows—including grass widows." Rule 5: "If possible, always marry an orphan." The essay concludes with rule 6: "If you find it difficult to follow all or any of these rules, you can keep on the safe side by remaining single. Most of our young men seem anxious to keep on the safe side."[17]

Unlike most young men, Chesnutt had married early, and he felt lucky to have married a woman who was "good," one whom he could "respect." What he found when he moved to the North, first in New York and then in Cleveland, were men who had married or were thinking of marriage along very different lines. The "young men" of Chesnutt's early stories consistently think of marrying women for their money or their beauty; an ideal wife, according to these young men, is one who possesses both. Chesnutt's stories disabuse young men of the time of such notions. He does so without preaching the virtues of good, respectable women, who may be neither pretty nor rich. Instead, he does so by making fun of the men who seek out beautiful or wealthy women for their wives. While Chesnutt began exploring the marriage theme in fiction first for McClure, he would develop it even further writing for literary journals like *Family Fiction, Tid-Bits,* and *Two Tales.* What we learn from these stories, generally longer more complex than those he submitted to McClure, is that young people suffer from following poor principles regarding marriage on both sides of the color line. The point of these and his later marriage stories was to show, rather than tell, readers that marrying for shallow reasons, like money and beauty, would lead only to heartache and pain.

The short stories Chesnutt published with McClure's syndicate, *Family Fiction,* and other such literary start-ups gave Chesnutt space to experiment with voice and character. He employed all kinds of voices—men, women, Black, white, voices of the rich and poor. He varied his stories between first-, second-, and third-person narrators. Some were set in the urban North, where he now lived, and others in the rural South he had left behind. Since McClure wanted stories for the syndicate to be short and he wanted them fast, Chesnutt would have spent little time revising these early stories. Unlike his later stories which he revised repeatedly over the course of months, sometimes years, Chesnutt kept no drafts of these early stories, suggesting that he wrote them by hand, sending his only copy directly to publishers. Those that were accepted were published, and those that weren't were simply discarded or sent elsewhere.

The two longest stories from this period—"Uncle Peter's House" and "A Grass Widow"—are the most serious of the bunch. In the case of Uncle Peter, we are left feeling some sorrow for having witnessed the suffering of a former slave, even though things come out all right in the end for him. In the case of "A Grass Widow," we are left morally shocked by the fate of Laura Wharton who, though "strikingly beautiful in face and figure," winds up alone and dead after her "unpleasant marital relations" lead her to a short life filled with lies and adulterous affairs. The rest of the stories present readers with a moral lesson by employing the rhetoric of irony and comedy rather than that of the sermon. The early short stories are funny; some, like "A Bad Night," are downright hilarious. The sense of humor Chesnutt employed in these early stories was witty and sly, a sense of humor that he would take further in the pages of *Puck*, a fairly new weekly magazine published out of New York City that relied wholly on humor to appeal to a new generation of readers.

Puck started up a few years after the publication of Mark Twain and Charles Dudley Warner's *The Gilded Age: A Tale of Today* (1873). Its first issue appeared on March 14, 1877, and featured a spirited cartoon cover of Puck, the fairy prankster from William Shakespeare's *A Midsummer Night's Dream*. Though Twain's writings never appeared in the magazine, the writings and illustrations that did appear in *Puck* were surely influenced by the success of Twain's work, a brand of literary realism that relied almost exclusively on political satire and racial caricature. *The Gilded Age* would go on to become one of the best-selling subscription novels ever produced and responsible for branding the era, known for corruption, greed, and get-rich-quick schemes.[18] The novel was notable not only for the dry wit and humor of its prose but also for its illustrations, which totaled over two hundred. *Puck* captured, or capitalized, on the collaborative, comic, and illustrative conventions that Twain deployed. It must have been something about *Puck*'s decidedly lowbrow literary form and its Twain-like methods that appealed to Chesnutt.

Why else would Chesnutt, a committed Republican, have decided to submit his work, already well received by a number of newspaper and magazine publishers, to one that openly supported the Democratic Party and denounced Republicans? Moreover, *Puck* had already become well known for its racist illustrations of Black, Jewish, German, and Irish Americans. And yet *Puck* proved to be an especially fertile ground for the emerging writer. Though he was paid less by *Puck* than McClure for his stories, the stories were a great deal shorter, and he was paid on time. *Puck*'s editors offered no suggestions or changes to the stories they accepted. It is unclear if they rejected any of the stories Chesnutt submitted. He kept only receipts from *Puck* for the money he was paid as well as notices of acceptances. These were form letters, typed, except for Chesnutt's name, "Mr. Chas. W. Chesnutt," the date, and the story's title, which were written in ink in the blank spaces provided on the form. It is not clear who read the story for review or sent the letter of acceptance. All notices concluded with the same line: "With thanks for your courtesy, Editors, PUCK." Chesnutt received nine such notices, one for each story that appeared in *Puck*. The first of these was for a story he called "Appreciation," which comprised a mere 370 words. It appeared in *Puck's* April 20, 1887, issue. Accompanying the story is an illustration of a smiling "old Negro" figure, one Chesnutt would employ repeatedly in his stories for *Puck*. The illustration of this figure appears with white whiskers, ill-fitting clothes, and a straw hat, signed "Dal," the abbreviation used by one of *Puck's* go-to illustrators, Louis Dalrymple.[19] Though brief, Chesnutt's story, with the accompanying image, over which he likely had little control, is disturbing.

The story relates a brief conversation between a Black man called "Old Pilgrim Gainey"—referred to as "Uncle Pilgrim" for most of the story—and the white "Mistah Dixon" in an unspecified "Missouri town." The story is narrated by Dixon, who speaks in standard English, while Uncle Pilgrim's speech is delivered entirely in dialect. Their conversation concerns Uncle Pilgrim's decision to return to the South, to his hometown, after having lived in the North for a short time. We learn from Uncle Pilgrim that despite the better wages, education, and civil rights he enjoyed in the North, he prefers to live in the South. For some reason, Pilgrim feels "dat cullu'd people ain't 'preciated at de Norf." The reason for this feeling and unusual preference is revealed when another white man called "young Tom Macmillan" enters the conversation when he "came up behind the old man, knocked his hat off, and saluted him with a playful kick." Addressing him as "Marse Tom," Uncle Pilgrim tells him to stop while grinning "which displayed all his wealth of ivory." He proceeds to request some "terbacker" from Tom, which he delivers without hesitation. For Uncle Pilgrim, the exchange between him and Tom allows him to feel the "'preciation" he desires: "I nevah had dat much terbacker give ter me all de time I wus at de Norf!"

Recent Chesnutt critics speculate that "the story's mix of parody and politics may have helped Chesnutt establish a relationship with *Puck*."[20] If this is the case, then Chesnutt would rightly be considered, as several of his critics have claimed, to manifest the quintessential qualities of the sellout. Chesnutt's *Puck* sketches suggest that he is willing to participate and perpetuate the rhetoric of racist caricature to fulfill his personal desire to have his work published. If this were the case, then Chesnutt should be chastised, even canceled as we say today, rather than celebrated as a great writer. What were the objectives Chesnutt had in mind when he wrote such stories for *Puck*, and, perhaps even more important, what were the consequences of their publication?

Puck was a magazine based almost entirely on satire of every variety. In Chesnutt's initial sketch for the magazine, it's not clear who or what is being satirized. The story is told in the first-person voice of a white Southerner who seems to play the role of an objective bystander. He is there to listen and report, as accurately as possible, the words of Uncle Pilgrim. Uncle Pilgrim appears to be the fool in Dixon's account; unable to appreciate the privilege of good wages and civil rights available to him in the North, he returns happily to the South, where he *prefers* to be deprived of both. Are readers to believe that most Black men are like Uncle Pilgrim? That the hard-fought battle for Black civil rights during Reconstruction was just a waste of time and resources? Or is the narrator the fool? Might such an overtly racist representation of Black people reveal the folly of white prejudices? Is the idea that Black people would take a plug of tobacco over civil rights and good wages plausible? In each of his sketches for *Puck*, especially those concerning relations between Blacks and whites, Chesnutt raises such questions about misperceptions that have potentially dire consequences. It was, after all, the prejudices held by whites against Blacks that Chesnutt was trying to expose. What better way to do this than to write directly to audiences who held such erroneous perceptions?

Chesnutt had been playing with the uncle or old Negro figure for a few years now. Since the publication of "Uncle Peter's House" back in 1885, Chesnutt had published at least four stories featuring such a character. He was now writing regularly for McClure and *Puck*, and now and again for other small magazines with decent circulations. It's not clear why Chesnutt decided to submit a story to the more established and weighted *Atlantic Monthly*. Chesnutt seemed to have been working on a longer story for some time, one that would not be suitable for either McClure or *Puck*, and one that perhaps dealt with themes that would not work for *Family Fiction* or *Tid-Bit*. In this longer story, he had woven together elements that he had been developing in his shorter pieces—a married white couple, an old Negro figure, and some insights into the South. Chesnutt had been gone from the South for almost four years. There were some things about it he missed, but he had no regrets. Still, it was home, he had grown up there, and the people and places were still a part of him. This story was set close to home, and it recalled all those features of his life he thought he had left behind. When "The Goophered Grapevine" appeared in the August 1887 issue of *The Atlantic Monthly*, Chesnutt knew he had arrived. He had become a successful writer.

7

Conjuring *The Atlantic*

But he is quite willing to leave to time and to the operation of natural laws the question of his reception into private white society; he recognizes in everyman an inalienable right to select his own associates.

—"An Inside View of the Negro Question" (1889)

Writing for McClure's syndicate and *Puck* had been gratifying, but Chesnutt was now looking to broaden and deepen his literary output. After his astonishing success on the bar exam, the *Cleveland Leader* reported on March 4, 1887, that "Chesnutt stood at the head of his class, having made the highest per cent in the thorough examination." Chesnutt resigned from the Nickel Plate Road and took a position with a law firm. Henderson, Kline, and Tolles, known at the time as "one of Cleveland's great law firms," employed Chesnutt as their in-house stenographer. He also worked with the partners on legal cases, particularly those dealing with matters of family law and divorce. Chesnutt's steady income from stenography and litigation furnished his growing family with all the pleasures of middle-class life. He could now purchase books, subscribe to magazines and newspapers, without having to worry about making ends meet. One of his singular pleasures was to cut articles from the papers and paste them into scrapbooks; these cuttings would later become an important source for future stories.

He was also beginning to dress the part of a professional writer. Just as he had studied stenography and shorthand from books he bought back in Fayetteville, he copied the rules of proper comportment—"How to

Behave," "How to talk, and "How to do Business"—from a book called *A Handbook for Home Improvement* published by Fowler & Wells, New York, in his journal.[1] He provided a lengthy discussion of what he learned from this book for the literary society a few years before leaving Fayetteville. Though Chesnutt had relied mostly on books to create an identity for himself, he recognized that reading books alone was insufficient to achieve his purpose. "But as our ancestors had no opportunity for association with well-bred people, except in a menial capacity; and as our opportunities are almost as limited: we ought to try to learn, either by reading or such observation as we can have, those simple forms and customs which are common to well-bred people throughout the civilized world. It is only by knowing and observing them that we can feel at ease in society, or properly enjoy the intercourse of people of refinement." Like other young professional men living in late-nineteenth-century American cities, Chesnutt was rarely seen without wearing a full suit, blazer, vest, collared shirt, and black necktie. His hair and mustache were perfectly groomed. He was fastidious about his appearance. It wasn't long before he decided to relocate the family to a bigger house, one where he would have room for a study or small library for his growing book collection, a space where he could read and write uninterrupted after a long day at the law office.

It was here that Chesnutt composed "The Goophered Grapevine," a story that explained the meaning of the unfamiliar word of its title from the lips of a former slave who called himself "ole Julius McAdoo." The story was different from the ones Chesnutt had been writing for *Puck* and McClure. Not only was it substantially longer, it also introduced a new element into Chesnutt's fiction, a story told almost entirely in the first-person voice of a former slave. Of course, slave narratives written by former slaves like Frederick Douglass, William Wells Brown, and Harriet Jacobs, were familiar to readers at the time. Most of these slave narratives were published before or during the war. Jacobs's *Incidents in the Life of a Slave Girl* was one of the later slave narratives to appear in print, in 1861.[2] Though slave narratives varied according to the experiences told by their authors, these slave narratives were, for the most part, deployed by antislavery activists and abolitionists like William Lloyd Garrison and Lydia Maria Child to reveal to their fellow Northerners the truth about slavery. Why would

Chesnutt, over two decades after the abolition of slavery, decide to deploy the first-person voice of a former slave in his fiction?

Chesnutt was surely aware of more recent fictions, by Thomas Nelson Page, Joel Chandler Harris, and, of course, Mark Twain, that had taken up the figure of the former slave. Chesnutt never mentioned any of them in his journals. He did, however, take these writers up in speeches delivered much later, explaining to audiences the power of their influence. In a speech called "The Negro in Books," delivered in 1916 in Philadelphia, he explained the motive of some of these writers and how they influenced the development of his own fiction. "The faithful servant motive—generally an old Negro uncle or mammy who loves the white folks better than his or her own black offspring—is one of the commonest types of Negro in fiction. Uncle Tom is the prototype. Thomas Nelson Page, in 'Marse Chan' and elsewhere has apotheosized this type. Joel Chandler Harris, in Uncle Remus, has delineated a delightful old Negro."[3] Chesnutt made his remarks on these authors without judgment. In fact, he saw himself as working within the same milieu, admitting that he used the "old Negro" figure himself in what he would come to refer to as *his* "conjure stories." Over the course of his life, Chesnutt would write over a dozen conjure stories, seven of which constitute his first book publication in 1899. "The Goophered Grapevine" would always stand out as being his first conjure story and his first publication in *The Atlantic*. Eventually, he would become more critical of those writers, particularly Thomas Nelson Page, whose stories he came to view toward the end of his life as "disguising the harshness of slavery under the mask of sentiment."[4] Looking back on his own work at the end of his life, Chesnutt took pains to distance himself from writers who deployed the "old Negro" in their fiction. But how was Chesnutt's "old Negro" different from those who appeared in American literature at the time?

Chesnutt seems to have started drafting various fragments that would comprise "The Goophered Grapevine" back in Fayetteville around the time he first read Albion Tourgée's novel *A Fool's Errand* in 1880. For Chesnutt, that novel revealed how Northerners "see in the colored people a race, but recently emancipated from a cruel bondage; struggling for education, for a higher social and moral life."[5] But what they *heard* was "the cry of the oppressed and struggling ones." This, for Chesnutt, was a one-dimensional, or just plain flat, depiction of former slaves and their descendants. Chesnutt noticed how former slaves depicted by writers like Tourgée seemed to want to "lend a willing ear to all that is spoken or written concerning their character, habits, etc."[6] But Northern writers and readers like Tourgée and Stowe, who included the voices of Black people in their fiction, had not *really* listened to them.

At least not as closely as he had. Chesnutt had been recording the voices of Black people in his journals for years. When he first started practicing stenography, Chesnutt would record the voices he heard at church, at school, and in the grocery store. Employing shorthand, Chesnutt had developed a combination of signs, lines, dots, a light stroke, a darker stroke of the pen, to follow the various patterns of speech he heard. Relying on the Pitman system of shorthand, Chesnutt developed a highly precise language to capture the sounds of voices that couldn't be spelled in longhand by a combination of letters. It wasn't just shorthand that gave Chesnutt a greater sense of intimacy with those who spoke Black dialect, a language that was transmitted orally, since most of its speakers were either illiterate or semiliterate. Unlike Tourgée and other popular postbellum writers like Joel Chandler Harris and Mark Twain, who integrated the sounds of "negro voices" in their fiction, Chesnutt, as he declared in his journal, was "a colored man, who has lived among colored people all his life; who is familiar with their habits, their ruling passions, their prejudices, their whole moral and social condition; their public and private ambitions; their religious tendencies and habits."[7] Chesnutt wanted to show Northern writers and readers who these Black people really were, and the kind of story that *real* Black people told was like nothing white Northern readers and writers had heard before.

The first of his conjure stories, in which he employed Black dialect at length, opens in the first-person voice of an unnamed white man from northern Ohio who is tethered to a sick wife called Annie. The couple decide to relocate to central North Carolina due to Annie's poor health and where the narrator hopes to continue his work in the field of "grape-culture." The story meanders along for a few paragraphs in the voice of this genial narrator as he describes his new Southern environs. A shift occurs around the fourth paragraph, when the couple from Ohio meet "a venerable-looking colored man."[8] The encounter causes a shift in the narration. The story's white narrator enters a conversation with the man. Once this happens, the "colored man," who reveals himself to be Julius McAdoo, a former slave who has lived on the plantation for much of his life, takes over the story, with only a brief interruption from the initial white narrator to explain the shift in voice:

> We assured him that we would be glad to hear how it all happened, and he began to tell us. At first the current of his memory—or imagination—seemed somewhat sluggish; but as his embarrassment wore off, his language flowed more freely, and the story acquired perspective and expression, and he seemed to lose sight of his auditors, and to be living over again in monologue his life on the old plantation.[9]

Julius delivers his story, unsurprisingly, entirely in what readers of the time would have dubbed "negro dialect." Chesnutt does not offer, as did Twain when he introduced his novel *Huckleberry Finn* a couple of years earlier, an explanatory note regarding his use of the dialect.[10] Instead, Julius just talks, and we, alongside the narrator and his wife, listen. What we hear is a story at once fantastic and horrifying. Julius explains that the property the narrator and his wife are thinking about buying, a vineyard that includes scuppernong grapes, is "goophered, cunju'd, bewitch." For the next several pages, Julius narrates the history of the vineyard, introducing its former owner, "Mars Dugal," the conjure woman "Aun' Peggy," whom he hires to put a spell on the vines to prevent slaves from stealing his grapes. After doing so, a new slave called Henry arrives on the plantation and, unaware of the conjure, eats the grapes from the vineyard. Henry looks to the conjure woman, Aunt Peggy, who creates a potion meant to protect him from the goophered grapevine. The result of the double conjure is that Henry takes on the qualities of the vines, losing his hair and shriveling up as the vines die in the winter, then coming to life in the spring, growing curly locks and gaining strength. The story concludes with the voice of the initial narrator, Annie's husband, who decides, against Julius's advice, to buy the vineyard. What results from the purchase, according to "the local press" cited in the story, is a fine example of "the opportunities open to Northern capital in the development of Southern industries."[11] The Northern couple not only make a small fortune from their newly purchased Southern grapes, they also employ Julius as their coachman and gardener, who, by the end of the story, they now affectionately call "Uncle" Julius. The Northern narrator wraps up *his* story by explaining that Julius's "goopher story" and "his advice to me not to buy the vineyard" were likely inspired by his desire to keep the grapes for himself, calling into question, if it hadn't already been, the story's purpose.

Was the story intended to keep the Northerners from buying the land so that Julius could continue occupying it? Or was it told as a genuine warning to the Northerners to be wary of transplanting their Northern ideas in grape culture to the differently composed Southern soil? Whatever its purpose, the Northerners recognize Julius's story to be a good one, so good that they decide to stay close to the goophered grapevine, not just for the sake of developing it for their profit but also to hear more of Julius's conjure stories about the Southern land they now call home. The relationship that develops between the Northern white couple and Julius was new. Julius's story helps to vivify Annie from her unknown illness while also aiding her husband's industry. For all the tragedy of the history of slavery Julius relates, Chesnutt's story ends happily, with our three characters engaged in a mutually satisfying relationship on a former plantation.

As Chesnutt worked on the story, drafting and knitting together its disparate elements, he hoped it would appeal to more literary readers. He seemed to have outgrown the constraints placed on him by McClure and *Puck*'s editors. A few years later, in conversation with Max Bennett Thrasher for the *Boston Evening Transcript*, Chesnutt explained his method and source material for this "first conjure story": "I remembered a remarkable yarn which had been related to me by my father-in-law's gardener, old Uncle Henry, to the effect that the sap of a pruned grapevine rubbed on a bald head in the spring would produce a luxuriant growth of hair, which would, however, fall out when the sap in the vine went down in the fall. To the creative mind this was sufficient material for the story 'The Goophered Grapevine.'"[12]

"The Goophered Grapevine" may have been based *mostly* on the "remarkable yarn" Chesnutt recalled from his Fayetteville days, but the story's Northern characters—the narrator, his wife, and the "Yankee" who swindles Mars Dugal of "mo'n a thousan' dollars" and whose bad advice on grape culture leads to the demise of both the vineyard and the slave Henry—are far removed from Fayetteville. The story's Northern characters are essential to the development of Chesnutt's conjure story—and its appeal. Without these Northern intrusions into Julius's life—and the South—there would be no story to tell. Moreover, without the story's Northern characters, it is unlikely Thomas Bailey Aldrich, *The Atlantic*'s conservative editor at the time, would have considered it worthy for inclusion in the precious pages of the magazine. Chesnutt's "Goophered Grapevine" was unrealistic, about magic spells that caused men to grow old overnight and then become young again. Moreover, it was told mostly in the voice of an "old Negro slave," speaking an almost incomprehensible regional dialect. The story's lack of realism and insistence on regionalism would have been anathema to the literary tastes of *The Atlantic*'s current editor.

Under Aldrich's editorship, *The Atlantic* had become the beacon of highbrow American literary culture. Julius's story at once chastises and seduces his Northern audience for their ignorance of Southern folkways. There was a delicious irony too in submitting this Southern story, featuring Black dialect, to a journal known for its defense and celebration of "Yankee Humanism" that Chesnutt must have savored. Rather than submitting to the well-known prejudices of *The Atlantic*'s genteel editor, known for his disdain of dialect and realist themes, Chesnutt created a narrator with whom Aldrich might identify. The Northern narrator exhibits the kind of disdain for Julius's story that would have resonated with Aldrich. Framing Julius's story, delivered entirely in a form of dialect that celebrates the cadences and cleverness of an illiterate former slave, with the voice of a highly literate, Northern gentleman was a stroke of genius. With its acceptance and publication in the August 1887 issue of *The Atlantic*, Chesnutt had achieved the seemingly impossible: he had penetrated the inner circle of America's literary elite. In doing so, "The Goophered Grapevine," as he would explain a few years later, had become the first purely imaginative contribution by "an American with acknowledged African descent" to appear in *The Atlantic*.

It wasn't only Chesnutt's racial background that made the publication of "The Goophered Grapevine" American literary history. It was also the fact that a story of its *kind*, one that featured a former slave telling a story to a couple of Northern landowners seeking to buy the very land where the slave had once toiled, had made its way into a journal committed to preserving the values of the literary elite. And it is *how* the Northerners are depicted listening to Julius, how they are at once baffled and in awe of the story, that revealed to readers how slaves, slave owners, and free Blacks lived tightly bound to one another; though their society had been destroyed, traces of it remained embedded in the land and the bodies of those still living.

Why would such a story appeal to a reader deeply committed to the cultural values of New England, one who had enjoyed wealth and social privilege for much of his life, and one known for venerating literature authored by elites? Thomas Bailey Aldrich, or TBA, as he signed off on correspondence with friends and associates, had been editor of *The Atlantic* for a little over five years when Chesnutt sent "The Goophered Grapevine" to the monthly magazine. Chesnutt was paid forty-five dollars for it, the most he had made on a single short story. Before he resigned his editorship a few years later, in 1890, Aldrich would accept two more of Chesnutt's "conjure" stories for *The Atlantic*; "Po' Sandy" appeared in the May 1888 issue and "Dave's Neckliss" shortly after in October 1889. It is not clear if Aldrich was aware that the appearance of this trio of conjure stories under his editorship would create a literary sensation, erasing the lines that had been drawn by editors like him over the years, lines that divided Black literature from white literature, Northern literature from Southern literature. Chesnutt's conjure stories showed them that such divisions were relics of the past. A new era in which Blacks, whites, Northerners, and Southerners lived and *wrote* together could begin, so long as we remembered, with a little help from a former slave called Julius, the horror of keeping them apart.

"The first of my conjure stories had been accepted for the Atlantic," Chesnutt would recall a couple of years before his death, "by Thomas Bailey Aldrich, the genial auburn-haired poet who at that time presided over the editorial desk. My relations with him, for the short time they lasted, were most cordial and friendly."[13] And that is all we know about Chesnutt's relationship with Aldrich. Aldrich did not mention Chesnutt in any of his writings or correspondence; letters between the two, if there were any, have been lost. We don't know if Aldrich suggested any revisions to the stories he accepted for *The Atlantic*. But we do know, because Chesnutt made a point of reminding his readers decades later, that it was Aldrich, known for his antipathy of literary realism, regional dialect, and ungrammatical phrasings during his reign over *The Atlantic*, who decided to publish the first, second, and third of Chesnutt's conjure stories, all of which relied on precisely the elements of literature Aldrich despised. One can more fully appreciate the novelty of Chesnutt's stories when reading his conjure stories in the context of their initial publication.

The May 1888 issue of *The Atlantic*, in which Chesnutt's second conjure story, "Po' Sandy," appeared, opened with the third and final installment of Henry James's esoteric novel set among the literary elite in Italy, *The Aspern Papers*. Alongside a couple of more forgettable works of short fiction by Agnes Repplier about "The Cavalier" and one concerning "A Child of Japan," there were essays on "The American Philosophical Society," "Cicero in the Senate," "Reform in the Celebration of Marriage," a celebration of the writings of America's first novelist, Charles Brockden Brown, and an account of "Mr. Ruskin's Early Years." Not only did the dialect, ungrammatical phrasings, apparent even in the story's title, set Chesnutt's story apart from all the other pieces published that month in *The Atlantic*, it also pertained to a subject and place far removed from the rest: the American South. What was Aldrich's purpose in publishing a story that so clearly did not fit with the rest? Why was Aldrich willing to risk incoherence and confusion by including stories by Chesnutt that so explicitly went against his literary taste for more classical themes?

Though Aldrich likely knew little about Chesnutt's work when he received that first conjure story in 1887, the same could not be said of Chesnutt. Chesnutt knew much about Aldrich's tastes, and he knew his likes and dislikes. He had been following Aldrich's work long before he sent "The Goophered Grapevine" to *The Atlantic*. Chesnutt was a voracious reader, especially of poetry, and had always been a big fan of Longfellow's. He copied lines from "The Song of Hiawatha" in his journal and used it to develop his first attempts at poetic verse. Being a Longfellow fan would have led him inevitably to Aldrich. Like Chesnutt, Aldrich was an avid admirer of Longfellow's poems, to which he attributed the development of his own highly successful literary career. Before becoming editor of *The Atlantic*, Aldrich had published an autobiographical work of juvenile fiction, *The Story of a Bad Boy*, which recounted an idyllic New England youth interrupted by his father's death when the boy was twelve.[14] His father's death prevented him from pursuing higher education at Harvard. Though the differences between Chesnutt's and Aldrich's childhoods were obvious, it is likely that Chesnutt found some of his own experiences mirrored in Aldrich's autobiography. Aldrich would go on to write books of poems in the style of Longfellow, calling on the past and celebrating New England seafaring life. Before moving to Boston with his wife, Lilian, Aldrich worked for several New York periodicals, including *The Evening Mirror* and *The Home Journal*. Having followed a somewhat similar path, from a small, rural town to working for a newspaper in a metropolis, Chesnutt may have identified with Aldrich's literary career, or at least aspired to attain the prestige that the older writer had achieved.

Knowing what he knew of Aldrich, he began his "old Negro" story not with the sound of the former slave's voice (so familiar to Chesnutt) but with the thoughts of a Northerner, a leisured, well-educated, and moneyed middle-aged man who could appreciate a fine wine as much as a well-crafted line of romantic verse. Reading the opening lines of "The Goophered Grapevine" smoking his pipe in his cozy office at 4 Park Street in Boston, Aldrich must have been struck by the intelligent, conversational, and inviting tone of Chesnutt's narrator:

> About ten years ago my wife was in poor health, and our family doctor, in whose skill and honesty I had implicit confidence, advised a change of climate. I was engaged in grape-culture in northern Ohio, and decided to look for a locality suitable for carrying on the same business in some Southern State. I wrote to a cousin who had gone into the turpentine business in central North Carolina, and he assured me that no better place could be found in the South than the State and neighborhood in which he lived: climate and soil were all that could be asked for, and land could be bought for a

mere song. A cordial invitation to visit him while I looked into the matter was accepted. We found the weather delightful at that season, the end of the summer, and were most hospitably entertained. Our host placed a horse and buggy at our disposal, and himself acted as guide until I got somewhat familiar with the country.[15]

Perhaps like McClure, Aldrich was impressed by the clarity of Chesnutt's prose and requested more. The story eases Northern readers into the South, promising that they will be "hospitably entertained" rather than reviled. And so, less than a year later, Aldrich accepted a second conjure story by Chesnutt, this even more powerful and tragic than the first.

"Po' Sandy" was a story of a slave marriage. Such a marriage was unrecognizable and shocking to a Northern couple who had become husband and wife in the conventional, legal way. Employing once again the storytelling talents of Julius McAdoo, Chesnutt took readers into what the story's Northern narrator called "the simple but intensely human inner life of slavery."[16] It is a place where most readers of *The Atlantic*, and certainly its aesthete editor, born and raised in Portsmouth, New Hampshire, had never been. Like "Goophered," "Po' Sandy" featured the spells of a conjure woman to deal with the greed and thoughtlessness of an otherwise benign slave owner called Mars Marrabo. This time, however, the conjure woman is Sandy's slave wife, Tenie, who conjures him into a tree so that he might avoid Mars Marrabo lending him out to other landowners. Sandy and Tenie are in love, but since Mars Marrabo owns them, their love is subject to *his* desires and whims. Despite their tremendous efforts to stay together, Mars Marrabo does what most slave owners looking to make a profit on his slaves do: he tears the slave couple apart, limb by limb. Perhaps even more horrifying than hearing about what happens to Sandy and Tenie is the fact that Mars Marrabo seems to be entirely ignorant of the violence and cruelty he inflicts on his slaves.

While aspects of the story were, obviously, unrealistic, there were other things about the story that were all too real. Here was a story about the harm slavery had done to a couple who were in love. Though the story was delivered in the dialect voice of Julius McAdoo, there was something timeless, even universal, about how "Po' Sandy" was turned into a tree by his wife, a conjure woman. It may have reminded the classically inclined Aldrich of the story of Daphne as told by Ovid in the *Metamorphoses*. Were Chesnutt's classical allusions what led Aldrich to swallow his distaste for regional dialect and romantic renderings of the poor and illiterate? It's hard to know for sure what precisely Aldrich liked so much about Chesnutt's conjure stories, only that he liked them, because he was the first to publish them. And we know that Aldrich never accepted anything for *The Atlantic* that he did not *like*. During Aldrich's editorship, the issue of aesthetic quality reigned supreme.

Whatever Aldrich's reasons were for accepting those first conjure stories, the effect of their publication on Chesnutt's literary career was profound. Whatever its limitations, few would dispute the fact that a publication in *The Atlantic* was, in the 1880s, a sign of one's literary prestige on the American literary scene. While *The Atlantic* under Aldrich's editorship was committed to defending literary tradition and individual talent, other periodicals were cropping up to respond to the growing demand for stories about current events, politics, and culture from alternative viewpoints, those that diverged from the high and mighty tones of the Bostonian elite. The dominance of Northern highbrow periodicals like *The Atlantic*, *Harper's*, and *The Century* was slowly beginning to erode around the end of the decade, just as Chesnutt's literary career was taking off.

The *Forum* was one such new magazine, founded by Isaac Rice, in 1885. Unlike Aldrich and McClure, Rice was neither an editor with an attention to a finely tuned line of literary prose nor a publisher with an enterprising spirit. He was trained as a musician but became a lawyer interested in breaking up the monopolies that seemed to have taken over almost every industry, from railroads to newspapers. Though Rice had great ambitions for *The Forum*, he needed help to run its daily operations, someone with experience in the periodical publishing business but not the kind of *insider* experience of men like Aldrich and Howells. The following year, Rice tapped Walter Hines Page to become its business manager. Page had moved to New York from Raleigh a couple of years earlier to work for *The Evening Post*. Page had earned a reputation as a Southerner with new ideas on the New York newspaper scene. Perhaps it was for this reason that

Rice thought he could launch *The Forum* onto the American cultural scene. Not the American scene of the Bostonians but one that had a broader scope, one that included Southern readers and writers like himself. Page joined *The Forum* first as business manager; a few years later, he took over the editorship from Lorretus Metcalf. Under Page's leadership, *The Forum* acquired a certain Southern flavor that set it apart from most magazines published out of New York and Boston. Unlike *The Atlantic*, articles in *The Forum* stressed current political and cultural issues. One of its most distinguishing features, which was characteristic of Page's literary sensibility, was the symposium. Recalling Plato's famous work, *The Forum*'s symposia would invite writers with opposing viewpoints to address the same question in the form of an essay. It was here, in the pages of *The Forum*, that Chesnutt saw his fiction appreciated and discussed by authors he had read and admired back in Fayetteville.

Shortly after the appearance of his second conjure story in the May 1888 issue of *The Atlantic*, *The Forum* ran a symposium series regarding the state of Southern literature, which included contributions from two of the best-known authors who dealt with the South in their fiction: Albion Winegar Tourgée and George Washington Cable. Their essays were prompted by one published in the October issue by Senator James B. Eustis, who, like Cable, was from Louisiana. But unlike the well-known Southern novelist, who had returned from a successful literary tour across the United States and Canada alongside Mark Twain in 1885, Eustis was a long-serving Southern politician and lawyer expounding on what he called "the Negro question." Bearing the provocative title "Race Antagonism," Eustis rationalized racial segregation by arguing that the country was "inhabited by two such distinct and antagonistic races" that were the result of a "separation" between the two races, leading to "a feeling of antipathy or *quasi* hostility between the two races, North as well as South, the only difference being that in the latter section, because the Negroes are more numerous, the manifestations of this suppressed antagonism are unavoidably more frequent." Though Chesnutt was likely unaware of Senator Eustis's view on the Negro question when he wrote his conjure stories, it offered a very different picture of the South and relations between "the two races" than the one Chesnutt presented in his conjure stories.[17]

Until *The Forum* published its symposium on the Negro question,

Chesnutt had been working in the field of literature, writing humorous stories, transcribing speeches, reading the classics. But with the publication of his conjure stories in *The Atlantic*, he seemed to have inadvertently entered the political sphere, not as a politician or activist but as a writer with a unique position. Though located in Cleveland, he was now considered a Southern writer, writing on the Negro question, from the singular point of view of a *colored man*. In his essay "The South as a Field for Fiction," Tourgée made reference to "a dialect story of Southern life written by one of the enslaved race."[18] Further along in the essay, he referred to "Chestnut's [*sic*] curious realism" that offered something new in American literature, to portray the "freedman as a man—not as a 'brother in black,' with the curse of Cain yet upon him, but a man with hopes and aspirations, quick to suffer, patient to endure, full of hot passion, fervid imagination, desirous of being equal to the best—is sure to be a character of enduring interest."[19] Tourgée was discussing Chesnutt's stories! Sure, he had misspelled his name and gotten a few facts wrong; but that was to be expected. Few knew much about Chesnutt's background when he appeared in the pages of *The Atlantic*. Tourgée mentioned his name, surname only, without offering specifics about who Chesnutt was, and little detail about the stories themselves; Tourgée just wrote about Chesnutt in a general way, to help him make a case for the literary potential of representing Black characters in fiction. But by just mentioning Chesnutt in his essay, Tourgée was effectively calling attention to his fiction. It wasn't exactly a positive review of the stories—Tourgée didn't provide sufficient detail for that— but Tourgée's essay was the closest Chesnutt had come to being publicly recognized as an author. With a little bit of courage and a great deal of anticipation, Chesnutt decided to write to Tourgée, to find out what the old judge he'd revered back in North Carolina *really* thought of him.

Chesnutt did not keep a copy of that first letter he sent to Tourgée, as he did with later letters he wrote. Perhaps he was embarrassed by it, perhaps he didn't think of keeping copies of personal letters at the time, or perhaps he just misplaced it. He did, however, keep Tourgée's response, dated December 8, 1888. From Tourgée's reply, we can surmise that Chesnutt approached the famous author with some trepidation, perhaps opening the letter by thanking him for mentioning his stories in *The Forum* and flattering the older writer by mentioning the important role *A Fool's Errand* and *Bricks Without Straw* had played in his decision to become a writer. Tourgée's quick and effusive response to Chesnutt not only marked the beginning of a new friendship, it was also the beginning of a literary movement that would transcend the political and racial divisions of the time. Chesnutt and Tourgée were writing to make the South a part of American Literature at a time when the division between North and South was an accepted feature of American political life. Spanning several handwritten pages, Tourgée began with a fulsome celebration of Chesnutt's work, offering him encouragement to pursue literature despite the difficulties he was sure to encounter. "My dear Mr. Chesnutt," he begins,

> Few things have given me greater pleasure than your letter. Of course, it was to you that I referred. I did not dare make the reference more explicit lest it should do you an injury. The fact of color is yet a curse, the intensity of which few realize. I have kept track of your work and noted the growth. Its realism is unique and true— true to nature and not to the fettering ideas of the narrow rules which makes our so-called realism the falsest of fiction. You have a great field before you, and your recent steps inside the gateway have been true and manly ones. You may do much—I trust you will do much to solve the great question of the hour—the greatest question of the world's history—the future of the Negro race in America.[20]

Chesnutt must have been more than a little overwhelmed by Tourgée's response. Did he really think that he, who had just a few years earlier been working at a colored school in Fayetteville and was now toiling away to support his family as a stenographer in a law firm, could solve "the great question of the hour"?[21] It seemed a bit over the top. Tourgée seemed a bit affected, with an inflated sense of his own importance, let alone Chesnutt's literary potential. But what if he was right? If Tourgée actually believed that he was the man to solve "the greatest question of the world's history," then he should probably get started. Maybe he should devote himself to writing the kind of literature that took up these big questions? Whatever the effect of Tourgée's letter on him, one thing is for certain: Tourgée had allowed Chesnutt to see himself as a writer on par with the *real* writers of the time—James, Howells, Twain, and of course Tourgée himself—but one with a point of view distinct from theirs. Tourgée called Chesnutt's realism "curious," but this was too vague. What did *curious realism* even mean? Chesnutt would need to clarify his point of view in black and white. Instead of answering Tourgée's effusive letter, he got to work on another conjure story that he called "Dave's Neckliss." After its publication in the October 1889 issue of *The Atlantic*, he would send a copy to Tourgée with a brief note apologizing for not having responded to his letter sooner.

As fate would have it, George Washington Cable arrived in Cleveland a couple of weeks after Chesnutt began his correspondence with Tourgée. What luck! Here he had just written to Tourgée about Cable's piece in *The Forum*, and now Cable was scheduled to arrive at the local Congregational church as part of the annual Forefather's Day celebration in a few days. This couldn't be just fortuitous—it seemed like it was meant to be, as if Chesnutt were destined to become part of a new literary movement, one that told the truth about the American South and segregation. Unlike with Tourgée, with whom he often disagreed, he found himself agreeing with most of what he'd read by Cable—not just his recent essay in *The Forum* but also his earlier political writings that had caused all that controversy. Chesnutt had been impressed that a white Southerner, and one who'd fought for the Confederacy, would write the kinds of things Cable did in "The Silent South" and "The Freedman's Case in Equity."[22] Of course, to Chesnutt, this was just common sense, but to have someone of Cable's stature write them was different. It gave Chesnutt hope that maybe all white Southerners didn't believe in the existence of inferior and superior races. He knew Cable had left his home in New Orleans after those essays were published. He wondered what life was like for Cable now that he lived far from the South in a small New England town. He wondered if the only way a Southern writer critical of the South could survive was by living elsewhere. He would love to talk with Cable, to ask him about his writing, to share his own with him, to finally talk to someone who cared about the same things he did.

Chesnutt didn't usually attend Forefather's Day celebrations. These celebrations had started long before Chesnutt had moved to Cleveland by the New England Society of Cleveland & the Western Reserve back before the war in 1853. Every year since, the Plymouth Congregational Church would put together a program of speakers to commemorate the Pilgrims' landing at Plymouth Rock. Usually, only members of the society attended these events, and Chesnutt, not being a "native or descendant of a native of a New England State," had no reason to attend.[23] Chesnutt had no desire to participate in events that celebrated blood and breeding. But when he heard that Cable would be there, he decided to go and hear what the Louisiana writer, now a resident of Northampton, Massachusetts, might say. Maybe there would be time for Chesnutt to speak to him? He would probably feel a bit out of place, but what did it matter so long as he could hear this unusual Southern writer speak for a few minutes?

Even before Page brought Cable and Tourgée together in the pages of *The Forum*, the connection between them was clear. Both were critics of the South and strong advocates of "the Negro." Chesnutt found common cause with both men but recognized differences, too. Chesnutt was impressed by how Cable's *Forum* essay, "A Simpler Southern Question," had so clearly and concisely explained the meaning of the otherwise elusive Negro question. Cable rephrased the question superbly: "Shall the Negro individually, enjoy equally with the white man, individually, the full measure of an American citizen's public rights?"[24] That was the right question to ask. Chesnutt appreciated Cable's iteration of *individually*. Chesnutt found it useless to think only of Black or white people as a group, as most people, like the senator from Louisiana, did. Doing so only embedded those on both sides of the argument more deeply in the racial categories that Chesnutt believed were the cause of the race problem in the United States. Perhaps buoyed by his recent correspondence with Tourgée, Chesnutt set out from his home on Brenton Street on a snowy December evening to meet Cable. That first meeting in Cleveland between two Southern writers, one who hailed from a family of slaveholders and fought for the Confederacy, the other whose parents had fled the South before the Civil War and led a colored school during Reconstruction, marked the beginning of an unprecedented collaboration, taking American literary realism beyond the bounds of the Northern elite.

How exactly Chesnutt was able to finagle an interview with Cable amid the celebrations of Forefather's Day is unclear. Chesnutt did not describe the meeting in any of his personal or public writings. But Cable did provide an account of his meeting with Chesnutt in his diary almost immediately after it occurred. Under the date December 21 in his diary from 1888, Cable took note of his trip to Cleveland, describing how

> as I turned to go to my room a man said "Is this" &c. I said it was. He said his name was Chestnut [*sic*]. Wanted to go to my room to ask me a question. I thought him an unskilful interviewing reporter, and met his proposition coldly. Asked him to state his question. He began that he had contributed some stories to *The Atlantic Monthly*—I said, "come upstairs." Up there he began thanking me for my political papers and surprised me with the statement that he was a "colored man." We talked an hour. He is very bright. Is a court stenographer here. I think he will be very valuable in our Open Letter Club work.[25]

Cable's brief description of his meeting with Chesnutt is remarkable not only for what it reveals about the beginning of their friendship. Cable unapologetically admits to having never heard of Chesnutt, that upon meeting him he made a series of false assumptions. First, that Chesnutt is "an unskilful interviewing reporter" and, second, that he is a white man. The only way Chesnutt was able to gain access to Cable, who at the time was almost as well known as Twain, was by using the fact of his authorship in *The Atlantic*. Writing for *The Atlantic* seemed to have been, for Cable at least, the only reason to engage a stranger in conversation. After Cable invited him to his room, Chesnutt made "the statement that he was a 'colored man.'" It is not exactly clear why the statement "surprised" Cable. Clearly, he had not connected the "Chestnut" mentioned by Tourgée in his *Forum* essay. Perhaps because Chesnutt did not look like how a colored man should look to Cable. Or perhaps Cable was surprised to learn that a colored man had had stories published in *The Atlantic*. Either way, Cable's ignorance and response did not seem to faze Chesnutt a bit. Chesnutt clearly impressed Cable, not just by flattering the older, more established writer but also by his knowledge and ability to hold his own in what sounded like a rather demanding conversation. So impressed was Cable by Chesnutt that he decided to invite an author he had never read to join his newly established Open Letter Club.

For Cable, Chesnutt could not have picked a better moment to introduce himself. A few months earlier, in the spring of 1888, Cable had put into place his latest plan to do something about the deteriorating situation in the South. Cable believed that the South's commitment to racial segregation had to end to secure its economic and cultural development. This was not the kind of argument he could make alone. His idea was to gather like-minded individuals to write and discuss the South's situation from multiple points of view. He called this gathering the Open Letter Club, and its purpose, Cable explained to prospective members, was "to keep under public discussion every aspect of the great moral, political and industrial revolution going on in the South, and to disseminate in printed form among thousands of good citizens, especially, though not exclusively, in the South, the most valuable matter printed on every branch of this subject." Most of the club's members were, like Cable, Southern and white. But there were also some Northerners, like Edward Atkinson, a New England capitalist who had written persuasively on Southern industry. Chesnutt must have felt more than a little flattered to have Cable include him as part of this learned group. He was, however, its only "colored" member, and Cable surely understood the importance of having Chesnutt join his club. Despite his desire to become a member of Cable's club, Chesnutt's desire to be a writer above all else would inevitably disappoint his new Southern friend.

A couple of weeks after their meeting in Cleveland, Chesnutt wrote to Cable at his suggestion, enclosing his own essay on the Negro question, which Cable read with considerable care, offering extensive revisions, having "spent well nigh a whole day on it." Perhaps the most notable change Cable suggested was to Chesnutt's title. "Why not call it 'The Negro's View of the Negro Question' instead of 'An Inside View of the Negro Question,'" which Cable felt was "indeterminate." Or perhaps "The Negro's Answer to the Negro Question." It was important to Cable that Chesnutt make his racial identity a central part of the essay. He made other changes, cutting sentences, even whole paragraphs, and then sent the whole thing back to Chesnutt with the request that he "not delay" in making the changes. Cable treated Chesnutt's essay with a great deal of urgency, explaining ominously that "there are reasons why the article should find publication as soon as possible."[26]

Cable's letter was dated January 30, 1889. Republican Benjamin Harrison had just defeated Democrat Grover Cleveland in the presidential election but had not yet taken office. It was a time of transition in the country. There was a sense that Harrison would use his presidency to defend voting rights for African Americans, and men like Cable were deeply involved in articulating arguments for the cause. Cable felt that having the argument "coming declaredly from a man of color" like Chesnutt would be persuasive, even more persuasive than having the same argument come from a white Southerner. Chesnutt agreed. He seemed eager to join the cause that the older, more experienced, writer stood for. After receiving Cable's letter and suggested revisions, Chesnutt wrote to him almost immediately: "MS. received, with accompanying note. I have adopted your suggestions literally, and have given the paper the title last suggested by you. I have only to look at the re-written MS. to see that your cuts have enhanced the dignity and effectiveness of the paper, and thereby more than compensated for any loss made by the excisions." Chesnutt promised that he would send "in a few days" revised "type-written copies of the MSS., of which you are at liberty to make any use you may see fit." But he could not keep this promise. Rather than just a few days, it took Chesnutt almost two weeks to revise the essay. Apologizing for the delay, Chesnutt explained, "I would have sent them sooner, but have really not had time to write them until now."[27] This would become a common refrain for Chesnutt in his correspondence with Cable. Cable was always asking Chesnutt to write more—essays, stories, novels—just as Cable was doing. Cable wanted Chesnutt to devote himself more fully, as he had, to the cause, regardless of the costs.

But Chesnutt had neither the time nor the money to meet Cable's demands. Chesnutt's stenography business had taken off. He'd left the law firm and was now working for himself. From his experience working at Henderson, Kline, and Tolles, he'd started his own court reporting firm. He had quickly developed a stellar reputation as a stenographer; the speed and accuracy with which he reported cases and speeches seemed to have impressed his clients. He had recently joined the Ohio Stenographers' Association and was slated to speak at its annual convention in August 1889. Shorthand continued to captivate Chesnutt's literary imagination and penchant for innovation. Chesnutt viewed shorthand not only as the best way to earn a living but also as a vital art form to which he remained committed. Shorthand, he explained to his fellow stenographers, "supplemented by the press, placed upon rash and inconsiderate utterance from platform and pulpit, and at the bar; it promotes truth and justice, and thereby is of positive moral benefit to humanity." Such remarks only added to Chesnutt's prominence as one of the most sought-after stenographers in Cleveland. His practice was growing rapidly. He decided to invite his sister Lillian to help with the business and help take care of the children. Dividing his time between his growing business and family was not easy. But he managed.

His literary business with Cable was a different matter altogether. He enjoyed their correspondence and was honored by Cable's attention to his writing. He knew Cable could help place his stories in the best periodicals. But Cable wanted more from Chesnutt than he could give. Cable wanted Chesnutt to work *for* his cause, to employ his writing for a specific political purpose. Though Chesnutt agreed with the purpose, he viewed his writing as more literary than political, even though he couldn't quite determine the difference between the two. For Chesnutt, literature and shorthand had a great deal in common. Literature had the potential to rise above the "rash and inconsiderate utterance from platform and pulpit." Chesnutt had a hunch that Cable's purpose and the methods he went about to achieve it were different from his own. But at the time, he was still working them out. Chesnutt was interested in telling stories, not preaching, and certainly not overt political statement. Chesnutt didn't want to offend Cable; he didn't want to lose his support. After all, Cable was a major American author; Chesnutt needed him, too. But he also knew he needed to be himself, to do what he needed to do for his children, and to write the kind of stories he thought were true, even if they didn't always toe the Republican party line. Chesnutt wanted to have it both ways, to have Cable's support and write the kind of stories he wanted to write. Not political essays written for a particular cause but stories with characters that readers could care about. He would soon learn that developing a friendship with writers like Cable and Tourgée took some delicate *political* negotiation; yet talking with them thrilled Chesnutt, giving him ideas for new stories that made these friendships essential to becoming the *literary* writer he wanted to be.

Cable's efforts to get his revised essay on the Negro question into the pages of *The Forum* in the end didn't amount to much. Despite the back-and-forth revisions, the hours both Chesnutt and Cable spent on it, Chesnutt's first political essay languished. Cable believed in Chesnutt and urged him not to give up. Cable blamed *The Forum*'s rejection of Chesnutt's essay partly on him taking too long to make the revisions. On May 30, 1889, Cable wrote to Chesnutt a letter filled with a series of injunctions: "You must admit the magazines and the press at large have for many months given large space to the discussion of the Southern Question. Your article would certainly have been published if it had been offered to the Forum ahead of Scarborough. But—as I know you contemplate already—it will have to be revised and readapted to suit the hour. Don't do this quite yet, please, unless you see special good reasons for doing it, for I have a matter in contemplation which will make a good place for your paper."[28]

Despite his best efforts, Cable was unable to deliver on his promise. Chesnutt's essay was rejected by *The Forum*, but he was pleased that they had published an article by another colored man, William Sanders Scarborough, whose views on the Negro question, in Chesnutt's words, were "substantially the same," though they did not, just because they were both colored, treat the topic "identically."[29] Cable agreed. He seemed to know, even though he had yet to consider Chesnutt's fiction seriously, that there was something different about Chesnutt's contribution. His work with and for Cable seemed to bring Chesnutt to a crossroads. Did he want to devote himself to "the discussion and settlement of the Southern question, and all other questions which affect the happiness of the millions of colored people in this country"? Or did he want to commit himself to stenography? He now had an opportunity to become an official county stenographer, earning a salary of $1,500 a year, with fees to the probable amount of $1,000 or $1,500 more, but if he took such a position, he would no longer have time to write fiction. Chesnutt didn't know what to do. He wanted to write, but he didn't want to be poor again. He was as devoted to giving his family every comfort and privilege he was once denied as he was to his writing. Not knowing what to do or having anyone he could talk to about his dilemma, he decided to write to Cable "in regard to a personal matter."

In his letter to Cable, dated March 4, 1889, Chesnutt took the unusual step of pouring out his soul. This is probably the most personal piece of writing Chesnutt had produced since his Fayetteville journals. But unlike the journals that were intended to be private, this letter was addressed to a reader. "My dear Mr. Cable," he begins, "Permit me to trouble you long enough to read this letter, in regard to a personal matter." Chesnutt proceeds to explain to Cable, in almost painful detail, the terms of his dilemma. He is qualified to work as a county stenographer, but he is not sure he wants the job. He appears to be terrified of failure, so terrified that he looks to Cable for advice. "In the event of failure on my part to apply for or to secure one of these appointments, I shall be compelled to turn my attention to other fields of labor. And my object in writing to you is to inquire your opinion as to the wisdom or rashness of my adopting literature as a means of support." Cable was a successful writer; he had made a great deal of money by writing and lecturing. Perhaps he could advise Chesnutt on how to do the same? Chesnutt wanted Cable to tell him what to do. Should he be a writer, like Cable, or should he devote himself to stenography? Could he support his family by writing alone? How had Cable done it, Chesnutt wanted to know. Chesnutt revealed much about himself, that he could write different kinds of literature, that he knew French and German, and that he was "only 31." He concluded his personal letter with a simple request: "If from your own experience and knowledge of the literary life you think it likely that I could make a success in it, and will take the trouble to write to me upon the subject, I will be under greater obligations to you than I am already."[30]

Cable did more than just offer Chesnutt advice. He invited him to come to Northampton, to live in Northampton, to work full-time for the Open Letter Club, serving as Cable's secretary. Cable's offer was sincere and, as everything he wrote to Chesnutt, urgent: "I want you now to think over the matter carefully and make up your mind for what salary you could come to Northampton as my secet'y. I do not know that we can meet each other on the pecuniary basis, but I will try if you will. So now please let me know what you can take that will make it in your judgment—all things carefully considered—desirable to come here & take up this work." Cable's response was intended to encourage Chesnutt's literary aspirations. But it is unlikely that Chesnutt, or anyone in his position, would have received Cable's response in the spirit the offer was made. Chesnutt wanted to be a writer, not a secretary. But to be the kind of writer he wanted to be required both time and money, both of which were in short supply. So Chesnutt's response to Cable, composed on May 3, 1889, is hardly surprising: "I regret to say that, after mature deliberation, I have reached the conclusion that I could not afford to come to Northampton for any sum which, judging from the figure you have already mentioned, you would probably feel justified in offering me. The contingency which immediately inspired my first letter to you did not happen—that is, the appointment of official stenographer—so that my business is not affected in that direction." After providing some figures on his present earnings, he explains that working for Cable would be "a sacrifice of half my income." It is a sacrifice, Chesnutt noted, that he would "personally" be willing to make, but it was a sacrifice that his duty to his family rendered impossible.[31]

Much to Cable's credit, Chesnutt's decision to decline his offer did not affect their burgeoning friendship. In fact, it seems to have strengthened it. Chesnutt did not work *for* Cable. If anything, Cable worked for Chesnutt, reading his fiction with greater care, helping him to publish one of his stories, which he first called "Rena" but would later become, with Cable's help, his first novel, *The House Behind the Cedars*. Chesnutt's decision to remain in Cleveland, to write and continue his stenography work on his own terms, would, among other events, lead to the end of Cable's Open Letter Club. By the end of the year, several of its members besides Chesnutt had become reluctant in supporting Cable's cause, which had grown increasingly radical. Despite the club's demise, Chesnutt continued to write essays and fiction that he would share with Cable, welcoming his advice and cherishing a friendship that would bear much fruit in the years to come.

8

The Novelist as Court Reporter

"Competition is the life of trade." The unsuccessful reporter is prone to say that competition is the death of shorthand. But I think that a little reflection will show that the first statement is the true one, and that a healthy competition promotes the efficiency of the shorthand art.
—"Competition," speech to the Ohio Stenographers' Association, 1892

Chesnutt had been admitted as an active member to the Ohio Stenographers' Association on August 27, 1889. Six years later, in 1895, he would be elected the association's president and serve in this role for two terms. Chesnutt seemed to be now spending most of his time on reporting—what he called "the shorthand art"—and less time on developing what Henry James called "The Art of Fiction."[1] The main difference between the two, at least for Chesnutt, had to do with money. He was paid substantially more for his shorthand because the demand for this art was high; and unlike fiction, there were fewer people who could meet the standards of a good stenographer. Chesnutt's rise through the ranks of the association was not surprising. Upon becoming a member, he had been selected by the association's executive board to open their seventh annual convention in Cleveland by delivering a paper on "Some of the Uses and Abuses of Shorthand." For Chesnutt, shorthand was "more than just a labor-saving invention." It was also more than just a way to make his living. Speaking both to and for his fellow stenographers, Chesnutt declared: "I do not think there will be any question among us that we should endeavor to maintain and elevate the character of the profession by which we live. Let us then strive to emphasize the higher uses of shorthand." Chesnutt believed that shorthand, like the press, helped to preserve the truth by "checking the utterances of public speakers—political speakers, preachers, lawyers, all men who earn their living by the sweat of their tongues." He evinced this rather lofty claim with a brief anecdote that was typical of the wit and sense of humor he displayed in his oral performances:

> When an impassioned orator, thrilling with anger or zeal, feels burning words of sarcasm, invective, recrimination, rising to his lips, his eyes happen to fall on the stenographer, who alone, perhaps, in all that vast audience, sits calm and cool—mentally (sometimes he is uncomfortably warm physically), and the orator feels the words grow cold upon his lips. "There's that confounded reporter," he says, "and every l—, every mistake of fact I may fall into, every grammatical slip, every mixed metaphor I make, he will dish up in his paper tomorrow."[2]

Chesnutt understood the work of the reporter as a way of preserving the truth, even preventing those occupying positions of power from falling into the clutches of political or moral corruption. He treated the professions that relied on stenography as a vocation, tantamount to a spiritual calling, and encouraged his audience to view shorthand as a "positive moral benefit to humanity." No wonder that W. H. Pritchard described Chesnutt's speech in the pages of *The Phonographic Magazine* published that year as "a learned and apt production."[3]

Given this public declaration on the moral and practical virtues of shorthand, it is surprising that in a letter to George Washington Cable, penned a few months after delivering his speech to the Ohio Stenographers' Association, Chesnutt bemoaned having to devote so much of his time to "court reporting." In his letter, Chesnutt described his court reporting business as interfering with the "higher work" of literature, which he claimed to prefer. Chesnutt used court reporting as an excuse to Cable for not having time to write literature, though he was likely being a bit disingenuous. Chesnutt *liked* being a court reporter, the branch of shorthand writing he devoted most of his time to; he was good at it, respected by others for his skill, and perhaps most importantly, he believed this work was of positive moral benefit to humanity. But for some reason, he didn't feel comfortable discussing the shorthand art with Cable. Instead, he mentioned his court reporting business "merely as an excuse for neglecting" the real work of writing literature. Chesnutt wanted to present himself as a *literary* man to Cable rather than as a court reporter. After sending the letter, Chesnutt went on with his business of court reporting and writing literature; the two, in fact, went hand in hand.

Cable was not alone in undervaluing Chesnutt's court reporting business. A few years later, in 1893, Albion Tourgée would make a similar mistake in his Bystander's Notes column he wrote for the popular weekly Chicago magazine *Inter Ocean*. Just as he had a few years earlier in his article for *The Forum*, Tourgée recognized Chesnutt's literary talent by mentioning him in a broader consideration of American literature. But Tourgée undercut his high praise of Chesnutt's writing with the claim that his "prosperity in other fields has smothered his rare gift." Writing in 1893, well before the publication of Chesnutt's books, Tourgée's comments referred only to the short stories that had appeared in top literary magazines of the time: Boston's *The Atlantic*, New York's *The Independent*, and San Francisco's *Overland Monthly*. Writing nostalgically of Chesnutt's "brief novels," Tourgée celebrated them as "something marvelous in their unpretentious realism," while in the same breath chastised Chesnutt for devoting too much time to his court reporting business. This time, however, Chesnutt was quick to set the record straight. Ten days after the appearance of Tourgée's column, Chesnutt wrote him a letter to correct the misimpression he had so haphazardly circulated in the pages of a major magazine.

> Permit me to thank you for the compliment in the *Inter Ocean* of April 8th. Such a statement from such a source is enough to make one determine that he will not permit such a gift to be entirely smothered, even by success in other lines. That I have not ceased altogether to write you may see from reading the story I send you by this mail. It is not as good as some other things I have written, and the publication in which it appeared, *Two Tales*, has suspended since the story appeared; I hope there was no relation of cause and effect between the two events.

The desire and intention on my part to write is, if anything, stronger even than when I was writing most. I am simply biding my time, and hope in the near future to devote the greater part of my time to literary production.[4]

Perhaps by enclosing his most recent publication, Chesnutt hoped Tourgée would issue an apology or retraction in his column. Surely, it was not in Chesnutt's interest as an author to have readers think that he was no longer writing "brief novels." Chesnutt was writing a great deal, not only short stories but also novels; most of these literary productions, as he went on to explain to Tourgée, have "never seen the light of day, and [have] not even been offered for publication." Tourgée did not issue a public apology or retraction concerning Chesnutt's writing. He did, however, respond to Chesnutt a few months later, offering him a job as his editorial assistant of a new journal he was attempting to start up called *The National Citizen*. As he did with Cable a few years earlier, Chesnutt initially declined Tourgée's offer, explaining that he had "always looked forward to the literary life, although not specially in the direction of journalism." Moreover, Chesnutt didn't think there would be enough readers interested in subscribing to a "publication devoted entirely to discussion of one topic, so to speak, even so important a one as citizenship." In fact, Chesnutt thought that such a journal "would have a tendency to repel the average white man rather than attract him."[5] After some discussion both by mail and in person, Chesnutt eventually agreed to accept the position of associate editor so long as Tourgée would employ him as a true colleague and not as a racial token; "I do not suppose that you want an associate editor merely for ornament," he wrote to Tourgée on November 21, 1893. "I certainly would not care to be a mere figurehead in such an enterprise, even for the honor of having my name coupled with such a distinguished one as your own." Such a proviso suggested he had learned much from his dealings with Cable and his efforts to use Chesnutt's racial status to further his political purpose. But just as with Cable's Open Letter Club, Chesnutt was right about the limited potential of Tourgée's *National Citizen*. Unable to raise sufficient capital to fund his newspaper enterprise, Tourgée was forced to give up on the editorial project in 1894. Chesnutt must have felt some relief when Tourgée finally dropped the idea. Not only did he get to keep the money he had pledged to invest, but he would no longer have to fulfill the onerous duties of an associate editor. Chesnutt had always been skeptical of demand for a journal offering readers "a monthly Lesson Leaf on the duties of the citizen, and a monthly record of outrages upon the citizen," as Tourgée had described his proposed journal. Instead, Chesnutt was looking to write stories that might attract, even amuse, the average reader to consider what he called "the subject of the wrongs of the Negro."[6]

The story Chesnutt enclosed in his letter responding to Tourgée's Bystander's Notes column was called "A Deep Sleeper." It had just appeared in the short-lived periodical *Two Tales*, which, for the five years it was in operation, was published every Saturday by the Two Tales Publishing Company on Beacon Street in Boston. It is not hard to see why the journal had been suspended after only a few years. Its objective was to publish just two stories each week by authors of some literary repute for, in the editors' words, "the average reader." There were no other articles about politics and culture or even illustrations, as there were in *Puck* and *The Century*, to entice average readers to pick up the magazine. Chesnutt's story appeared alongside one by Walter Leon Sawyer called "A Boy's Love." Like Sawyer's story, Chesnutt's concerns, in a roundabout way, the experiences of a boy. Chesnutt's boy is called Tom, "a lubberly, sleepy-looking Negro boy of about fifteen, related to Julius's wife in some degree, and living with them." But the story is not really about Tom, it is about the marriage of his deceased grandparents, two former slaves called Skundus and Cindy.

Departing slightly from his earlier conjure stories, "A Deep Sleeper" does not feature a conjure woman who possesses magical powers to transform living creatures. This former slave story is more in the vein of a fairy tale or mystery story, reminiscent of well-known stories like "Sleeping Beauty" by the Brothers Grimm or "Rip Van Winkle" by Washington Irving. And unlike the majority of Chesnutt's conjure stories, which end tragically, "A Deep Sleeper" ends with the slave couple living happily ever after. Though set among slaves in the South, Chesnutt's story is, like the one with which it was published, a love story. But it is a love story between *slaves*, and it is told by an illiterate former slave to a small group of literate, wealthy, white people.

In his letter to Tourgée, Chesnutt remarked that he thought the story was not as good as some of his others. Perhaps he thought it was not as good because it was more romantic than his other stories. In this story, nobody is killed or tortured. Though the slave owner Marse Dugal threatens to torture Skundus for having fallen asleep for a month after he has been lied to and separated from his betrothed, "eve'ybody knowed Marse Dugal' bark uz wuss'n his bite." Though Marse Dugal and his wife believe they exert absolute control over their slaves, it turns out that these slaves have the upper hand over their owners. While the story gives readers a good sense of the cruelty and ignorance of slave owners, it does not *criticize* or blame them for being slave owners. They are just ineffectual and tend to make bad decisions, whereas the illiterate slaves who work the land day and night are presented as shrewd, loving, and industrious. In the end, those viewed as lazy and stupid turn out to be smart and hardworking, while those who seem smart and industrious, because they are wealthy and white, turn out to be the opposite. At first glance, the story appears to be just amusing, filled with hilarious jokes by Julius that, if understood, inspire laughter. But the story, like Chesnutt's sense of humor, had an edge. The story functioned as a kind of allegory or myth of the origin of certain racial stereotypes. It was perhaps a story that not every *average* reader would get, but it was a story that would attract an average reader, like the ones Chesnutt depicted in the story, because it was funny and had a happy ending. Chesnutt's style of writing about the race problem of the time was so different from that of his contemporaries that they hardly recognized his stories to be making a political point about the race problem. "A Deep Sleeper" dramatized the bond between a husband and wife as being natural and more powerful than the control exerted by slave owners over slaves. The power wielded by slave owners appears unnatural and unreasonable; the story pokes fun at their deluded sense of ownership over human beings. Chesnutt's stories may not have had an explicit political message, as did Cable's and Tourgée's, but they did have a positive moral that, he hoped, would benefit humanity.

Though Chesnutt stood apart in some respects from Cable and Tourgée on the matter of literary methods, the three men still had a great deal in common. While their attempts to form concrete literary and political collaborations never worked out as they'd hoped, they were constantly reading one another, offering suggestions, discussing, encouraging one another to write more and to find new venues for publication. On June 12, 1889, Cable wrote a short note to Chesnutt, letting him know that he had just read his article "What Is a White Man?" "with care and great pleasure."[7] The article had appeared a couple of weeks earlier, on May 30, 1889, in *The Independent*, a long-running and well-respected magazine "Devoted to the Consideration of Politics, Social and Economic Tendencies, History, Literature, and the Arts." *The Independent* had begun in the 1840s as a religious periodical, but under the editorships of Henry Ward Beecher and Theodore Tilton had taken sides on various political questions, most notably on slavery and women's suffrage. *The Independent* maintained an important position among American periodicals. It was one of a very small group of religious papers to hold the attention of a general audience in a period that saw most such periodicals degenerate into denominational newsletters. By the time Chesnutt's association with the magazine began, *The Independent* was run by its owner and founder, Henry Chandler Bowen, a committed member of the Republican Party. Chesnutt's "What Is a White Man?" marked his foray into the field of nonfiction writing. His name appeared beneath the essay's provocative title as "Charles W. Chesnutt, ESQ.," signaling his professional status as a lawyer.

"What Is a White Man?" provided readers with a meticulous discussion of the "laws in different states of the Union defining the limit which separated the white and colored races."[8] In this essay, we see Chesnutt flexing his legal muscle. Unlike his unpublished essay on "The Negro's Answer to the Negro Question," which Cable had revised heavily and was still shopping around to New York editors at *The Century* and the *North American Review*, "What Is a White Man?" made no mention of Chesnutt's race. He referred to himself in the essay only as "the writer." Chesnutt had published the essay without much input from Cable. Though Cable had read the essay in *The Independent* as any other reader would have, he felt a particular connection to its central argument that he expressed to Chesnutt: "I have long thought of this branch of the question and have constantly and patiently watched opportunities to bring it forward. You know that all my earlier stories about quadroons really ask this question, 'What is a white man, What is a white woman?'"

Cable's response to reading Chesnutt's essay was a little odd. Instead of congratulating Chesnutt on having published his first essay in the pages of one of the leading political periodicals of the day, as a friend and fellow author might do, Cable focused his reading of Chesnutt's essay on his own writing, going so far as to tell Chesnutt that he had already thought of most, if not all, of the points made in the essay long before reading it. He even went so far as to scold Chesnutt for publishing the essay because the question it asked readers to consider—"What Is a White Man?"—might distract readers from focusing on "the solution of our great question."[9] As he put it, "I thought in my beginning that it was an initial question but believe now it is not, yet it is one that must have its place and time and value in the solution of our great question." Perhaps Cable thought Chesnutt should have checked with him before submitting his essay to *The Independent* or at least told him about its publication so that he didn't have to discover it on his own. Chesnutt would be careful to avoid ruffling Cable's feathers in the future. Chesnutt would inform Cable of a subsequent story and essay that were accepted by *The Independent* well before they appeared in print.

Chesnutt did not respond directly to Cable's letter. Instead, he wrote to his new secretary, Mary Adelene Moffat, who had taken the job that Chesnutt had declined a couple of years earlier. In this brief letter, Chesnutt explained that he was working on fulfilling Cable's latest request for "information he wants in regard to North Carolina laws."[10] He also asked Moffat to relate to Cable that he had "read his 'Haunted House,' 'Attalie Brouillard'—if that is correct—and the *Independent* paper with the pleasure I always derive from his writings." He went on to let her (and Cable) know "that the *Independent* accepted a story of mine last week, and that another will appear in the October *Atlantic*." The two writers now seemed to be engaged in something of a publishing competition; rather than asking for Cable's help or advice on how to get his work published, he was merely informing him where he could read his already-published work. The story that had been accepted by *The Independent* for its November issue was "The Sheriff's Children," appearing just a month after "Dave's Neckliss" was published in the October issue of *The Atlantic*. Cable remained silent on both.

These stories had been accepted by major magazines and had a wide readership. The stories themselves were good, *really* good. Both were complex tragedies. "Dave's Neckliss," narrated once again by Julius McAdoo, relates the horrifying torture and death of the literate, hardworking slave Dave, who is falsely accused of stealing a ham by one of his fellow slaves, Wiley. Wiley is jealous of Dave's accomplishments and his intimate relationship with one of the most sought-after female slaves on the plantation. The jealousy and sexual tension between the slaves are reminiscent of the story of Achilles and Agamemnon in the *Iliad*, which Chesnutt had read avidly back in Fayetteville. Chesnutt forwarded a copy of the story to Tourgée shortly after writing to Cable, calling "Dave's Neckliss" "the best of the series."

"The Sheriff's Children" is also a tragedy. But this is a very different kind of story from his conjure stories and his amusing sketches for *Puck*, *Two Tales*, and *Family Fiction*. Chesnutt described it as "a Southern Story, dealing with a tragic incident, not of slavery exactly, but showing the fruits of slavery." This was a story about a lynching, told entirely from the point of view of the lynchers. It would become the first of Chesnutt's "color line" stories, which would be collected a decade later and published as part of *The Wife of His Youth, and Other Stories of the Color Line* a decade later. Though the story presents its characters speaking in dialect, Chesnutt insisted that "it is not in dialect, and while it has a moral, I tried to write as an artist and not as a preacher." Published among stories regarding "The Centenary of the Catholic Church," "The Hebrew Question," and "The Negro Problem in the Episcopal Church," in the November issue of *The Independent*, Chesnutt took pains to distinguish his story from those surrounding it. "The Sheriff's Children" was different too from the stories he had been publishing. Rather than relating the "tragic incident" from the point of view of a former slave or a particular character within the story, the story is told by an unnamed third-person narrator. By doing so, Chesnutt was attempting to render the people, places, and events it describes from an "artistic" or objective point of view.

The story opens with an overview of its setting. "Branson County, North Carolina, is in a sequestered district of one of the staidest and most conservative States of the Union." We don't know anything about the story's narrator. The narrator seems to be perched high above the action, looking down on the place and the people who live there, with an ability to see and hear everything. But this narrator, unlike the narrators of his earlier stories, does not participate in the activity being observed. The narrator proceeds to explain or *report* on a murder, a rare event, in Branson County. The narrator provides all the details concerning the who, what, when, where, and how of the murder, and then the narrator moves closer to the action: "Toward noon there was an informal gathering of citizens in Dan Tyson's store." Here the narrator records what he hears, exactly as it is spoken. "I hear it 'lowed that Squire Kyahtah's too sick ter hole co'te this evenin,'" said one, "an that the purlim'nary hearin' 'll haft er go over tel nex week." The misspellings, elisions, and diction offer readers a closer look into the case than that provided in the newspapers. In this murder case, it is the mob, what the narrator delicately calls "an informal gathering of citizens," that takes the place of a judge and jury in a court of law.

So the story takes us through the murder, how the suspect is found, tried, imprisoned, and eventually found dead in his cell. None of the story's action takes place inside of a courtroom; it all happens *outside* the court. Yet our narrator reports the case as if it were a legal trial, providing a verbatim report of the case from both sides, even though there is no defense or prosecution. By telling the story in this way, the accused is granted something like a fair trial, in which the reader acts as judge. Of course, the point of the story is that the accused has been denied his right to a trial, having been pronounced guilty by a mob who view him as "a strange mulatto" and therefore the likeliest suspect. The story concludes with a twist. The accused turns out to be the unacknowledged son of Branson County's respected sheriff.

Unlike their ongoing conversations and letters concerning Chesnutt's work in progress, Cable and Tourgée remained silent on these new stories. Cable likely didn't have anything to say about these stories to Chesnutt because he could not improve upon them and had no critique to make of them. Tourgée was likely more interested in Chesnutt's Black characters than the white ones of "The Sheriff's Children." Now it seemed that Chesnutt was publishing as much fiction as these older and more-established writers with whom he was corresponding regularly. The shift in their relationship became apparent in Chesnutt's second political essay, published in *The Independent* a couple of years later.

On April 2, 1891, Chesnutt published "A Multitude of Counselors," again bylined "Charles W. Chesnutt, ESQ." *The Independent* was the only magazine that published *both* Chesnutt's fiction and nonfiction. In the pages of the politically oriented *Independent*, we see a new side of Chesnutt's writing emerge; he was just beginning to explore how, and why, to take a political position on the page. In this new literary venture, he was certainly influenced by Cable and Tourgée; but he was also working out a position of his own, one that was based on his unique situation and point of view. In "A Multitude of Counselors," Chesnutt discussed those writers who had taken it upon themselves to offer advice to the "colored people of this country" about the "race prejudice" that "pervades every department of life."[11] He mentioned only two writers by name: "Mr. George W. Cable" and "Judge Tourgée." After discussing the current historical situation for a couple of paragraphs, Chesnutt opened the essay's third paragraph by listing the writers who have addressed the "series of outrages" that have occurred "within the last month" against "self-respecting colored people." He begins with "Mr. George W. Cable," who "advises the colored people to unite and by every peaceable means—by word, by voice, by pen, to forward their own cause." As he developed the paragraph, he mentioned several others, but not by name, referring to them only as "One writer" or "One friend," who advise, or counsel, "colored people" on what to do about their "lacking to the completeness of their citizenship." He concluded the paragraph, however, with the only other named writer who constitutes the essay's "Multitude of Counselors." In contrast to Cable's unity and peace with which the paragraph opened, Chesnutt concluded the paragraph with the proper name and professional title "Judge Tourgée," who "openly predicts a guerilla warfare of races, and can only advise the colored people to defend themselves in an uneven and hopeless conflict." In emphasizing the differences between Cable's and Tourgée's positions, Chesnutt reinforces a connection between the three of them. He did not privilege one writer over the other. For him, the "conflicting advice which his friends have given him" only proves they are "as much in the dark as to what is best for him to do, or as to what will be the outcome of his presence in the United States, as he himself is."

This observation turned out to be a major revelation. Not just for Chesnutt personally but also, he hoped, "for the ten million colored people in the United States." Chesnutt spent several pages of the essay showing that despite the diversity of opinion offered by the multitude of counselors, all their advice is "impracticable." Chesnutt concluded the essay by pointedly *not* offering advice or a solution to those who "are the victims of a cruel race prejudice," as most writers on the race problem of the time tended to do. Instead, he began the essay's final paragraph with an observation:

> The colored people can speak out for themselves, and ought to whenever they can safely do so. The right of free speech is as sacred to a freeman as any other right, for through it he sets in motion the agencies which secure his liberty. Whether or not he can exercise his rights is not to the point; he should nevertheless assert them.[12]

Chesnutt's essay must have come across as something of a rebuke to those writers who were working so hard for "the cause of the colored people"—especially those he called out by name.

If Cable or Tourgée felt miffed by Chesnutt naming them in his essay as two of the most prominent and perhaps misguided of the multitude of counselors, they never mentioned the slight to him. At least, not in written form. It is possible that he discussed the points he made in the essay with Cable and Tourgée on one of his visits with them. In November 1889, a couple of years before the publication of "A Multitude of Counselors," Cable stopped at Chesnutt's home during one of his lecture tours. We don't know if Chesnutt discussed "A Multitude of Counselors" with him on this occasion. We do know from his daughter Helen's account of the visit that Chesnutt showed Cable "his books and manuscripts" and even read "the new version of 'Rena Walden.'" Helen recalled that during Cable's visit, Chesnutt "was glowing, his eyes were beaming, he was bubbling over with happiness." Cable stayed for dinner that night, and Helen described how the whole family "sat spellbound as they listened to the little bright-eyed man who seemed to be having such a delightful time with Papa." Their close friendship would continue uninterrupted long after the appearance of "A Multitude of Counselors." In fact, it would intensify when Helen and Ethel moved to Northampton to attend Smith College years later, a move that Cable facilitated at various stages.

Andrew Jackson Chesnutt (father), ca. 1910.
COURTESY OF THE CHARLES W. CHESNUTT COLLECTION,
FISK UNIVERSITY LIBRARY

Howard School in Fayetteville, North Carolina, where Charles W. Chesnutt was a pupil-teacher, c. 1865-1884. COURTESY OF THE CLEVELAND PUBLIC LIBRARY DIGITAL GALLERY

Charles Chesnutt and his brother Lewis in 1865. Charles is at the left.

Thomas Edison seated with a phonograph, April 1878.

Albion Winegar Tourgée, c. 1868.

Frederick Douglass, 1876, by
George Kendall Warren.

Hon. John P. Green, 1902.

T. Thomas Fortune, editor of
The New York Age, and brilliant
politician, author and speaker, 1900.

Cyrus West Field, c. 1860,
by Matthew B. Brady.
COURTESY OF THE NATIONAL
PORTRAIT GALLERY, SMITHSO-
NIAN INSTITUTION

S. S. McClure, 1883-1903,
by George Collins Cox.
COURTESY OF DIVISION OF WORK AND
INDUSTRY, NATIONAL MUSEUM OF AMERICAN
HISTORY, SMITHSONIAN INSTITUTION

Walter H. Page (1899), from a photograph taken when he was editor of *The Atlantic Monthly*.
FROM THE LIFE AND LETTERS OF WALTER H. PAGE (VOLUME I), BY BURTON J. HENDRICK, GARDEN CITY, NY: DOUBLEDAY, PAGE & COMPANY, 1923

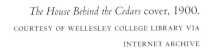

The House Behind the Cedars cover, 1900.
COURTESY OF WELLESLEY COLLEGE LIBRARY VIA INTERNET ARCHIVE

Booker T. Washington, c. 1890-1900
COURTESY OF THE LIBRARY OF CONGRESS PRINTS AND PHOTOGRAPHS DIVISION, WASHINGTON, D.C.

Edward Christopher Williams, son-in-law of
Charles W. Chesnutt, between 1902-1929.
COURTESY OF THE CLEVELAND PUBLIC LIBRARY
DIGITAL GALLERY

Helen Maria Chesnutt, Smith College, Class of
1902, c. 1902.
COURTESY OF SMITH COLLEGE ARCHIVES

Ethel Perry Chesnutt, Smith College, Class of
1901, c. 1901.
COURTESY OF SMITH COLLEGE ARCHIVES

William Dean Howells, c. 1900,
by George Collins Cox.

Bliss Perry.

Charles W. Chesnutt and others seated at Delmonico's for Mark Twain's seventieth birthday.

Charles Waddell Chesnutt at age fifty-two, 1910.

Group portrait of men and women, including Chesnutt, attending the NAACP-sponsored Amenia Conference in Amenia, New York, August 24-26, 1916.

In late July 1891, a few months after the essay appeared in *The Indepen-dent*, Chesnutt visited Tourgée at his home at Point Chautauqua, New York. This was a big trip. It was the first time he'd left his family since Dorothy was born. His fourth child was only seven months old when Chesnutt boarded the train for New York. He felt a little guilty about taking this trip alone, leaving the family behind, especially Dorothy. "My next long vacation will be spent with my family," he promised in a letter to Susan sent during the second week of his stay. "It is very pleasant, but it seems a little selfish to take it all alone."[13] We don't have Susan's response to this letter, if she did respond. But by this time, she must have grown accus-tomed to being left mostly alone with the children. She did have the help and company of her sister-in-law Lillian, who was still living with them at the time; but Chesnutt's long absences would likely have begun to grate on her nerves. Sensing this, Chesnutt's letter was perhaps intended to soothe her, making a promise to spend more time with the family. Chesnutt kept this promise, as he did most of his promises to her. By his daughter Helen's account, Chesnutt was always a devoted husband and father.

From his letter to Susan, we can surmise that he spent a couple of weeks in and around Tourgée's spacious home at Mayville, on Chautauqua Lake, spending most of his time writing, attending lectures and concerts, reading, and talking with Tourgée. Just as it is now, Chautauqua Lake was a niche tourist destination for writers and artists who could afford a sum-mer vacation fishing and boating while also engaging in more intellectual pursuits. Chesnutt seems to have been enamored with the environs, visiting Tourgée's home on more than one occasion. He wrote little about the subject or tone of these visits. It is likely that he met Tourgée's wife, Emma, and their daughter, Aimee, with whom he would correspond years later. He did reveal about this visit that he had been trading manuscripts with Tourgée, insist-ing that he "is a very interesting fellow, and improves on acquaintance."[14] As with Cable, Tourgée seemed entirely unaffected by Chesnutt's com-ments about him in *The Independent*, suggesting a mutual respect and pro-fessionalism as the foundation of their friendship. Tourgée was probably glad that Chesnutt mentioned him in his essay; he, more than most writers, enjoyed being read and discussed, particularly among African Americans, whom he felt did not always appreciate the time he spent and the sacrifices he had made on their behalf. Perhaps the three of them, having all spent considerable time in the South and now living in the North, understood themselves as members of what Henry James had called "the brotherhood of novelists," those joined by their ability to give and take criticism from one another in a spirit of camaraderie for the sake of their art.[15]

Chesnutt returned from his vacation at Point Chautauqua with Tourgée, refreshed and ready to get back to his court reporting business. He had found a more spacious office in the recently completed Society for Savings Building, located on the public square in downtown Cleveland. His new office was located on the seventh floor of the high-rise, the tallest building ever constructed in the city at the time. The building had opened its doors on June 23, 1890, and Chesnutt moved in soon after it opened. He took some pride in occupying a space inside Ohio's first skyscraper. It must have reminded him of his days in New York City. But rather than toiling away as an unnamed reporter for the *Mail and Express*, living alone in a rented room in a boardinghouse, he was now running his own court reporting business, owned a beautiful home, was surrounded by his family, and was publishing stories and essays in the nation's top journals. Chesnutt must have taken a great deal of pride in how far he'd come. But he still had not accomplished what back in Fayetteville he called the dream of his life: to write a novel.

A couple of weeks after returning to work, Chesnutt traveled to Dayton to deliver another speech to his colleagues at the Ohio Stenographers' Association convention. This speech delineated the qualifications of those, like Chesnutt, who had become court reporters in the nascent stages of the profession. Of course, court reporters had been employed by state and federal courts for decades in the United States. But the use of shorthand in court reporting had begun only in the late nineteenth century. Chesnutt had never been formally trained in the art of shorthand. Everything he knew about it was learned on his own, from reading textbooks and practice. In the 1880s, when Chesnutt was working as a court reporter, the requirements and qualifications for the position were still being developed. Certificates and licenses in court reporting were not yet being issued by schools or training programs. Chesnutt's speeches to the association from this time reveal that he was on the cutting edge of developing the proper methods and practices of court reporters.

Based on his personal and professional experience, Chesnutt was called on to delineate "Some Requisites of a Law Reporter" for members of the association at their annual convention on August 25, 1891. One of the most critical aspects of the judicial process is the requirement that a verbatim record be created for virtually all judicial activities. The earliest records of judicial proceedings were recorded by pen and ink. This usually involved a scribe quickly writing briefs of court proceedings during or immediately after court. Different forms of shorthand writing were developed and implemented in the nineteenth century, but there was a great deal of variance in methods and training among shorthand court reporters at the time Chesnutt began to specialize in court reporting. His speech was intended to clarify both the work of a court reporter and its distinction from other forms of shorthand writing.

Though enumerating the qualifications of a good court reporter, Chesnutt's speech also revealed a great deal about his evolving storytelling methods. A natural requisite for being a good reporter, Chesnutt explained, was "quickness of apprehension" or "the ability to 'catch-on' quickly."[16] This quality is necessary because a court reporter "must understand, superficially at least, what is going on, and he has not time to study it out." A second natural requisite for a court reporter to possess is "good hearing." A court reporter had to hear everything that was being spoken not merely to understand the meaning of words but to create an accurate transcription of the entire proceeding. "When listening merely to understand, one word or sentence explains another; but when listening to record, each word, at least each sentence, must explain itself, and therefore must be heard distinctly." Aside from such natural skills as hearing and apprehension, Chesnutt also listed several natural qualities that a good court reporter should possess or at least work to develop. These are: "a cool head, an even temper, as much modesty as is consistent with a proper self-respect" and, finally, "patience and perseverance."[17]

The "acquired" skills for a court reporter were more numerous. He listed six acquired skills for court reporters and prefaced his list with a warning, reminding his audience that becoming a court reporter was *difficult* and therefore should not be attempted unless one is willing to work hard and to devote a great deal of time to the profession:

We must bear in mind the duties of a law reporter; that he is expected to take down correctly and write out intelligibly whatever takes place in a court of justice. The proceedings of a court in one year, in the present age of commercial and scientific activity, are likely to embrace, in one of our great cities, a large part of the field of human knowledge. To be thoroughly at home in this work, to do it easily and well, a reporter should know everything.[18]

Chesnutt's audience must have been more than a little taken aback by his pronouncements. Surely, he was not seriously suggesting that court reporters be omniscient. All they were paid to do, as he noted belatedly, at the very end of the speech, was "to write shorthand rapidly and correctly, and to read it back readily." But for Chesnutt, these skills were just "a secondary consideration." Obviously, the speech made plain that he was not talking about just "some requisites of a law reporter," as he'd titled the speech. He was talking about how to write good literature. The kind of literature that offered readers both sides of a case, not the kind of one-sided reporting one read so often in partisan newspapers. This speech was not just about how to be a good court reporter, it was also about how to be a good writer; the techniques for both occupations, at least for Chesnutt, were virtually the same.

No wonder he begins his list of acquired skills with a thorough study of language. As he put it: "A good law reporter should be an accomplished linguist. Not only should he be thoroughly acquainted with the principal languages of Europe, but with the chief dialects, for he does not know at what moment he may be called up to report the testimony of a German, a Frenchman, a Pole, a Dutchman, a Russian, or a Spaniard."[19] In his speech, he offered an example of a German immigrant, whose English some might view as incomprehensible. Not for the court reporter. It is the job of the court reporter to at once transcribe and translate the voices of those whom most cannot or choose not to understand so that their side of the case can be heard. He might have added to his set of examples an illiterate American Southerner, since it was the voices of these people that he *reported* in his fiction. But these voices were not often heard in the Cleveland courts where Chesnutt and his fellow stenographers spent most of their time. Chesnutt's peculiar brand of court reporting skills would become a singular feature of his narrative style and could be seen in his most recently published story, "The Sheriff's Children." But this new narrative technique was also something he was experimenting with in the development of longer works of fiction, novels that he was working on alongside the political essays and stories he was publishing. Chesnutt had told Tourgée that he was just "biding his time"; but he was doing more than that. He was developing a narrative technique that would distinguish his soon-to-be-published realist novels from those of his contemporaries.

During these years, Chesnutt had been working on three novels simultaneously, all featuring female protagonists: *Mandy Oxendine*, the nascent "Rena Walden," and Stella Merwin of *A Business Career*. These novels were reminiscent of popular realist novels of the time that had been appearing serially in literary magazines. Henry James's *Daisy Miller: A Study* had been published as a novel in the United States in 1879; after making its first appearance serially a year earlier in London, England, in the pages of *The Cornhill Magazine*. A couple of years later, *The Portrait of a Lady* had created a sensation when it first started appearing in the pages of *The Atlantic*, beginning in November 1880. Both featured strong female protagonists who are undone by making poor choices among their male suitors. Though James's fiction had captivated critics, it was William Dean Howells's novel *An Imperative Duty*, published as a serial novel a decade later in the pages of *Harper's Monthly*, that captivated Chesnutt. Published as a novel in 1891, it is the only one of Howells's novels—he published over twenty in his lifetime—that Chesnutt owned and kept in his library. In many respects, the plight of Howells's female protagonist, Rhoda Aldgate, raises the same question Chesnutt was asking in his political essays. For Howells, the question was not only "What Is a White Man?" but also "What Is a White Woman?" The answer seems to have been slightly different, as the question, when pertaining to a woman, almost always involved the question of marriage rather than, as Chesnutt discussed in his essay, the question of voting rights. In Howells's novel, Rhoda experiences the discovery of her Black identity as "the loss of her former self."[20]

Although her lost self is a white self, what she most laments is no longer being able to own what she is—both in the sense of admitting publicly her African American heritage and in the sense of being descended from owners of Black property. Rhoda's white suitor, Dr. Edward Olney, to whom she does "own up" about her Black heritage, further eases her fears of being dispossessed through his willingness to continue to regard her as "the daughter of slave-holders."[21] Unlike James's female protagonists who meet death or tragedy, Howells's Rhoda marries and lives happily, though the couple must live, as husband and wife, outside the United States, where such a union, if discovered, was outlawed.

Chesnutt would later refer to Howells's novel "on the race question" as "a very pleasing story" and a "very pretty novel."[22] *Pretty* and *pleasing* are not the first adjectives that come to mind when reading Howells's story of interracial marriage. As one contemporary reviewer of the novel for *The New York Times* put it: "You conclude 'An Imperative Duty' with spirits which are depressed." The reviewer for *The Times* was probably referring to the racism exhibited by the characters. What Chesnutt likely found pleasing and pretty about the novel was the invention of a character "that expressed itself in the sunny sparkle of her looks, that ran over with a willingness to please and to be pleased, and to consist in effect of a succession of flashing, childlike smiles."[23] Eschewing the well-known conventions of the tragic mulatta character popularized by an earlier era of nineteenth-century writers, Howells's Rhoda Aldgate manages to overcome the tragedy of race to create a life for herself that is at once dignified and happy.

Mandy Oxendine was Chesnutt's first experiment in novel writing. The opening chapters of the novel focus on the love story between Mandy Oxendine and Tom Lowrey. That love story is soon overtaken by an attempted rape, a murder, a series of false accusations, a near lynching, and a surprise escape. The book concludes mysteriously, even though the murder case has been solved, with Mandy and Tom acquitted and "married among the friends of their youth. With their after life," we are told, "this record of their period of storm and stress has nothing to do."[24] The story's final line—"They deserved to be happy; but we do not all get our deserts, as many a lucky rogue may congratulate himself, and as many an ill-used honest man can testify"—was both a pronouncement and a prognostication. Chesnutt ended the story on a high note, but the low note was not far behind. We also don't know what the future holds for our couple. Neither do we know if the couple decide to pass together or if they decide, in the parlance of the time, to stay true to their race. In Mandy and Tom's unusual romance, Chesnutt had presented both Mandy's and Tom's sides of the love story as a kind of objective observer, just reporting on the outcomes of his characters without passing judgment. Mandy and Tom's tale was Chesnutt's first crack at writing a novel; it would also help to develop the plot of his first *published* novel, but that would be an event that would require a few more drafts and revisions, a story of interracial love and passing that would again be rejected; but this time, with a little help from his old friends, Chesnutt's unsafe novel would prevail over his first negative readers and find new readers who appreciated the novel for what it was rather than who its author was.

Mandy was in form at least a distant Southern relation to Howells's Rhoda Aldgate. She spoke in the vernacular of her upbringing, she had grown up in a small town in rural North Carolina, a descendant of "free colored people" whose efforts to seek greater opportunities elsewhere were "met by the iron barrier of caste."[25] Despite the many obstacles to her happiness, Mandy eventually marries the man she loves, Tom Lowrey, who is also in search of greater opportunities, like those that elude her by living on the Black side of the color line. So she decides to move, or pass, onto the other side. The story of Mandy's passing, the love between her and Tom, and the obstacles that lie between them constitutes the plot of the novel. The copy of the novel that survives is likely not the final draft that Chesnutt composed, but it is the only one we have. It is fortunately a *complete* draft, which gives us a good sense of the rising action, the development of the characters, and the way things turn out for them. Chesnutt spent years working on *Mandy* and finally submitted it to *The Atlantic* in March 1897 for serial publication. He probably should have anticipated their negative response: "We are not able to persuade ourselves that we should find publication a safe venture," they wrote six weeks after he submitted it. The letter was signed by Walter Hines Page; it marked the beginning of their correspondence. However, there is no evidence that Page actually *read* the novel. The reader's report was signed by SMF, not WHP, suggesting it was read by only one of the magazine's hired readers, not the magazine's editor. The reader's comments on the novel are brief but revealing: "A not ill-told, but in no wise remarkable story, by an octoroon writer, of the fortunes of a pair of lovers of his own kind. There are touches of naturalism which are pleasing, but the short tale is not one to make much of." Calling Chesnutt "an octoroon writer" perhaps gave the story greater credibility, but it was also a bit dismissive, suggesting that the story was based merely on the author's life experience and would appeal only to people like him, or "his own kind," in the reader's terms. But the reader's summary of the novel concluded on a more upbeat tone: "There is some originality in the tale & it is readable, though in more ways than one it shows the hand of a writer unused to long flights."[26]

This reader did not indicate whether to publish or not. That decision was left to Page. And Page decided, based on the reader's summary of the novel, it would not be a safe venture for the press. There was nothing safe about *Mandy Oxendine*. This novel, like five others he would write that would be rejected, would languish, unpublished, among his papers for decades after his death. But it was his first investigation into novelistic fiction, his first experimentation with narrative conventions, the first inklings of the descriptive, court-reporter style he'd employ in his future writings.

PART III

New England

9

Stories of the Color Line

The United States is perhaps the only country in the world where a man's color is the paramount consideration in fixing his social and civil status and determining what opportunities he shall have in life.

—Chesnutt to Sarah Alice Haldeman, February I, 1896

On Friday, April 10, 1896, Albion Tourgée boarded a train to Washington, DC, from his home in Mayville, New York to make his case against Louisiana's 1890 Separate Car Act before the United States Supreme Court. The case, better known as *Plessy v. Ferguson*, would prove to be "epoch making," as Chesnutt described it about a decade later.[1] But when Homer A. Plessy appeared before the Supreme Court with Tourgée as his lawyer, the case drew little attention among members of the American public. Other than Tourgée, who had been writing about the case since at least 1893 in his Bystander's Notes column, few were reporting on the case in the nation's major newspapers. Frederick Douglass had been dead for a little over a year; Booker T. Washington had just delivered his now infamous speech at the Cotton States and International Exposition in Atlanta, Georgia, where he introduced the "hand simile" to describe the new relationship between Black and white Americans. "In all things purely social we can be as separate as the fingers, yet one as the hand in all things essential to mutual progress."[2] The verdict in the *Plessy* case seemed to be a foregone conclusion. For many, distinguishing between American citizens on the basis of their perceived racial differences seemed to be the only peaceful solution to the race problem. Tourgée had been working on arguments against racial separation for about five years, but apparently never discussed his work on *Plessy* with Chesnutt. It was, to say the least, a peculiar omission.

Chesnutt doubtless had read about Tourgée's work on the *Plessy* case in his weekly column in Chicago's *Inter Ocean* magazine. In fact, in the very same column in which Tourgée mentioned Chesnutt's "brief novels" as "something marvelous in their unpretentious realism" on April 8, 1893, Tourgée provided a full discussion of the Separate Car case, which "will for the first time be presented to the Supreme Court in *ex parte* Plessy, from Louisiana now pending, wherein the Bystander is of counsel for the plaintiff in error."[3] Like Chesnutt, Tourgée had the tendency to move easily between the language of literature and that of the courts. But Chesnutt never once mentioned *Plessy* in his extant correspondence with Tourgée, not even in his letter that referred specifically to "the *Inter Ocean* of April 8th," in which Tourgée discussed the case. In that letter, Chesnutt seemed interested only in literary matters, particularly the reception of his own fiction. After explaining to Tourgée how much literature he had produced, he expressed interest in literature written by others. Chesnutt returned to Tourgée's column by asking him for "the names of the publishers of the two books reviewed by you in the *Inter Ocean—Dessalines* and the other. I should be glad to buy them and read them and write a word of appreciation to the authors." The two books Tourgée had reviewed in his column were *Dessalines* by William Easton and *A Voice from the South* by Anna Julia Cooper. Both authors were classified at the time as Black, and both were born in Southern states—Easton was from Texas and Cooper from North Carolina. Chesnutt seemed interested in reading these authors and even connecting with them. But Chesnutt did not offer any description, nor did he inquire about the *Plessy* case that Tourgée discussed in considerable detail. Why not? Did Chesnutt, in 1893, not care about the case? Did he think it was none of his business, that it had nothing to do with him? If so, he was gravely mistaken. Only after the case was decided three years later would he recognize its importance, not just to him personally but to the entire constitution of the United States.

The similarities between Chesnutt and the plaintiff in Tourgée's case, Homer Adolph Plessy, were striking. Like Plessy, Chesnutt was, as he put it in a letter to American activist and philanthropist Sarah Alice Haldeman, "really seven-eighths white."[4] Chesnutt was responding to Haldeman's request for information concerning "negro" contributions to science and literature. In using the fraction to describe his identity, Chesnutt was playing with the infamous "one-drop rule" legal principle of racial classification essential to maintaining slavery. Acknowledging heterosexual unions between people belonging to different racial categories, the one-drop rule mandated that the children from these unions were to be considered "negro." Nodding to and dismissing this outmoded principle, Chesnutt admitted that he would not call himself "much of a negro," though he went on to say that he has "never denied the other, and would be quite willing for the colored people to have any credit they could derive from anything I might accomplish."[5] There is no record of Haldeman having responded to Chesnutt's letter; but it must have made her rethink the racial conventions that she seemed to take for granted in making her initial request. This was Chesnutt's way of resisting the racial classification system that sought to determine who he was. By employing the term *seven-eighths* as he did, he seemed to be pointing out the absurdity of it all without offending his interlocutor. Was he Black or white? Was *she* Black or white? He seemed to be suggesting that the whole system by which people were determined to be one thing or another made no sense; yet the nonsensical system persisted, so he would, like the rest of us, have to figure out how to live within the system. And this was the convoluted way in which Chesnutt explained, to Haldeman and others, the *kind* of writer he was. As far as Chesnutt was concerned, he was just a writer, but if others wanted to view him as a "negro" writer, that was their business. Still, he did celebrate the accomplishments of eighteenth-century "negro" men and women like Phillis Wheatley, "the poetess of colonial and revolutionary times," as well as Benjamin Banneker, "the negro astronomer and almanac maker."[6]

That was in February 1896, just a few months before the now-famous "separate but equal" verdict was delivered by the Supreme Court. After *Plessy*, Chesnutt could no longer call himself "seven-eighths white." He was 100 percent Black. Or as he would put it later in *The House Behind the Cedars*: "One drop of black blood makes the whole man black." Like Plessy, Chesnutt would have to abide by a system of racial classification that maintained a division between those classed as white and those as Black. The clearest manifestation of this separation would be separate cars on trains to ensure that people understood their racial designation, not simply, as we are now, seated according to the price we pay for our tickets. Dividing passenger trains by racial categories was just the beginning. Many Americans took the Supreme Court's decision as a signal or affirmation that racial divisions were a natural, normal, and even necessary aspect of everyday life in the United States. The problem for Chesnutt, and Plessy, and hundreds of thousands of other Americans was that they did not see themselves as either Black or white; they saw themselves as having a mixed racial ancestry, seven-eights, or three-quarters, or whatever. Some did not even know who or what race their parents or grandparents were. Based on the *Plessy* decision, your race was not something you could determine for yourself; race was a matter left to others, the courts, the government, society. The strict division between the categories, in fact the categories themselves, made no sense in determining a person's individual identity. And yet the Supreme Court's ruling in the *Plessy v. Ferguson* case rendered the color line, an imagined division between Black and white people, to be real.

Most Americans are familiar with the phrase *separate but equal* and know something about the complicated legal case from which it was derived. *Plessy v. Ferguson*, according to the transcription provided by the Supreme Court (the name of the court reporter who transcribed the case is not included on the transcript), was originally filed in the Supreme Court of the state of Louisiana by Plessy, the plaintiff in error, against the Honorable John H. Ferguson, judge of the criminal district court for the parish of Orleans. Though the case focused on the circumstances of one man, it was actually the product of a collective effort of the Comité des Citoyens to test the constitutionality of a Louisiana law that segregated the state's trains. The group had solicited Tourgée to represent them in the case, and he worked tirelessly on the case pro bono. When the case reached the U.S. Supreme Court and Tourgée delivered his arguments defending Plessy—and others who might find themselves in a similar position—few were aware of the case's ramifications. On May 18, 1896, the Supreme Court handed down its decision, upholding the constitutionality of de jure segregation. Justice John Marshall Harlan was the sole voice of dissent, writing, "The judgment this day rendered will, in time, prove to be quite as pernicious as the decision made by this tribunal in the *Dred Scott* case." Justice Harlan was referring to another civil rights case, concerning an enslaved man named Dred Scott, decided nearly forty years earlier in 1857. In that case, the Supreme Court decided that all people of African descent, free or enslaved, were not United States citizens and therefore had no right to sue in federal court. In addition, the court decided that the Fifth Amendment of the U.S. Constitution protected slave owner rights because enslaved workers were their legal property. The *Dred Scott* case had made slavery into a legally protected institution and diminished the citizenship of Black Americans. The case was rendered moot by the abolition of slavery with the passage of the Thirteenth Amendment on January 31, 1865.

About a month before the verdict in *Plessy* was delivered, perhaps a week after Tourgée had concluded his arguments on behalf of Plessy and the Comité des Citoyens on April 13, 1896, Chesnutt wrote to him. The tone of this letter conveyed a new formality and distance between the once intimate friends that was surprising. In his previous letters, Chesnutt always addressed Tourgée as "My dear Judge." The use of the moniker was a sign of affection. But this letter, which would turn out to be Chesnutt's penultimate letter to Tourgée, began with "Dear Sir." What had changed between them? The occasion for the letter dated April 25, 1896, was to clarify the Cleveland address of one of the subscribers Chesnutt had secured to Tourgée's latest journalistic venture called the *Basis*. Chesnutt also expressed his hope that "the *Basis* was doing well," which, he knew, was not. But mostly Chesnutt was writing, in a formal way, to express gratitude. "Permit me as a citizen of this State, desirous of social order and good government, and also as one of those for whose benefit the work was in part at least undertaken, to thank you for your kind collaboration with our Mr. H.C. Smith in securing the passage through the State legislature of the anti-lynching bill."[7] Harry Clay Smith was the founder and editor of one of Ohio's most important Black newspapers, *The Cleveland Gazette*. He had also been elected as a Republican to the Ohio House of Representatives in 1893.

Smith had been a fan of Tourgée's work. It is possible that they met years earlier, when Smith had been a member of an orchestra that performed during the summer months near Tourgée's home on Chautauqua Lake. However they met, their collaboration, according to Chesnutt, proved successful in the passage of an anti-lynching law that has come to be known as Ohio's Smith Act of 1896, one of the severest state-sponsored anti-lynching laws of its time. In his letter, Chesnutt did not mention the *Plessy* case, nor did he mention literature, either his own or that of his contemporaries. Instead, he continued with the theme of gratitude, concluding on a rather ominous note. "You will never get an adequate reward in this world for your efforts in behalf of the oppressed and the humble, but you believe in a hereafter, and I hope there is one, if for no other reason than that you and those like you may receive their reward."[8]

The deep gratitude Chesnutt expressed to Tourgée had a note of concern to it. Tourgée's despair after the *Plessy* verdict had been well known. Tourgée stopped writing and took a well-deserved break from politics. This letter seemed to mark the end of an era. It certainly indicated the end, without a specific rupture or falling-out, of their close friendship. The letter anticipated a farewell to Tourgée and their almost decade-long correspondence. It had started with Chesnutt reading Tourgée, then Tourgée reading Chesnutt, and admiring each other's literary accomplishments. It ended with the *Plessy* verdict. Some months after the case, Tourgée's daughter, Aimee, wrote to Chesnutt, soliciting a letter of support for her father's appointment as U.S. consul to Glasgow and relating that other African Americans, including Harry Clay Smith, had already offered letters. Chesnutt hardly needed convincing. He gladly sent his letter in support of Tourgée's appointment to Aimee. About a year after his loss in the *Plessy* case, Tourgée was appointed by President William McKinley to occupy the post of United States consul in France; he took residence in Bordeaux shortly after the announcement. Chesnutt's final letter to him, written on May 24, 1897, was never answered. Its contents revealed their divergence from each other since their friendship began about a decade earlier.

Dear Sir:—

I learn from the newspapers that you have been appointed U.S. Consul to Bordeaux, France. While it is not what I understood you had made application for, I have no doubt, from what I know personally of Glasgow, that so far as climate and natural surroundings are concerned, you will find Bordeaux a much pleasanter place to live in; for Glasgow, even in midsummer, is in appearance as sordid and depressing a place as I ever saw. I suspect, too, that your daughter, if she accompanies you, will like it better; and no doubt we will have in the course of time some Franco-American literature from the family. With cordial congratulations, I remain, Sincerely yours, Chas. W. Chesnutt[9]

Though he had to learn of Tourgée's appointment from the newspapers, there is no sign that Chesnutt begrudged Tourgée's continued silence. Instead, Chesnutt wrote to him as if little had changed between them. Chesnutt recalled in this letter his first trip to Europe, taken in the summer of 1896, just a few months after the *Plessy* verdict was delivered. He was speaking of Europe, particularly Glasgow, which he had visited briefly on a whirlwind trip to Europe, with authority. Chesnutt seemed to be showing off a bit his familiarity with the place in this brief congratulatory note to his old friend. Ironically, the two had discussed a few years earlier, in 1893, the possibility of Chesnutt relocating to Europe to pursue his literary career. It was only three years later, following the disappointing verdict in the *Plessy* case, that Chesnutt decided to set sail for Europe. Perhaps *Plessy* had spurred him on. Perhaps he was seeking a new society, one in which he would not be forced to conform to the new racial caste system being imposed on the United States.

Whatever his reasons for taking off to Europe may have been, Chesnutt's European tour turned out to be a brief affair. Tourgée was not so lucky. He died, after seven years living in Bordeaux, on May 21, 1905. However, he was buried close to his beloved home in the Mayville cemetery at Chautauqua Lake, where he and Chesnutt had once spent a pleasant summer reading each other's manuscripts. Chesnutt joined several other African American writers and social activists to celebrate Tourgée's contributions at his funeral. While Tourgée ended his literary (and political) career in Europe, it was where Chesnutt experienced a rebirth of his own.

For a fan of the fiction of Dickens, Thackeray, and Dumas, being in Europe was a dream. Especially London and Paris, where, according to the journal he kept from the trip, he spent the bulk of his time—and money. Chesnutt spent days walking on the boulevards of Paris. He ascended the Eiffel Tower, drank lemonade and champagne at cafés. He bought a seat at the Theatre Français, where he watched an obscure play called *Ritzau par Erkman Chatreau*. Though the theater was full of people and excitement, Chesnutt found himself too tired to enjoy the performance, deciding to leave after just the first act. He strolled through the Palais-Royal and Champs-Élysées, where he bought a pair of gloves and socks for himself. Then he sauntered down to Brentano's on the Avenue de l'Opéra, where he bought a life of the Three Dumas, photographs of other literary celebrities, and "all of Maupassant's works."[10]

He seemed to have spent most of his time alone. He made the occasional new friend on a train ride or in one of the many cafés he visited. He did not mention missing his family or friends back home. This trip was all about him. This was Chesnutt's version of the nineteenth century's conventional Grand Tour—that Continental itinerary that capped off the American education of young men seeking to become gentlemen. Usually, such a trip was taken before marriage and the start of a career. But Chesnutt's tour was taken well after his marriage and the births of his four children. For Chesnutt, taking a grand tour of Europe provided him with the credentials to be an author. Visiting Europe was the next best thing to a college degree or a literary pedigree, both of which he lacked. Moreover, he paid for the trip from his earnings as a court reporter. Unlike other aspiring American authors who had toured Europe, he had no wealthy relatives to foot the bill for him.

The journal he kept from his first trip to Europe was brief, written in haste, by a man on the move. His notes suggest that he is in a perpetual state of awe, happy to be traveling, to be in Europe, surrounded at every turn by culture and art. There is not a single mention of the race problem. While traveling, he observed "colored" men and women, speaking French, but there was not much to distinguish them from their compatriots. At one point during his time in Paris, he observed a "diligent assortment of the demi-monde, including several colored women, creoles." His use of the term *demi-monde* was a reference to a play by Alexandre Dumas *fils* published in 1855. Dumas seemed to be always on his mind now; he visited his statue at the Place du Général-Catroux in the seventeenth arrondissement, his home, and burial place. Dumas was a French "colored" author, but no one in France, or elsewhere, seemed to care much about his race. This was the kind of author Chesnutt hoped to be. Chesnutt would reflect on his first visit to the square and Dumas's influence in a speech on "Race Ideals and Examples" delivered to the Literary Societies at Wilberforce University in June 1913.

> When I was in Paris upon a former visit some years ago this square contained a handsome bronze monument on a granite base, designed by Gustave Doré, a famous French artist, in honor of Alexander Dumas, *père*, the elder Dumas, so called. On the summit of the monument is a seated figure of the great romancer, and on the front and back of the base are two marble sculptress in bas-relief, one representing the figure of a musketeer, suggest Dumas' famous novel, *The Three Musketeers*, and the other a group composed of a young girl reading one of Dumas' romances to two workingmen.[11]

Such details of street names and monuments he recalls from his first trip to Paris gives a sense of the growing importance of Dumas to him.

But there were so many other artists, aside from the Three Dumas to read and know in France. He hit the usual tourist sites. The Louvre, the Palais Garnier, Père-Lachaise Cemetery, where he "stood by the tomb of Abelard and Heloise and the great men of France; plucked a leaf from the grave of Moliere and Racine, another from that of Balzac and another from that of Chopin." It was being so close to these great European writers and artists that Chesnutt savored. He was no longer just dreaming of becoming an author, he was now living among them. He even saw himself as one of them.

But Chesnutt was interested in more than just the literary scene in Europe. He was also interested in its social life. He noted having "seen many colored people," spending time with a "Miss Mason," who was studying art.[12] She lived with her mother in the Fontainebleau area of Paris. Perhaps Chesnutt was imagining what it would be like to live in Paris with his own family. Might they be able to make a life for themselves here in Paris like the Masons? He probably saw a little of Helen and Ethel in Miss Mason. But would Susan be happy in Paris? She had been so unhappy when she first came to Cleveland, having to live so far away from her family. But she had found a fine social circle and made a beautiful home in the very city she once loathed. Would she be willing to leave all that behind and start over in Paris? It was hard to picture Susan in Paris. Cleveland seemed to suit her so well. And the girls were becoming young women. Would they want to leave their friends behind for the chic culture of Paris? Or would they end up like those women, the demi-monde? Would they fall in with the wrong crowd? Would they start going out with white men? What would their social circle in Paris be like? As much as he longed for a bigger social circle, a life not constrained by racial divisions, he had grown up with them. What would life in Europe be like without being a member of a racial community? Chesnutt could speak French; he could get along all right, but would Susan? Her skin was darker than his. She couldn't speak French, and she had given up her teaching career when they married. Despite her devotion to being a wife and mother, she had become a permanent fixture in their Social Circle club, organizing dinners, picnics, and musical programs with Cleveland's other "colored" wives. Who would be her friends in *Paris?* Moving to Europe as a Black American with a wife and four children involved a different set of considerations, chief of which was money.

Most Americans who had relocated to Europe, those expats who populated the novels of Henry James and William Dean Howells, were loaded. Chesnutt was nothing like them. He had to work for his money; he'd neither inherited any nor could he rely on political appointments that granted some lucky Americans access to European high society. So the more he thought about it, the more he thought of the United States as home, despite its ubiquitous race problem. Europe was fun to visit but not a place to live. He returned home, "to Ameriky," as he affectionately called it in his journal, after spending a few days in England. There he visited Stratford-upon-Avon to gaze at Shakespeare's tomb, visited his memorial, "and admired the statue of W.S. in the garden with his figures and Prince Hall, Falstaff, [Lady] Macbeth." Finally, "visited the birthplace of W.S., the museum, saw the Red Horse Inn where W. Irving stayed, the foundations of the New Place house where W.S. died."[13] England was the final stop on Chesnutt's

European tour. It was from there that he boarded the *Lucania* in the port of Liverpool and set sail for Newfoundland. From there, he took a train on the Erie Railroad for Cleveland, where he was greeted at the station after his long journey by Susan and the children. He was eager to get home— and back to work.

Before Chesnutt left for Europe, he had sent the latest version of his "Rena" story to Richard Watson Gilder, editor of *The Century Magazine*. He wrote to Gilder directly, without relying on George Washington Cable to act as his middleman. Gilder had been Cable's editor when he first started publishing stories for *Scribner's Magazine*, through which they developed a friendship. Gilder remained committed to Cable's fiction even after most editors felt that he had given up his literary talent to speak for what he called the "Silent South." It was Cable who first sent Chesnutt's essay "The Negro's Answer to the Negro Question" to Gilder several years earlier. Gilder rejected that essay, writing to Cable that "Mr. Chesnutt's . . . is a timely political paper—so timely & so political—in fact so partisan— that we cannot handle it."[14] Cable continued to press Gilder on Chesnutt's behalf, sending him an early version of Chesnutt's "Rena," which he rejected with similar cutting remarks. Still, Chesnutt persisted to solicit Gilder. He must have felt that his support for Cable's fiction, which was close at least in theme to his own, would eventually lead Gilder to accept his stories for publication. But Chesnutt was not Cable. Gilder responded to Chesnutt's letter asking him if he "would be willing to read this story again with view to its publication in the *Century*" coolly. Gilder's response seemed to confirm what Chesnutt already knew: he would never be seen by Gilder as an equal to what he considered Cable's genius. What Chesnutt needed was an editor of his own, an editor who appreciated his writing for what it was and could see his potential as a first-class American writer.

When he returned from Europe, the American literary world was ringing with the death of Harriet Beecher Stowe. She died at her home in Hartford, Connecticut, at the age of eighty-five on July 1, 1896. She had been one of the founding members of *The Atlantic* and a regular contributor to the magazine long after the publication of her best-selling fiction, *Uncle*

Tom's Cabin in 1852, and tributes to her life and work took up considerable space in its August and September issues. Though Chesnutt had not contributed any stories to *The Atlantic* since "Dave's Neckliss" in 1889, he remained an avid reader of the magazine. Upon his return from Europe, Chesnutt would have been eager to read the latest issue, which opened with a touching personal essay by Annie Adams Fields, the widow of former *Atlantic* editor James T. Fields, called "Days with Mrs. Stowe."

Much had changed at *The Atlantic* since Stowe published her first story in its first issue back in November 1857. "The Mourning Veil," unlike her antislavery fiction upon which her fame mostly rested, opened with an epigraph by the era's most popular poet, Henry Wadsworth Longfellow, and was set, like most of *The Atlantic's* writers and the literature they wrote, in the six states constituting New England. Located at its center in Boston, *The Atlantic* made no secret of its literary commitments. "The Mourning Veil" anticipated Stowe's historical novel, written after her two antislavery novels, *Uncle Tom's Cabin* and *Dred: A Tale of the Great Dismal Swamp. The Minister's Wooing*, set in eighteenth-century Rhode Island, first appeared as a serial in the pages of *The Atlantic*, before being published as a book in 1859. With its publication, Stowe had put the slavery issue behind her, at least in her fiction, to focus on religious and domestic issues. She found *The Atlantic* to be an ideal venue to showcase her writings on these topics. Unlike her earlier fiction set primarily in the South, her *Atlantic* stories were all set in the familiar territory of New England.

Chesnutt had been a huge fan of *Uncle Tom's Cabin*. He first mentioned *rereading* the novel back in the summer of 1874, shortly after his sixteenth birthday. But his first encounter with Stowe's novel was much earlier; it was one of the first books he remembered reading. When rereading it in his mid-teens, he considered "it was no ways old to me." It was one of the books Chesnutt would return to repeatedly throughout his life. He even bought a beautifully bound copy of it, published by Houghton, Mifflin and Company in 1886, as a Christmas present for Susan. But he never mentioned any of Stowe's other stories. Reading Annie Fields's tribute to Stowe, about their first encounter in Europe, and of her long literary career must have been one of the reasons Chesnutt decided to send his own stories to the magazine a few months after returning from Europe. *The Atlantic,* of course, had accepted Chesnutt's first conjure stories a decade earlier. While he wrote nothing during his travels in Europe, he was eager to get back to his writing desk when he returned. His trip abroad, away from his court reporting business, his family, and the race problem, seemed to have inspired him to write—and to *publish* his stories after taking a break from the world of magazines.

Stowe's death in the summer of 1896 marked a long closing chapter in the history of *The Atlantic*. After Emerson, Longfellow, and the magazine's other founding fathers had passed on, she was the last, and its only female founder, to go. Horace Elisha Scudder was its current editor, having taken over from Thomas Bailey Aldrich in June 1890. Scudder came from a Boston family, and after receiving a thorough classical and religious education a couple of hundred miles away at Williams College, nestled in the Berkshire Mountains of northwestern Massachusetts, he moved to New York City. There he developed a talent for writing children's literature and eventually edited a magazine for children. He returned to Boston in the midst of the Civil War, where he started *The Riverside Magazine for Young People*. It was through this literary venture that he developed his long connection with Houghton. He worked as the company's chief literary advisor and eventually found himself at *The Atlantic*'s helm when Aldrich resigned. Scudder was open to new talent and publishing writers beyond the tight New England set that had been the mainstay of the magazine. Still, he was no less a member of the inner circle and had not traveled or thought much about literature beyond the New England writers who were an essential feature of the magazine since its founding.

When Chesnutt had first pitched the idea of a collection of short stories to be published by Houghton back in 1891, Scudder was complimentary and reaffirmed the publisher's interest in his fiction but counseled waiting while he developed a reputation through publishing more stories. "The place you have won," he wrote, "is an honorable one, yet as good as your work is, we question whether it has secured for you so general a recognition that a book would be at once welcomed by a large enough number to insure success."[15] Chesnutt decided to follow Scudder's well-intentioned, though slightly shortsighted, advice. Scudder's narrow, somewhat risk-averse editing style was upended when he decided to hire Walter Hines Page as his assistant editor in 1895. Born a few years before Chesnutt in Cary, North Carolina, Page was the first Southerner to occupy the hallowed editorial office of *The Atlantic*. Page's entry into *The Atlantic*'s building at 4 Park Street in Boston in the summer of 1895 initiated a seismic shift in both the content and format of the magazine. It would also result in making Chesnutt's dream of becoming an author come true.

Page's association with *The Atlantic* had begun over a decade earlier, when he published an article in the May 1881 issue with the sleepy title "Study of an Old Southern Borough." The essay appeared back when Chesnutt had been principal of the normal school in Fayetteville. Though he never mentioned reading it, its portrayal of the South would have likely struck a chord. It was based mostly on the towns of rural North Carolina, the kind of town where Chesnutt lived and worked. Though written in the voice of a third-person objective observer, Page drew heavily on his personal experience of growing up in Cary to develop the essay's narrative and argument. Page introduced "elements of two distinct civilizations" that were asynchronous. The first and "most notable personage" is the *"antebellum gentleman."* This personage, in Page's rhetoric, was the greatest obstacle to progress and explained to readers why. "He is now an old man, for he was in the prime of life before the war. He inherited his broad acres, and by his slaves he accumulated something of a fortune."[16] Page went on to draw a portrait of the antebellum gentleman in considerable detail, quoting him, revealing what he read, where he went, and the routine of his daily life.

Page's critique of these men and their effect on Southern society was unrelenting and scathing. It was not just in the details and animated portrayal he provided; it was also the proximity with which he spoke of the people and places he described. Page *knew* the people who were the subject of his critique; and he was willing to tell the world, but mostly the New England audience whom he addressed in the pages of *The Atlantic*, what the South was *really* like. "The whole town has a languid and self-satisfied appearance. There is little animation in man or beast. The very dogs look lazy. It would require twice the energy to put forth the same effort that it would cost in New England." That last line was the zinger. Page, a Southerner, was admitting, affirming, what everyone in the North seemed to already know. The New England town was the model of American civilization, the pinnacle of culture and progress. But to become more like New England, to follow its noble example, would take a monumental effort, which Page concluded was possible. "The growth of a civilization is always slow. But with the proper fusion of the old and the new, greatness can here be achieved, and that rapidly."[17] This became Page's dictum for progress, not just in the South but in all of the United States. It is no wonder that he found common cause in Chesnutt's stories. Chesnutt and Page were united not just by a common understanding of their Southern origins but also in their philosophical outlook and the methods by which they hoped to make their vision of the South a reality.

When Page joined the editorial staff at *The Atlantic* in 1895, he was a man on a mission. He had been hired by the magazine's editor, Horace Scudder, and its publisher, George Harrison Mifflin, to bring *The Atlantic* into the new century. Page's personal mission to reform the South and his commitment to upholding the principles of democracy in the United States became a key function of the magazine. He manifested these principles in an aggressive editorial style that at once alienated members of the magazine's old guard while it brought new writers from outside New England into its fold. That Page's influence over the magazine coincided with Chesnutt's return from Europe and his burst of literary production was more than just fortuitous. It had the whiff of an unplanned Southern invasion of *The Atlantic*.

It is uncertain when Chesnutt sent his new stories to *The Atlantic* for consideration. His daughter Helen described his submission process as both a personal and family affair. As Helen tells it, Chesnutt "took stock of his literary output" some time in February 1897, "selected three stories that he considered of *Atlantic* caliber, and sent them on to Houghton, Mifflin and Company. Then suspense filled the air at 64 Brenton Street as the family waited for the verdict."[18] However, there is no record of Chesnutt's initial submission to Houghton, nor are there any reader's reports for these stories. More likely, the stories were sent directly to Horace Scudder, who passed them along to Page, who was now in charge of accepting or rejecting manuscripts from new writers. Though Chesnutt had published with *The Atlantic* in the past, he had not published a story with the magazine for almost a decade and so was put, it seemed, in the new writer category. It isn't clear if

Page had read Chesnutt's earlier *Atlantic* stories or had even heard of him before reading his three new stories. If he had, he didn't mention it in his first letter to Chesnutt, dated February 16, 1897. Page's letter, like most of his correspondence with writers whose stories he accepted for publication, was formal, polite, and encouraging. He began, "We have in hand three contributions by you, 'The Wife of His Youth,' 'The March of Progress,' and 'Lonesome Ben.'" Page was particularly impressed by the first two stories and wanted to publish them immediately. He had an instinct for the right story at the right time and felt that these stories, more than "Lonesome Ben" "illustrate interesting phases of the development of the Negro race."[19] Page, unlike other editors at the time, always made it a practice to capitalize "Negro." The story Page rejected, "Lonesome Ben," was written more in the manner of his previous conjure stories, featuring Julius McAdoo as the central narrator, framed by the white married couple John and Annie. It was set like his other conjure stories back in North Carolina and related incidents that occurred, as Julius put it in his now familiar phrase, "befo' de wah." The story itself concerned the life of a slave called Ben, married with a couple of children, who decided to leave his family and run away from the plantation in order to avert a beating from his owner. Getting lost after more than a week in his pursuit of freedom by following the North Star, he winds up back where he started. But rather than return home and confront the wrath of his owner, Ben hides out by the creek that borders the plantation. There he finds himself so hungry and alone that he turns to the outcroppings of clay along the creek for sustenance. Eating the clay transforms Ben from being a "six foot high an' black ez coal" man to one with a "yellow hue." The change in his skin tone caused by eating clay made it impossible for Ben to return home; his wife and child no longer recognize him, nor does his owner, from whom Ben had been trying to run away. Suspended between his slave home and freedom, Ben dies a few yards from his owner's plantation, alone and heartbroken.

Ben's fate manifests not only the tragedy of slavery but also the impossibility of progress for the slave. Ben, perhaps like the former slave Julius, who told the story to John and Annie to explain the high quality of the clay, a natural and distinctive feature of the soil in North Carolina, is stuck in the place where he came from. Julius is less interested in developing the

land than in the history that lies buried beneath it. That Page decided to reject Lonesome Ben suggested that he was more interested in Chesnutt's stories that were set in the present, not the past, and the kind of progress of the
"Negro race" he developed in his other stories, "The Wife of His Youth"
and "The March of Progress." These stories were set in the present, *after*
the war, relating the circumstances of men and women who had moved *past*
slavery. These stories portrayed characters who were trying—and sometimes even succeeding—to leave the racial and economic constraints of
slavery behind them.

Page was partial to stories about or set in the South. He was also interested in publishing Black writers who manifested divergent perspectives on
the race problem. Around the time Chesnutt had submitted his new stories to *The Atlantic*, Page had requested and received papers from Booker T.
Washington explaining his "Tuskegee system" of education for both Black
and white Southerners. He also solicited and published several articles by
W. E. B. Du Bois. The most famous of these was published in the August
1897 issue of the magazine. "Strivings of the Negro People" has become a
classic piece of African American literature in which Du Bois first used the
now-familiar phrase *double-consciousness*.[20] Page's hand in coordinating the
Washington–Du Bois dispute is not widely recognized; but putting such
divergent ideas next to one another in the pages of *The Atlantic* was typical
of his editorial style, which he had learned and perfected during his days at
New York's *Forum*. Page courted controversy, inviting dispute among writers to achieve social reform and exposing corruption in government. That
Page took a special interest in Chesnutt's stories was hardly surprising.
Chesnutt's relationship with Page was always professional and cordial, his
support unstinting. It helped that Page believed Chesnutt's stories had the
potential to be "very profitable" and encouraged him to write more stories
so that he "might make a book."[21]

It is hard to know for certain if Chesnutt would have been able to make
a book without Page's support. In discussing this unprecedented relationship between a Black author and a white editor, literary critics have referred
to Chesnutt as "Page's protégé." But the historical facts of their relationship
refute such a characterization. Chesnutt was already an established writer
by the time Page encountered his fiction. He had already published three

stories in *The Atlantic* when Aldrich was its editor and was already known to its current editor, Page's boss at the time, Horace Scudder. Scudder dissuaded Chesnutt from making a book in 1891 not only because he felt that Chesnutt lacked a high-profile reputation but also because of his firm commitment to promoting New England writers like Henry James, Sarah Orne Jewett, and Kate Douglas Wiggin. He had always been skeptical of including Southern authors or submissions dealing with the South in the magazine. Even after hiring Page as his assistant, Scudder remained suspicious of his methods and his efforts to reshape the magazine. Page made no secret of his Southern convictions or his interest in soliciting Southern writers to publish with the magazine. Chesnutt's fiction suited Page's literary tastes to a tee. Rather than taking Chesnutt on as his "protégé," Page pursued Chesnutt, imploring him to write more and to work with him directly, even exclusively.[22] Page needed a writer like Chesnutt to remake *The Atlantic*, to take the magazine into the twentieth century, a magazine that could compete with the plethora of new magazines that had started up in the past decade or so, one that could attract readers from a wide range of political and cultural interests, not just the old New England elite who had started it back in the mid-nineteenth century.

Shortly after returning from Europe in 1897, Chesnutt had submitted five stories to *The Atlantic*. With the exception of "Lonesome Ben," Page wanted to publish all of them. But he had to move cautiously. The Washington–Du Bois debate had just begun to take off in *The Atlantic*. He didn't want to overwhelm readers with race stories. He had first suggested to Chesnutt publishing "The Wife of His Youth" and "The March of Progress" "under a common heading" believing "they would produce a better effect than if published separately."[23] He asked Chesnutt what he thought. Chesnutt was quick and enthusiastic in his reply. Not only did Chesnutt like Page's idea, he also wanted to expand on it and offered another story to be included with the couple Page had already accepted. Enclosing "A Matter of Principle," which he thought could be read as a companion piece to "The Wife of His Youth," Chesnutt suggested to Page that "if it should be found available, and the exigencies of magazine space would permit the three might be published under the general head 'Forward, Back, and Cross Over,' adapting one of the figures in a quadrille—'The March of Progress' coming first 'The Wife of His Youth' next, and 'A Matter of Principle' for the cross over." Chesnutt choreographed connections between his stories, weaving them together as if part of a longer sequence in which characters moved together in harmony toward a common understanding of one another and the world in which they lived. Chesnutt proceeded to offer Page more suggestions, offering more material, a short novel called *Mandy Oxendine*, set entirely in the sand hill region of North Carolina, that he thought might interest Page. He wanted Page to know that he had sufficient material (and could produce more) to fill whatever space Page had available.

Soon after writing to Page, Chesnutt wrote to Cable in February 1897 to tell him of recent developments in his writing. "I have thought it might interest you to know that *The Atlantic Monthly* has accepted for early publication two of three stories that I sent them recently." It's not clear if Chesnutt was writing to Cable to gloat, for approval, or merely to keep him updated on his literary activity. Their friendship seemed to have cooled somewhat. The apparent rift may have been caused by Chesnutt no longer seeking Cable's literary advice. Chesnutt was publishing again in *The Atlantic*; he didn't really need Cable to act as his representative as he had done for *The Century* and other such journals in the past. Chesnutt also informed him that he "made the trip across the water, of which I spoke to you, and enjoyed it very much, visiting England, Scotland, Belgium, Germany, Switzerland, and France." He didn't offer any more details on the trip, but the long list of countries he visited seemed to suggest that he had gained much experience since their previous conversation. Chesnutt concluded the letter warmly, trying to rekindle their correspondence and former close friendship. "My wife and family join me in regards to you and yours, and a line from you at any time would be welcomed, and placed among the things we like to keep."[24]

Despite his request for "a line" from him, Cable did not respond to Chesnutt's letter. Perhaps Chesnutt's letter recounting his recent literary accomplishments and travels did not interest the older writer. Perhaps Cable was too busy with more urgent matters. Together with his secretary, Mary Adelene Moffat, Cable was immersed in taking his social activism in a new direction. Based in the old Methodist church a block from Northampton's Main Street, not far from Cable's home on Paradise

Road, he had established the headquarters of the Home Culture Clubs. The clubs had started out in residential homes in the small New England town; its purpose, Cable wrote, was "for the educational and social culture of working men and women, the improvement of their home life and the establishment of friendly relations between widely separated elements of society."[25] Cable and Moffat organized weekly gatherings in Northampton and eventually expanded their activities throughout Massachusetts. An 1896 advertisement for the clubs stated "their purpose is to combine the stimulations and pleasures of mutual improvement with the promotion of a kinder, fuller, and more active neighborliness than ordinarily results from merely drifting with the current of one's social preferences." Cable was still involved in literary activities; he had established a new illustrated literary magazine called *The Symposium*, which Chesnutt was eager to read, though Cable never sent him a copy.

Seemingly undeterred by Cable's silence, Chesnutt decided to write to him again. In this letter, written a couple of months later, he revealed little about himself. This time, he was writing on behalf of his daughters Ethel and Helen. Chesnutt had decided that his daughters should attend Smith College in Northampton to further their education after graduating from Central High School in Cleveland that year. It was a huge decision. Smith had opened a couple of decades earlier as a women's liberal arts college by Sophia Smith in 1875. By the time Helen and Ethel were thinking about college in the spring of 1897, Smith had become the premier institution of higher learning for women in the United States. Rather than pigeonholing women into careers in teaching or the domestic arts, Smith was one of the few colleges at the time that offered women the same kind of classical educational programs offered to men, at least those women whose families could afford to pay its tuition.

But there was another reason Chesnutt decided to send his daughters to Smith. As Helen explained in her biography, in her senior year at Central, she and her sister "realized with shock and confusion that they were considered different from their classmates; they were being gently but firmly set apart, and had become self-conscious about it." It would seem the effects of the *Plessy* case, decided a year earlier, had already begun to take root, even among high school students in Cleveland. Helen recalled one of her white classmates had explained the situation to them. "'After all,' she had said, 'you are Negroes. We know that you are nice girls, and everybody thinks the world of you; but Mother says that while it was all right for us to go together when we were younger, now that we are growing up, we must consider Society, and we just can't go together anymore.'"[26] Susan was particularly incensed by the way her daughters were treated, by the way race was determining their prospects and making them feel different. She turned to her husband, as she always had, to fix things. Chesnutt sought to remedy their family's race problem by departing from Cleveland to expand their horizons in Northampton.

Cable's home in Northampton was adjacent to Smith College, with which he had many associations. Many of Smith's professors had become involved in the Home Culture Clubs, hosting gatherings. Cable was also well acquainted with the college's president at the time, Laurenus Clark Seelye. So Chesnutt wrote to him. But this time, it was not about his writing, and it wasn't for advice about getting an essay or short story published by drawing on his connections with editors like Richard Watson Gilder at *The Century*. This time, Chesnutt needed Cable and his connections to help him get his daughters settled at Smith. In the fall of 1897, Ethel and Helen Chesnutt became the first African American students to enroll at Smith College.

This time, Cable replied almost immediately to Chesnutt's letter. Cable was eager to help Ethel and Helen settle in at Smith. He told Chesnutt he should feel free to refer to him when looking for a boardinghouse for his daughters. He advised that they share a room off campus, "to take one room together, and I should urge their finding some place where very few others are lodging; for however kind and just their hostess might be there is always the risk of small-minded young people (fellow-students or others) making them uncomfortable."[27] Cable's prompt reply was at once comforting and disconcerting. Cable confirmed what Chesnutt, and of course his daughters, already knew. Even at an expensive liberal arts college, situated in the heart of abolitionist, progressive New England, they would encounter prejudice. But at least they would have access to a great education, the kind of education Chesnutt had so badly wanted, but was denied, at their age. As he and Susan prepared their daughters for leaving home, attending college with the brightest and wealthiest young women in the country, Chesnutt grew nervous.

He wrote to Cable again in late August. In this letter, he included clippings from newspapers concerning the case of Anita Florence Hemmings, an African American woman at Vassar College, a slightly older women's college in upstate New York. Hemmings had hidden her Black ancestry from the admissions office, passing as white for all four years of her education, only to be outed a few days before graduation. It became a public scandal. Chesnutt shuddered to think of the kind of ridicule his daughters might face at Smith. Once again, Cable responded immediately to quell Chesnutt's fears and reassure him that he was doing the right thing. Beginning by discounting the story in the papers as "written with great carelessness of the truth," Cable went on to "discredit *the whole thing*." He concluded the letter by offering Chesnutt a resounding endorsement of Smith College as the ideal place for his daughters.

> As to Smith College, I have already said all I know that I believe the president & board to be without vulgar prejudice on this subject. And yet I don't see why you need hesitate to write to President Seelye and tell him the facts and your feelings of delicacy. You may refer him to me if you care to do so. But I <u>know</u> there is no rule of the institution excluding any on the score of race. That is a preposterous supposition and I doubt not is as false a charge against Vassar as it would be against Smith.[28]

There is no evidence to suggest that Chesnutt wrote to Seelye. Cable's spirited response seems to have set Chesnutt's mind at ease. He left Cleveland with his daughters a few weeks later. The three would board a northbound train for Northampton. Helen and Ethel would begin their college life in Northampton. Both would earn their AB degrees from Smith in 1902 and go on to pursue successful careers as teachers.

Their years at Smith gave them, and Chesnutt, an inside view of New England. Cable played the role of advisor and mentor to Chesnutt and his daughters during their years living in New England. They appreciated his presence, but Ethel and Helen would have to make their own way through college. It was a struggle, both financially and emotionally. But they made it. Though Chesnutt was grateful for Cable's advice, he turned to Boston, *The Atlantic*, and Page. With Ethel and Helen at college, and their brother, Edwin, to follow at Harvard a few years later, Chesnutt was ready to join the world of the American literati by making books of his own.

Takes Up Literature

I have taken the step I contemplated when I saw you last, and have retired
from business since October 1, with the intention of devoting my time
henceforth to literary pursuits of one kind or another.

—Chesnutt to Walter Hines Page, October 11, 1899

When "The Wife of His Youth" first appeared in the July 1898 issue of *The Atlantic*, it met with rave reviews from critics and readers
alike. One reviewer summed up the story's virtues by exclaiming that it
was "marvelously simple, touching and fascinating." But the reader whose
opinion mattered most appeared a couple of years later, in the May 1900
issue of *The Atlantic*. Under the title "Mr. Charles W. Chesnutt's Stories,"
William Dean Howells looked back on the story's publication as a singular
literary event. He wrote his review from the vantage point of a critic who
possessed the rare talent of distinguishing between good and bad literature.

From his elevated critical perspective, Howells deemed "The Wife of
His Youth" to be "good" and dared readers to disagree with him. Howells
was the premier influencer of the period. If he gave an author his stamp
of approval, that author could count on book deals, solicitations from
magazines, and invitations from societies to read from his work. If Howells decided an author's work fell below the bar of "good art," that author
would be doomed to obscurity or would have to work hard to write something new that might change his mind. Fortunately for Chesnutt, Howells
approved, even celebrated, his story, declaring:

Any one accustomed to study methods in fiction, to distinguish between good and bad art, to feel the joy which the delicate skill possible only from a love of truth can give, must have known a high pleasure in the quiet self-restraint of the performance; and such a reader would probably have decided that the social situation in the piece was studied wholly from the outside, by an observer with special opportunities for knowing it, who was, as it were, surprised into final sympathy.[1]

Calling "The Wife of His Youth" "a remarkable piece of work," Howells extolled "the novelty of the material; for the writer dealt not only with people who were not white, but with people who were not black enough to contrast grotesquely with white people—who in fact were of that near approach to the ordinary American in race and color which leaves, at the last degree, every one but the connoisseur in doubt whether they are Anglo-Saxon or Anglo-African." The doubt cast on whether a person was Black or white was only half of the story. The other half concerned a marriage plot. It was hardly a love story since Mr. Ryder, the story's protagonist, winds up giving up his first choice for a wife to submit to the wife of his youth. Liza Jane is a dark-skinned former slave Mr. Ryder had married before the Civil War. She had spent her life since emancipation in search of her husband, whom she had advised to run away when her owner threatened to enslave him. The two are reunited just as Mr. Ryder is about to propose to another woman, Mrs. Dixon, a wealthy, young, fair-skinned widow. With the publication of "The Wife of His Youth," Chesnutt single-handedly turned the familiar conventions of the romantic love triangle upside down.

Despite Howells's self-aggrandizing tone and culturally insensitive remarks in discussing the story, he was mostly right about the novelty of "The Wife of His Youth." This was a new kind of story. Of course, there already were stories about the unique position light-skinned Black people occupied in the United States. There was, for instance, the fantastic story about Ellen Craft, who used her light skin to pose as a slave owner and managed to escape from slavery with her dark-skinned husband masquerading as her loyal slave. Then there were the popular fictional stories written by the abolitionist and feminist Lydia Maria Child and the former

slave William Wells Brown featuring mixed-blood heroines who managed to resist the white men who were in hot pursuit of them. But these
were all love stories set during or immediately after slavery, and these
light-skinned Black characters were almost always the product of illicit
and sometimes forced sex between white slave owners and their female
slaves. Chesnutt's story was not just a post-slavery story, it was also a
post-Reconstruction story set in the North, making it a *modern* American short story that featured Black characters who were *not* slaves living
lives not so different from those of white characters. This, as Howells
insisted, was a new kind of American story. "The Wife of His Youth"
was set in the present, in 1890s Cleveland, featuring light-skinned Black
people who were free, educated, employed, and, in the case of Chesnutt's
fictional Mr. Ryder, owned property.

This was Chesnutt's first story that drew on his personal experience of
Cleveland, where he had been living with his family now for over a decade.
It portrayed the social circle in which he, his wife, and his children were
active members. His rendering of this new world, of a Black society comprised mostly of the descendants of slaves and free colored people from
the South, was complex, subtle, and shocking. The story had been in the
making for a couple of years. He had discussed it with George Washington
Cable back in the winter of 1895, well before the *Plessy* verdict and his first
trip to Europe. But both had been on his mind when he began crafting a
story about Mr. Ryder, the "dean of the Blue Veins," which "were a little
society of colored persons organized in a certain Northern city shortly
after the war."

The distinguishing feature of this "little society" was its obsession
with racial divisions. Comprised of "individuals who were, generally
speaking, more white than black," the Blue Vein Society Chesnutt introduced in the story was committed to protecting the interests of those
"people of mixed blood" who found themselves outside the prevailing
Black and white racial categories of the time. Based on many of his own
features and experiences, Chesnutt's Mr. Ryder was an altogether new
kind of American character. Mr. Ryder devoted himself to maintaining
racial distinctions, serving as the leader of the Blue Vein Society and using himself as an example for others of "mixed blood" to identify with.

"'I have no race prejudice,' he would say, 'but we people of mixed blood are ground between the upper and nether millstone.'" The purpose of Chesnutt's story was to reveal a different side of "race prejudice" to readers, one that was not discussed much in the mainstream press. Rather than describing the strained, even violent, relations between Blacks and whites, Chesnutt took aim at people of mixed blood, people like himself and his friends, who claimed not to practice "race prejudice" but then devoted much of their time to organizing little societies in which membership was determined by skin color. This same topic would become standard fare for a later generation of writers associated with the Harlem Renaissance, writers like James Weldon Johnson, Nella Larsen, and Carl Van Vechten, who would pay homage to Chesnutt for breaking new literary ground as they developed their own modern treatments of the theme of racial passing.

With the publication of "The Wife of His Youth," Chesnutt seemed to have left, at least temporarily, Uncle Julius and the South of *his* youth behind. Chesnutt now turned to Mr. Ryder and Groveland—the name he used for present-day Cleveland in his fiction—taking aim at *Northern* prejudice among well-to-do colored people. These shifts in his fiction caused readers and fellow writers to take notice. "Who—in the name of the Lord!—is Charles W. Chesnutt?" the best-selling novelist James Lane Allen inquired of Walter Hines Page. Born in Lexington, Kentucky, before the Civil War and now a permanent resident of New York City, Allen was one of the few Southern authors who had managed to break through the cultural barriers put up by the New England elite. Though mostly forgotten and out of print today, Allen's many short stories and novels, bearing titles such as *A Kentucky Cardinal* and *Two Gentlemen of Kentucky*, were popular during his lifetime. Allen was a frequent contributor to both *The Atlantic* and *Harper's*. His effusive praise of "The Wife of His Youth" surely assured Page, though he hardly needed reassurance, that Chesnutt was a writer worth investing in. Anticipating Howells's later review, Allen called Chesnutt's story "the freshest, funniest, most admirably held & wrought out little story that has gladdened—and moistened—my eyes in many months." Allen wrote to Page but indicated he was really writing for Chesnutt: "Send the man my thanks, and my blessings in his pathway." Page complied with Allen's request and more. Rather than paraphrase Allen's remarks, Page decided to send Allen's entire letter to Chesnutt with a short personal note: "The enclosed letter will, I am sure, please you. I send it to you in confidence and with uncommon pleasure."[2]

Chesnutt received the letter about a week after his fortieth birthday. Page hadn't intended the letter to be a birthday present, but the letter turned out to be the best gift Chesnutt could have received. With the publication of the story in the summer of 1898 and the immediate critical acclaim it received, everything seemed to have changed. Chesnutt was so moved by Allen's letter that he wrote to Page almost immediately after receiving it. The tone between Chesnutt and Page had also changed. Their relationship had grown, become more intimate. Page was now more than just Chesnutt's editor at *The Atlantic*; they had become friends, keeping confidences, developing a mutual respect. For Chesnutt, receiving Allen's letter from Page was a sign of his trust in him. It was also a symbol of their friendship.

> I had written the other letter that I send you herewith, and it was lying on my desk, when I received your favor, enclosing Mr. Allen's letter. It is needless for me to say that I experienced genuine emotion at so spontaneous and full an expression of approval from one who speaks with authority, as one of the scribes. If there is any quality that could be desired in such a story that Mr. Allen has not found in it, I am unable to figure out what it is. His letter has given me unfeigned delight, for I have read his books and know how to value his opinion. If you will be good enough to let him know that his praise and his good wishes are both a joy and an inspiration to me, I shall be obliged to you. You don't say anything about my returning Mr. Allen's letter. Of course, I should like to keep it, but if you think it would not be right to do so, I will content myself with a copy, which you will doubtless permit me to retain, in confidence, of course.[3]

Page's reply dated about a week later, on July 6, 1898, kept up the intimate tone of Chesnutt's. It began with an injunction: "Keep Mr. Allen's letter. Do not say anything about it for the present, because I really had no clear right to give it to you, but I do not feel sufficiently guilty to ask you to return it." Page continued, "Keep it as long as you like—permanently, in fact, and if by accident it ever comes out that I took the liberty to give it away, I am sure Mr. Allen will forgive me: but I should prefer at present that he should not know it."[4] Why all the secrecy? Was it just a matter of Page's function as an editor, that he was obliged to keep his correspondence with authors private? That he was expected not to share private letters that he had received on behalf of the magazine with authors, even if those authors were the subject of the letters? Whatever were Page's reasons for giving Chesnutt Allen's letter and for asking Chesnutt to keep the letter a secret between them strikes one as more than just a question of editorial propriety. Page signed off his letter to Chesnutt, "Very truly yours, with Tar-heel cordiality, Walter H. Page."

This was not the first time Chesnutt and Page had exchanged confidences. Several months earlier, before "The Wife of His Youth" had been published, Chesnutt had sent a long letter to Page. Page had already accepted the story, along with "The March of Progress," for publication back in February, but neither had appeared yet in print. In October, Chesnutt had sent Page twenty stories. Some had been published before, some were new, at Page's request. Page had suggested that by sending all the short stories Chesnutt had produced, he might present them to the readers at Houghton, Mifflin and Company with the intention of selecting several of them to make a book "to put upon the market." It was early December then, almost the end of the year, and none of the stories, not even the ones that had been accepted for *The Atlantic*, had been published. Chesnutt was beginning to worry. What if the stories never appeared? What if Page couldn't find room for them? What if there had been a shake-up at the magazine and Page's authority had been somehow undermined by Scudder? What if the readers at Houghton didn't like his stories? How was Chesnutt to know what was happening with his stories? Chesnutt was completely in the dark when it came to how the editorial decisions at the magazine were made. He was just a Cleveland court reporter, hoping to get his stories into print by the premier literary magazine and publisher in the country. He didn't really know anyone at *The Atlantic* or Houghton whom he could ask.

But he needed to know what was going on with his stories. Would they be published or not?

So he wrote Page a long letter in which he confided to him his "literary plans." He began:

Dear Mr. Page—

I felt in a somewhat effusive mood the other day, and I sat down
to write a long letter in which I was going to tell you something
about my literary plans, how long I had cherished them, the
preparation I had made for them by study in our own and other
languages, by travel in our own country and in Europe; how I had
in a measure restrained myself from writing until I should have
something worth saying, and should be able to say it clearly and
temperately, and until an opportune time should have come for
saying it; how I had intended, for reasons which were obvious,
and had in a measure paved the way financially, to make my
literary *debut* on the other side of the Atlantic, and follow it
up immediately by devoting my whole time to the literary
life—etc.[5]

This was Chesnutt laying bare his soul to Page. He wanted Page to know who he was, what he had been through, what he had done, and what he hoped to do. It was a deeply personal letter, unusual for an author to send to an editor of a magazine. Chesnutt had never sent such a letter to an editor before, even though he had worked with many over the years. His correspondence with S. S. McClure had been curt and professional. Chesnutt had little noteworthy correspondence with *The Atlantic*'s previous editors, Thomas Bailey Aldrich and Horace Elisha Scudder. They just accepted or rejected his stories as they saw fit. But there was something different about Page.

Page had joined the Houghton, Mifflin and Company publishing firm in 1895, a week before its founder Henry Oscar Houghton's death on August 25. George Mifflin, Houghton's partner, was now in full charge of both the press, the publishing house, and *The Atlantic* magazine. Mifflin was eager for Page to bring the magazine and the publishing house into the twentieth century by soliciting new authors to publish their books with the old, but not yet obsolete, press. Chesnutt had met Page in Boston a few years later in the summer of 1898 to discuss his new stories for *The Atlantic*. Page had been encouraging, even solicitous of his work. It was then that Page had promised his stories would come out in the December or January issue of *The Atlantic*. Now it was December, and there was no sign of publication. Had Page changed his mind? Perhaps he was just busy. Or had Page forgotten him?

Having heard nothing from Page about either, Chesnutt decided it was time to reach out to him. He wanted to remind Page of their conversation, of the commitment Page had made to him and his interest in publishing with Houghton. "It is not difficult to find a publisher of some kind, on some terms—but there are publishers and publishers," Chesnutt explained. He made it clear to Page that he wanted his first book to bear the imprint of the Riverside Press, one of the oldest and most respected book printers in the country.

Based in Cambridge, Massachusetts, on the banks of the Charles River, Houghton, Mifflin and Company functioned as the publishing arm of Henry Oscar Houghton's prized Riverside Press. He had founded the press in 1852 and had almost immediately earned a reputation as a printer of discrimination who perceived the essential relationship between the author's words and the paper, page, and type, through which thoughts conceived in isolation would become public property. Houghton conceived of a book in terms of the whole, taking great care in its outward form so that readers could take the greatest pleasure in reading. His press achieved a reputation for fine workmanship, and his publishing house solicited authors who were equally interested in producing material that would match the beauty and care taken with the production of the book.

Chesnutt's development as a bibliophile had begun when he was in his teens, shortly after his mother's death. Because he could not afford to continue his education at college, he turned to books in pursuit of greater knowledge. As he worked as a schoolteacher to earn money for himself and his family, his love of books only intensified. But Chesnutt was poor. Most of the salary he earned from teaching was spent on necessities—rent, food, clothes. He also had to send money back home, to his father, to help AJ take care of his siblings, to his new young wife and their children. Much to the chagrin of his father, whatever money Chesnutt had left over he spent on books. As a youngster, Chesnutt had dreamed of having his own library. He imagined keeping his books in "a large apartment." He mused on his imaginary library in his journal: "If you should travel day and night, by the swiftest means of conveyance, for three whole months you could only make the circuit of its walls. As for the books, you would not have time to look at them. You might see some of their handsome covers and gilt edges as you hurried past, but you could have no idea of your contents."

Chesnutt always loved the feeling of being surrounded by books, having direct access to knowledge that was produced centuries before. It was this love of books, for their beauty and knowledge, that led him to try his hand at making books of his own once he could afford the time to devote to write literature. But for Chesnutt, reading—not writing—books was his first love. "What a blessing is literature, and how grateful we should be to the publishers who have placed its treasures within reach of the poorest," he declared to himself on March 7, 1882. It seems strange that Chesnutt would express such gratitude to *publishers* for making literature accessible to people like him rather than to the authors who created the literature without which publishers would have nothing to make into books. Chesnutt's paean to publishers was made shortly after being named principal of Fayetteville's normal school and the birth of his second daughter. Books, at this busy and anxious time of life, provided him with great joy and respite. "Shut up in my study, without companionship of one congenial mind, I can enjoy the society of the greatest wits and scholars of England, can revel in the genius of her poets and statesmen, and by a slight effort of the imagination, find myself in the company of the greatest men on earth. Can work procure success? My only fear is that I will spoil it all by working too much." A great deal had changed for Chesnutt since he wrote these lines in his journal. He was now a budding author, he had traveled to Europe, he owned a home, he was the father of four, three of whom were attending elite colleges in New England. Yet the anxieties of his youth persisted. Especially now, it seemed, when he was so close to sating his desire to make a book of his own, not just reading and collecting books written by others.

In response to Chesnutt's December letter, Page assured him that his stories and novel had been received and not forgotten. He elaborated, "Your stories are undergoing a rather unusual experience here; because they are being read, I believe, by our whole staff of readers and I hope to have in a very little while word to send you."[6] The four readers, including Page, at Houghton came to their decision to decline both the collection and the novel more than three months later, on March 29, 1898. It was not the "most favorable" decision Page had hoped for; but the situation was not, as he insisted to Chesnutt, hopeless.

The novel was deemed by Houghton's reader "impracticable from a publisher's point of view."[7] Page softened the blow by explaining that the novel "would be a doubtful venture on our list. It does not follow, of course, that it would not succeed on some other list, for it might very well do so; but it has been impossible for us to reach the conclusion, after very careful deliberation and discussion that it would be a wise venture for this firm to undertake." Page went on to encourage Chesnutt not to give up on *A Business Career*, which he felt "may be a success" despite "Messrs. Houghton Mifflin and Company's conservative attitude toward it. You will doubtless be able to find a publisher, and my advice to you is decidedly to keep trying till you do find one." But this time, Chesnutt did not heed Page's advice. He remained steadfast in his commitment to Houghton, Mifflin and Company.

Though the readers declined Chesnutt's untitled collection of short stories and novel, Page explained that Houghton were still very much interested in his "'conjure' stories to make a book, even a small book."[8] Rather than dwell on the rejection, Chesnutt decided to focus on the positives, of which Page assured him there were many. A couple of months later, on May 20, 1898, Chesnutt sent Page six new conjure stories. He listed the titles of the new stories and made his purpose clear. "In writing them, I have followed in general the lines of the conjure stories you have read already, and I imagine the tales in this batch are similar enough and yet unlike enough, to make a book."[9] And so, with Page in his corner at Houghton,

Chesnutt's first book was published and printed by the Riverside Press in March 1899.

The Conjure Woman comprised a total of seven stories, three of which had been previously published, in a slightly different form, in *The Atlantic* magazine. Another of the stories, "The Conjurer's Revenge," had already appeared in the June 1889 issue of *The Overland Monthly*. The title of the book was most likely suggested by Page, as were the stories ultimately selected from the thirteen conjure stories Chesnutt had submitted to him over the course of a year and a half. But the book had been in the making for over a decade, several years before Chesnutt met Page; he published his first conjure story, "The Goophered Grapevine," in the August 1887 issue of *The Atlantic*.

These stories were thematically intertwined by the phenomenon of conjure, which appeared in one form or another in all of them. But they were formally realized by the dialect voices of the slaves and former slaves, particularly that of Julius McAdoo, who stood at the center of all the stories and became *The Conjure Woman*'s standout hero. Some, like the Yale literary critic Robert Stepto, preferred the title *Uncle Julius Stories* to *The Conjure Woman*. Readers' dissatisfaction with the title of Chesnutt's first book was hardly surprising. Chesnutt hadn't given a title to the collection of stories he submitted to Page back in late October 1897. He had just provided a list of the titles of the twenty stories. When he submitted six more stories about six months later, he gave them the general heading "'conjure' stories," listing the titles of the six stories separately. Three of these, "The Gray Wolf's Ha'nt," "Mars Jeems's Nightmare," and "Sis' Becky's Pickaninny," were included in the book. Page sent Chesnutt a "personal note" on September 6, 1898, letting him know that "Messrs. H.M. and Company will publish the book of Conjure stories" and that "a formal letter will follow in a day or two."[10] When the formal letter arrived, the book was still missing a title. The letter began, "It gives us pleasure to report that after thorough consideration we feel disposed to publish for you your collection of short stories which we have nick-named 'conjure' stories, (for we think that a better title may possibly be found)." Chesnutt remained undecided on a title when he replied on September 19, 1898, returning the manuscript, having revised it according to the readers' instructions. In his reply, he "arranged the stories in what I think good order. The 'Goophered Grapevine,'" he insisted, "cannot well be anything but the first story, 'Po' Sandy' is a good second, and 'Hot foot Hannibal' winds them up well and leaves a good taste in the mouth."[11] As to the arrangement of the stories, Houghton followed Chesnutt's rather exacting instructions, but there was still the question of the book's title. Regarding it, Chesnutt said only, "You speak in your letter of a better title for the book than 'Conjure Stories.' I send with the MS. a list of suggested and most of them 'suggestive' titles. I would be glad to have your views on the subject, or to have you select a title from this list or independent of it."[12] Unfortunately, Chesnutt's list of titles has not been recovered from the Houghton archive.

So we don't know exactly how or why Chesnutt's first book came to be called *The Conjure Woman*. It might have been on the list of titles Chesnutt sent to Page, who could have simply chosen it as the best of the bunch. Clearly, the word *conjure* was an important key term that knit the stories together; but in one of the stories, "The Conjurer's Revenge," the conjurer is a man. Still, *most* of the stories do feature Aunt Peggy as the conjure woman, and she certainly emerges in the collection as a powerful fictional force who existed, in the stories' narrator's terms, "befo' de wah." Since each of the stories straddle the period before and after the Civil War—the antebellum and postbellum periods of American history—it is difficult to pin down the precise moment of the stories. Perhaps this was the reason Chesnutt remained irresolute about the book's title. But since this was his first book, it is not surprising that he would be tentative about what to call it. Chesnutt seemed to feel that his publisher would know better than he how to pick a title for the book that would entice readers to buy it. He was just thrilled the book was being published by Houghton, Mifflin and Company. As he put it to them, "Permit me to assure you that I appreciate the privilege of 'coming out' under the auspices of your House, and I thank you for the complimentary terms in which you announce your decision."

While Chesnutt equivocated on the matter of its title, he showed a marked interest in the physical features of the book and how it was marketed. Decades after Houghton decided to publish *The Conjure Woman*,

Chesnutt recalled the exact details of the publication of his first book in meticulous detail:

> After the book had been accepted for publication, a friend of mine, the late Judge Madison W. Beacom, of Cleveland, a charter member of the Rowfant Club, suggested to the publishers a limited edition, which appeared in advance of the trade edition in an issue of one hundred and fifty numbered copies and was subscribed for almost entirely by members of the Rowfant Club and of the Cleveland bar. It was printed by the Riverside Press on large hand-made linen paper, bound in yellow buckram, with the name on the back in black letters on white label, a very handsome and dignified volume. The trade edition was bound in brown cloth and on the front was a picture of a white-haired old Negro, flanked on either side by a long-eared rabbit. The dust-jacket bore the same illustration.[13]

This was the first book Houghton had printed and published by an African American author. It was a big deal. At the time *The Conjure Woman* appeared in print, its publisher never referred to him by this twentieth-century racial title. Instead, the firm's readers referred to Chesnutt among themselves as a "slightly colored author." They did recognize that a book written by a slightly colored author was different from those Houghton had produced in the past and would require a different set of marketing strategies to appeal to the readers who usually bought their books. They worked closely with Chesnutt on marketing the book to new readers and book collectors. As soon as he received the acceptance letter from Houghton, Chesnutt told his close friends and colleagues in Cleveland about it. They were impressed. Judge Beacom, whom Chesnutt had gotten to know while reporting cases in his courtroom, was also interested in literary affairs. He started the Rowfant Club, the Cleveland literary society that had ordered the limited edition of copies of *The Conjure Woman*. He had even hoped Chesnutt would join the society at some point. But not yet; it was too soon for the society to admit "colored" men—even "slightly colored" ones—to their all-white, all-male society. Now that Chesnutt had written a book of his own, maybe his fellow members would be more willing to admit him. Chesnutt was of course pleased by Judge Beacom's interest in him and the book. Beacom understood that Chesnutt's book was not just another book of plantation fiction, a genre of postbellum American writing that enjoyed considerable popularity at the time. Though his publisher too seemed to understand the distinction of Chesnutt's book, they felt they needed to appeal to readers of plantation fiction to sell *The Conjure Woman*. Their marketing strategy was evident in the book's original cover design, a portrait of an elderly Black man flanked on both sides by rabbits, as Chesnutt described it. The portrait was an obvious reference to Chesnutt's narrator, Julius McAdoo. But what was the purpose of the rabbits? Surely they did not refer, even in an obscure way, to John and Annie's presence in the conjure stories. There were no real or imaginary rabbits in Chesnutt's stories.

About a year before Houghton accepted Chesnutt's book for publication, they had published a book of folktales by the white Southern author Joel Chandler Harris called *Tales of the Home Folks in Peace and War*. Harris had become popular almost two decades earlier for his "Uncle Remus" stories, first published by the well-known New York firm of D. Appleton & Company. Houghton had reviewed and accepted Harris's most recent collection in December 1897, right around the time they were considering Chesnutt's collection of stories. Though Page found Harris's stories to be "very uneven in quality," he felt that with his "diplomatic editorial suggestions," he could improve the book.[14] Moreover, Harris had established his reputation as a popular author with his Uncle Remus stories, in which the African trickster figure Br'er Rabbit played a major role. All the stories in Harris's latest book had appeared in magazines and newspapers "of all grades during the last ten years," and several of them included illustrations. In other words, Harris's book was a sure thing, it came with a built-in audience, so the firm could count on making a profit on the book without expending too much effort. Hence, the rabbits on the cover of Chesnutt's *Conjure Woman*.

Chesnutt's book, on the other hand, was the opposite of a sure thing. It was a risk. But it was a risk the firm, mostly because of Page's personal interest in Chesnutt, decided to take. As they explained to Chesnutt, "Let us say first it gives us unusual pleasure to add a book by you to our list;

and then we ought frankly to say that this particular book we cannot help regarding with some doubt as to any great financial success. The workmanship is good—of some of the stories, indeed, we think it is exceedingly good; but whether the present interest in this side of the Negro character is sufficient to carry the book to the success we hope for can be determined only by experiment."[15]

Never in the history of American publishing had a major publishing firm produced a work of fiction by a non-white, or slightly colored, or African American writer. Of course, books by African Americans had been published in the United States. Frances Ellen Watkins Harper had published her sentimental novel *Iola Leroy* in 1892 with a small publishing firm and bookseller in Philadelphia called Garrigues Brothers, which published mostly religious and juvenile fiction. Prior to the Civil War, novels by William Wells Brown, Frank J. Webb, and Harriet E. Wilson were published by and for small abolitionist circles to further the antislavery political cause. But a work of fiction by and about Black people in the United States directed at a mainstream audience was unheard of. Most books written by Black people in the United States were self-published, having only very small distributions.

The experiment of *The Conjure Woman* published by Houghton probably never would have worked if Chesnutt hadn't met Page. They found common cause in their North Carolina experience, and they truly valued each other's opinions. As a Southerner himself, Page had noticed something in Chesnutt's stories that most at Houghton had missed. For all the magical and unreal aspects of the conjure stories, they were *real*, true representations of life in the South. Julius was decidedly not Uncle Remus, telling childish stories about animals and slaves. He was telling complex, layered, ironic stories that were as provocative as they were moving and beautiful. While reading the conjure stories individually as they appeared in *The Atlantic* and elsewhere offered readers a brief encounter with Julius McAdoo and the history of slavery he narrated, reading the stories consecutively, in book form, the ongoing narrative beginning with "The Goophered Grapevine" and ending with "Hot-Foot Hannibal," presented a panorama of slavery and its aftermath. It gave readers a full sense of the slave culture Chesnutt transcribed, permeating and enriching every aspect of American culture.

The appearance of *The Conjure Woman* in print in late March 1899 changed Chesnutt's world. It also changed the world of American literature.

On October 4, 1899, the *Cleveland Plain Dealer*, Ohio's largest and most read newspaper, ran an unusual story under the heading "Takes Up Literature." "Charles W. Chesnutt," they announced, "Abandons Stenography for a New Field." It is not exactly clear why this story, next to one about England's role in the South African Boer War and another about a Warren Line vessel wrecked on the Newfoundland Coast, was newsworthy. Yet there it was, a story about Chesnutt ending his "very lucrative stenographic business he has built up in Cleveland during the past fifteen years" to take up literature full-time. Though the story did not include any direct quotes from the author, it was clear that the reporter had spoken to Chesnutt for the story. "The success of 'The Conjure Woman,' a volume of negro dialect stories, of which he is the author, led him to take this step. He blossomed into a litterateur at the early age of sixteen years, when his first effort was accepted by one of the well known periodicals. Since that time he has been a frequent contributor to the best magazines." The reporter also announced that "Houghton Mifflin & Co. are at the present time printing his latest volume of short stories and preparing for an early edition."

Chesnutt had been contemplating the move for some time. He had discussed the prospect of stepping back from stenography to take up literature full-time with Page when he visited him in Boston back in July. *The Conjure Woman* had just come out, he had been in discussion with Herbert Small, head of another Boston publishing firm, Small, Maynard & Company, to write a biography of Frederick Douglass for their Beacon Series of Biographies of Eminent Americans. He had also been thinking about a second book, "a volume of stories along the line of 'The Wife of His Youth.'" And of course, there was "Rena," which he had been working on for over a decade. Though Houghton had already rejected "Rena," Chesnutt refused to give up on her. Nor did Page want him to. Page continued to encourage Chesnutt to keep writing and revising. So despite the rejection, Chesnutt believed he had found his *"metier* as a story writer."[16] "The Wife of His Youth," "Rena," and the new stories of the color line that he was developing dramatized the negative effects of "color distinctions" that had become endemic in the United States since the 1896 *Plessy* verdict.

Even though reviews of *The Conjure Woman* were overwhelmingly positive, Chesnutt knew, as Houghton had rightly predicted, that it would not make him a fortune, perhaps not even a living wage. The firm knew they would be lucky to break even with the costs of its publication, but they, and especially Page, remained committed to the book and to Chesnutt. They were eager to bring out Chesnutt's second book; this one at an even greater cost than the first. When "The Wife of His Youth" first appeared in *The Atlantic* in July 1898, it had become a sensation, a convergence of artistic genius in line with realist stories by Henry James and William Dean Howells. But unlike their stories, Chesnutt's had found readers on *both* sides of the color line.

In the months before closing his office, Chesnutt was working around the clock. His days continued to be occupied with his court reporting business, but he devoted his nights and weekends to writing. He was also traveling. He made frequent trips to Boston, often making quick stops in Northampton. He wanted to make sure Ethel and Helen had everything they needed to study and thrive at Smith College. Chesnutt took a great deal of pride in his daughters' academic accomplishments. He wanted them to have the college career he never had. He was also planning on sending Edwin to Harvard once he graduated from high school. Harvard was the destination of the sons of the elite, and he wanted his son to be one of them. In Boston, he met with Page to talk about his future work, North Carolina, and the publishing industry. Page was always full of good ideas and encouragement. Through Page, Chesnutt met other editors and publishers—Herbert Small at Small, Maynard & Company, M. A. De Wolfe Howe, an associate editor at *The Youth's Companion*, and Joseph Edgar Chamberlin, who wrote for the *Boston Evening Transcript*. All wanted Chesnutt to write for their publications. Howe wanted Chesnutt to write more stories along the lines of "The Wife of His Youth." This story, it seemed, even more than the conjure stories, had opened the door to new opportunities.

Amid all this travel and literary activity, Susan was beginning to worry. Chesnutt was working too much. She wrote to Ethel and Helen in Northampton to express her concern, perhaps also to persuade them to come home. Smith was expensive. Maybe if they switched to Western Reserve University, which was a short walk from their home on Brenton Street in Cleveland, Chesnutt wouldn't have to work so hard to pay their college fees. They still had two more years at Smith to graduate. Between paying for college and writing new stories to meet the new requests, Chesnutt had little time to help Susan at home. She had to take care of Edwin and Dorothy herself. "I was out yesterday for the first time in two weeks," she complained in her letter to Ethel and Helen. "Edwin's shoes had given out and I had to go downtown with him to get another pair, as his father is too busy now to think of things of that kind." Susan's tone of resentment was hard to dismiss. She was unhappy. Though she concluded her letter on a high note, her resentful tone remained high, too. "I am glad that he gets so much encouragement in his literary work, as that keeps his spirits up, and helps him to slave along without thinking too much about it. I am only sorry that he didn't get this encouragement ten years ago."[17] Susan chose her words carefully. She felt that her husband, born as she was to free colored people and having never been a slave, was now working *like* a slave for his white publisher.

After receiving their mother's letter, Helen and Ethel felt guilty and ashamed for making their father work so hard just so that they could attend a fancy liberal arts college in the Northeast. When his daughters wrote to him, telling them they thought they should quit Smith and come home to save money, he would not hear of it. Dismissing Susan's concern, Chesnutt told his daughters "that it was very dutiful and considerate of them to make such a proposal, but that he was quite able to keep them at Smith and was in no sense overweighted by the burden."[18] We don't know what he said to Susan to get her to stop worrying. We do know that he decided to pull back from his court reporting business to avoid overwork. Perhaps this was enough to put Susan's mind to rest. They both knew that his break from court reporting would be temporary. They couldn't afford to live on his earnings from writing, at least not while putting their children through college. But for now, he needed to focus on his writing to meet his new and ever-increasing literary commitments. Aside from his homelife, the ever-worsening situation in North Carolina weighed on his mind, too. He wanted to write about it. In fact, he wanted to take a trip there. It had been years since he'd returned home to visit his father and his sisters. He had been too busy with work. But now he wanted to see—and hear— what was going on there for himself. He knew firsthand that the reports he read in the papers about the events in Wilmington were all slanted or just plain false. There were so many reasons to write more, but there were also reasons, as Susan reminded him, to stop writing, or at least write less and report more cases. He could earn three or four times as much court reporting than he could writing stories.

But when Page decided to trade off "The March of Progress" for another conjure story, Chesnutt managed to sell it for a good sum to *The Century*. This was a major coup. Gilder actually liked something he wrote enough to publish it. It was his first (and last) story to be published in *The Century*. And "Rena" kept coming along. Meanwhile, he was giving lectures and readings at several important venues, meeting new people, making contacts, becoming something of a literary celebrity. Maybe there was a chance he could make a living from writing. Could he make enough to keep his family living well? It was a risk that he had to take. He decided to devote his time to literature, to strike while the iron was hot; if he got burned, he knew his way back to the office.

So in the fall of 1899, Chesnutt closed his swank office at the Society for Savings Building to take his business home. The family made space for Chesnutt to work from home. He still reported a few cases to help make ends meet, but mostly he was writing stories of various kinds— long fiction, short fiction, nonfiction, and even a play. By the end of the year, *The Wife of His Youth, and Other Stories of the Color Line* was done. It was illustrated by the well-known artist Clyde O. DeLand with a very pretty cover of red and gold. It was beautifully bound. Houghton, Mifflin and Company had gone all out. This was exactly the kind of book Chesnutt had dreamed about writing. But he had no time to celebrate. By the time *The Wife of His Youth* was done, he got the news that Page had resigned his editorship of *The Atlantic*; he would leave Boston and Houghton for the newly formed publishing house of Doubleday & McClure in New York by the end of the year. Shortly after the move, Page took over from

McClure the role of senior partner, to form Doubleday, Page & Company in 1900. Page's move did not end the friendship with Chesnutt. In fact, their friendship only grew. Page remained committed to bringing out Chesnutt's stories. After all, he knew he needed Chesnutt to help save the North Carolina of their youth. Chesnutt got right to work on writing a new North Carolina story while readying "Rena," finally, for publication.

PART IV

Home

II

——— • ———

Passing on Rena

> It will be observed, however, that well-nigh every great work of fiction
> was inspired by some worthy motive, and that those to which no purely
> altruistic end can be imputed, have served some purpose beneficial to
> mankind.
>
> "The Writing of a Novel" (ca. 1900)

Since at least the late 1880s, after the publication of his first conjure
story in *The Atlantic*, Chesnutt had been writing and rewriting one story
that he called "Rena." By the time it was published, over a decade later,
in the fall of 1900, it had gone through multiple iterations and revisions.
He had shared it first with George Washington Cable in 1889, who made
suggestions, which Chesnutt presumably took, and sent it off to Richard
Watson Gilder, editor of *The Century*. When Gilder rejected it, Chesnutt
continued to work on it, expanding it, condensing it, adding characters,
removing others. About five years later, he tried sending it again to Gilder,
who remained uninterested. So he kept revising while working on the
conjure stories and his stories of the color line, featuring descendants of
former slaves and free people of color struggling to navigate the postbellum world in which they had all become "blacks" living separately from
"whites," according to the new terms stipulated by the *Plessy v. Ferguson* case.
In the meantime, "Rena" had grown from a short story to a novelette, into
a full-fledged novel. As Chesnutt explained to Walter Hines Page in late
December 1898, "I have put in more of the old town, and its people. I have
tried to draw, in Rena's character, a fine character forced inevitably into a

false position. The heroine, instead of being the interesting lay figure of the story as you read it before, I have tried to make a living, loving, suffering, human woman."[1]

From its earliest manifestation, Chesnutt had believed that *Rena* was his magnum opus, his masterpiece, his rendering of everything he knew and experienced about the race problem in the United States. *Rena* couldn't offer any solutions to the problem, but the work could show readers its harmful effects, not just on society but on individual Americans. *Rena* was a tragedy written in the classical conventions of the form that he had studied so closely back in Fayetteville as a young schoolteacher. It was there he first encountered Homer, Virgil, Horace, and Shakespeare. Dickens, Balzac, and Dumas. Chesnutt had no interest in writing *Black* literature, Negro literature, or African American literature. From his earliest days as a writer, he seemed to believe that he might write a truly *great* American novel, something along the lines of Hawthorne's *Scarlet Letter*, or Melville's *Moby-Dick*, or, closer to his time, Stowe's *Uncle Tom's Cabin*, or James's *Portrait of a Lady*. He seemed to feel that the books by Black writers that had been published were not "good," at least as Howells employed the term in his literary criticism of the time. For Chesnutt, books by William Wells Brown and Phillis Wheatley lacked coherence, form, and beauty. As he put it to himself in his journal, "If they were not written by a colored man, they would not sell enough to pay for the printing. I read them merely for facts, but I could appreciate the facts better if they were well presented." Chesnutt wrote to escape the racial constraints of his time, not just personally; he, after all, was light-skinned enough to pass as white, if he had thought that passing would solve the race problem. But passing was not the solution. He wrote to understand the effect of racial categories on *all* Americans, how being categorized as Black or white shaped, even determined, an individual's life. But Chesnutt's own experience was shaped not exclusively by race; he had formed who he was and hoped to be by his experience of reading.

It was unsurprising then that Chesnutt started out wanting to publish his stories with mainstream, well-established publishers and magazines like Houghton, *The Century*, and *The Atlantic*. But these firms and magazines didn't publish stories by or about men like Chesnutt. Chesnutt was writing about "new people," the sons and daughters of former slaves, interracial unions, mostly set in the South. The now-classic nineteenth-century American novels by New England authors like Hawthorne, Stowe, James, and Melville focused on a different side of American life: abolition, seafaring, adultery, money, and marriage. "The problems of people of mixed blood" that Chesnutt was writing about were not yet a subject that mainstream publishers were generally interested in. How would Chesnutt get publishers interested in a novel that focused mostly on people like him?

Decades after its publication in 1900, *The House Behind the Cedars* would be touted for its passing plot. For later writers and critics, Chesnutt's first published novel exemplified a form that gained attention a couple of decades later in popular American culture. *The Autobiography of an Ex-Colored Man, Passing, The Imitation of Life, The Human Stain*. These novels were all about racial passing in the twentieth century that made it big, a few became bestsellers, and a couple were adapted into full-length feature films. Passing had become an *American* cultural phenomenon, like life, liberty, and the pursuit of happiness. But unlike these universal principles, passing was available only to a select few: those individuals born into Black families but with skin so fair they could, if they chose, leave their Black families to become white. The stories about passing were often based on real-life cases that people first encountered in the newspapers. They depicted men and women who had left their Black families to pass as white, pursuing high-powered jobs in politics, art, and science. Such characters got married, to start new, white families of their own. There was the sensational story of Belle da Costa Greene, who had become the first director of the Morgan Library, a personal confidante and perhaps even lover to the financier John Pierpont Morgan. She was just one example, of the hundreds, maybe even thousands, of others who had, as the nonsensical logic of racial passing went, been born Black and become white.

And Chesnutt, as those close to him knew, was one of those, with skin so light that he could be white, who could pass. But he never did. At least not for long enough to make a difference in who he was. Throughout his life, he was given a few labels that were supposed to determine who he was: mulatto, octoroon, quadroon, colored, slightly colored, negro, Black, Afro-American. Chesnutt saw himself as all of these and none of these.

He was always Charles W. Chesnutt, born to free people of color before the Civil War. What would his life have been like, he wondered, if he had been born white? Or if his skin were dark brown instead of olive, his hair curly instead of wavy, and his eyes brown instead of gray? Would these differences in his appearance have made him a different *person*? A different kind of writer? Would he have been a writer at all?

In his early stories, the ones he wrote for *Puck* and the S. S. McClure Syndicate, Chesnutt rarely wrote of race. If Black characters appeared in these stories, they were usually figures of humor or irony, without making a political statement, at least explicitly. His conjure stories were almost all framed by white characters, the married couple John and Annie, who appeared as listeners, and sometimes (mis)interpreters. Julius's stories, delivered in his characteristic Black dialect voice, were made more accessible to the white readers to whom they were mostly directed. *Rena* had started out as a short story based on his observations of growing up in rural North Carolina. It is the story of a failed marriage, driven by the characters' obsession with skin color and racial ancestry. But in its early versions, there were no white characters. *Rena*, like his later stories about members of the "Blue Veins," focused entirely on the struggles of light-skinned or mixed-blood characters. But as the story developed, over the course of a decade, *Rena* evolved from a story about one woman's unhappy marriage into an American tragedy, touching the lives of all those who had been shaped by the racial categories into which they were born. *Rena* was also Chesnutt's labor of love; it was a story he believed in, even though publishers predicted "nothing but failure" for it. "I have not slept with that story for ten years without falling in love with it," he wrote to Page on March 22, 1899, just after Houghton had, once again, "turned down my novel 'Rena' in great shape." Chesnutt was disappointed and uncharacteristically incensed. "They have condemned the plot, its development, find the distinctions on which it is based unimportant," he complained. Despite their criticisms, Chesnutt remained committed to *Rena*. Unlike with *Mandy Oxendine* and *A Business Career*, which he gave up on after Houghton declined to publish them a few years earlier, he refused to accept the publisher's rejection as the final word on the novel. Considering their latest rejection, Chesnutt turned to Page for advice and consolation. "The fact that it met with your approval in the rough, was my chief incentive in rewriting it. Whether I took the wrong tack in my revision I don't know; perhaps I did; but if you find the time, I should like you to read it—even if it is already disposed of—in order that I may be able to discuss it with you when I see you again."[2]

After multiple revisions and rejections, and some discussion with Page, Chesnutt sent *Rena* "in her latest and finished form" to his trusted editor in the summer of 1899.[3] Chesnutt had just returned from Green Acre Farm in Eliot, Maine, where he delivered one of his first public lectures, "The Negro in the South." Situated so far north and east, Chesnutt would have to work hard to make the topic accessible to his audience. The organizer of the lecture series, Sarah Jane Farmer, had originally invited Page to deliver the lecture. Farmer was born into a wealthy New Hampshire family. Her mother, Hannah Tobey Shapleigh Farmer, was a prominent philanthropist. Her father, Moses Gerrish Farmer, was an electrical inventor and professor who boasted more than one hundred patents, including the fire alarm pull box. Under Farmer's energetic direction, the Green Acre Conference had become a summer destination for New England intellectuals to network and discuss the social and political problems of the day while enjoying the stunning views of the Maine coast. Page knew the extent of Farmer's influence among the New England elite. Page astutely passed Farmer's invitation onto Chesnutt, exhibiting the diplomatic skill that he would employ decades later as ambassador to Great Britain. Page likely thought Chesnutt was better qualified to speak on the subject than he was and could use the event to spread the word about *The Conjure Woman*, which had hit bookstores in mid-March.

Chesnutt spoke on the closing day of the conference, Saturday, August 12, 1899, at eight o'clock in the evening. The *Boston Evening Transcript* provided a full, though not verbatim, account of Chesnutt's lecture, calling it one of the best of the season and referred to him as "A Well-Known Story Writer," according to the anonymous "Special Correspondent" who reported on his lecture. The reporter remarked on Chesnutt's eloquence and assessment of slavery. "There was nothing good about slavery. Conceived in iniquity, born in sin, cradled in shame, drowned, it had been believed, in blood, and buried beneath the Constitutional Amendments, slavery still rears its noisome head and poisons the air of this republic."

Chesnutt's own account of the lecture was less bombastic. As he put it in a letter to Page sent a couple of days after returning to Cleveland, "The subject was a little large, and I am afraid I dwelt more on the political and civil status of Negroes in the South and didn't have time to properly consider remedies." Chesnutt seemed a little overwhelmed by the crowd and the event, but noted that his lecture "was vigorously applauded" and that he also "read them a story after the lecture," though neither he nor the special correspondent revealed which of his stories he decided to read to his mostly white audience. Chesnutt was now becoming a regular fixture of the New England literati. He laid the foundation for later years when the *Boston Evening Transcript* published lengthy, glowing reviews of his fiction, and Chesnutt became a favorite of its literary editor, Joseph Edgar Chamberlin, with whom he enjoyed a rewarding friendship. Chesnutt owed Page, at least partly, for his entry into the Bostonian intellectual circle. He was quick to thank Page for the "opportunity" to visit a new part of the country and to get "a number of nice people interested in my work." He concluded the letter on a more personal note, bidding farewell to Page, now that he had left Houghton to work for Doubleday & McClure in New York. "I have to thank you for all this, as another manifestation of the friendship that has resulted in so many good things. I hope that you may find your new work congenial, and am sure that the world will be the gainer by enlargement of your field of opportunity."[4]

It took Page a few months to reply to Chesnutt's warm letter, in which he also hinted that he was still awaiting a response from him on *Rena*. Page had been busy moving to New York City from Boston, and then he had to settle into his new job in the office of Doubleday at Union Square. Doubleday was a different operation from Houghton. It was a relatively new publishing house, started by a partnership between Frank N. Doubleday and S. S. McClure, who had once been, and perhaps still was, a great fan of Chesnutt's stories. The pair had started the firm just a year before they reached out to Page, seeking his financial and editorial expertise in structuring the newly established publishing house. Page was obviously preoccupied by his new post when Chesnutt had written him. Page explained and apologized to Chesnutt for his silence on January 24, 1900. "One change has followed another so rapidly here and the work of getting my family settled has been so much more difficult than I anticipated, and my absences from my desk have been so numerous that I neglected the very things that I cared most to do." This was Page's way of not just apologizing to Chesnutt but also of letting him know that he still cared about him and his work. Now that he had settled into his new office, he had finally found time to reread *Rena* and to share it with his new colleagues, "and we have all read the manuscript with very great pleasure." Page wanted to publish the novel under the imprint of his new firm, but he knew he had to tread carefully; he knew how important *Rena* was to Chesnutt. "My own judgment about it has been confirmed by the judgment of my partners, and I write to ask whether you care for it to be brought out by us. I ask this because I do not have the slightest wish to draw you away from Houghton, Mifflin and Company who are my good friends as well as yours, but since you had this submitted there once and it was declined, I do not know what your feeling is about re-submitting it; and so I put the question to you with directness and frankness."[5]

Chesnutt was so overcome with joy and relief while reading the letter he could barely read the rest. He started getting ready to go see Page in New York. Chesnutt wanted to discuss the terms of the contract with him in person, to think about resubmitting to Houghton, and the new title Page had suggested for the novel. "We all agree," Page wrote, "that the best title is *The House Behind the Cedars*." There was so much to think about, so much to do. He telegraphed Page, told him he had received his letter and wanted to discuss the terms of publication in person. He started to pack. He went to look for Susan, told her the good news and that he was going to take a train to New York, probably the following day, or that day, if he could get one. She wasn't thrilled, as she complained to Ethel and Helen after he left. "Your father has just left for New York, so we are alone once more. He intended to go East the first of February, but received a letter from Mr. Page yesterday about publishing his novel *Rena*, and as Mr. Page wished to know at once, he concluded he had better go on so they could talk the matter over before deciding."[6]

As Chesnutt boarded the train, Page's words were still floating before his eyes: "I congratulate you on the local color and the accuracy of your descriptions of the town and the country. You seem to have caught the very spirit of the whole community. Then, too, the story of Rena herself is most admirably and dramatically unfolded."[7] He had done it. Finally, after years of writing, revising, rejection, and more revising, Chesnutt had finished *Rena*. He had written a novel, and, according to Page, a really good novel, maybe even a great one. Page would know. He was, as many at the time believed, the best literary editor in the country, regardless of which firm employed him. Chesnutt trusted Page's opinion more than anyone else's, more than George Cable's or Tourgée's, and certainly more than that aloof New Yorker Gilder, with whom he had little in common. Page knew the South like he did, and he had always told him the truth about his writing. Could his long hours of work and worry be finally paying off? It seemed almost too good to be true.

The House Behind the Cedars had started out as a longish short story. Set in Patesville, Chesnutt's pseudonym for Fayetteville, like that of so many of his stories, this story's plot focused on two characters. Mis' Molly, "a free colored woman who was despised by the whites for her taint of negro blood and envied by the blacks for her fairness of complexion and her material prosperity."[8] Though Mis' Molly never married, she had entered an intimate relationship with a white man, "an ex-member of congress, the owner of a large plantation." When this man, called "Mr. Ferrebee" in one version of the story, died, he left Mis' Molly with a house and several children, "there was but one daughter," whom he named Rowena, after the heroine of Walter Scott's popular romance novel *Ivanhoe*. But everyone called her Rena because it "was easier to say." The allusion to Scott's romances was central to Chesnutt's portrayal of the South. As the novel's narrator explained: "The influence of Walter Scott was strong upon the old South. The South before the war was essentially feudal, and Scott's novels of chivalry appealed forcefully to the feudal heart." Though her name derived from Scott's Scottish romance, Rena Walden and the post-slavery South in which her story was set seemed to be light-years away from the Anglo-Saxon medieval world of *Ivanhoe*.

Once Chesnutt introduced his heroine, the narrator focused his attention on her beauty and devotion to her mother. Chesnutt's original unnamed narrator told the tragic story from a distance, related to the action only tangentially, as someone who had known Mis' Molly and heard the story. He related the tragic story in the objective third-person voice, describing the details of Rena's marriage, poorly arranged by Mis' Molly, to a fair-skinned colored man who misrepresents himself as a man of wealth and property. Rena seemed to prefer the company of a kind-hearted Black man named Frank Fowler, but Mis' Molly refused any "so-cial intercourse between the two households, the one family was black, the other 'light-complexioned.'" Chesnutt's early story of "Rena" is about an unhappy marriage caused by a commitment to endogamy—the custom of marrying only within the limits of one's local community—among light-complexioned colored people in the South, that leads almost inevitably to the heroine's death.

The novel that was finally published by Houghton, Mifflin and Company in late October 1900 was a different story. After sharing early versions with Cable, Page, and others at the publishing house, *Rena* had become a love story between a beautiful, fair-complexioned colored woman and a wealthy white man from South Carolina. Aside from the changes in the marriage plot, Chesnutt decided to include another character, John Walden, Rena's older brother, who had left home years before the story be-gins to pass as a white man. The story is told mostly from his point of view. John is also the architect of his sister's romance with George Tryon, while his mother unwittingly ruins the romance because of her commitment to outmoded racial categories. The changes to the story's plot were intended to broaden its scope and appeal to white readers, though the results for the novel's central characters were mostly the same. Rena still winds up shar-ing a home with the wrong man and dies, but her tragic fate is caused not only by her mother's "ambitions" that "Rena should make a good match," wanting her to marry a "smart" man and a man of substance. The tragedy is also caused by George Tryon, the white man who falls in love with Rena and breaks off their engagement when he learns of her association with "the colored race." The novel's penultimate chapter, entitled "The Power of Love," reveals George's folly, that he has chosen race over love, to his eternal detriment. The reader is left with a warning not to repeat George's mistake; instead they, presumably white men like George, should follow their hearts rather than the laws and customs of race. Despite its uplifting moral message, *The House Behind the Cedars* is a sad tale, and those readers in search of a satisfying happily-ever-after marriage plot would have found the ending disappointing, even downright dispiriting.

There is no formal record of the conversation between Chesnutt and Page that took place on January 27, 1900. But Chesnutt did provide Susan with a brief account of it. After all, he owed her some explanation for his absence and when he would return home.

> Got here all right, and saw my man. They are real anxious to publish *Rena*, but I will not let them know until I have been to Boston where I think I shall go tomorrow afternoon. I don't need to worry about getting publishers at present.
>
> Page is a fine fellow, wants my novel and wants it bad, but doesn't want it unless I want him to have it. Leaves it all to me, and if I say so will publish spring or fall, as I say. This is between us—you and me, of course.[9]

Chesnutt went off to Boston to tell them that Doubleday wanted his novel but that he would hold off from publishing with them if Houghton decided they wanted to publish it, too. For the first time in his career, Chesnutt was in a position of power: he was negotiating with publishers, he was in the driver's seat; he could go with New York or Boston. After his meeting in Boston, he did not go home to Cleveland as he'd planned. Instead, he returned to New York not only to see Page again but also to meet with William Dean Howells. Once again, he wrote to Susan to explain his absence:

> Am in this village again. Had an interview with the famous Mr. Howells this morning. He is going to write me up for the *Atlantic*. Have got my name on the books of all the lecture bureaus from Major Pond down. Made a speech in Boston yesterday.
>
> I may stay over here until Monday, or may go home sometime tomorrow. Saw T. Thomas Fortune today, and some other folks, I may go by Northampton and see the girls, but as the chances are that I shall come back East in March, I may wait until then before seeing them. Will write you again. Hope you and children are well.[10]

We don't know if Susan responded to this breathless letter. It seems unlikely since he had promised to return home the following day, which, this time, he did. He explained to Helen and Ethel that he could not visit with them in Northampton as he'd hoped because he had to "hurry home," catching the next train from New York to Cleveland, expecting to arrive "there 9:30 tomorrow a.m." It was a whirlwind trip that had convinced him that he had finally *arrived*, metaphorically speaking. He had met with Page and Howells in New York, Francis Jackson Garrison at Houghton in Boston. Though the January days during his travels were bitterly cold, he hardly noticed while enjoying conversation with these literary men. But he needed to get home, he had to "hustle" the "MS of a certain novel in the shortest time possible" and had "to send that tuition money" to Smith, which, as Susan surely reminded him, he had neglected to pay before leaving home.

When Chesnutt returned to Cleveland on February 5, 1900, a more purposeful and experienced writer than when he had left a week before, he had to deal with various household matters. Edwin, or Ned, as the family called him, was getting ready to graduate and enter Harvard, and Susan was feeling lonely. It was a long winter, and she comforted herself in Chesnutt's absence by making summer plans. She wanted to rent a cottage for the summer, where the children could play on the beach and she could entertain her friends. But Chesnutt was preoccupied by preparing the novel, writing new stories for publication, and lecturing. Aside from Howells's glowing review of his stories, there was also a piece about him in *The Outlook* by the well-known literary journalist Hamilton Wright Mabie under the title "Two New Novelists" that appeared a couple of weeks after he returned home, on February 24. Chesnutt was gratified by Mabie's attention and appreciation of "the artistic value" of his work. Despite the accolades, he was still not making enough money to pay the bills, and his family expenses seemed to be growing daily. He wrote to his daughters in early March, enclosing a bank draft to cover their expenses and explained that he had "been working downtown for the last ten days, in an old matter, left over." Even though he had given up his court reporting business, Chesnutt was still working as a shorthand reporter while writing stories. It was impossible for him not to. He told Helen and Ethel that he considered this work "not an unpleasant diversion," because it helped him to pay the bills. But Chesnutt would later complain to Edward Williams, Ethel's future husband and already a good family friend, that the work was a "vulgar toil" he was forced to take on in order "to pay the rent for our summer cottage."[11]

Everything was happening all at once. The children were growing up, he was about to publish his first novel, he had been recognized as a great writer by the foremost literary critic in the country, but the money he was bringing in from writing was not enough. He was sure that when *The House Behind the Cedars* was published, he could slow down. The money from the novel would be enough to pay the bills. The year 1900 was big. He was, after all, on the cusp of a new century. Chesnutt was forty-two and poised to become a novelist, a great writer like his heroes Dumas, Dickens, and Thackeray, not just another colored writer.

After some back-and-forth with Page at Doubleday and Garrison at Houghton, Chesnutt decided to stay at Houghton. Though the publishing house had not too long ago rejected *Rena*, Chesnutt remained partial to the tradition and history Houghton, Mifflin and Company represented. Garrison was the son of the famed Boston abolitionist William Lloyd Garrison, and Chesnutt wanted to be part of that literary tradition. A lot had changed in a year. Garrison informed Chesnutt of the firm's decision on March 24, 1900. "We have decided to take *Rena* (under the title *The House Behind the Cedars*) in place of *The Rainbow Chasers*, and to publish it next fall on the same terms as *The Wife of His Youth*, with the understanding and agreement that this shall be the only book of yours published this year, and understanding that this will be agreeable to you, we shall forward the contracts to you at Cleveland early next week."[12] This was not exactly a form letter. It was brief, to the point, and bore, mostly, good news. But the warmth, camaraderie, and support that characterized his correspondence with Page was missing. Of course, Chesnutt did not know Garrison the way he knew, and liked, Page. He supposed he would develop a relationship with this new editor over time, after he signed the contract and worked with him on any changes to the book they had accepted. But in accepting

Rena, they had rejected another short novel he had submitted previously to *The Atlantic* as a serial called *The Rainbow Chasers*.

Garrison also made the unusual request that this should be "the only book" of Chesnutt's to be published that year. The terms of their acceptance were not entirely unfavorable, but Garrison insisted that in accepting *The House Behind the Cedars*, Chesnutt was to work with Houghton *exclusively*. They knew he had been still talking to Page at Doubleday, who, while they were considering his novel, was soliciting him to write a new, expanded "life of Douglass," for an "ambitious biographical plan" that he was cooking up in New York. "A biography is not going to sell, of course, to the same extent that fiction sells, but we expect to make a success of this series by keeping it alive over a long period of years,"[13] Page told him. He also assured Chesnutt that "there would be no conflict between this book and your little book in the Beacon Series." That "little book" was the first biography of Douglass that Chesnutt had written, which had been out for about a year. Page felt that its publication had made Chesnutt an authority on the subject, believing that he "can make a most interesting contribution to the history of the anti-slavery agitation." But once the letter from Garrison arrived, about a month after Page's offer, Chesnutt decided against Page's plan. Page was now working for the competition. He had committed to Houghton not just because of their prestige but also so that his new novel could find a home among his earlier works. The same day that he received Garrison's letter, he wrote to his daughters: "*Rena* will be published early next fall by Houghton, Mifflin and Co. I thought best to keep the three southern books together, and they asked the privilege of reconsidering *Rena*."[14] He seemed now to consider these three books as a kind of Southern trilogy—*The Conjure Woman*, *The Wife of His Youth*, and *The House Behind the Cedars*. This was the way Chesnutt rationalized his decision. The books should be read together, as developing a singular theme, the ways in which state-sanctioned racial divisions inhibited, even destroyed, human relationships. Chesnutt's decision to stick with Houghton as his publisher for his third book was a big one, with numerous ramifications.

Chesnutt had been treated well by Houghton. He had always enjoyed his association with one of the oldest and most prestigious literary presses in the country and found their connection with *The Atlantic* convenient for his purpose. Doubleday, Page & Company was a newer, much smaller operation. In its first year of publication, they put out about sixty books, compared with Houghton's ninety. The plan Page offered was attractive, but it was risky. With his wife and children to support, Chesnutt could not afford to take such a risk. He knew Page would respect his decision and their friendship would remain intact, despite the slight snub. So he did what he thought best for *Rena* and especially for his family. Once the decision was made, he turned his attention to writing something new, political *nonfiction* essays, that would give *Rena* some historical context; *The House Behind the Cedars* was to be published, at long last, on October 27, 1900. Chesnutt received his advance copy the following day from the press and was thrilled by its "very handsome dress." The book was beautiful, the ideal cover for the story of its tragic heroine, Rena. But there was still the question of how the novel, "a story of a colored girl who passed for white," as he "bluntly" put it in a letter to Harry D. Robins, would sell.[15]

Now that Page was no longer his man at Houghton, the question of how to market Chesnutt's new book had to be answered. Page had made a reputation for himself not only as an astute editor but also as a salesman. He was an editor who thought just as much about how to sell a book as to what made a book worth reading. Without Page directing the marketing of Chesnutt's novel at Houghton, the task fell to a relatively unknown member of its staff, Harry Douglas Robins. Robins was fairly new at the press, having joined the staff about a year earlier in the fall of 1899. Shortly after his arrival, he had become involved in helping to market Chesnutt's previous book, *The Wife of His Youth*. Unlike Page, Robins was keen on emphasizing the racial content of Chesnutt's fiction over its Southern realism, believing that with the recent publication of Booker T. Washington's book *The Future of the American Negro* and what he called "the public notice attracted to the general subject of the colored people," the firm should appeal to this relatively new public interest. In deciding on a marketing plan for Chesnutt's novel, Robins seemed to be at something of a loss. This was a novel about colored people *passing*; it featured a white man as the colored heroine's lover and potential husband. It was essentially a love story between a Black woman and a white man. This was not the kind of story about colored people that would, Robins expected, appeal to general readers, readers interested in stories of resilience and triumph in the style of Booker T. Washington's life story. This was a novel that, as Robins believed, would "in certain quarters raise a commotion."

Chesnutt appeared to be confused and a little irritated by Robins's request for his "cooperation in presenting" *The House Behind the Cedars* to the public. He told Robins that he knew of readers in Cleveland and Washington, DC, who were interested in his books but knew less about readers in other American cities such as Boston and New York, or Philadelphia and Chicago. He also made clear to Robins, who seemed still to want to push Chesnutt's "racial identity," that his book was not just about race. He elaborated: "I rather hope it will sell in spite of its subject, or rather, because of its dramatic value apart from the race problem involved. I was trying to write, primarily, an interesting and artistic story, rather than a contribution to polemical discussion." Shortly after it was released, Chesnutt remained skeptical of Robins's marketing strategies. On November 19, he wrote a short letter to Robins that began, "I hope you are doing what you can to call attention to *The House Behind the Cedars*." Even after meeting Robins on his last visit to Boston and being impressed by the "very handsome and appropriate dress" that were given by the press to the novel, Chesnutt remained unsure about Robins. "I did not see it mentioned at all in any of your advertisements in the New York papers of November 11th," he complained. He went on to remind Robins of the novel's quality. "The verdict around here is that it is a novel of the sort that one having begun doesn't want to lay down until its finished: and the least friendly of the few criticisms I have seen concerning it admits that it is a well constructed novel." Chesnutt seemed not to trust either Robins's marketing skills or his ability to recognize a good novel from a bad one. Robins had obviously not read the novel closely, at least not as closely as Page had. "I hope it is one of those novels that will work its way on its merits, which is of course the best sort of success."[16]

Of course, Chesnutt was anxious for *The House Behind the Cedars* to sell well. It was his first novel, and he had put his heart and soul into it. He also needed the money from its sales to fund his writing career. If sales were poor, he would have to return to court reporting sooner rather than later. Relatively speaking, the novel had sold well. Compared to Theodore

Dreiser's first novel, *Sister Carrie*, published the same year by Page at his new firm, *The House Behind the Cedars* was a success. Dreiser's novel had sold around 750 copies, compared to Chesnutt's almost 3,000. But like Dreiser, Chesnutt was disappointed by the novel's sales. As with Dreiser's controversial novel concerning the life and love stories of its unlikely heroine, the public did not seem to welcome the tragic story of love and race Chesnutt told in *The House Behind the Cedars*; it did not yield widespread attention, despite its critical acclaim. As Helen recalled, "although the book had gone into its fourth printing by April, Chesnutt was not satisfied, he had hoped for a much larger sale."[17]

Despite the novel's disappointing sales, Chesnutt was proud of his work. Shortly after its release, he had Houghton send copies to his father in Fayetteville and his daughters in Northampton. This was a novel about his past and his future. It held love and marriage against racial boundaries, so long as its readers, unlike its hapless characters, followed their hearts. Several months after it was published, when Chesnutt had moved on to writing a new novel, he received a short note from Horace Scudder, the former editor at *The Atlantic* and at Houghton, who had been skeptical of Chesnutt's literary abilities. It had been a few years since he'd spoken to Scudder, since Page took over editing the magazine back in 1898. He'd heard from Page that Scudder had been ill. Chesnutt was surprised by Scudder's letter. He opened the envelope and read its contents with a feeling of worry and anticipation.

My dear Mr. Chesnutt:

I have been ill this past five months, and am only slowly
recovering my usual vigor. I had many thoughts as I lay on my
bed, and among others I thought of you and your work, and
remembered that I had never written to tell you how much I
admired your skill in making the change in the plot of the *House
Behind the Cedars*. I found fault with the earlier version, but in this
I think you have retained the magic element which marked the
book in its first form and have given a more reasonable and far
less irritating dénouement. As a work of art, the book seems to

me to have gained distinctly, and as I said I admire greatly the literary skill which could so remodel the book. This faculty of seeing one's work from another's point of view is not common and argues well certainly for your power to do things in more than one way![18]

Chesnutt had tears in his eyes as he read the last sentence. The use of the exclamation point to conclude was a nice touch. He hardly ever employed the effusive punctuation mark in his own writing. He had always approached Scudder with trepidation, believing him to be something of a literary snob. But there had been nothing to fear. Scudder was a man of generosity, literary talent, and sympathy. Scudder died a few months later, unable to read Chesnutt's second novel. Chesnutt wondered if he would have liked it as much as he did *The House Behind the Cedars*.

12

Future Americans

I hope you will see my new novel, "The House Behind the Cedars," which runs along the "color line." My next book on the subject will be square up to date, & will deal with the negro's right to live rather than his right to love.

—Chesnutt to Booker T. Washington, October 29, 1900

In late 1899, just after his first three books were published—two short story collections by Houghton, Mifflin and Company and a biography of Frederick Douglass by Small, Maynard & Company—Chesnutt was asked to review Booker T. Washington's first book. Of course, Chesnutt had been aware of Washington well before he published *The Future of the American Negro*. Washington had gained a great deal of attention as founder and principal of the Tuskegee Institute in Alabama back in the early 1880s. Washington distinguished Tuskegee by emphasizing "education in theoretical and practical agriculture, horticulture, dairying, and stock-raising," which he believed were essential skills for "lifting up any race." But it wasn't until September 1895, seven months after Frederick Douglass's death, that Washington was thrust into the national spotlight with his now-infamous speech delivered at the Cotton States and International Exposition in Atlanta.

It was here Washington presented a full-throated defense of racial segregation. His speech was attended by thousands, including reporters from all the major newspapers in the country. A single sentence from the speech would become Washington's ideological trademark: "In all things that are purely social we can be as separate as the fingers, yet one as the hand in all things essential to mutual progress."[1] The speech catapulted Washington to the center of American culture and politics. A month after the Supreme Court delivered its verdict in the *Plessy v. Ferguson* case, Washington received an honorary degree from Harvard University on June 24, 1896. A few years later, Doubleday and Page brought out his autobiography *Up from Slavery*, detailing his rise from slavery, illiteracy, and poverty to developing one of the most successful institutions for higher education in the South. Calling the book and the man both "remarkable," Howells's glowing review of *Up from Slavery*, published shortly after its release in the August 1901 issue of the *North American Review*, compared Washington's autobiography approvingly to Chesnutt's biography of Douglass.[2] Washington's accomplishments told in "simple prose" and Chesnutt's rendering of Douglass's in "heroic poetry" were proof, Howells maintained, that there was "no color line in the brain."[3]

Booker T. Washington's popularity among Black and white audiences led Theodore Roosevelt, who had just become the U.S. president after the assassination of President William McKinley on September 14, 1901, to invite him to the White House for dinner. The presidential invitation was intended to be a symbolic gesture of healing and renewal after McKinley's violent death. But the presence of the Black Washington in the White House had the opposite effect. The mainstream press lambasted Roosevelt for crossing the color line so openly. As the most popular Black man in the country, Washington was controversial. Perhaps it was this quality that Chesnutt both admired and feared. When asked by Harry Robins in December 1899 if he could reach out to Washington for a blurb or review to help Houghton publicize *The Wife of His Youth, and Other Stories of the Color Line* to Southern audiences, Chesnutt responded with ambivalence and caution. "About Booker Washington, I don't know. Anything he might say would doubtless be valuable, if he would venture to express himself favorably on a book supposed from the Southern standpoint to preach heretical doctrine. Perhaps one ought not to ask him, however, until the Southern reviews come in." The "heretical doctrine" Chesnutt was alluding to was relationships between individuals, ideally through marriage, that crossed established racial barriers, a central theme of his fiction at this time. Chesnutt, like those who had heard or read Washington's speeches in the papers, knew that Washington's work at Tuskegee required him to toe the color line.

Yet Chesnutt and Washington were alike in many ways. Though Washington's skin was a shade darker than Chesnutt's, his father, as far as he knew, was a white man and so would have been considered, like Chesnutt, to be a "mixed blood Negro." The two men found common cause in their commitment to higher education as a method for reforming the conditions of the South. Though they wrote in different styles and from a different vantage point about the South, Walter Hines Page had strongly supported both Washington's and Chesnutt's work as their editor. Both were voracious readers, both were mostly self-taught, both worked as educators in the South, and both served as principals of colored normal schools. Washington's essay "The Case of the Negro" appeared in the same November 1899 issue of *The Atlantic* as Chesnutt's short story, "The Bouquet." While Washington's essay expounded the benefits of industrial education, Chesnutt's story developed a relationship between a Southern white woman who decides to take a position as a teacher at a "colored school."

Mary Myrover in the story becomes enamored with one of her pupils, a dark-skinned girl named Sophy Tucker. Mary senses Sophy's devotion to her, and in return, Mary sympathizes with her student. Mary's sympathy, however, does not diminish the racial superiority that lingers in her view of Sophy. Despite their differences, the two form a close and complex bond. That bond is soon broken by the teacher's untimely death and Mary's mother refusing Sophy an opportunity to pay her respects to her dead teacher at her home. When Sophy arrives at the cemetery to lay a bouquet of her teacher's favorite flowers on her grave, she is met with "a small sign in white letters on a black background—'Notice. This cemetery is for white people only. Others please keep out.'" The irony of the sign is not only the primary colors, which reinforce its message of racial segregation. It is also the fact that "Sophy, thanks to Miss Myrover's painstaking instruction, could read this sign very distinctly." What harm was there in Sophy laying the bouquet on her teacher's grave? The sign is a cruel, though relatively minor, injustice in the grand scheme of racial segregation. But it was a moving one. Sophy and her teacher would be insignificant figures in the political debates raging in the country over education and race, yet it was their story, rather than a story about grand institutions and social policies, that Chesnutt wanted to tell. Chesnutt had originally submitted "The Bouquet" to *The Youth's Companion* in early April 1899. But that magazine rejected it, "less on account of its handling the difficult subject of race than because its quality is perhaps too delicate for an audience so large and varied as *The Companion's*."[4] It would be included in Chesnutt's book of *Stories of the Color Line* with an illustration by the artist Clyde O. DeLand, memorializing Sophy at the cemetery. Though Washington's story was delivered in a more straightforward manner than Chesnutt's "delicate" story of racial segregation, Page felt that both Chesnutt's and Washington's stories needed to be told and read together to form a completer picture of the problem.

It is somewhat surprising Chesnutt and Washington became friends, given their differences over how best to solve the race problem still dividing the United States. It was not an easy friendship; it was one that required considerable generosity and negotiation on both sides. Washington came to have a special place in the Chesnutt family. Upon graduation, Chesnutt's daughters Ethel and Helen would both work at Tuskegee under Washington's guidance. Ethel started working for Washington in 1901, while Helen made her way there a few years later, after completing a second degree at Columbia University. Washington ensured they were well taken care of and well paid. Chesnutt's only son, Edwin, would later follow in his older sisters' footsteps, taking a job as Washington's personal stenographer, transcribing his speeches and business correspondence to earn money before continuing his education in dentistry. Washington seemed to adore Chesnutt's children, considering them models for the staff and students at Tuskegee on account of their professional manner. It was Washington who initiated the friendship when he extended an invitation to Chesnutt to visit him at his home on October 19, 1900. When Chesnutt accepted Washington's invitation to visit Tuskegee in February 1901, he returned with greater appreciation for Washington's accomplishments. He called Tuskegee "a revelation," remarking on the efficiency and cleanliness of the school Washington had built. But their first meeting occurred a few years before, on Chesnutt's home turf in Cleveland.

In the first and least well known of Washington's autobiographies, *The*

Story of My Life and Work, published a year before *Up from Slavery,* he related a humorous anecdote about their first encounter.

> A year or so ago I took lunch in Cleveland with Mr. Chesnutt him-
> self. That was before his books had called world-wide attention to
> his color. I had read his stories in the Atlantic and said: "Tell me,
> Mr. Chesnutt, how did you ever come to know the Northern dar-
> key so well?" Mr. Chesnutt replied that he had had rather unusual
> opportunities for observing the Northern darkey at close range.
> Six months later I learned I had the pleasure of lunching with a
> cultured "Negro," and that Mr. Chesnutt had been bubbling with
> merriment ever since. I did not suspect it at the time.[5]

Washington did not explain the occasion for their lunch date. Perhaps it was as *Atlantic* authors they had come together in Cleveland. Perhaps he had been invited to give one of his stirring speeches to a crowd of Clevelanders, which included Chesnutt. Whatever the occasion for their meeting, it was unusual that Chesnutt chose not to reveal himself as a "colored man" to Washington, as he had to George Washington Cable when the two had met not too long before in Cleveland. Perhaps he felt he didn't need to. From the story Washington told about their meeting, it seemed that Chesnutt could joke around with Washington in a way he could not with Cable. For all the seriousness of their later disagreements, particularly regarding voting rights, their friendship was characterized by a camaraderie, even playfulness, absent from Chesnutt's friendships with other authors.

Washington's anecdote about meeting Chesnutt first appeared in print in the pages of the *Boston Evening Transcript* on August 25, 1900. It was part of Washington's speech to the National Negro Business League at their first meeting in Boston at Parker Memorial Hall. When the anecdote re-appeared in Washington's first autobiography, he decided not to mention the occasion or the context for his remarks. In the summer of 1900, when Washington was speaking in Boston, Chesnutt had been writing a series of essays under the title "The Future American" that had become something of a literary sensation among Bostonians. Aware of Chesnutt's popularity among his audience, Washington decided to invoke his personal connection to the author. He prefaced his remarks about his meeting with Chesnutt in his speech by referring to "The Future American" essays, suggesting the controversy they had stirred up. "Readers of Mr. Charles W. Chesnutt's current series in the Transcript would view that colored Southerner with a keen ethnological interest."[6] Washington was suggesting that Chesnutt *embodied* the ideas he presented in his theory of the future American. But leaving out the reference to Chesnutt's "series in the Transcript" caused readers of Washington's autobiography to wonder what Chesnutt was doing in the story of his life. Perhaps Washington wanted to avoid stirring up controversy by mentioning the essays that went against his strategy of compliance when it came to the racial segregation issue.

Following their first meeting, Chesnutt would play an increasingly important role in Washington's life, helping him to shape and defend his theory of education. Chesnutt's appearance and writing seemed to beguile, even undermine, Washington's theory of "the American Negro." Chesnutt wrote on topics like those Washington wrote and spoke about, but his writing was different in form and purpose. Published in the fall of 1899, around the same time and by the same publisher as Chesnutt's biography of Frederick Douglass, Washington's *The Future of the American Negro* is a curious amalgam of his speeches and articles, written after his Atlanta exposition address. Historians view the book as central to Washington's political career as it constitutes the "most inclusive and systematic statement of his social philosophy and racial strategy."[7] Washington's description of the future relied, in large part, on understanding the relationship between the past and present. Though Washington never claimed to be a historian in the conventional sense of the term, he began his study of *The Future of the American Negro* with a history lesson that today would be considered textbook.

> The first slaves were brought into this country by the Dutch in 1619, and were landed at Jamestown, Virginia. The first cargo consisted of twenty. The census taken in 1890 shows that these twenty slaves had increased to 7,638,360. About 6,353,341 of this number were residing in the Southern States, and 1,283,029 were scattered

throughout the Northern and Western States. I think I am pretty safe in predicting that the census to be taken in 1900 will show that there are not far from ten millions of people of African descent in the United States. The great majority of these, of course, reside in the Southern States.[8]

Washington's prediction of the growth of "people of African descent in the United States" became his raison d'être. Someone would have to help organize and administer to the needs of this growing body of the population. Who better than someone who had experienced life as both a slave and freeman? Washington believed that his plan for the industrial education of people of African descent, based almost entirely on his personal experience as described in his later autobiography, would bring about economic prosperity. A commitment to industrial education would serve not only those classed as "Black" in the 1900 U.S. census; industrial education had the potential to serve all Americans, regardless of their race or country of origin.

In the final months of the nineteenth century, Chesnutt "was on the go all the time." He was traveling throughout the Atlantic Seaboard, from Maine to Washington, DC, giving lectures and reading stories. He began to gain a reputation "as a wit" in his speaking style and was receiving requests to address audiences almost daily. Just before the turn of the century, when *The House Behind the Cedars* was positively reviewed and accepted for publication, he accepted a couple of invitations to review *The Future of the American Negro*. Chesnutt was considered an ideal reviewer. As the editor of *The Critic* explained: "Mr. Chesnutt is particularly well equipped for the writing of Mr. Washington's book. By birth he belongs in part to the race of which it treats, and by education, in pedagogy and the law, he brings sympathy and intelligence to bear upon the subject."[9] Curiously, that assessment of Chesnutt's "sympathy and intelligence" was based on his work as a teacher and lawyer, rather than on the publication of his own books and articles. Chesnutt accepted both requests to write about Washington, seeming to enjoy the opportunities afforded him from his growing literary reputation. He also approved of Washington's work and was ready to ally himself with Washington publicly. "Dr. Washington has a great deal of ability, and I have no doubt will succeed in endowing Tuskegee handsomely; and his idea will doubtless spread and be fruitful of good," he wrote to his future son-in-law Edward Williams months before reading Washington's book. Despite his support of Washington's "idea," Chesnutt also expressed misgivings about Washington's narrow, even shortsighted, point of view when it came to his vision of *The Future*.[10]

In his review for *The Saturday Evening Post*, Chesnutt christened Washington "the prophet of the practical."[11] The future usually signals the unknown, a time far beyond our own, so far beyond what we know it can only be *imagined*. Though the future is related to an assessment of the past, it is often imagined as something new, a break with the past. But Washington's rendering of the future, for Chesnutt, was still stuck in the past; he "indulges in no flights of fancy, no gilded speculations about the condition of the American Negro generations hence; indeed, the author frankly dismisses the question as one that does not concern him." Chesnutt determined Washington's *Future* not to be about the future at all since he "gives to the present a large part of his attention."[12] As a book about the present, Chesnutt found it to be "a logical and forceful" defense of Washington's "theory of the industrial education of the Negro." In a second review published about a month later in *The Critic* entitled "A Plea for the American Negro," Chesnutt delved more deeply into the shortcomings of Washington's theory.

> This volume, which is Mr. Washington's first extended utterance in book form, cannot fail to enhance his reputation for ability, wisdom, and patriotism. It is devoted to a somewhat wide consideration of the race problem, avoiding some of its delicate features, perhaps, but emphasizing certain of its more obvious phases. The author has practically nothing to say about caste prejudice, the admixture of races, or the remote future of the Negro, but simply takes up the palpable problem of ignorance and poverty as he finds it in the South.[13]

For those looking for an account of "the Negro's" present conditions, Chesnutt suggested, "the book is in all respects worthy of the attention of thoughtful minds." But those looking for insights into the "remote future," "caste prejudice," and "the admixture of races" would have to look elsewhere. Washington could hardly have expected that Chesnutt's reviews would become his way of teeing up his own vision of the future, one that would take up the thorny issues that Washington couldn't tackle for fear of upsetting Tuskegee's donors. Reading and writing about Washington's future seemed to inspire Chesnutt to publish his own thoughts about the future. But in writing about the future, Chesnutt would do what Washington avoided: he would indulge in flights of fancy and gilded speculations. What he came up with went so far beyond the conventions of his (and our) present that it sent shock waves through the thoughtful minds that read "The Future American" essays when they first appeared in the pages of the *Boston Evening Transcript* in the summer of 1900.

Chesnutt's association with the *Boston Evening Transcript*, the largest daily paper in New England, had begun a couple of years before the publication of his "Future American" essays. It all started with the Boston journalist Joseph Edgar Chamberlin, who had become a huge fan of Chesnutt's fiction. Chamberlin likely attended Chesnutt's lecture and reading at Green Acre Farm in Maine in the summer of 1899. Shortly after, Chamberlin wrote to him, inviting him to his home in Wrentham, Massachusetts, known to locals as Red Farm. It had become a gathering place for an eclectic group of writers, artists, and thinkers of the time, including the young Helen Keller and the elderly Unitarian minister and author Edward Everett Hale, whose stories Chesnutt admired. While his daughters were attending Smith in Northampton, Chesnutt made frequent trips to Red Farm and encouraged Ethel and Helen to do the same, which they did. Just a short train ride out from Boston, Red Farm became a kind of intellectual retreat for Chesnutt, where he spent hours, sometimes days, chatting with the Chamberlins, Ed, his wife, Ida, and their five children. When Chesnutt met him in 1899, Chamberlin was well known for his humorous Listener column, which was a regular feature of the *Transcript*. He was also an editor at the nationally distributed *Youth's Companion* magazine in which one of Chesnutt's stories, "Aunt Mimy's Son," appeared in its March 1900 issue. That same month, Chesnutt, as he explained to his wife, "went out to Wrentham, Massachusetts with my friend, Mr. Chamberlin, of the *Boston*

Transcript, and stayed all night."[14] The two friends had stayed up all night talking about books, politics, and the future.

Almost a decade older than Chesnutt, Chamberlin came from an old, but not wealthy, New England family. They were Republican and abolitionist. Chamberlin had recently completed a biography of the radical abolitionist John Brown, who had been executed on December 2, 1859, for leading a raid on the federal armory in Harpers Ferry, Virginia. Chamberlin's biography was one of the first published about the radical leader and was released around the same time and by the same publisher as Chesnutt's on Douglass. The two books were considered, like their authors, companions. Even though Chamberlin had never traveled to the South, he and Chesnutt held a common view of culture and education. Neither had been to college, though both had wanted to go. Chamberlin's description of his unconventional education could just as well have described Chesnutt's experience: "When a boy passionately desires an education, unquestionably he obtains it in some sort, college or no college."[15]

That night in March, Chesnutt told Chamberlin about Rena and his novel *The House Behind the Cedars.* At the time of the visit, Chesnutt was still waiting on Houghton's response; though he knew, given Page's positive response, its publication was imminent. Chamberlin sat spellbound listening to Chesnutt narrate Rena's tragic love story. The two men talked about their own marriages. Chamberlin was having marital trouble of his own with his wife, Ida. It was not too long after their conversation that Chamberlin left his wife and the idyllic views of Red Farm behind him. He moved to New York City by himself to report for Chesnutt's former employer the *Mail and Express.* Both Chesnutt and Chamberlin had married young; their wives had been even younger. Chesnutt still considered himself lucky in his marriage, but he worried about his children, especially his three daughters.

Around this time, Ethel, his oldest, had become engaged to her longtime sweetheart, Edward Williams. Chesnutt always enjoyed his company; he was smart, well read, and decent. Edward was considered Black even though his mother was considered white. It wasn't clear how Edward's mother, Mary Kilkary, with Irish Catholic roots, had met his father, Daniel Williams. They were both living in Cleveland and had fallen in love despite all the barriers to their relationship. It was nothing short of a miracle that they'd gotten married and raised their fine son, who would go on to study library science at New York University; he and Ethel later moved to Washington, DC, where he became head librarian at Howard University and published a novel of his own that was surely influenced by his ongoing conversations with his father-in-law. Edward was handsome, with smooth brown skin, a Roman nose, slightly darker, and a few years older than Ethel. They made an attractive couple. Chesnutt was delighted by their union and looked forward to becoming a grandfather in a few years.

Thinking about Ethel and Edward got him thinking about Helen and Dorothy. What if they weren't so lucky? Who would they marry, and where would they live? Would they too have the good fortune to meet someone with Edward's intelligence, good looks, and prospects? What if one of them fell in love with a white man? Of course he wanted his children to be happy, to marry whomever they chose, but he knew from experience and his knowledge of the law that marrying someone outside their tightly knit colored Cleveland community would limit their opportunities, would change the whole course of their lives. Edward was a fine fellow, but his parents had struggled against prejudice just for falling in love. It seemed ridiculous, this stigma, these laws, that prohibited marriages just because of perceived racial differences. On and on Chesnutt talked, while Chamberlin listened to him ramble about love, marriage, race, and caste prejudice until it really was time to go. He still had to get back to New York to talk with Page after his visit with the Chamberlins. He said goodbye to Ida, who was sick in bed, but had insisted on seeing Chesnutt before he left. They were, as he told Susan, "lovely people."[16]

A couple of months after returning home, while "struggling with a careful revision of *Rena*" in mid-May, a letter from Chamberlin arrived. As literary editor of the *Transcript*, Chamberlin was in search of new material, something that might attract the attention of the elite Boston crowd who subscribed to the paper. There was quite a lot of chatter about a new book by a Harvard professor. William Z. Ripley's *The Races of Europe*, published in 1899, had become widely read, and Ripley was giving lectures at Harvard and other locations in and around Boston to promote the book. Recalling their conversation at Red Farm about marriage and race, Chamberlin asked if Chesnutt might like to write something of his own, a kind of response to Ripley, something that dealt with the races of America, interracial marriages, and their effect on the development of society.

Preoccupied with *Rena* when the request came, Chesnutt put Chamberlin off. He would first need to revise and send the manuscript off to Houghton before thinking about writing something new. He sent the completed manuscript to the press by the end of the month, however. That left the summer months to think about Chamberlin's request, perhaps considering its connection to the passing and marriage plots he'd been reworking in the novel. But Chamberlin didn't want fiction. Chamberlin wanted an *essay*, something along the lines of the clear, simple prose Washington, Ripley, and other such "race men" of the time were writing. But the essay, at least the kind of dull nonfiction prose narrative of Washington and Ripley, was not Chesnutt's modus operandi; he was a storyteller, a stenographer, and a lawyer. Chesnutt wore these different hats at once, placing one on top of the other, as he sat down to write his version of "The Future American."

"The future American race is a popular theme for essayists," Chesnutt began his satirical three-part essay series for the *Boston Evening Transcript*.[17] Chesnutt decided to take down the "popular" race theories circulating at the time, pointing out their absurdity while also praising "recent scientific research" for having "swept away many hoary anthropological fallacies." "Most expressions upon the subject," he continued, "have been characterized by a conscious or unconscious evasion of some of the elements involved in the information of a future American race." His purpose in writing on this well-worn topic was to address "some of these obvious omissions," with the hope of offering readers "a new point of view." That new point of view was a highly ironic one, rooted in his reading of the history and literature of ancient Rome.

Chesnutt had been employing irony as a regular feature of his fiction as far back as his sketches for *Puck*. In his 1889 sketch "A Roman Antique," Chesnutt introduced an unusual former slave who "uster be Mars Julius Caesar's fav'rite body-sarven'."[18] This slave, never named in the story, purported to have ties to "imperial Rome" and described "its glory and magnificence and power" with such captivating detail that he managed to swindle the unnamed naive New York narrator out of a "twenty-dollar gold piece." Whether or not the slave was thousands of years old and served the famous Roman emperor as he claimed was beside the point. The point of the story is that the illiterate slave is an awfully good storyteller and has a surprisingly intimate knowledge of ancient Rome. Indeed, the reader of the story comes to believe, as does the narrator, that the former slave has rightfully earned the money the narrator handed to him "in a fit of abstraction."

Chesnutt's "Roman Antique" was an example of his ongoing engagement with the literature and politics of ancient Rome. As a youth, he had mastered Latin and spent hours translating passages from Cicero's speeches and Virgil's *Aeneid*. That he endowed his former slave narrators with knowledge of ancient Rome was Chesnutt's way of playing on his readers' late-nineteenth-century prejudices and assumptions. Chesnutt's former slaves were not to be pitied like Stowe's Uncle Tom or Twain's Jim. Instead, Chesnutt's stories developed an elevated sense of humor, full of irony and double entendre. As we see in "A Roman Antique," the kind of irony Chesnutt developed was subtle; he had no interest in making enemies or offending the delicate sensibilities of readers of *Puck* or the *Boston Evening Transcript* who generally accepted the opinions of the "race scientists" that he decided to take up in his essay for the *Transcript*. Chesnutt employed irony to make it difficult for readers to tell if he (like the subject of "A Roman Antique") was telling the truth or just joking, in the same way that Washington, among others, had a hard time figuring out his race. The tendency was to divide people into categories: you were either Black or white. Not being able to tell the difference between Black and white, truth and fiction, was central to Chesnutt's message on race. Who was a white man? Who was a Black man? And who had the authority to determine the difference? Just as when he met with Washington, Chesnutt seemed to be "bubbling with merriment" as he took apart popular race experts who claimed to have accurate knowledge of who people were and where they came from.

Before writing his essay trilogy for the *Transcript*, Chesnutt's most sustained and effective use of irony appeared in his story "A Matter of Principle," published as part of *The Wife of His Youth, and Other Stories of the Color Line*. The social customs and laws regulating marriage and other forms of sexual intimacy in the United States were often a subject of Chesnutt's fiction, but in his *Color Line* stories, Chesnutt focused his attention on the ways in which marriage was used to propagate race. Unlike his other tragic marriage plots, including that of Rena's in *The House Behind the Cedars*, there is not even a whiff of romance in the story about Cicero Clayton and his failed attempt to arrange his daughter's marriage according to his racial principles. Because of their skin color, Cicero and his daughter, Alice, are members of a community who, when it came to marriage, privileged racial affiliation—namely, skin color—over love.

> Marriage among Miss Clayton's set were serious affairs. Of course marriage is always a serious matter, whether it is a success or a failure, and there are those who believe that any marriage is better than no marriage. But among Miss Clayton's friends and associates matrimony took on an added seriousness because of the very narrow limits within which it could take place. Miss Clayton and her friends, by reason of their assumed superiority to black people, or perhaps as much by reason of a somewhat morbid shrinking from the curiosity manifested toward married people of strongly contrasting colors would not marry black men, and except in rare instances white men would not marry them. They were therefore restricted for a choice to the young men of their own complexion.[19]

Those fans of romantic comedies would likely recognize the ironic tone found in the novels of Jane Austen, particularly her most famous, *Pride and Prejudice*, at play in Chesnutt's story. Though the pride and prejudice at work in Chesnutt's story are far removed from the problems that keep Mr. Darcy and Elizabeth Bennet apart for much of Austen's novel, there is a similar critique of the ways in which the characters of both stories are blinded by material interests that lead them to make bad choices when it comes to marriage.

"A Matter of Principle" did not receive the same reception as "The Wife of His Youth." Though they were both set in Groveland and detailed the inner workings of "the Blue Vein Society"—Chesnutt's euphemisms for Cleveland's middle-class colored community to which he and his family, by virtue of their skin color, belonged—Cicero Clayton was a less sympathetic figure than Mr. Ryder. Though Mr. Ryder is similarly race-obsessed, he acts out of personal interest and in the end gives up his commitment to skin color by recommitting himself to the dark-skinned wife of his youth. Cicero Clayton claims to "have no prejudice against color" but does everything in his power, short of breaking the law, to keep his daughter from marrying "a black man," regardless of his fine character and her feelings for him. Perhaps Chesnutt identified with Cicero Clayton's bad impulses as a father and so was ruthless in his satiric portrayal of him and his "principles." The story concludes, comically, with Alice Clayton disappointed that she missed her chance to marry a Washington congressman and is left with a "last chance" to marry Jack, a man with light skin like hers, but lacking the pedigree to be viewed as an ideal husband. Jack assures Alice that they will be happy together because he plans to prove himself "a better man than the Congressman." The two, we assume, will get married and live happily ever after. But their marriage is based on a series of compromises, not love. It is not clear, at the end of the story, whether Cicero has changed his mind about the racial principle of color to which he had so tenaciously clung. All we know is that "when the vexed question of the future of the colored race comes up, as it often does, for discussion, Mr. Clayton may still be heard to remark sententiously:—'What the white people of the United States need most, in dealing with this problem is a higher conception of the brother-hood of man. For of one blood God made all the nations of the earth.'"[20]

Of course, white supremacy was no laughing matter. But in the story, Chesnutt renders Cicero Clayton's belief in the natural superiority of "the Anglo-Saxon race" ridiculous. Chesnutt drew on his hilarious portrayal of Cicero and Alice Clayton to sketch his portrait of the future American race. This singular "race"—Chesnutt defined the word in his first article to mean "a people who look substantially alike and are molded by the same culture and dominated by the same ideals"—would be the result of an inevitable "amalgamation" between "the three broad types—white, black, and Indian—" of Americans identified by the U.S. census. Then, as now, the racial language employed by the census determined how its citizens understood themselves and their relation to one another. In his essay, Chesnutt predicted amalgamation between the races of the United States, echoing the sententious voice of Cicero Clayton, through marriages between individuals belonging to different "types," resulting in a composite and homogenous people in which racial difference has "been entirely eliminated." But Chesnutt did not stop there. He went on to explain that if people did not desire to marry those belonging to a different type, then the solution was to *arrange* such marriages: "One could imagine a government sufficiently autocratic to enforce its behests, it would be no great task to mix the races mechanically, leaving to time merely the fixing of the resultant type."[21] In one fell swoop, Chesnutt took down the laws, language, and social customs that were intended to maintain the integrity of racial categories by preventing intimate relations between different types of people. Chesnutt's first installment of "The Future American" showed how laws aimed at *mechanically* separating people are ridiculous. Once "the processes of nature are not too violently interrupted by the hand of man," Chesnutt imagined, "the formation of a uniform type out of our present racial elements will take place within a measurably near period."

In his second essay on "The Future American," Chesnutt decided to take his argument a step further. Here he claimed that amalgamation "has already been going on" and looked back on slavery as "a rich soil for the production of a mixed race." Alongside this shocking assessment of slavery, Chesnutt listed several well-known white Americans who were actually Black. Then there were all the people he'd known "during a residence in North Carolina in my youth and early manhood" who were classed as Black but were actually white. The confusion over who was white and who was Black reached a kind of climax in the essay when Chesnutt related "a little incident that occurred not long ago near Boston" concerning "three light-colored men, brothers, by the name, we will say, of Green, living in a Boston suburb, [who] married respectively a white, a brown and a black woman." Chesnutt didn't support this "little incident" with any historical detail or evidence; all readers knew was that it had occurred in *Boston*, close to the homes of the majority of its readers. This would have left many wondering if they knew the Greens or a branch of one color of the Green family. But the rainbow of colors Chesnutt employed to discuss their marriages made matters even worse. The colors, and the readers, are all connected, regardless of our best efforts to keep the colors separate. But the story isn't told as a fact. It is told in the form of a humorous anecdote, like the kind that peppered Washington's famous speeches on the "American Negro." But when Chesnutt concluded telling the story of the three Green brothers and the result of their brown, black, and white marriages, he got serious, listing several real, current draconian laws aimed at prohibiting marriages between people belonging to different races: "In North Carolina, marriage between white persons and free persons of color was lawful until 1830. By the Missouri code of 1855, the color line was drawn at one-fourth of Negro blood, and persons of only one-eighth were legally white." These laws were no joke. The state was continuing to implement such measures "which retard the development of the future American race type."[22] For all their serious consequences, these laws, in Chesnutt's account, are ridiculous because they don't work. Those we label black, brown, or white are actually all just members of the Green clan!

The third and final installment of Chesnutt's "Future American" showed that despite all the state's efforts to interrupt the mixture of the races it is a "fait accompli."

> That it must come in the United States, sooner or later, seems to be a foregone conclusion, as the result of natural law—*lex dura, sed tamen lex*—a hard pill, but one which must be swallowed. There can manifestly be no such thing as a peaceful and progressive civilization in a nation divided by two warring races, and homogeneity of type, at least in externals, is a necessary condition to harmonious social progress.[23]

Chesnutt disguised "the heretical doctrine" of absolute unity among citizens of the United States in Latin, as if to say, *This is not what I, as author of these essays, condone; it is just the way things have been since ancient times and there is little I or you, dear reader, can do about it. The law is harsh, but it is the law nonetheless. We might as well accept the natural unity among people and let our children marry, or not marry, whomever they choose.*

Edwin and Helen would choose not to marry, while his youngest daughter, Dorothy, would marry John Slade, a doctor who had graduated from Howard University. Chesnutt was not thrilled with Helen's decision but did not interfere with his daughter's love life. Perhaps he had learned from Cicero Clayton's mistakes. Those like Cicero who act or speak against the law by interfering with their children's marriages will bear the high cost of their interference. Chesnutt's essays were intended for public consumption, aimed at the thoughtful readers of the *Boston Evening Transcript*. The essays took up serious social issues, read not as literature but as a sociological study. But for Chesnutt, the essays allowed him to poke fun at himself, his community, and the conventions that determined their relations with one another.

In accepting Chesnutt's articles for publication in the *Transcript* on August 15, 1900, Chamberlin found them to be "very interesting and significant." But he pointed out "some factors in the problem which," he felt, Chesnutt had "omitted." Its most glaring omission, according to Chamberlin, was a consideration of class differences as they related to the topic. As he put it, "The fact that the fusion between the races is likely to take place in the main among the poorest and least-cared for classes" will make it difficult for "their progeny" to multiply as fast as "the pure whites" who, he went on to point out, "will always multiply in more rapid proportion than the mixed race."[24] Chamberlin, like many who read Chesnutt's "Future American" essays when they first appeared, seemed to have missed their point entirely. As far as Chesnutt was concerned, there was no such thing as pure whites; we are all like the Boston Greens—impure Americans. The two probably worked out their differences on another one of Chesnutt's visits to Red Farm.

13

Southbound

For instance, from the town of Wilmington, N. C., since the "revolution," as the white people call it, or the "massacre" according to the
Negroes—it was really both—over fifteen hundred of the best colored
citizens have left the town.
—"The White and the Black," *Boston Evening Transcript*, March 20, 1901

A few months after the publication of "The Wife of His Youth," there
occurred in Wilmington, North Carolina, a coup d'état, the likes of
which had never been seen before (or since) in the United States. Chesnutt
wrote to Page almost immediately after he heard about the events in Wilmington to express his outrage as a fellow "tar-heel." "I am deeply concerned
and very much depressed at the condition of affairs in North Carolina
during the recent campaign," he began. Chesnutt continued to decry what
had happened in Wilmington, calling it "an outbreak of pure, malignant
and altogether indefensible race prejudice." Strangely, Chesnutt ended the
letter less concerned about the violence, destruction, and tremendous loss
of life in Wilmington than in the event's connection to his story.

But I would not inflict my views on you in this manner, except for a
circumstance you may find interesting. The colored people's newspaper *The Daily Record*, the office of which was burned yesterday by
a mob of the "best citizens" of Wilmington, numbering in their
ranks many "ministers of the gospel," and the editor of which has
been compelled to flee for his life, republished "The Wife of His

Youth" in installments running over about a week, sometime ago, and somebody sent me several copies of the paper. It gave credit to the *Atlantic*, but I rather doubted whether it had obtained your permission to copy the story. If I had the heart to joke on a subject that seems to me very seriously and hopelessly tragical, I might say that the misfortunes of the newspaper were a sort of divine retribution, or poetic justice for a violation of copyright.[1]

Chesnutt was disgusted and depressed about the violent turn in politics that had occurred in what he still considered his home state. But he also wanted Page to know that he had readers down there, *Black* readers. Though these readers didn't count to his publisher because they didn't buy the story or later his books in the conventional way, they were still readers. That *The Daily Record*, North Carolina's most-read Black newspaper, had printed "The Wife of His Youth" was a sign of Chesnutt's broad reach among an audience that Houghton, Mifflin and Company had never considered before. The question for Chesnutt and he hoped for his publisher too was how to tap into this market, to sell his books to Black readers, most of whom lived in the South.

With a population of roughly twenty-five thousand, Wilmington was then the largest city in North Carolina. Chesnutt still had family there. During his years in North Carolina, he would take frequent trips to Wilmington along North Carolina's southeastern coastline. His wife, Susan, shortly after the birth of their first child, had spent a month in Wilmington while he was busy in Fayetteville with work. She, perhaps more than he, loved the town. Situated on the lower Cape Fear River, it offered Susan a much-needed break from Fayetteville's sand hills. She felt comfortable there, enjoyed frequenting the shops and restaurants along the boardwalk with her friends and family. But all that changed on November 10, 1898, when a mob mainly of white men armed with rifles took to the streets of Wilmington, burning Black-owned businesses, including the office of *The Daily Record*. Its editor, Alexander Lightfoot Manly, fled the city after being threatened by the mob for printing an editorial that acknowledged consensual sexual relations between white women and Black men. Just a few months before the violence, *The Record* had republished "The Wife of

His Youth" in installments running over about a week. It was this literary
event, Chesnutt explained to Page, and not "the outbreak of pure, malignant and altogether indefensible race prejudice" that had compelled him to
write to Page. Just a day after news of the violence in Wilmington broke,
Chesnutt was already telling his own story about it, giving it a literary spin,
that would, a few years later, turn into *The Marrow of Tradition*.

The "misfortunes of the newspaper" that reprinted "The Wife of His
Youth" without permission would come to play a prominent role in the
novel. Though few copies of *The Daily Record* survived when its office was
burned and its editor forced to flee his home, Chesnutt provided a detailed
description of the paper in the novel's ninth chapter. As an avid reader
of newspapers, particularly those in which his stories appeared, Chesnutt
described the newspaper that was said to have been a catalyst of the riot as
accurately as possible in his novel, from multiple points of view. *The Daily
Record* was

> an eighteen by twenty-four sheet, poorly printed on cheap paper,
> with a "patent" inside, a number of advertisements of proprietary
> medicines, quack doctors, and fortune-tellers, and two or three
> columns of editorial and local news. Candor compels the admis-
> sion that it was not an impressive sheet in any respect, except when
> regarded as the first local effort of a struggling people to make
> public expression of their life and aspirations. From this point of
> view it did not speak at all badly for a class to whom, a generation
> before, newspapers, books, and learning had been forbidden fruit.

While the novel's white characters mocked the paper as "an elegant
specimen of journalism," Chesnutt's narrator teaches us how to read the
paper sympathetically, "as the first local effort of a struggling people to
make public expression of their life and aspirations." He would go on
to describe the editorial without quoting directly from it, explaining to
those who had not read the original editorial how much of its meaning
derived from the context in which it was printed. "Such an article in a
Northern newspaper would have attracted no special attention, and might
merely have furnished food to an occasional reader for serious thought
upon a subject not exactly agreeable; but coming from a colored man, in

a Southern city, it was an indictment of the laws and social system of the South that could not fail of creating a profound sensation." In this way, *The Marrow of Tradition* would become more than just a novel. It also functioned as a historical document, recording the experiences of those who had been vanquished.

For Chesnutt, *The Marrow of Tradition* was a way, he said, of overcoming his feeling of despair and reaffirming his "belief that the forces of progress will in the end prevail." Chesnutt started his second novel in September 1900. A few weeks after sending his "Future American" essays to Chamberlin at the *Transcript*, he bought a new notebook. He wrote his name and the date in his characteristic cursive style with his favorite fountain pen at the top of the book's woven hard cover and printed in hand lettering the words *Literary Memoranda* in its center. Chesnutt took his time printing these words. Each letter was drawn with a bit of a flourish, as if animated to inspire and introduce the thoughts that he would write in the book's pages.

Chesnutt's Literary Memoranda, unlike his earlier Fayetteville journal and notebook, was not a personal diary. The term *memoranda* has a legal-sounding quality to it; it was impersonal, something more along the lines of a formal document or office memo than a journal or diary. Like his earlier journal, this was a place for rough drafts, first takes, or story ideas. But there was something different about the Literary Memoranda. His title for the notebook lent these ideas a kind of ontological weight—these handwritten ideas were important; they would be used later for stories that would be published and earn him a living. The reader of Chesnutt's Literary Memoranda meets an author at work, not just a naive schoolteacher who dreams of becoming an author someday. Unlike his journals that are now falling apart from the wear and tear of having been read and reread in the Chesnutt archive at Fisk University, his Literary Memoranda, despite its age, is in almost immaculate condition. Few seem to have recognized its importance, perhaps mistaking it as part of Chesnutt's legal, rather than literary, career. This was Chesnutt's way of taking literature seriously, a way of seeing himself as a *professional* author, putting himself next to other professional authors, the realists he admired most at the time: Henry James, Mark Twain, and William Dean Howells.

On the first page of his Literary Memoranda, Chesnutt sketched a plot for a short story, calling it simply "Race Riot."[2] Chesnutt's handwriting had not changed much over the years. He wrote in a looping, right-leaning hand. Though he was likely writing quickly, every word of his handwriting is entirely legible. He did not write in complete sentences; he was writing as he was thinking. He did not pause to add details, and the characters and places lacked proper names. It was hardly even a rough draft of a story. These were notes, ideas, reflections toward a story, something he would transform into a novel, eventually type up, and send to Houghton. Later, he scrawled in pencil on the top of the page "Marrow of Tradition" and "(see p. 9)" as he developed what would become the plot of his second novel. This novel was something new for Chesnutt, a real experiment in fiction, and unlike his previous attempts at novel writing, he wrote this one without interventions from external readers or rejections from editors.

He did, however, tell a select few about *Marrow*, only those he thought would appreciate what he was doing. "One finds appreciation from those who *know*, a very agreeable thing. I think you understand how difficult it is to write race problem books so that white people will read them—and it is white people they are primarily aimed at," he wrote on December 1, 1900, to his old friend John P. Green, who had recently become the first Black senator in Ohio. He explained further that he was planning another book, "but of broader scope" from his previous ones, this new novel was his attempt "to sketch in vivid though simple lines the whole race situation." The plot Chesnutt first sketched in his Literary Memoranda is the first and perhaps best account of his yet-to-be written novel. He would offer several other plot summaries, in speeches, readings, and articles after it was published. Though the plot would change and develop in different directions, the characters and events he first described in his Literary Memoranda would launch the book that would over the years slowly rise to the status of a great American novel. This was how he began to write it.

Young colored man, educated, decides to settle in a Southern city, where he can be of more direct use to his people, personally as well as by example. He must be of some pursuit or profession, preferably medicine, and must have distinguished himself in some specialty. A race riot breaks out, in which he suffers terribly, his house and drugstore being destroyed, and his child or mother being killed or dying of fright. There is no redress & no hope of redress. The doctor prepares to leave the town. The child or wife of one of the chief promoters of the riot is taken suddenly & violently ill. There is only one white physician in the town who is capable of treating the case, which requires immediate attention and this physician is out of town. The colored physician is called. He refuses; is persuaded, wavers, argues, yields, and saves the child's life. Is begged to remain in the town, and is offered the white man's protection but wants the rights and opportunities of a man. His new found friend would not be able to stop or turn aside the forces he had set in motion.[3]

The "young colored man" became Dr. William Miller. The Southern city would be called Wellington, an obvious allusion to the real-life Wilmington. He called Miller's wife Janet, devoting an entire chapter to her story. The Millers had a little boy of six or seven, who would become one of the first and youngest fatal casualties of the riot. As a devoted mother and wife, Janet came closest to being the novel's hero. But the novel did not have heroes in the conventional sense of the term. The novel did, however, have a clear and unredeemable villain in Captain McBane. "His broad shoulders, burly form, square jaw, and heavy chin betokened strength, energy, and unscrupulousness." There was something slightly Dickensian in Chesnutt's rendering of him. But all of Chesnutt's characters, Black and white, were flawed. They were struggling with their positions in society, with its constraints, and the ways in which their pasts determined their futures. The "chief promoter of the riot" was Major Philip Carteret, editor of the town's daily newspaper, *The Morning Chronicle*, and had the good fortune of being married to a wealthy Southern heiress, Olivia Merkell. The novel opened with Olivia in the throes of childbirth, an event complicated by her age and state of mind. But she managed to give birth to a boy they gave "two beautiful names," Theodore Felix. Olivia is related to Janet Miller; they have the same white father but different mothers. Janet is Black, and Olivia's white. The white physician was called Dr. Burns. He and Dr. Miller are friends and colleagues. Though Dr. Burns rejected the unscientific logic of racial categories, he was forced to submit to them when he found himself on a southbound train, alongside Dr. Miller. These were just the main characters. But there would be others, Black and white minor characters who interact, assemble, and dissemble, as each would play a role in the novel's central event, a race riot that destroyed lives and property, mostly belonging to the town's Black residents, with the potential to spread. The real-life Wilmington massacre could be rendered as the beginning of another civil war or a chance to reassert the forces of Reconstruction. Chesnutt used the event that had left him despairing of the future to begin telling a new story of race in America, a story in which characters bound to racial histories by the law must break out of them to live.

The novel's plot is complex. There are several subplots, and the time line moves seamlessly between the past and present. This is not exactly historical fiction. Rather, it is a history of current events. The events and characters it presents had not yet become history; the novel writes them into history. This history begins with a familiar scene of a woman in labor, with her worried husband by her side, hoping for the best but expecting the worst. The urgency of the present moment is emphasized by the lush description of the setting. "The night was hot and sultry. Though the windows of the chamber were wide open, and the muslin curtains looped back, not a breath of air was stirring." We know we are in the Deep South by the "stifling heat," "the shrill chirp of the cicada and the muffled croaking of the frogs in some distant marsh," and the "heavy scent of magnolias."[4] To release us from the oppressive present, we are taken into the not-so-distant past, when our characters were younger, without the burden of their present situations weighing them down. In the past, we meet a young Major Carteret, returning home from Appomattox "to find his family, one of the oldest and proudest in the state, hopelessly impoverished by war." But amid the ruins, Carteret finds love and a source of income from his wife, Olivia Merkell. With her money, he started a newspaper, which he "had made the leading organ of his party and the most influential paper in the State." We are back in the present, in Olivia and Philip's home. Dr. Price and Mammy Jane, Olivia's childhood nurse, join them. All four anticipate the birth of the Carterets' first child, a boy who will inherit the legacy of his parents and grandparents. The conjunction between childbirth and the founding of a newspaper is hardly a coincidence. Olivia is the source of the state's future generations and its news. Though her husband functions as father and editor, without her wealth and body, Major Carteret would be nothing more than a victim of the lost cause.

By the time Chesnutt started writing his novel, the mixture of politics and nuptial relations had become a regular feature of American novels. Likely, Chesnutt had the novels of William Dean Howells on his mind, particularly his 1889 novel *A Hazard of New Fortunes*, that similarly wove together a real-life outbreak of political violence, a story of marriage and family, with the work of a magazine editor. *Hazard*, as Howells came to believe, was the "most vital of my fictions" and has become, according to some later critics of American literature, one of the century's most important American political novels. But at the time of its publication, *Hazard* had almost destroyed the career of its author.[5]

Hazard presented readers with the inner workings of the late-nineteenth-century magazine business. Much of the novel's action and characters were based on Howells's experience as a magazine editor and writer in both Boston and New York City. The novel opened with a character he called Fulkerson, who looked and sounded a lot like Sam McClure, with whom Chesnutt was personally acquainted. It had been the S. S. McClure Syndicate that helped to launch Chesnutt's career as a professional author right around the time Howells published *Hazard*. The plot followed Fulkerson's relationship with Basil March, a writer and editor with a keen sense of aesthetic taste. The novel had begun to appear in *Harper's Weekly* in late March of 1889, just as Chesnutt was making a reputation for himself by publishing stories in *The Atlantic*. He was surely following the weekly appearances of Howells's latest novel that proved controversial for its depiction of political events. A couple of decades later, reflecting on his novel, Howells explained the circumstances leading to its inception.

Opportunely for me there was a great street-car strike in New York, and the story began to find its way to issues nobler and larger than those of the love-affairs common to fiction. I was in my fifty-second year when I took it up and in the prime, such as it was, of my powers."[6] The

1889 New York streetcar strike formed both the backdrop and climax for Howells's novel. It is a story about class conflict and the distribution of wealth. The characters he developed in the novel are defenseless when the labor strike turns violent, resulting in a riot that ended with the death of the saintly son of one of the novel's key characters from a stray bullet. Though the work of the magazine was not directly involved in the outbreak of violence, the novel's protagonist acknowledged his own participation in the disorder in his efforts to represent it faithfully. *Hazard* was the most explicit manifestation of Howells's emerging political position. A couple of years earlier, Howells had become embroiled in the Haymarket affair, in which a bomb was thrown into the police ranks during a public protest in the streets of Chicago. When the police opened fire on the crowd, killing several of their own men and civilians, the peaceful protest turned into a bloodbath. To pay for the crime, police arrested several men known for espousing anarchist ideas and suspected as organizers of the protest. But there was no evidence they had been responsible for the bomb. Later, these men were executed. Howells was deeply moved by the event and its outcomes. He felt it was his duty, as a writer and citizen, to speak out. These men were charged and executed without due process. They were ostensibly killed for their political beliefs. Alongside the letters to newspapers that he wrote and were printed with his name, his novel functioned as an extended response to the violence and the violation of rights that Howells felt were threatening the democratic principles of the United States. Howells's novel, like Chesnutt's, concluded with his characters arguing about the strikers. What starts out as a peaceful protest to demand better wages for streetcar operators erupts into a violent riot that ends with a tragic death scene of one of the novel's central characters. But in writing about these recent political events in the form of a novel, creating characters who were involved in the events, Howells was criticized for overstepping the literary boundaries of his profession.

Chesnutt met Howells about a decade after the publication of his most controversial novel. By this time, much of the controversy over Howells's politics had subsided, and he was looking back on the novel he had written a decade or so earlier with a sense of critical distance, through the eyes of an older and wiser author who was more cautious when mixing politics with literature. On February 3, 1900, Chesnutt was in New York. He had been visiting with Walter Hines Page at his new office in Washington Square and discussing the publication of *The House Behind the Cedars*. A meeting with Howells was arranged by his publisher. Page's former assistant at Houghton, William B. Parker, was working closely with Howells to bring out a review of Chesnutt's work for *The Atlantic*. While the occasion for the interview was Howells's article on Chesnutt, it may also have been an opportunity for Chesnutt to ask Howells about his own literary career, what he thought about future directions in American literature and politics. Perhaps they even discussed Howells's views on the race problem. Chesnutt, as most writers of his generation, was thrilled by Howells's attention. As former editor of *The Atlantic Monthly*, with a weekly column called Editor's Study published in *Harper's Magazine*, in which he presented his opinions about current literature, Howells had become known as the dean of American Literature. Howells's public profile gave him the power to make or break literary careers. When Chesnutt returned to his hotel, he wrote to Susan to tell her about his conversation with Howells. He could hardly contain his enthusiasm. Chesnutt also wrote to his literary-minded son-in-law Edward Williams about the meeting; he knew Williams would appreciate its importance. Williams's response put into words Chesnutt's thoughts about the role he anticipated Howells would play as he was getting ready to publish his first novel: "I am very glad to hear that Mr. Howells is going to write you up, for, with his appreciation of the aesthetics of style and diction, he should be able to say something worthwhile, and his dictum on any subject commands the respectful attention of the cultured East. With their attention once at your command, I think you can be trusted to do the rest."[7]

As Williams predicted, Howells's appreciation of style and diction led him to say something "worth while" about Chesnutt's stories. Appearing in the May 1900 issue of *The Atlantic*, just a few months before the publication of *The House Behind the Cedars*, the timing of the review was perfect. Howells opened the review by addressing "the critical reader." By doing so, Howells was drawing an important distinction, a distinction based not on skin color but on reading experience. For Howells, a critical reader is "any one accustomed to study methods in fiction," those who possess the ability "to distinguish between good and bad art, to feel the joy which the delicate skill possible only from a love of truth can give." Critical readers would appreciate and feel "a high pleasure" in reading Chesnutt's stories. Howells also explained that Chesnutt's stories are not for everyone and that "they will possibly not reach half a million readers in six months, but in twelve months possibly more readers will remember them more than if they had reached the half million." On and on Howells praised "Mr. Chesnutt's Stories," leaving little doubt as to their quality and importance. He also made a point of setting aside Chesnutt's "sixteenth part of a race" to view him above all as an author who presented "character, the most precious thing in fiction," faithfully.[8]

Chesnutt was, of course, delighted by Howells's review and told him so almost immediately after reading it. "I want to thank you very cordially for your appreciative review of my books in the May *Atlantic*. It would have been pleasant coming from any source, and it has a very great value coming from you." Howells's review had material value; it meant that Chesnutt had the stamp of approval from the dean of American Literature and could expect entry into its hallowed halls. Perhaps it was Howells's "appreciative review" of Chesnutt's books that gave him the confidence to try something new, something that addressed "issues nobler and larger" than the tragic love affair he'd depicted in *House*. As he described it in a letter to Booker T. Washington about a month after sketching it out in his memoranda: "My next book on the subject [of the color line] will be square up to date, & will deal with the negro's right to live rather than his right to love."[9]

Until this time, Chesnutt had steered clear of the kind of overtly political novels written by his literary friends Albion Tourgée and George Washington Cable. But the violence in Wilmington had changed all that. Chesnutt felt compelled to write about it, to make sense of the tremendous loss of life and property that ensued from the riot. He sought to make sense of this issue not only for himself but also for all those who were watching the events unfold from afar. Curiously, Chesnutt did not mention his idea for the novel to Tourgée, Cable, or Page, his usual literary interlocutors. Of course, Tourgée had moved on to Bordeaux, where he was recovering from the *Plessy v. Ferguson* verdict, and Page had left Boston for New York. But why not Cable? They were still in close touch when he had begun sketching out the novel's plot; both Helen and Ethel were still at Smith, so talking with Cable would have been convenient when he visited his daughters in Northampton. Perhaps he felt that Cable would not appreciate the concept or that he would even disapprove of his rendering of the race riot. Shortly before its publication, Chesnutt explained that "the incidents of the race riot described in the story were studied from two recent outbreaks of that kind—one in Wilmington, N. C., and the other in New Orleans."[10]

Just a couple of months before sketching out his "Race Riot Story," riots had broken out in New Orleans in July 1901. Known now as the Robert Charles riots, violence erupted in New Orleans after a Black man named Robert Charles shot and killed a white police officer while resisting arrest. Rioting lasted for several days, and dozens lost their lives or were badly hurt as a result. New Orleans was Cable's territory. Though he had left it long ago to settle among the more like-minded citizens of New England, he still considered New Orleans home. While the story was set in a different part of the South, it was conceivable that Cable would take issue with Chesnutt using the event as a source for his fiction. Or, perhaps Chesnutt felt, after the publication of *The House Behind the Cedars*, he no longer needed Cable's advice. He was now a novelist in his own right, not just a writer of stories and amusing sketches. This would be a novel he would write on his own. Whatever were his reasons for keeping *Marrow* under wraps until it was completed, it is safe to assume that he believed this was a story that belonged to him, it was about people he knew, and the events it described had affected him in a way that few other political events had.

He knew it was a risky literary venture, but he also knew that any author who mixed politics with literature in the United States, from Harriet Beecher Stowe to his contemporaries Cable and Howells, was taking a risk. And like these other novelists, he believed that current events demanded him to do something. It could become a bestseller, like *Uncle Tom's Cabin*, or it could cost him his personal reputation, as *Hazard* had for Howells, at least in the short term. Either way, he knew he had to write this book, whatever the consequences. If he didn't, he would be a coward or, worse, a sellout. He didn't want to write books just for entertaining readers. He wanted to move them, even shock them, into doing something about the lawlessness, violence, and loss of life that were ruining the lives of law-abiding, freedom-loving Black and white American citizens.

Chesnutt read Howells's review as an invitation, encouraging him not just to keep writing the kind of short fiction he had been writing but to take his fiction further, to delve deeper into the race problem, to continue to present the problem as *he* saw it. His point of view veered away from the unrealistic, sentimental way in which other writers had depicted the problem. Chesnutt concluded his letter to Howells with a literary promise: "I shall try to keep in mind the heights to which you point me, both by precept and example, and shall hope to meet the condition which you prescribe for my success." Howells's review also marked for Chesnutt his formal entry into the field of professional literary authorship that he had so long craved. "I am very grateful for your kindly notice and encouragement, after which I feel that I can safely subscribe myself a man of letters and hope for a worthy career in that field of effort."[11] He sealed the letter with a token of friendship. "Permit me to count myself among your friends as I have numbered you with mine."

There seems to be a bit of literary gamesmanship underlying Chesnutt's brief note to Howells. Chesnutt met with Howells once, perhaps twice, at most. Though they were well acquainted with each other's work, they did not travel in the same circles. Unlike his friendships with Chamberlin, Page, Tourgée, and Cable, Howells never invited Chesnutt to his home, nor had Chesnutt hosted Howells in Cleveland. This was a little unusual since Howells hailed from Ohio and visited his family home not too far from Cleveland frequently. Not having met each other's families, Howells and Chesnutt were, at best, literary colleagues; both were engaged in the project of developing American realism. Shortly after their meeting in New York City, Howells published a work of nonfiction, something along the lines of a literary memoir, but not quite. Called *Literary Friends and Acquaintance: A Personal Retrospect of American Authorship*, Howells's latest book was filled with pictures and effusive descriptions of various famous authors—Longfellow, Emerson, Thoreau, Hawthorne, Twain, among others. Unlike his novels and stories, this book was a conservative document, looking back at America's literary past with a heavy dose of nostalgia. Though it was written in the style of a memoir, Howells opened the book with a note to the reader explaining its distinction from the popular form. "But I wish to make my own personality merely a backdrop which divers important figures are projected against, and I am willing to sacrifice myself a little in giving them relief."[12] By declaring Howells his friend, with the expectation that the declaration would be reciprocated, Chesnutt included himself in the company of important American literary figures with whom Howells had been friendly, even if Howells had excluded him. It was, to say the least, a bold move.

A few months after his exchange with Howells, Chesnutt made considerable headway on his novel before taking a trip to Wilmington in February 1901. This was Chesnutt's first trip to the South since leaving Fayetteville for New York back in 1883. So much had changed since then. His daughters were about to graduate from Smith; his son was finishing up high school in Cleveland and hopefully heading to Harvard. He had built a successful court reporting business and had earned enough money from it to resign and pursue a career in literature. Though he felt relatively secure with his decision to leave the South, Chesnutt remained interested in its affairs, both in its development and its stagnation due to its isolation. Despite having made a life for himself far removed from the people and environs of the South, he still identified with it. As he explained to an audience in Cleveland, gathered to hear him read from his published and unpublished books on November 15, 1900, "I spent the most impressionable years of my life in the picturesque old town of Fayetteville," and it remained the primary subject of most of his fiction. While he no longer lived in the South, he kept in touch with it through letters from friends and family as well as reading its newspapers, which kept him up to date on most of its happenings.

Chesnutt had been planning the trip for a while. Though he intended to reconnect with friends and family in Fayetteville, the primary purpose of his southbound journey was professional, not personal. Booker T. Washington was eager to host Chesnutt at Tuskegee. He wanted Chesnutt to write about the place, tell his literary friends and acquaintances in the Northeast about its virtues. As he delved more deeply into writing his novel, Chesnutt realized he needed to return to Wilmington, where the novel was set. Washington's invitation to visit Tuskegee was just the excuse Chesnutt needed to make the long journey back to the South. As if marking the literary significance of the trip, Chesnutt sketched out his itinerary in his Literary Memoranda. The plan was to take the southbound train from Cleveland to Wilmington, from which he would take another train to Tuskegee to meet with Washington and spend a few days touring the campus. From Tuskegee, he would make his way back up to Atlanta, where he would spend several days at Atlanta University, with "Dr. W.E.B. Dubois, whose studies in sociology have won him a wide reputation."[13] He documented his Southern travels in a couple of essays, published shortly after his return, in late March 1901. All in all, Chesnutt spent a month traveling throughout the South to witness its developments since he had left it a couple decades before.

What emerged from these travels was a portrait of striking contrasts between Tuskegee and Atlanta. "In the one, the busy note of industry was predominant; in the other, an air of scholastic quiet pervaded the grounds and the halls."[14] Chesnutt did not privilege one over the other; he viewed both as essential to the development of the South. He saw beauty in both institutions, one led by Du Bois, the other by Washington. Chesnutt was also critical of both for having accepted the constraints of racial conditions, upon which both institutions were ultimately built, though in different ways. He presented his critique plainly, qualifying it as coming from someone who was not *from* there. "The present writer does not believe in the wisdom of the segregation of the races which prevails in the Southern States, and thinks that it is carried to an extreme which is not only short-sighted, expensive, and troublesome, but which, to an outsider, borders upon the ridiculous."[15] For all their differences in purpose and method, Chesnutt wound up his Southern tour by offering a critique of both Du Bois and Washington, viewing them as joined in "accepting the situation as inevitable." Chesnutt's observations and conversations while in the South seemed to help him clarify his position as a writer who wrote about its race problem as an "outsider."

Soon after returning from his Southern tour, he wrote a letter to Washington, thanking him for his hospitality. "I arrived safely home, after a roundabout trip with numerous stops, and have brought with me many pleasant impressions of Tuskegee, and of the great work you have under way there." He also admitted that for all the pleasant impressions he formed during his visit to Tuskegee and of Washington's "great work," he left the South with a bitter taste in his mouth. "But, personally, I don't like the South."[16] It was these more current *unpleasant* memories of segregation in Wilmington, Tuskegee, and Atlanta, rather than those formed during his "impressionable years" in Fayetteville, that he poured into *The Marrow of Tradition* over the next few months, fleshing out its chapters and shaping it into a novel about the South as he saw it rather than as he *remembered* it.

What began as a race riot story in September 1900 had become a novel of thirty-seven chapters. It included a family drama, a romance, a murder mystery, an inheritance plot, and, of course, the story of a newspaper editor whose racial rhetoric stoked the hearts and minds of its readers to riot against their democratic institutions. The novel's concluding chapter, called simply "The Sisters," united what Chesnutt's essay for the *Transcript* called "The White and the Black." When the Black Janet is finally reunited with her white sister, Olivia, readers are left wondering, still waiting, for a happy end to the tragedy caused by their separation. We imagine it will happen, but not in the pages of the novel; the happy end is left to the readers to imagine what will happen after the moving reunion between the sisters, the death of Janet's son, and, we hope, the recovery of Olivia's. Will they live happily ever after together as a family, forgetting the past that separated them, or will they carry the resentments of the past with them and continue living apart as sisters segregated by the fiction of race? Chesnutt offered a cryptic response to the question in the novel's unforgettable final sentence: "There's time enough, but none to spare."

Chesnutt submitted the complete manuscript of *The Marrow of Tradition* to Houghton, Mifflin and Company on July 25, 1901. In the past, Chesnutt would address his letter to Walter Hines Page, they would have a back-and-forth about it, and perhaps Page would suggest a different title, stylistic revisions, and the like. But now that Page had left the company to head up his own firm in New York, Chesnutt addressed his letter to the head of the firm, George Mifflin, with specific instructions.

My Dear Mr. Mifflin:

I send on today, under another cover, the manuscript of the novel upon which I have been working for the past eight months. Recurring to our conversation in Boston, I should like to have you put it at once in the hands of your readers—and decide whether or not it is a novel for which, so far as experience can predict or conjecture, a good sale can be reasonably expected—by which I mean a sale much better than that of *The House Behind the Cedars.*

I have put a great deal of work into it; it is entirely sincere, and it is certainly a much better book than any I have heretofore written. If you decide that there are possibilities for it, I shall be glad, as I said, to have you publish it.[17]

The shift in Chesnutt's tone is striking. He is a confident, assertive, and altogether new man. Chesnutt is an author in this letter, not the man who, just a couple of years earlier, had complained to Walter Hines Page that "your house has turned down my novel 'Rena' in great shape."

While he had worked on *The House Behind the Cedars* for "ten years," he had worked on *The Marrow of Tradition* for only eight months. Yet he believed it to be "a much better book than I have heretofore written." He seemed not to worry about the publisher rejecting it. Even if they did reject it, he knew there were other publishers—namely, George P. Brett, an editor at the Macmillan Company, who had already expressed interest in publishing it. But he knew, rightly as it turned out, that he didn't have anything to worry about. He knew this was a good novel, the best he'd written; he was totally confident that the readers at Houghton would agree. He was also able to make demands of his publisher, with whom he had now published three books. He was a known commodity, and he expected to be treated with respect. So he told Mifflin that he wanted a quick turnaround on this book; he didn't have time to wait. There was a sense of urgency around the publication of *The Marrow of Tradition* that was new. Chesnutt wanted this novel to be *read*; he wanted this novel to make a political difference, to have a social impact. Mifflin seemed to concur with Chesnutt about the novel; he complied without hesitation, putting the book "at once" into the hands of his readers. The manuscript was received on July 29, 1901. Mifflin gave it to Parker to read on the same day. Parker read it and submitted his report two days later. Parker provided a close and rigorous reading comprising over three manuscript pages. He concluded that it was "a novel full of intensity, well though not brilliantly written and capable of wide popular success."[18]

Chesnutt was informed of the firm's decision on July 31. "We have read the manuscript of your 'Marrow of Tradition' with great interest, and are much impressed by its power and intensity."[19] The firm's faith in the novel was unequivocal. Chesnutt's years of struggle and sacrifice seemed to have finally paid off. That *The Marrow of Tradition* was accepted so quickly was surely a sign of Chesnutt's ability and status. He could now turn his attention to writing full-time, not worrying anymore about finances and making ends meet. Perhaps he could start sketching the plot of another novel or story. At any rate, the publication of *Marrow* brought him some much-needed respite from constant work and worry. The novel was sent to the printers without any major revisions on August 6. Publication was planned for early October. In the meantime, Chesnutt accepted an invitation to chair the Committee on Colored Troops for the Thirty-Fifth National Encampment of the Grand Army of the Republic that was to gather in Cleveland in early September, where President William McKinley was scheduled to give a speech to honor the troops.

On September 6, 1901, McKinley was shot twice by Leon Czolgosz in Buffalo, while attending the Pan-American Exposition. The president died from his wounds eight days later, becoming the third president of the United States to be assassinated. His assassin was known for espousing anarchism, a conjecture that led some to draw connections between McKinley's assassination and the Haymarket affair. Both events were blamed on a rising tide of anarchism in the United States, brought about, it was believed, by European immigration. Though Chesnutt's work on the Committee for Colored Troops continued, he was shaken, as were most at the time. Shortly after McKinley's death, the vice president, Theodore Roosevelt, took the reins of the presidency and invited Booker T. Washington to dine at the White House.

The reward of writing a novel of great power was delayed indefinitely. The novel appeared on bookshelves across the country while news of Washington's visit to the White House dominated the papers. Despite the shift in media attention from the riots to McKinley's assassination and Washington's dinner with Roosevelt, Houghton still expected *The Marrow of Tradition* to do well. They were meticulous with its book design and distribution. Though Chesnutt was pleased by his publisher's attentiveness, he appeared to be more realistic, perhaps even pessimistic, in his expectations. Shortly after the novel's release, Chesnutt wrote to his eldest daughter, Ethel, a rather dispirited letter, complaining of a "touch of rheumatism in my right knee" and an overall feeling of "revulsion" from which he hoped to recover. Though he was glad that his "publishers believe in the book, and we all hope it may do well," the enthusiasm and confidence he had felt for it when he submitted it to the press a few months earlier had clearly waned. He revealed to Ethel that he had moved into the Williamson Building in downtown Cleveland, returning to "business this winter, as unless my book does very well indeed I shall need the money. Also need the pressure to keep me straight and make me work."[20]

Chesnutt seemed to have sensed the literary consequences of the political shift in the country. *The Marrow of Tradition* sold barely three thousand copies in its first year. Despite his disappointment with its sales, Chesnutt seemed prepared for the novel's poor showing on the literary market. He recalled Howells's explanation of this phenomenon not too long before when he spoke of the distinction between critical readers. Moreover, Chesnutt had, like Stowe half a century before, taken aim at Southern political and cultural institutions. He knew Southern audiences would be unsparing in their critique of the novel. As if following a familiar literary convention of assessing American political novels, the reviews by critical readers located in the North of *The Marrow of Tradition* were overwhelmingly positive. The Boston-based monthly magazine *The Literary World* offered it effusive praise. "There is real power in this novel of Southern life. It deals with present conditions, with the inextinguishable race prejudice, with the struggle to keep the negro down and deprive him of his constitutional rights, with the grisly tendency toward mob execution."[21] Aside from the northeastern reviews that praised the novel, Chesnutt seemed more interested in appealing to Black readers with his latest work. He cherished a letter from Timothy Thomas Fortune, editor of the popular Black periodical *The New York Age*, who wrote, "I have just finished reading *The Marrow of Tradition*. I thank God that He has given you genius to write such a work. It is the strongest work of fiction on our side since *Uncle Tom's Cabin*, which it equals in dramatic power and excels in the plot and literary finish. I would not be surprised if it should work such a revolution in public sentiment as *Uncle Tom's* wrought, at any venture it will accomplish a vast good."[22] Chesnutt was heartened by Fortune's remarks, but it was not enough to counter the backlash of negative criticism that he would later confront over the publication of his most political novel.

While Chesnutt anticipated a division in the novel's reception between Northern and Southern readers, as well as its appeal mainly to critical readers, he had not expected a negative or, as he put it in a letter to his publisher, "not a favorable" review, from one of his most ardent supporters. By the time *The Marrow of Tradition* appeared on the literary scene, Howells's years of political radicalism and optimism for the future of American literature had waned. In the fall of 1901, Howells had removed himself from the centers of literary culture to live among wealthy retirees off the coast of Maine. He had grown ornery and cranky after McKinley's assassination, having experienced family tragedies of his own. His reviews reflected this change. Regretting a damning review he had written in 1901 of an academic survey of American literature, he decided that it didn't do to let oneself go. Thirteen years later, he apologized to the author, Barrett Wendell, for the "abominable spirit" of his review. There is no record of Howells apologizing for his unfavorable review of *The Marrow of Tradition* that appeared in the December 1901 issue of the *North American Review*. But his remarks on *Marrow* proved to be a blow to its author. Subsequent critics would pick up on Howells's review, taking his remarks out of the context and spirit of the times, viewing them as a personal attack on Chesnutt rather than Howells's more general assessment of a "time when most novels are not worthwhile."[23]

Divided into eight discrete sections, each dealing with a book of recent fiction, Howells devoted the review's sixth section to *The Marrow of Tradition*. This review, so different from the tenor of his previous assessment of Chesnutt's stories, dwells on the author's race. Howells begins his assessment in a tone of innocent speculation that renders his critique sharper when it is delivered. "Mr. Chesnutt, it seems to me, has lost literary quality in acquiring literary quantity, and though his book, 'The Marrow of Tradition,' is of the same strong material as his earlier books, it is less simple throughout, and therefore less excellent in manner." Howells would continue in much the same spirit, delivering his admiration for an author he once had faith in. "At his worst, he is no worse than the higher average of the ordinary novelist, but he ought always to be very much better, for he began better, and he is of that race which has, first of all, to get rid of the cakewalk, if it will not suffer from a smile far more blighting than any frown." Whereas Howells had previously viewed Chesnutt as an "artist," here he views him as a member of what he calls "the black race," pitting him against "the whites." Recognizing the critical shift in his view of Chesnutt, Howells explained that "I am not saying that he is so inartistic as to play the advocate; whatever his minor foibles may be, he is an artist whom his stepbrother Americans may well be proud of; but while he recognizes pretty well all the facts in the case, he is too clearly of a judgment that is made up. One cannot blame him for that; what would one be one's self?" Howells seems to take issue with the novel's determination that those who were its victims had not been, at least in part, responsible for the violence. He dismisses its rendering of "the bloody revolution at Wilmington, North Carolina, a few years ago." Howells asked, "If the tables could once be turned, and it could be that it was the black race which violently and lastingly triumphed in the bloody revolution at Wilmington, North Carolina, a few years ago, what would not we excuse to the white man who made the atrocity the argument of his fiction?" The question is worth asking. But the racial terms in which Howells understood the problems seems to miss entirely the point Chesnutt was making in the novel. What we take to be two distinct races of people, a Black race and a white one, is an illusion, a fiction made up to justify the violence and resentments. The two are intertwined, they are related, they are in fact *one family*. The mistake that Olivia and her husband made was to view themselves as existing apart, as members of a distinct race. They come to realize their mistake, but the question the novel asks is different. Will we see race as a deadly mistake, or will we see it as a way of asserting our rights by depriving others of theirs? But Howells only sees race. He concluded his reading of the novel by making race rather than character the novel's central problem: "No one who reads the book can deny that the case is presented with great power, or fail to recognize in the writer a portent of the sort of negro equality against which no series of hangings and burnings will finally avail."[24]

Howells's review of *The Marrow of Tradition* marked a shift in his view of the potential of American literature. Howells was bemoaning the end of American realism. The movement he had led with such vigor was now just a distant memory; the public craved a different kind of literature, novels full of romance, intrigue, and false characters. They sought novels like *Trilby* by George du Maurier, which had outsold all of Howells's realist novels by an incredibly wide margin. Howells seemed to transfer his sense of despair over the future of American literature to those he had once expected to carry on the mantle of realism. Howells's somewhat flippant assessment caused Chesnutt to rethink his own sense of the kind of literature he was writing. As he put it in a letter to his publisher shortly after the appearance of Howells's review, "I am beginning to suspect that the public as a rule does not care for books in which the principal characters are colored people, or with a striking sympathy with that race as contrasted with the white race." Though he remained committed to writing literature, Chesnutt was beginning to doubt the value of the kind of literature he was writing, since his books were not meeting his hope of achieving "popular success," which to Chesnutt meant "a sale of 20,000 or 30,000 copies, enough to produce a modest return for the amount expended in writing it."[25]

Indeed, *The Marrow of Tradition* had not come close to becoming a popular success. Chesnutt wondered if it was time to change tack. Perhaps the novel was not the only or even the best way to convey his solution to the race problem. Howells had criticized Chesnutt for writing a "bitter" book about "the relations between blacks and whites." Perhaps his quarrel was not with Chesnutt's novel but any novel about the relations between Blacks and whites. Novels about such relationships did not sell. Relations between Blacks and whites were so unpleasant at the time that it was far easier to avoid literature that grappled with its challenges. To write a different kind of novel, Chesnutt would have to present his characters engaged in different kinds of relationships, but he felt such characters would be false. Howells had given up on novels as a way of appealing to the public. Chesnutt looked to his publisher for answers, but they had none to give. They seemed baffled by the public and critical response to *Marrow*. Chesnutt would find answers elsewhere. He gave up writing novels for a while and searched for a new form in which he could address the public more directly.

14

The Novelist as Public Intellectual

Personally I belong to the more radical school, in which I should class such organs of thought as the *New York Evening Post* and the *Independent*; as I do not think the matter of race or racial development under our constitution and theory of government should be considered by the law at all, and I believe the political and social structure of the South to be destructive of liberty.

—Chesnutt to Robert C. Ogden, May 27, 1904

On Wednesday, January 23, 1901, the *Boston Evening Transcript* opened its Books of the Day column with a glowing review of a recently published book called *The American Negro: What He Was, What He Is, and What He May Become* by William Hannibal Thomas. Under the title "A Negro on the Negro Question," the reviewer called the book, brought out earlier that month by the Macmillan Company, "very remarkable." The unnamed reviewer's praise of the book was qualified by a graphic statement that would drive Chesnutt's yearslong campaign to remove *The American Negro* from bookshelves. "Nevertheless," the reviewer explained, "Mr. Thomas puts the knife into the body of the unfortunate American Negro deeper than I have ever seen it put before." This was a story of betrayal, *racial* betrayal. Thomas claimed an insider's knowledge of what he called "negro characteristics" because he was born of "legitimate race admixture" in "a log cabin, on the fourth day of May, 1843, in Jackson Township, Pickaway County, Ohio." In the foreword to the book, Thomas offered a brief personal history, recounting his "mixed blood" ancestry, especially as it pertained to his time spent as a teacher in the summer of 1861, "supplying the place of principal of the Union Seminary, which at that time was the sole academic school in America managed by Negroes."[1] He also served in the Civil War, losing his right arm in battle, from a gunshot wound, "on the evening of the 21st of February" in Wilmington, North Carolina. Based on these facts, one might assume that Thomas and Chesnutt would have a great deal in common.

Despite having much in common biographically, they couldn't have been more different. From Thomas's vantage point, as a member of Ohio's free Black community, he observed "everywhere the same fixed traces of an environing heredity cropping out through selfishness, insincerity, and servility as the bar sinister of negrology." The claims and rhetoric of *The American Negro* were so specious and unsubstantiated, it is difficult to see what the reviewer saw as "remarkable" in the book, other than a confirmation of racial stereotypes. Comparing the book and its author to Booker T. Washington, whose autobiography *Up from Slavery* had just come out under Walter Hines Page's direction from Doubleday, Page & Company, the *Transcript*'s reviewer surprisingly claimed that Thomas "is a deeper thinker than Mr. Washington, and the ideas he presents are more orderly than those contained in Mr. Washington's recent volume." Following this rather unfavorable comparison, at least from Washington's side of things, the reviewer went on to distinguish Thomas by comparing his ideas with Chesnutt's. "Unlike Mr. Charles W. Chesnutt," referring to his "Future American" essays, which had appeared in the paper a few months earlier, "Mr. Thomas sees little hope for the race in the prospect of amalgamation with the whites."

This was just one of many points, as Chesnutt would go on to outline, on which he and Thomas differed. Chesnutt took issue with the idea of inherited racial characteristics. As a lawyer, Chesnutt was a close reader of the Constitution and agreed passionately with the nation's founding principle that "all men were created free and equal." Perhaps the most important divergence between them rested on the issue of "the disfranchisement of the blacks," as the *Transcript*'s reviewer put it. "Mr. Thomas himself advocated a strict educational suffrage qualification and the modification of the fifteenth amendment." Since the early 1890s, disfranchisement had become a major issue among Southern state legislatures. Chesnutt was involved in protesting efforts that deprived Black men of the right to vote. For Chesnutt, the Fifteenth Amendment "was one of the finest acts of statesmanship ever recorded." Its only flaw was that it wasn't being properly applied or defended by the federal government. Chesnutt's position on the Fifteenth Amendment marked a radical departure from *both* Thomas and Washington. There was no more important political issue for Chesnutt than the franchise, what now goes by the name "voting rights," following the passage of the 1965 Voting Rights Act. In 1901, at the time Chesnutt was writing, voting rights were stipulated by the Fifteenth Amendment alone. The amendment was brief. It was proposed on December 7, 1868, and ratified on February 3, 1870. Section one of the amendment states that "the right of citizens of the United States to vote shall not be denied or abridged by the United States or by any State on account of race, color, or previous condition of servitude." Section two grants Congress "the power to enforce this article by appropriate legislation." These two sentences of the U.S. Constitution formed the cornerstone of Chesnutt's political position.

In *The American Negro*, Thomas expressed a radically different view. In one of the book's longest and most detailed chapters, Thomas blamed the Republican Party that was, he wrote, "directly responsible for the political debauchery of the Southern negro." He accused Republican politicians of investing "civic functions" on those who were "ignorant beings clothed in patches, sleeping in hovels, and scarcely one remove in intelligence from their inseparable animal companions of plantation life." For Thomas, the enfranchisement of the "freedmen" was nothing more than "the partisan tool of designing white men" to maintain political power by using them for their votes without regard to their actual needs. Thomas's argument against the foundational democratic principle of voting rights incensed Chesnutt.

After reading the review of *The American Negro* in the *Transcript*, where glowing reviews of his own books had also appeared, Chesnutt went out and bought the book for two dollars, probably from the Arthur H. Clark Company over on Prospect Avenue, and read it in the quiet of his study. While the review had described its contents accurately, it did little to prepare him for the scope of Thomas's attack on all those connected with "the Negro race." Chesnutt was outraged. But before formulating his own response to it, he decided to write to his friend Joseph Edgar Chamberlin, the *Transcript*'s literary editor at the time, to find out who wrote the review of *The American Negro*. Chesnutt was dumbfounded by Chamberlin's response. It was Chamberlin himself who'd written the review. Chamberlin, who had written reviews of Chesnutt's books, with whom he'd dined, who'd hosted him and his children at his New England home, a man whose taste in literature and judgment of people he trusted. How could Chamberlin review Thomas's book, full of lies and misinformation about Black people, *favorably*? "I was bound to assume," Chamberlin explained, "that the house of Macmillan would not publish a book which was not genuine or allow a preface to be put forth which contained a false statement of the author's life."[2] Chesnutt understood Chamberlin's position. But he didn't accept it. If Chamberlin *appreciated* a book like Thomas's, one that claimed "negroes lack the ability to acquire clear and concise knowledge of ideas and things," how could he also appreciate Chesnutt's books, which presented Black people as complex, articulate, and ultimately no different from white people? Perhaps it was not the responsibility of a reviewer to fact-check a book; it was the publisher's responsibility.[3] How could the Macmillan Company *publish* such a book? But why would Chamberlin promote the book in his column? These and other such questions swirled through Chesnutt's mind as he corresponded with Chamberlin.

Chamberlin agreed that Thomas's position on race was troubling. But "if it be false, it should of course be controverted with facts." He went on to say that "if Thomas is a fraud he should be fully exposed, and the house of Macmillan should be riddled for giving him a hearing. If he is what he says he is, he is entitled to the hearing."[4] Chesnutt was dismayed, yet understood Chamberlin's logic as grounded in the First Amendment principle of free speech. But Chesnutt took Thomas's remarks *personally*. How could someone born in circumstances similar to his own come to such false conclusions about race? He knew it was up to him to expose Thomas as a fraud, to show readers, even such a well-informed and sympathetic reader like Chamberlin, the truth. Though Thomas and the publication of *The American Negro* have since fallen into the dustbin of history, both the book and its author had a profound effect on Chesnutt.

Shortly after his exchange with Chamberlin in early February 1901, Chesnutt would embark on his Southern journey that would result, several months later, in the publication of *The Marrow of Tradition*. But his Southern travels had done little to quell his outrage over the publication of *The American Negro*. To the contrary, they only sharpened his critique. Chesnutt started to compose a detailed memo he called "IN RE WILLIAM HANNIBAL THOMAS, AUTHOR OF 'THE AMERICAN NEGRO,'" which he distributed to several recipients between 1901 and 1904. Somewhere between legal brief and character sketch, Chesnutt's memo began in the tone of a memoirist: "In the month of February, 1901, while traveling through the Southern States, I made inquiry from time to time with reference to the career of one William Hannibal Thomas, author of a defamatory book against the Negro race, published by the Macmillan Company." Though Chesnutt wrote this in the first person, it revealed little about its author. It was *all* about the life of William Hannibal Thomas. Chesnutt conceded that Thomas had served in the Ninety-Fifth Regiment and the capture of Vicksburg during the Civil War, eventually earning the title of sergeant in Company I of the Fifth United States Colored Infantry Regiment. However, Chesnutt also discovered that Thomas's record was blemished. Thomas had been expelled from the Western Theological Seminary in Allegheny, Pennsylvania, during 1868 for engaging in "criminal intercourse with the woman whom he subsequently married."[5] He also learned from Dr. J. W. E. Bowen, whom he met in Atlanta, that Thomas "while connected with Clark University, had misappropriated funds that came into his hands as an officer of said school." These were just a couple of several criminal charges against Thomas that Chesnutt discovered and recorded in his memo regarding the "AUTHOR OF 'THE AMERICAN NEGRO.'"

During Chesnutt's stay in Tuskegee with Booker T. Washington, they had long conversations about Thomas and his book. Unlike Washington, who assigned a few of his employees at Tuskegee to investigate Thomas, Chesnutt continued his own separate investigation into Thomas's affairs. A couple of months after returning home, Chesnutt sent Washington and George P. Brett, head of the Macmillan Company, the results of his investigation. Washington's letter of thanks suggested that Chesnutt's investigation into Thomas had been effective. "My dear Mr. C," it began,

I thank you for your kindness in sending me transcript of the evidence which has been compiled describing the character of

the execrable William Hannibal Thomas. I am very glad to learn
of your efforts to have this book withdrawn from circulation. I
believe that the effort is succeeding because the MacMillans are
not pushing it in any of the advertisements as I have taken pains
to notice.[6]

Chesnutt's memo into Thomas's life was a private document that he
circulated to have the book "withdrawn from circulation." He would also
go public with his campaign against Thomas in a series of personal essays
that broadened his attack against *The American Negro* and clarify his own
political position.

Shortly after returning from his Southern journey, he wrote a personal
essay for the *Boston Evening Transcript* describing his travels and observations.
Published in its Literature section on March 20, 1901, Chesnutt's essay
was a good deal more political than the articles concerning literature between which it appeared. The byline that appeared under the title "The
White and the Black" alluded to Chesnutt's status as a writer of fiction.
"By Charles W. Chesnutt, Author of 'The Wife of His Youth.'" The essay
drew on all of Chesnutt's literary and reporting skills to provide an eyewit-
ness account of the South since the passage of the *Plessy v. Ferguson* decision
in 1896. "I could almost write a book about these laws, their variations,
their applications and curious stories that one hears continually concerning
them."[7] Instead of writing a book about the disastrous consequences of new
segregation laws that the *Plessy v. Ferguson* decision had enabled, Chesnutt decided to tell *true* stories about "these laws" in the form of what now goes by
the name *creative nonfiction*. The label didn't exist when Chesnutt was writing.
The advantage of writing essays, rather than books, was that they could be
published quickly as articles, in daily or weekly periodicals. Several prominent realist writers—William Dean Howells, Henry James, Mark Twain,
and Constance Fenimore Woolson—also wrote nonfiction personal essays
about their travels abroad. Perhaps Woolson's essays, published in *Harper's
Monthly* twenty years earlier about her tour of the South shortly after the
Civil War, in the 1870s, can be read as closest in form to Chesnutt's nonfiction writing. But Chesnutt's essays were more political than that of these
authors. He wanted to offer a vivid and explicit argument against the *Plessy*
decision by showing readers how it had changed the South of his youth for

the worse. If something wasn't done to appeal the decision, those changes would become embedded, perhaps even spread beyond the South. These new laws were indicative of what he called "these reactionary days," a step backward, "perilously near to that of slavery."

Chesnutt's nonfiction essays read like an extended opinion piece based on personal experience, backed up by conversations with Southern men and women, train conductors and passengers, conjure doctors and their patients. He concluded "The White and the Black" with "some reflections suggested by a book recently published." This marked the beginning of Chesnutt's public campaign to denounce *The American Negro* and its author. "Mr. Thomas," Chesnutt's investigation revealed, "has lived in Ohio, in Georgia, in South Carolina, and elsewhere. I have recently been in all these States, and find a universal disposition everywhere to let Massachusetts claim him; she is perhaps, better able to bear the burden than any other State." Chesnutt deemed the book to be so offensive that it was "unquotable." He summarized it for readers as consisting of "five or six hundred pages of defamation of a race with which he admits close kinship" in which the author "denies the Negro intellect, character, and capacity for advancement." To refute Thomas, Chesnutt declared, "With my own eyes I have seen, upon revisiting places which I knew eighteen or twenty years ago, that the colored people are acquiring property, in large amounts."[8]

"The White and the Black" was the first of a series of essays he published that described his return to the South. These essays were intended, as he explained in his letter to Washington on March 13, 1901, to provide readers insights into the changes in the South he observed since having left his Fayetteville home almost twenty years earlier. "I have put some of my impressions in the shape of letters to the Boston *Transcript*, which will no doubt see the light, unless I have delayed them too long." But the essays were more than just "impressions." They were a close study of the people, culture, and politics of the South that were based on personal experience, more personal and political than any of his previous publications. Chesnutt was working on his novel *The Marrow of Tradition* while he penned these essays, hence the delay in completing them for publication. Perhaps he used the essay form as a repository for his personal thoughts and opinions of what was going on at the time so they would not intrude on the multiple points of view he was developing in his fiction. Or perhaps they were a way of keeping his name in the public eye as he worked away on his great novel. Chesnutt was now a literary celebrity; he was frequently being called on to offer his thoughts on current events and literature. After Howells's *Atlantic* review appeared, Chesnutt was solicited by several editors for stories or essays they might include in their periodicals.

The *Transcript* published two of Chesnutt's Southern essays. The second, entitled "The Negro's Franchise," appeared a few months later, on May 11, 1901. He opened the essay by making clear that he was "asked by the *Transcript* to express any thoughts which may occur to me upon the very interesting and thoughtful address of Dr. Donald of Trinity Church, delivered at the dedication of Dorothy Hall." Elijah Winchester Donald, whose religious sermons often contained reflections on current political events, was rector of Trinity Church in Boston and was well known to readers of the *Transcript*. There was nothing fictional about Chesnutt's second essay for the *Transcript*; it was more a work of reportage. This one appeared alongside "A Realistic Pen-Picture" of the recent "Jacksonville Fire" written "By an Eye-Witness." There was no mention of Chesnutt being a literary author of stories in his byline this time. Instead, Chesnutt's essay was introduced by offering political context: "Mr. Charles W. Chesnutt Takes Issue with Dr. Donald's Tuskegee Address—The Thirteenth Amendment of Little Value Without the Fourteenth and Fifteenth—The Negro Must Continue to Appeal to the North for Help—A Stirring Article." The *Transcript* was pitting Chesnutt against Donald. Donald, like Thomas and Washington, felt that education, not voting rights, was the most important issue for improving the lives of former slaves and their descendants. The *Transcript* was presenting Chesnutt as engaged in a political and particularly public debate on the issue of the Fifteenth Amendment, a debate in which Chesnutt was now an authority, even a spokesman. Chesnutt put into print his opinion not just about a local political event, a speech by "Dr. Donald," but about national political issues.

Chesnutt also wrote other essays about his Southern travels that were published elsewhere. "A Visit to Tuskegee" appeared in the *Cleveland Leader* on March 31, 1901, and another called "Superstitions and Folk-Lore of the South" was published in the May 1901 issue of *Modern Culture*; in both,

Chesnutt continued to develop the form of his current "impressions" of the South and the importance of the Fifteenth Amendment to its progress. He was also asked to write a review of Thomas's book for *The Critic: An Illustrated Monthly Review of Literature, Art & Life* by its editor Jeannette Leonard Gilder for its April 1901 issue. As sister to Richard Watson Gilder, who ran *The Century*, Jeannette Gilder had been acquainted with Chesnutt for some time. But they had become literary allies when she published his review of Washington's book *The Future of the American Negro* in February of the previous year. It was clear that Gilder had a great deal of admiration for Chesnutt's work. She introduced Chesnutt's essay with a brief editorial that made plain his status at the time. "Mr. Charles W. Chesnutt, the writer of this review, speaks freely and forcibly of the man who has defamed his race. Mr. Chesnutt, who is himself allied by blood to the Negro race, is also a writer of wide reputation. He knows his subject thoroughly and speaks not only with feeling, but with the facts at his fingerends." The note was signed, simply, "EDS. *CRITIC*."[9] This combination of fact and feeling characterized Chesnutt's nonfiction writing that comprised an increasingly large share of his literary oeuvre.

The publication of *The American Negro* and his return to the South after an almost twenty-year hiatus seemed to coincide magically, cementing Chesnutt's new status as a twentieth-century public intellectual. The term *public intellectual* had only recently entered discourse via the political pronouncements surrounding the 1898 Dreyfus affair made by renowned French novelist Émile Zola. The case of Captain Alfred Dreyfus began a few years earlier, in December 1894, when Dreyfus, a Jewish artillery officer, was convicted of treason. The accusation was baseless, but Dreyfus was convicted and sentenced to life in prison. He had been in prison for several years before Zola decided to take up his case. Zola gave voice to a critique of the government's case against Dreyfus not by staging a coup d'état or by supporting acts of terrorism but by publishing an opinion piece in a newspaper that enabled the literate public to consider an opposing view to the consensus that accepted Dreyfus's guilt. Zola genuinely believed that the pen was mightier than the sword.

Chesnutt found himself in a similar position. Having witnessed the aftermath of the Wilmington massacre and dissenting from the increasingly popular view that Black education should trump questions of Black political rights, particularly the right to vote, Chesnutt turned to writing sharp political essays to critique the government—and individuals—that supported the racial logic fostered by the *Plessy v. Ferguson* decision. Though the court had issued its verdict in 1896, and Tourgée had lost his legal battle in favor of "color-blind" justice, Chesnutt continued to write, speak, and argue against the decision. That Chesnutt expressed a decidedly unpopular position at the time goes without saying. Despite the considerable toll on his future *literary* career, it was a position he never regretted.

After the publication of *The Marrow of Tradition* in the fall of 1901, Chesnutt was forced to deal with its poor showing on the literary market. Around the end of the year, he was contemplating taking a different tack with his fiction, writing stories that featured white characters, rather than the "colored people" that had become the mainstay of his stories and novels. Amid these musings, on January 12, 1903, he received a surprising invitation from the New York publisher James Pott to write an essay "on the general subject of the disenfranchisement of the negro of the south." Pott's idea was to create a single book comprising essays from "representative leaders of the race." Chesnutt accepted the invitation only after he was assured that his essay would appear next to essays by Booker T. Washington, W. E. B. Du Bois, Paul Laurence Dunbar, and Timothy Thomas Fortune. When Chesnutt sent his essay to Pott on June 16, 1903, after a considerable delay, he offered a half-hearted apology, explaining that the essay had become "at least twice as long as what you asked me for."[10] The essay had grown in size and importance. He asked Pott if he could submit it for periodical publication as well, to broaden its audience and increase his income from it. Pott refused. But he did agree to Chesnutt's request to have him increase his remuneration from the fifty dollars he had originally promised to one hundred. Chesnutt's essay appeared third, after Washington's "Industrial Education for the Negro" and Du Bois's "The Talented Tenth." Chesnutt's "The Disfranchisement of the Negro" was followed by four others. Pott's placement of the essays in the collection was significant.

Pott was known as a publisher mainly of religious and theological books, appealing primarily to clergymen and students, particularly of the Church of England and its affiliates. His decision to solicit essays to compose a book on "the Negro Problem" seemed a bit out of his publishing wheelhouse. None of the essays in the collection addressed religious matters. Du Bois and Washington were preoccupied with discussing systems of education while essays by Fortune and Dunbar were interested in "the Negro's" cultural contributions to American life. Pott didn't offer an introduction to the collection, but he did offer a brief biographical note, introducing each of the authors he invited to contribute. In introducing Chesnutt's essay, Pott explained that he "presents a straightforward statement of facts concerning the disfranchisement of the Negro in the Southern States. Mr. Chesnutt, who is too well known as a writer to need any introduction to an American audience, puts the case for the Negro to the American people very plainly, and spares neither the North nor the South."[11]

This was the first of Chesnutt's essays published in book form. It was also the only one to be published in that format. With this single exception, all of Chesnutt's nonfiction essays, amounting to well over fifty, were published in periodicals or delivered as speeches in front of Northern audiences. He also wrote dozens of essays that remained in manuscript form, having never attempted to submit them for publication. It is surprising that Chesnutt never considered collecting some of his essays, those published in journals and newspapers, for book publication as Du Bois, Washington, Howells, and James had. Doing so might have broadened his literary profile, as essay collections by these authors had done for them. It is difficult to speculate on Chesnutt's reasons for refraining from doing so. Chesnutt's political essays were almost always part of a contemporary debate, taking up current events in highly specific ways. Perhaps he felt that essays on such timely topics would not have much of a shelf life. The reading public's attention span then, as now, was short.

But it was also the case that Chesnutt did not seem to derive as much pleasure from writing political essays as he did from writing fiction. Fiction writing, for Chesnutt, was a labor of love; he wanted to do it full-time but couldn't afford to do so with his family obligations. Despite his celebrity status, his primary source of income was stenography, not literature. Yet it was to fiction that he turned again to portray the inner life of this brave new post-*Plessy* world.

PART V

Age of Problems

15

Victims of Heredity

I am pretty fairly convinced that the color line runs everywhere so far as the United States is concerned, and I am even now wondering whether the reputation I have made would help or hinder a novel that I might publish along an entirely different line.

—Chesnutt to Houghton, Mifflin and Company, December 30, 1901

By 1903, the great disappointment Chesnutt had felt over *The Marrow of Tradition*'s poor showing on the literary market had worn off. The sales of the novel fell so far short of what Chesnutt and Houghton, Mifflin and Company expected, particularly given the success of his previous books, that Chesnutt abandoned his attempt to make a living as a professional author and returned to his work as a court stenographer. The stenography business was going strong; Chesnutt's skills remained in high demand.

Chesnutt was now forty-five. He entered middle age with a good deal of optimism. Though *The Marrow of Tradition* had not fulfilled either his or his publisher's expectations, he had secured an excellent reputation as a literary author and public intellectual. While earning a good income from his court reporting business, he remained active on the lecture circuit, delivering lectures and writing articles relating to the race problem. His oldest daughter, Ethel, was enjoying married life and expecting her first child. Helen had secured a teaching position at Central High School in Cleveland after a short stint in the South. Edwin entered Harvard as a sophomore in the fall, to join the class of 1905. Helen recalled this time as being happy and prosperous for the entire family. "Susan and Charles were content—the plans for their children were working out exactly as they wished."[1]

Since Ethel and Helen's happy departure from Northampton, Chesnutt no longer had an excuse to travel east. But during his daughters' years at Smith, Chesnutt had become familiar with the New England literary scene. He'd made frequent trips to Boston to discuss the publication of his books at the office of Houghton on Park Street. He'd also grown fond of the city, visiting the corner bookshop that had displayed his books so prominently, meeting fellow authors for lunch, frequently visiting the Museum of Fine Arts, then located in the city's Copley Square, in a now-destroyed building designed by the Boston-based architecture firm of Sturgis and Brigham. As a frequent contributor to the *Boston Evening Transcript*, he was careful to keep up with the cultural and political events of the city.

On one of Chesnutt's visits to Boston, he had been introduced to Bliss Perry. Perry, or *Professor* Perry, as Chesnutt addressed him, had just been appointed editor of *The Atlantic*, following Page's decision to resign the editorship to pursue book publishing in New York City. If Page stood in Chesnutt's mind as a Southern kindred spirit, a man like Chesnutt, raised in North Carolina, Perry was a New England man through and through. Before accepting the editorship of *The Atlantic*, Perry had occupied the position of Holmes Professor of English Literature at Princeton University. Page's abrupt departure from the press caused Chesnutt some consternation. Page and Chesnutt shared much besides their ongoing interest in Southern affairs; they were equally ill at ease with the customs of the New England educated elite with whom they regularly associated. Those who found Page's Southern habits and impatience with New England's academic traditions off-putting welcomed Perry as his replacement.

But Chesnutt had been comfortable with Page. It was Page's presence at both *The Atlantic* and Houghton that Chesnutt trusted. Page understood Chesnutt's vision and welcomed him into the fold of American authors as few editors at the time had been willing to do. Now that Page was gone, Chesnutt would have to form new connections at 4 Park Street, chief of which was with the man who'd replaced Page at the helm of *The Atlantic*. Returning to Cleveland after dropping off his daughters at Smith and spending a few days in Boston in late summer of 1899, Chesnutt wrote to

Perry. "I was not aware, nor had I received any intimation, at the time I was introduced to you at the Atlantic Office a few days ago, that you were going to assume control of the magazine, or I should have grasped the opportunity to become better acquainted with you, and should have congratulated you, as I do now, heartily, upon the very important post which you have assumed in the world of letters."[2]

Perry was born and raised in picturesque Williamstown, nestled in the Berkshire Mountains of northwestern Massachusetts. His father, Arthur Latham Perry, was professor of economics at Williams College and was known as much for his adherence to Christian ethics as he was for his economic ideas. Bliss was the eldest son of a large family that lived just a stone's throw from the campus. He had grown up surrounded not only by the books and languages of a classical education but was also blessed with easy access to the pleasures of nature; he fished and hunted, studied birds and all manner of wildlife. He entered Greylock Institute, a boarding school, at a young age, which was a little more than out of sight of his father's house—the school was just as essentially New England as his home had been. And Williams College was a continuation of this New England of open skies and invitations to meditate. From birth, he had lived where it was taken for granted that things of the mind, of the spirit, must have first consideration. For Chesnutt, Bliss Perry's life was so far from the life he knew growing up in rural North Carolina he found it difficult to find common ground with the new editor. So he turned to literature, just as he had with Tourgée and Cable about a decade earlier, to strike up a connection with someone so well established in the exclusive literary circles of the time.

Chesnutt approached Perry more tentatively than he had Page, revealing little of himself but hoping Perry would take just as keen an interest in his work as had his predecessor. He concluded his first letter to Perry with a tentative query: "I do not know whether your connection with the Atlantic carries with it the function of literary advisor, but if it does, and in looking over the stories there should occur to you any more effective arrangement than the one I have given them in the MSS., which I have just forwarded to the house under another cover, I shall be glad to have the book get the benefit of your idea."[3] Chesnutt was referring to his second collection of short stories, *The Wife of His Youth, and Other Stories of the Color Line*, which Page had accepted and ushered through much of the publication process. But Page had left the press before the book had entered its final production and marketing phase. Page had played an active role in the publication of Chesnutt's first collection of stories, suggesting the final title, *The Conjure Woman*, and deciding on which of the twenty stories Chesnutt had originally submitted to include.

Before leaving his desk at Houghton and *The Atlantic*, Page had left a note for Perry, suggesting that he look over Chesnutt's stories, "with a view to finding one that might be suitable for publication in the Atlantic in advance of the book," which was to appear on bookshelves in late November. In his letter, Chesnutt reminded Perry about the note, which he had discussed with Page, and asked for more. Chesnutt wanted Perry to take up the mantle of "literary advisor" that Page had left behind. "I am sure the general subject considered in the stories would be viewed by you sympathetically, if I can judge from 'The Plated City,' which I read with great interest and pleasure several years ago, and regarded as a contribution on the right side of the same great theme." He concluded this uncharacteristically awkwardly phrased letter by wishing Perry "an entirely congenial career" in his "new work" as editor of *The Atlantic*.[4]

Published in 1895 by the New York–based publishing house Charles Scribner's Sons, Perry's second novel dealt with the race problem from the vantage point of a highly educated white New Englander. The novel introduced readers to Tom Beaulieu and his beautiful sister, Esther, both considered colored in a working-class Connecticut town called Bartonvale. Tom is the star third baseman for the Bartonvale Nine local baseball team. Perry opened the novel in the middle of the ninth inning, in which Tom miraculously steals home base after having been intentionally walked by the pitcher, clinching an unexpected win for his team. Though Tom is appreciated for his prowess on the field, he is shunned by the town's white residents as a member of its "colored quarter." In the novel, Perry exposed not only the folly of New England caste prejudice but also the tragedy of racial segregation as practiced in the North. Published less than a year before the *Plessy v. Ferguson* verdict, *The Plated City* offered a view of segregation from an author who spent almost all his life in elite academic circles in the Northeast.

While Perry described the occupants of the town's library and base-ball field in detail, his so-called colored characters, like the entirely baffling Mrs. Calhoun, who runs the boardinghouse where Tom lives, remain wooden in manner and speech. After explaining to Esther, who has recently moved to the town from Québec, that she is, like himself, considered colored in Connecticut, Mrs. Calhoun proceeds to set Tom straight. "Tom," she exclaimed, "you mustn't keep that po'critter heah. T'won't do nohow. Look a heah! I'se watched her and Cy's watched her when she wa'n't looking, and I tell you yo' sistah's white!" Based entirely on Mrs. Calhoun's words and apparent observation, Tom and Esther de-cide they are indeed "white" and make their way to the "other side of the river, where the white people are," as instructed by their self-appointed Black benefactor.[5]

That Chesnutt had read Perry's insipid representation of Black charac-ters and novelistic take on the race problem "with great interest and plea-sure" was not surprising. The book indicated to Chesnutt that he and Perry were, despite his use of racial stereotypes and embarrassing Black dialect, on the "right side of the same great theme." What was surprising was that Chesnutt had never mentioned Perry or his book before he had become editor of *The Atlantic*. Chesnutt had been quick to seek out like-minded au-thors, Black and white, who wrote on the race problem. Chesnutt had also become well known for his stories and essays on the "great theme." How odd, then, that these two writers' paths never crossed before Perry joined *The Atlantic*. Perhaps it was Perry's academic position and New England roots that kept the writers apart. In fact, Perry's novel dealing with the race problem was mostly a New England romance in which a young librarian called Sally Vance and an up-and-coming architect called Craig Kennedy have their marriage virtually arranged for them by the town's autocrat, Dr. Atwood. Esther also ends up married to a wealthy lawyer, though Tom dies, trying to save Dr. Atwood from a burning building. Perry's Northern view of the race problem seemed to be less urgent, and a little more roman-tic, compared to Chesnutt's literary approach to the problem.

Perry, as a writer and editor, was mostly interested in literature dealing with the people and places most familiar to him. Chesnutt's *Southern* stories of the color line did not interest him in the way the writings of Emerson,

Longfellow, Hawthorne, and Whitman had. Perry's response to Chesnutt's query and request that he might become his literary advisor—continuing the relationship he had forged with Page—nipped in the bud the prospect of the two forming a literary alliance in the great war against racial segregation. On August 30, 1899, Perry responded to Chesnutt's letter. He opened the letter by explaining—not apologizing for—why he had not responded sooner and relied almost entirely on his assistant, William B. Parker, a recent Harvard grad, to continue communication with Chesnutt. "I have asked Mr. Parker's attention to your question concerning the order of the stories in the book, and if he has any suggestions to make he will communicate them directly to you. As I have been unable to read the book as a whole, I cannot propose any better order than that which you have already given them." Perry had read enough of the book to accept one of them, "The Bouquet," the only one of Chesnutt's *Stories of the Color Line* to feature a white character called Mary Myrover, for publication in *The Atlantic*. Though not a New Englander herself, Mary did occupy the position of "white schoolteacher" in the story, occupying the role that most New Englanders played in Southern fiction of the time. He closed the letter cordially, "Let me thank you for your courteous word about 'The Plated City' and beg you to accept my assurance of interest in your further literary work."[6] True to his word, Perry left all further correspondence with Chesnutt to Parker, who took even less interest in Chesnutt's Southern stories than had his boss.

Parker was consistent and courteous with his rejections. In a particularly poignant and revealing rejection to a story Chesnutt submitted about a year later called "A Limb of Satan," Parker delivered a blow couched in velvet. Parker opened his letter with an enthusiastic endorsement only to dash Chesnutt's hopes in the next breath. "I have thoroughly enjoyed reading 'A Limb of Satan,' but, as I have just been writing a minute ago in the case of another negro story, we feel a little dubious about printing more negro or dialect stories for the present—we feel it wise to call a halt for a time at least." In the same letter, Parker also rejected a novel that Chesnutt had submitted earlier that year called *The Rainbow Chasers* for serial publication in *The Atlantic*. Here too Parker's rejection seemed especially cynical because he acknowledged, even enthusiastically praised, the quality of the work but rejected it in the end solely because he had already contracted other writers—namely, romances by popular female authors.

> Now as to the serial—here, too, you find us on the off side. We have arranged, however, for as much serial matter as we can use, probably up to the middle of 1902; namely:-a historical novel by Sarah Orne Jewett to begin in November; a series of Penelope's Irish Experiences—travel and humor—by Kate Douglas Wiggin to begin in November; another novel, historical, by Mary Johnston, of a period earlier than she dealt with in "To Have and to Hold."
>
> These are all considerable pieces of work, and, as you will see, make it almost impossible for us to accept any other serial story for fully a year and a half. If it were not for this embarrassment of riches we should be glad to consider your novel, with which we wish you all success.[7]

Chesnutt received Parker's, and by proxy Perry's, message loud and clear. They were not interested in publishing Chesnutt's "negro stories." Chesnutt found himself in good company, however. Kate Chopin's story "The Demon" was similarly rejected, despite its "excellent craftsmanship," because "the sad note seems to us too much accented." Like Chesnutt, Chopin wrote with an accent, presenting her Southern characters and situations with considerable complexity and so could not penetrate the New England sensibility that had returned with a vengeance since Page's untimely departure from 4 Park Street.

Chesnutt responded to Parker's rejections by writing another novel, this one intended either to appeal to their New England sensibility or to mock it. Perhaps he intended it to do both at once. Chesnutt's purpose for his new novel that he called *Evelyn's Husband* is unclear because he either destroyed any mention of it in his correspondence and personal writings or because he decided not to discuss the novel with any of his usual literary interlocutors. Published in 2005, almost seventy-five years after his death, the novel has languished from a lack of critical attention since it was rejected by both Houghton and by McClure, Phillips and Company in 1903.

The reader's reports from Houghton, which Chesnutt likely never read, reveal a great deal about why the novel was kept from the public for so long. "Mr. Chesnutt," the anonymous reader at Houghton explained in a report dated October 13, 1903, "has written a story dealing mainly with Back Bay Bostonians, and has travelled, in my judgment, much beyond his depth. In other words, he has attempted to handle materials with which, either through lack of social experience, or opportunities of observation, he is unfamiliar. The result is a display of bad taste, ignorance of the ways of people decently brought up, and the obtrusion of an unmitigated and selfish cad on the attention of the reader in the person of Manson, Evelyn's lover and husband."[8] The full name of Chesnutt's hero was Hugh Manson, who is, in the words of a second reader at the press, "a poor Kentucky Mountain Boy, rescued and educated and turned into a brilliant architect doing business in Boston." Chesnutt's hero is a self-made man unlike Edward Cushing, the man originally engaged to marry Evelyn before Manson enters the romance. Curiously, none of the novel's first readers mentioned Cushing, who opened the novel, as "a man of taste, of culture, and of wide experience. He occupied a beautiful old home on a historic street, in the same spot where his ancestors, solid men of Boston, had dwelt, in successive houses, for two hundred years." Cushing, like most of the men who occupied the offices of Houghton, had graduated from Harvard "*cum laude*, and then went abroad." Upon returning to Boston, Cushing took another degree at Harvard Law School, "hoping to develop a taste for the profession, or at any rate to prepare himself for a career in politics or the diplomatic service, should he feel inclined to enter either;—some of his ancestors had won distinction in both, and the family name carried a certain prestige which might be counted upon to help him with either the electorate or the appointing power."[9] While respectful of Cushing's education and wealth, the narrator remains dubious of his accomplishments since they were achieved through inheritance rather than hard work.

When *Evelyn's Husband* was rescued from the decaying folders of his archive at Fisk University by the literary critic and editor Matthew Wilson, it was understood that Chesnutt was "writing in the genre of the white-life novel, in which African Americans write exclusively about white experience."[10] It is true that the novel features white characters, but it is not *exactly* about "white-life." It is a story about inheritance, not too far from the inheritance plot that drove much of the narrative that culminated in the race riot of *The Marrow of Tradition*. But *Evelyn's Husband* was more of a romance in which a wealthy, middle-aged, New England gentleman, and a Harvard man to boot, is left at the altar by a beautiful young woman whose family he has supported for much of her life. She elopes, a few hours before she is scheduled to marry Cushing, with a man "born in eastern Kentucky, thirty years ago."[11] Though lacking breeding and wealth, Manson is, in Evelyn's eyes at least, the better man. The man Evelyn chose for her husband is not only a Southerner; he is educated at the tuition-free, private, nonsegregated Berea College, about a hundred miles south of the state's more prestigious and segregated University of Kentucky, located in the heart of Lexington. Fittingly, Manson's "people were not descendants of cavaliers, proud of the deeds of their ancestors—not all of them noble—nor slave-holders drawing their wealth from the toil of other men. They were poor-whites." The poor white Southerner, much to the chagrin of the novel's first readers, is presented as the hero, while the wealthy Bostonian who'd earned multiple degrees at Harvard finds himself humiliated by the fickle Evelyn.

But Houghton's readers were right, in some respects, about the novel. The dialogue between the lovers revealed Chesnutt's lack of experience with the inner workings of Boston's elite society. He had, after all, just come to know it as an adult, when his first story, "The Goophered Grapevine," was accepted by *The Atlantic* when he was twenty-nine. That story added Uncle Julius to the cast of characters making up the American literary canon, alongside Rip Van Winkle, Hester Prynne, Ishmael, Uncle Tom, and Huck Finn. The characters in *Evelyn's Husband* lacked Julius's humor and charm.

Evelyn's Husband suffered from the trappings of popular romance, unlikely coincidences, the occasional corny monologue, and too-direct dialogue, tending to spell out what ought to be implied. It also lacked the sense of humor and irony that had become a trademark of Chesnutt's marriage stories and sketches, like "A Matter of Principal," and those published in his early years as a regular contributor to *Puck* magazine. But the contrast between the lovers who vie for Evelyn's hand in marriage is unmistakable. Chesnutt pits the young, poor white Southerner against the middle-aged, wealthy, Harvard-educated New Englander to great effect. The two coincidentally find themselves the sole occupants of a deserted island, somewhere off the coast of Brazil. Manson has lost his sight following the shipwreck, and Cushing opts not to reveal his identity. What so irritated the novel's first readers was not just that the Southerner defeated the Northerner in winning the beautiful maiden's hand in marriage but that Manson and Cushing are rescued, and Manson miraculously recovers his sight and is reunited with Evelyn. Upon their return to civilization, Cushing finds a more appropriate wife in Evelyn's mother, Alice, and all live, as in most popular romances of the time, happily ever after. But the novel did succeed in presenting readers a new kind of American family, one in which the Northerner must confront the vanity and privilege derived from his racial inheritance, accepting in the end the superiority of his "poor-white" Southern rival. It is a modern American David-and-Goliath story that drew upon Chesnutt's personal experience of Boston social life.

After receiving another rejection from Houghton, Chesnutt sent the manuscript almost immediately to Witter Bynner, who had just started working as an editor for McClure, Phillips and Company in New York City, after graduating from Harvard. Bynner offered Chesnutt a more personal but no less "harsh" rejection. On November 6, 1903, Bynner sent Chesnutt his opinion of the novel. "If you will let me talk to you as frankly as I judged from your manner you would not resent, I must say that I doubt if 'Evelyn's Husband' will do your reputation very much good. It might be published to fair advantage, perhaps; but we are convinced that in leaving your earlier kind of work you have made a literary misstep." This was Bynner's nice way of telling Chesnutt to stick to writing "negro stories." He continued: "I don't want you to think for a minute that we are not appreciative of the many excellent and charmingly written passages through the book, particularly in your narrative and running comment, which is so vastly better than your dialogue." He summed up his reading on a more positive note, urging Chesnutt to write more. "Though we are returning this, I shall be decidedly interested to hear of the progress of the novel you sketched to me, centering about an Octoroon. There is no doubt, I trust, that you will let us have first chance at your next book?"[12]

The book Chesnutt most likely sketched out to Bynner was *Paul Marchand, F.M.C.*, which, like *Evelyn's Husband*, would languish in the archive for several decades after his death.

Chesnutt seemed not to have taken Bynner's rejection of *Evelyn's Husband* personally. Now that Edwin had found a home at Harvard for himself, Chesnutt returned to Boston having put the development and rejection of *Evelyn's Husband* behind him. Though Chesnutt was critical of the Harvard elite who rejected his novel, he neither resented nor envied their privilege. Chesnutt was proud of Edwin for having earned entry into Harvard. And though the cost of tuition, room, and board took their toll on the family's finances, Chesnutt delighted in having his son included among the nation's "best and brightest" men Harvard accepted. With his frequent visits to Boston, ostensibly to see Edwin during his junior year, it was only a matter of time before Chesnutt encountered Perry again. After a few years of publishing nothing in *The Atlantic*, Chesnutt wrote to its editor on March 1, 1904.

Dear Mr. Perry:-

In pursuance of my threat the other evening when I saw you at the University Club, I enclose the manuscript of three stories entitled respectively, "Baxter's Procrustes," "White Weeds", and "A Close Shave"—I had thought of calling the last "The Jointed Doll" as an alternative title. If you can use one or more of them for the Atlantic, I should be glad to have you do so.[13]

Perry's response to Chesnutt's letter was unusually warm and swift. On a cool Saint Patrick's Day in Boston, Perry wrote to accept, finally, another story from Chesnutt for *The Atlantic*.

I have taken the earliest opportunity to read the three stories which you were good enough to send to the magazine. You must not think me unmindful of the eternal significance of the race question when I tell you that of the three stories I prefer "Baxter's Procrustes" for our particular purposes. It is an ingenious and amusing story, extremely well told. A good deal of our Atlantic fiction deals with serious, not to say tragic, problems, and it is a pleasure to us to accept a story of the other sort whenever its literary excellence warrants us in doing so.[14]

It's hard to overstate the significance of this exchange. Chesnutt was now working full-time, even overtime, as a court reporter and stenographer. He was running his own reporting firm, supervising several full-time employees, in an office located in the swank Williamson Building of Cleveland's downtown. He and Susan had just bought a new, more spacious home on Lamont Avenue, where Ethel and his first grandson could spend weekends, playing in the garden, while Susan relished hosting gatherings of her ever-growing circle of friends. Amid his booming business and family life, Chesnutt somehow found the time to take the train to Boston, visit with Edwin, and hobnob with the literati at its University Club. Founded in the early 1890s, located on the fashionable side of Beacon Street, the U Club was frequented mainly by wealthy and well-read Bostonians. Chesnutt and Perry likely discussed his new stories over a glass of brandy, with cigar or pipe in hand. No wonder "Baxter's Procrustes," a story about a fraternal group called the Bodleian Club, written in the first person of one of its members, appealed most to Perry. It seemed to be written with him in mind.

The Bodleian Club "is composed of gentlemen of culture, who are interested in books and book-collecting." The story was not just about book collecting, however. The club also boasted "quite a collection of personal mementoes of distinguished authors among them a paperweight which once belonged to Goethe, a lead pencil used by Emerson, an autograph letter of Matthew Arnold, and a chip from a tree felled by Mr. Gladstone."[15] The story is, quite frankly, hilarious. Neither realism nor romance, it is closest to satire in form, though kinder than most stories associated with the form. It is a story about men who claim to love literature but who, in fact, don't read books at all. Not that they don't know how. They just choose not to. Chesnutt poked fun at the pretensions of such men of culture, men like Perry. That Perry got the joke and still published it in the June 1904 issue of the *Atlantic* spoke volumes about his character and his own deep love of literature, especially the kind kept in the library of the Bodleian. It would be the last of Chesnutt's stories to be published in *The Atlantic* during his lifetime. The race stories Perry rejected would be published years later in magazines, such as *The Crisis*, edited by W. E. B. Du Bois, that were more interested in keeping the race question before its readers. Perry would stay on as editor of *The Atlantic* for a few more years, until he resigned the editorship to chair the English department at Harvard University in 1909, where he would remain until his retirement, at the age of seventy in 1930. Though mostly forgotten today, Perry is remembered by a few literary critics for having taught the first class devoted to the writings of Ralph Waldo Emerson at his alma mater and having written one of the first book-length appreciations of Walt Whitman. He lost touch with Chesnutt after the publication of "Baxter's Procrustes" in 1904.

Chesnutt remained active on the literary scene during the first decade of the twentieth century. Rather than wallow in the rejections of *Evelyn's Husband* and the disappointment in the low sales of *The Marrow of Tradition*, Chesnutt entered a new, experimental phase of his literary career. The appropriation of the white point of view that Chesnutt had long experimented with became a preoccupation, and he started using the term *sympathetic*—associated mostly with nineteenth-century sentimental literature—to describe his white characters from this period. Around the same time that he had submitted his three stories to Perry for consideration in *The Atlantic*, Chesnutt had also been working on a long short story, "perhaps 40,000 words," he'd been calling "The Colonel's Dream." It introduced Henry French, a Southerner hailing from a once wealthy slave-owning family who had lost its fortune after the South's defeat in the Civil War. The story opened sometime in the 1890s, at the height of the Gilded Age, a time during which, as Mark Twain illustrated in his novel of that name, a lot of people suffered from an obsession with speculation. Coincidentally, the character in Twain's *Gilded Age* who suffered most from the speculation disease also went by the title of colonel. Unlike Twain's infamous Colonel Sellers, Chesnutt's colonel is a Southerner who earned the title at the young age of nineteen, after fighting for the losing side in the Civil War. Colonel

French is now a wealthy merchant in New York City who decides to return to his Southern hometown after remaking his fortune as head of the "firm of French and Company, Limited, manufacturers of crashes and burlaps and kindred stuffs, with extensive mills in Connecticut, and central offices in New York."[16] The colonel is already wealthy when the novel begins. But when he sells off his firm, by taking a great risk at the start of the novel, he becomes a millionaire. The colonel has made so much money that once he decides to leave his apartment overlooking Central Park and relocate to the South to live in his childhood home with his young son, he can continue to live in high style without working another day in his life. "The Colonel's Dream" is a kind of Gilded Age tale in reverse. It is a story not so much about making a fortune through savvy investments and speculating on the expanding railroad; it is instead a story about how a former Confederate soldier attempts to remake the South he left behind in ruins with the fortune he acquired while investing in the North. "The Colonel's Dream" is a far cry from the *American* dream. It is instead the story of a *Southern* dream that, like so many dreams, goes up in smoke when confronted by reality.

Chesnutt sent "The Colonel's Dream" to Houghton in the spring of 1904. Though the readers liked it better than they had *Evelyn's Husband*, they were not fully convinced it should be accepted for publication. As one reader put it, "It might be published without discredit—though of course Southern critics would not like it. It does not seem to me, however to have enough positive strength to be a desirable book, and as we declined the author's latest book before this (a much weaker and poorer story, it should be said) I think we may well let this one go also."[17] The second reader was more equivocal in his negative assessment of "The Colonel's Dream," criticizing it for being "didactic" and "written in a wooden style." This reader felt that the "colonel and his friends are not very clear to the eye, and the human relations are amateurish. There are one or two scenes where negroes are brought in which are worth while, but by and large the story is not worth publishing."

Houghton rejected "The Colonel's Dream" on May 12, 1904. The letter was signed by the head of the firm at the time, Francis Jackson Garrison, the son of the famed Boston radical abolitionist William Lloyd

Garrison. While echoing the sentiments expressed by the press's readers, Garrison also seemed to be genuinely impressed by the novel. "It is simply and naturally told, too, with your wonted restraint and moderation; and one can but feel the pathos of the climax, as of any like dashing of a brave hope and effort in real life." Despite Garrison's sense of the novel's beauty and importance, he explained why Houghton could not publish "The Colonel's Dream." "If we could follow our wish and impulse, we should like to publish the book, but we cannot shut our eyes to the fact that the public has failed to respond adequately to your other admirable work in this line, and that we have netted a large aggregate loss on the several volumes of which we expended far more for advertising than the results justified."

Garrison's reference to the poor showing of Chesnutt's previous books must have stung. But it was the truth. It was the *public* that had failed to respond to Chesnutt's "admirable" books on the race problem. Chesnutt remained steadfast in his commitment to writing literature. Without missing a beat, Chesnutt sent the manuscript to Page at Doubleday in New York City. On June 24, 1904, a little over a month after receiving Garrison's kindly worded rejection letter, Page sent his response to "The Colonel's Dream." Page loved Chesnutt's use of "old Fayetteville" as the setting and found his presentation of "the race problem in a most vivid and pathetic way." But in its present form, the story was too short, by Page's standards, to justify publication as a novel. So, just as he had suggested with "Rena"—Chesnutt's early version of *The House Behind the Cedars*—Page suggested that he expand "The Colonel's Dream" into a full-scale novel. "Can you give it more body? Make it a larger structure; introduce, if necessary, more characters, and round it out to something like a good hundred thousand words able bodied novel? I hope you can. If the subject admit of this treatment and you are in a mood to do it, I should be very proud indeed to publish it for you."[18]

Chesnutt was relieved and elated by Page's response. Chesnutt said nothing to Page about his rejection from Garrison. He could not understand Chesnutt's literary project as Page had. Since Page's departure from Houghton, and his dealings with the men who'd replaced Page, Chesnutt seemed to have lost interest in the firm that had published his first book. Only someone who knew the South like Page did could get what Chesnutt was doing. And only someone who was willing to do what was right, not just satiate the public's desire for squishy romance and racial caricature, would be willing to risk a marginal loss on the literary marketplace. Garrison made clear to Chesnutt that Houghton, for all their commitment to publishing great books, could no longer be his publisher. "We feel morally certain," Garrison had explained from his cushy office at 4 Park Street, with the portrait of his father hanging on the wall behind his desk, "that we should make no more of a success with 'The Colonel's Dream' than we did with 'The Marrow of Tradition,' and that, on business grounds alone, we are not justified in assuming the risk of its manufacture and publication."[19] Garrison's rejection paved the way for another collaboration with his trusted fellow Southerner.

"My dear Mr. Page," Chesnutt began his letter on June 29, 1904. "I received your letter which gave me much pleasure, concerning my story 'The Colonel's Dream.' I have always considered you the best judge I knew of a Southern story of that sort, because in addition to the other necessary qualities, you combine a sympathetic knowledge of the South and a freedom from prejudice which are rarely found together."[20] After making considerable additions, revisions, and much conversation with Page, *The Colonel's Dream* was published as a novel in September 1905 by Doubleday, Page & Company.

The Colonel's Dream was the first of Chesnutt's books published outside Boston. The first edition appeared with a simple red hard cover, the title printed in embossed gold letters at the top, with Chesnutt's name, in the same gold lettering at the bottom. When Chesnutt received his copy, he complained of "several typographical errors which escaped" the attention of both the "office proof-reader and myself," including the misspelling of his name on the cover. In a letter to Isaac Frederick Marcosson, his new editor at Doubleday, he enumerated several other errors that he hoped would "be corrected as early in the publication of the book as the condition of publication will permit." Unlike his books published by Houghton that were advertised in major newspapers across the country, Doubleday could not afford to advertise the book as heavily. A month after it was released, Chesnutt again wrote to Marcosson worrying that he had "not seen the book advertised anywhere, except about half an inch in the last number of the *World's*

Work."[21] He also noted "a curious but interesting fact" about the reviews he'd read. "The most appreciative reviews have come from the South. They disagree with my conclusions, they deprecate the publication of the book, but they treat it with respect and do not deny its correctness as a picture of widespread conditions."[22] Though *The Colonel's Dream* never became the bestseller that Chesnutt longed to write, he took considerable satisfaction in the reviews.

Around the time Chesnutt had first started working on the novel, there appeared an article in *The World's Work*, the magazine Page had started when he became a senior partner at the firm, that had a considerable impact on the form and function of American literature. In "The Novel with a 'Purpose,'" Frank Norris, who worked alongside Marcosson at Doubleday, and whose own novels had been published by the press a few years before *The Colonel's Dream*, wrote that the best class of books "proves something, draws conclusions from a whole congeries of forces, social tendencies, race impulses, devotes itself not to a study of men but of man."[23] Norris's definition of literature spoke directly to the kind of novel Chesnutt was writing. There is no evidence that Chesnutt ever met Norris while he worked at Doubleday. Norris died suddenly in 1902 a few years before *The Colonel's Dream* appeared on the literary scene. Chesnutt's novel revealed an affinity between the two authors that was plain as day to those, like Marcosson, who worked closely with both.

For starters, there were interesting similarities in the appearance of Norris's and Chesnutt's books. Like Chesnutt's, Norris's *The Pit: A Story of Chicago*, published by Doubleday a couple of years after his death in 1904, was outfitted with a simple red cover and gold lettering. Just as with *The Colonel's Dream*, *The Pit* opened with a dedication by the author. Norris dedicated his novel to his brother, while Chesnutt's was dedicated more broadly and abstractly. "To the great number of those who are seeking, in whatever manner or degree, from near at hand or far away, to bring the forces of enlightenment to bear upon the vexed problems which harass the South, this volume is inscribed, with the hope that it may contribute to the same good end."[24] Both novels also provide readers with a useful list of characters before the action begins. Neither author included titles or chapter headings, which was unusual, at least for Chesnutt, as chapter titles were a significant feature of his previous novels published by Houghton. Norris's and Chesnutt's novels were similar in other, less material, ways as well. Both took the responsibility of the novelist to exposing the lies and falsehood perpetrated on the reading public by major newspapers seriously. And even though the truth did not sell as well as the sensational lies published in the daily papers and elsewhere, they were willing to sacrifice popularity to tell the truth. As Norris put it in another of his articles, "The People have a right to the Truth as they have a right to life, liberty and the pursuit of happiness."[25] And Norris believed that only the novelist who refused to submit to the popular appetite for "the sordid and brutal," as Chesnutt put it, could provide readers with the truth.

Amid all the false stories being told about the race problem in the South, from the novels of Thomas Dixon and the nonfiction of William Hannibal Thomas, Chesnutt wanted to tell a story that presented the South as it really was. That he decided to tell that story ironically through the eyes, blurred by nostalgia and privilege, of a former Confederate soldier who had spent most of his adult life working in New York City was just one reason why most readers of the time were baffled by it. In Colonel French, Chesnutt created a character at once detestable and remarkably likable; he would call him sympathetic. Readers were invited to *sympathize* with the character's position as a now rich, white Southerner, someone so imbued with the racial precepts of the time he hardly noticed the ways in which he benefited—and others lost—from them. We don't cheer for Colonel French when he tries to improve his Southern hometown, marry his childhood sweetheart, take back the home of his ancestors that now belongs to a hardworking Black barber, or bury his son, against the laws of racial segregation, beside his trusted Black servant. But we do begin to see and sympathize with his blindness. When he finally comes to see the South, his former home, for what it really is and the role he has played in making it what it is, he is compelled to leave it again, brokenhearted, yes, but a man in possession, for perhaps the first time in his life, with the truth.

Ignoring those critics and editors who insisted that Chesnutt write more "negro stories," sticking to situations that they thought he knew well, Chesnutt wrote a novel, the last that would be published in his lifetime, from the perspective of someone living on the other side of the color line. He wrote about how wealthy white men were victims of their heredity, those whose social status, experience, and education blinded them from seeing the truth. In *The Colonel's Dream*, Chesnutt attempted to help readers see the United States—North and South—for what it was, regardless of which side of the color line you lived on.

16

Literary Celebrity

> For if the element of race prejudice were removed from our national life,
> there would be an end to the race problem, even though other conditions
> should remain exactly as they are. Grave questions there would be, of
> poverty, of ignorance, and of other things; but the Negro would have no
> special grievance.
>
> —"Race Prejudice: Its Causes and Its Cures," speech to the
> Boston Historical and Literary Association, June 1905

In late spring 1905, Chesnutt was planning another trip to Boston. This would likely be his last—and longest—trip to what he referred to as "the most intellectually advanced city of our land." Chesnutt had been invited by William Monroe Trotter, founder and editor of the "colored weekly" newspaper *The Guardian*, to a gathering of the newly formed Boston Historical and Literary Association. Trotter's newspaper had become known for its radical ideas and opposition to the ideas espoused by Booker T. Washington. Chesnutt had put off Trotter's invitation to help, as he put it, "improve intellectual life of the Colored people of Boston."[1] Though Chesnutt was sympathetic to some of the views and the mission of the association, he found Trotter's relentless attacks on Washington unproductive, even offensive. He explained his position on Washington to Trotter when their correspondence began back in 1901. "I am willing to approve the good, and where I disagree with him, to preach the opposite doctrine strenuously. But I aim to be a literary artist, and acrimonious personalities are the death of art."[2]

Despite announcing his dedication to art, Chesnutt joined the Committee of Twelve for the Advancement of the Interests of the Negro Race shortly after putting the final touches on *The Colonel's Dream*. The Committee of Twelve, as it came to be called, was formed a year earlier as a way of bringing together prominent race men—namely, Washington and W. E. B. Du Bois—on the issues of the day. Chesnutt was asked to join the committee by its secretary, Hugh M. Browne. Browne explained that the committee was comprised of prominent writers and thinkers; aside from Washington, there was also Timothy Thomas Fortune and, before he resigned, Du Bois. Its stated purpose was "the Advancement of the Interests of the Negro Race" in all areas of public life. When Du Bois resigned from the committee over differences with Washington in 1904, Browne wrote to Chesnutt to fill the vacancy. Chesnutt was unaware of the unfolding schism between Washington and Du Bois when he decided to join. As he put it to Browne, "There is probably room for every phase of thought and opinion in regard to the race question. I think, however, that we are all united in the wish to overcome as far as may be the prejudice against the colored people and to promote good feeling so far as that is possible without the sacrifice of vital principles." As if furthering his commitment to join with "men whose views vary so widely," Chesnutt accepted Trotter's invitation to speak in Boston, just as he was beginning to work closely with the man Trotter detested.[3]

The association met at Parker Memorial Hall, an imposing building located on the corner of Berkeley and Appleton Streets in the South End of Boston's bustling downtown. It just so happened that Edwin was scheduled to graduate from Harvard in late June. The ceremony would be at Harvard's breathtaking Memorial Hall, perhaps the grandest monument in New England commemorating the North's victory over the South, honoring those students who died fighting for the Union. On Wednesday, June 28, 1905, forty years after the Civil War, Chesnutt attended his son's graduation, with President Theodore Roosevelt slated to deliver the commencement address. Roosevelt won the election in 1904 following McKinley's assassination and was serving his first full year in office. Shortly before the election, Chesnutt had publicly endorsed Roosevelt for president in the pages of Fortune's *New York Age*. Setting aside his commitment to nonpartisan forms of speech, the ideal he believed to guide the work of literary artists, Chesnutt declared: "The man who with one drop of black blood who would vote against him, and to place the destinies of this nation for four years to come in the hands, or even subject to the direct influence, of the horde of Negro-burning, Negro-hating, Negro-disfranchising and 'Jim-Crow'-ing Democratic politicians of the South is, not to mince words, both an ingrate and a fool." Chesnutt's strongly worded endorsement "For Roosevelt" was only one of many reasons he was eager to hear the Republican president speak at Harvard so soon after his victory over the Democrats.[4]

Chesnutt wanted to savor this moment. It was what he had been working for as long as he could remember. They were staying at the home of Walter Sampson, Chesnutt's New England relations on his mother's side. He would speak to Trotter and the association shortly after their arrival on Sunday. The following day, he and the family would be "entertained at a luncheon on Monday by Mrs. Booker T. Washington at her summer residence at South Weymouth."[5] A couple of days later, the Chesnutts would head across the bridge over the Charles River to watch Edwin accept his diploma as he shook hands with Charles W. Eliot, Harvard's president at the time. Eliot had been heading up Harvard since 1869; he'd graduated from the college back in 1854 and served as a professor of chemistry and mathematics. Like several members of the faculty, Eliot left Harvard for Europe during the Civil War; he returned after the war, eager to reinvigorate and reunite the college upon the Union's victory. Eliot's presidency marked a new era in Harvard's history; his mission had been "to broaden, deepen, and invigorate American teaching in all branches of learning."[6] After the ceremony, the Chesnutts hosted a "spread" in Hollis Hall on Harvard Yard, inviting all their friends, both Black and white, to celebrate Edwin's graduation.

Here was a place where the color line, at least for a moment, did not divide. Chesnutt and Susan were a long way from where they'd started out in Fayetteville. It had cost them a great deal to send Edwin to Harvard, but there was no doubt in Chesnutt's mind that it had been worth the price. Edwin was now "a Harvard man." And Chesnutt, having been deprived of a college education, knew more than anyone seated in Memorial Hall that steamy day in June what a diploma from Harvard meant. Chesnutt and his family were beginning to reap the rewards of their hard work and the reputation he had built over the years. There could be no doubt in Chesnutt's mind that his decision to leave Fayetteville, as principal of its "colored school," all those years ago had paid off.

The speech Chesnutt delivered to the Boston Historical and Literary Association was so different from the one he heard Roosevelt deliver a few days later at Harvard, it was hard to believe they were speaking just a few miles apart about the political conditions of the same country. Of course, the audiences to which they spoke and the occasion for their speeches were radically different. Roosevelt was speaking to Harvard's graduating class about "College Ideals in American Business Life."[7] Chesnutt was speaking about "Race Prejudice" to a group of Boston's "Colored people," a few of whom, including Trotter, had graduated from Harvard. Yet Chesnutt's speech was all about diminishing these differences. He saw these differences as the "cause" of the "race problem." The solution, he said, was in developing "education," a kind of education that put Washington's Tuskegee industrial education right next to Harvard's classical education, the kind of education Trotter and Du Bois had imbibed. Though separated by geography and ideology, Chesnutt saw Harvard and Tuskegee as *equally* important and necessary. Chesnutt was proposing to "Afro-Americans of Greater Boston," as *The New York Age* described his audience, that the country needed both kinds of institutions, the one down the road *and* the one far from home, in the Deep South, to end race prejudice. While men like Trotter and Du Bois wanted to diminish the influence of institutions like Tuskegee for espousing what they felt was the wrong kind of education, Chesnutt was proposing something different. He saw Americans in need of a multiplicity of schools to meet the needs of the nation and all its people, those living in the North and the South, Black and white. What seemed like a straightforward, perhaps even obvious, solution to the race problem turned out to be a radical one. No wonder some of the self-proclaimed radicals in the audience—namely, the man who'd invited him to speak—disagreed so loudly with him.

Under the headline MR. CHESNUTT SAYS RACE PREJUDICE MAY BE REMOVED, *The Age*'s unnamed "regular correspondent," most likely the paper's editor, Timothy Thomas Fortune, announced that Chesnutt BELIEVES BOTH HIGHER AND INDUSTRIAL EDUCATION INDISPENSABLE. The correspondent also reported that "what Mr. Chesnutt said appealed to all sensible auditors present. The only dissenting view was that of the editor of a local paper, who was not backed by any other speaker." The fact that the reporter did not name the editor of the newspaper all but gave away his identity. As another member of the Committee of Twelve, Fortune was no fan of Trotter's. Fortune likely delighted in the opportunity to diminish Trotter and the influence of his "local paper."[8]

The Age also reported that expectations for "the address by Mr. Charles W. Chesnutt" had been high. His speech was the "chief attraction among the Afro-Americans of Greater Boston"; it was slated as the event of the season, a kickoff to a typical summer in Boston filled with various cultural events. The hall was packed with well-to-do Black Bostonians eager to catch a glimpse of "the eminent novelist and lawyer from Cleveland" whose success and stories they admired. Chesnutt appeared onstage in his usual three-piece suit, perfectly groomed mustache, carrying his typed remarks in one of his well-worn hardback notebooks. Though he was scheduled to speak on a rather serious topic, "Race Prejudice: Its Causes and Its Cures," he opened with a joke. "Mr. Chesnutt announced at the opening of his address that an ambulance might be required to take his remains from the building after his utterances." The joke was a sly reference to Washington's 1903 speech to Boston's National Negro Business League at the AME Zion Church. It was there that Trotter climbed onto a pew to heckle Washington. His fellow radicals covered the alter in cayenne pepper and laughed as those who'd invited Washington to speak tried to talk through their sneezes. The protest was jocularly referred to as "the Boston riot" and got Trotter arrested. Trotter was of course seated prominently when Chesnutt took the stage. Chesnutt's joke was intended to poke fun at Trotter's "protest," not to diminish it entirely. Trotter's aggressive methods were different from Chesnutt's, but Chesnutt still respected Trotter's point of view. Chesnutt's joke was also his way of preparing his audience for another controversial speech. But this time, Trotter's response to Chesnutt's dissenting point of view was drowned out by the majority in the audience who agreed with Chesnutt.[9]

Chesnutt spoke for over an hour, about everything from scientific racism and poverty to slavery and the Civil War. The part that appealed most to the staff of *The New York Age* was how he "surprised many of his audience stating what in his opinion the remedies are. He declared that prejudice will be removed slowly and that in this removal we shall need more of both industrial and higher education than we now have." This surprising *political* statement from an "eminent novelist" distinguished Chesnutt from other writers and leaders on the race question of the time, particularly popular race men like Washington, Du Bois, and Trotter. So impressed was his audience with Chesnutt's remarks the reporter declared that "we shall print in THE AGE next week extracts from Mr. Chesnutt's address." The printed version of Chesnutt's speech was read by thousands, mostly Black readers, who were beginning to see Chesnutt not just as an eminent novelist and successful stenographer but as a man-about-town, someone worth listening to.

Chesnutt returned to Cleveland in high spirits. Work at the office was humming along at a steady pace; he was anticipating the response to *The Colonel's Dream*. A few weeks after the novel hit book stands, on September 22, Chesnutt wrote to Alice E. Hanscom, a local literary critic and long admirer of his fiction. "I have already heard many good words concerning *The Colonel's Dream*, and I hope it may commend itself to a wide circle of readers—for the sake of the cause as well as for my own sake."[10] Hanscom had already expressed her thoughts on the novel privately to Chesnutt in an earlier letter to him. "I don't quite see how you can so successfully keep the impartial, unimpassioned tone, though I realize the wisdom and finer literary art in doing so."[11] Her public—and unsurprisingly positive—review of the novel appeared a couple of months later in Cleveland's *Union Gospel News*. According to Hanscom's review, Chesnutt's novel was a great success; he had done what he set out to do, to write a *literary* novel about the political and economic conditions of the nation, both North and South, Black and white. He'd set aside acrimonious personalities to write about someone who held a point of view so different from his own. *The Colonel's Dream* featured a former Confederate soldier who had risen to the rank of colonel and managed to make a fortune in New York City after the war. With his novel now out, his fourth book to be published under Page's direction, Chesnutt could confidently call himself a "literary artist."

Exalted by the critical success of *The Colonel's Dream* but not yet aware of its disappointing sales, Chesnutt was delighted when his invitation to Mark Twain's seventieth birthday party arrived in the mail. The party was to be held at Delmonico's, the most fashionable restaurant in New York City, located on the corner of Twenty-Sixth Street and Fifth Avenue, on Tuesday, December 5, at eight o'clock. It was hosted by Colonel George Harvey, a successful businessman, editor of the *North American Review* and president of the publishing firm Harper and Brothers. The party became known as the literary event of the new century. Harvey invited 170 guests, mostly well-known writers and humorists, had a forty-piece orchestra perform, provided everyone with elaborate party favors, including a foot-tall plaster-of-paris bust of Twain, and printed a special menu with sketches by the popular cartoonist Leon Barritt, showing various episodes of Twain's spectacular rise to literary fame and fortune. The party was a grand celebration of Twain's life and work, but it was also meant to be a celebration of American literature and its writers. *The New York Times* described the event on its front page the following day: "Never before in the annals of this country had such a representative gathering of literary men and women been seen under one roof. They were representative in every conceivable respect—even geographically. There was no corner of this country that did not have at least one favorite son—or daughter—present. The Far North and the extreme South, the New England States, and the Pacific slope—all sent delegates."[12] This was a gathering not just to celebrate Mark Twain; it was a symbol of the spirit of American democracy manifested by its most beloved literary men and women. Chesnutt fit right in.

Chesnutt had taken the train from Cleveland to New York City almost immediately after enjoying Thanksgiving dinner surrounded by his family. Susan had been busy preparing the meal and getting Chesnutt ready for his trip. She had packed a new dress suit that she had custom made by Cleveland's most sought-after tailor, the German-born Elias Rheinheimer. It fit much better than his old suit, which was, in her opinion, getting too tight around the waist. Susan knew that Chesnutt would be dining with other famous literary figures and would have his picture taken among them, a photograph that would be seen by thousands in the pages of *Harper's Weekly*. Other than the presence of Dr. Charles Eastman, a member of the Dakota Sioux Tribe and well-known author of *Indian Boyhood*, Chesnutt was the only "colored writer" in attendance. Susan wanted her family and friends to see him as part of the inner circle, so she made sure he looked the part of an author of America's Gilded Age. Perhaps Susan would have liked to accompany her husband on this occasion. But she wouldn't have known what to wear among all those stylish literary types. Anyway, her name had not been included on the invitation; she would have to wait and hear all the juicy details when Chesnutt returned home a week later.

The dinner was a formal white-tie affair. All the men wore black tail-coat and a white bow tie tucked under a stiff collar. The women wore floor-length ball gowns of varying colors and styles. Chesnutt was seated between the journalist and proto-conservationist Ernest Ingersoll and Anna Parmly Paret, an author of advice columns and manners for *Harper's*. Across from him sat Caroline King Duer, the stylish editor of *Vogue* magazine, then, as now, setting trends in the world of American fashion. She had written to Chesnutt a few years earlier requesting a portrait of Chesnutt for *Vogue's* Literary Department. Duer had regarded Chesnutt to be a "leading author of the day" and was delighted to meet him in person. She was also a writer of short stories and essays, known for her sense of humor and wit. Although there is no transcript of their dinner conversation, it was undoubtedly full of laughter and high-spirited storytelling.

Chesnutt also mingled with other guests at the dinner. There was his old friend George Washington Cable, who, alongside Richard Watson Gilder and William Dean Howells, delivered one of the evening's more memorable toasts to Twain. But he would have also been introduced to new, decidedly *modern* American writers, like Willa Cather and Emily Post, who were just beginning to make names for themselves in the ever-changing world of American Literature at the dawn of the twentieth century. Though held a few days after his actual birthday on November 30, Twain's birthday party at Delmonico's on December 5, 1905, signaled a major shift in American Literature. No longer the bastion of the New England, Harvard-educated elites, its center was now located in New York City, with Mark Twain, born Samuel Clemens on the bank of the Mississippi in midwestern Missouri, at its helm.

Chesnutt was a few years from his fiftieth when he helped Twain celebrate his seventieth. Despite the differences in their age and stature, Chesnutt seemed poised to join "the King" of American literature, as Howells dubbed Twain that night, as a member of this singular American

"aristocracy of brains." After spending a week in New York City, hobnob-
bing with his literary fellows, revisiting his favorite haunts still around
from his reporting days on Wall Street, and a "rather long interview" with
his friend and publisher Walter Hines Page, Chesnutt returned home. Little had changed on Lamont Avenue since he'd left. He slowly unpacked his
suitcase, hanging up his coattails and placing his souvenir, a bust of King
Twain, on a shelf in his library. There it would remain until Charles Jr., his
young grandson, dropped it while showing it off to educator Leslie P. Hill
and his wife, friends of the Chesnutts visiting from Tuskegee.

Chesnutt was more relieved than angry when Mark Twain fell to
pieces. In response to Hill's apologetic letter, thanking Chesnutt for hosting him and his wife but sorry for having intruded on his library, Chesnutt
explained that the souvenir had lost much of its importance. "It had long
since ceased to be ornamental, if indeed it ever had been, and my library
really looks better without it."[13] Chesnutt remembered the celebration of
Twain at Delmonico's in 1905 fondly. But now, five years later, Chesnutt
no longer felt the need to keep the king of American literature so close to
his writing desk. He had become "the best known novelist and short story
writer of the race," as Benjamin Brawley dubbed him in his 1910 survey
of The Negro in Literature and Art.[14] A professor of Latin and English at Atlanta Baptist College, now more commonly known as Morehouse College,
Brawley would become the preeminent critic of the newly emerging field of
African American literature, with Chesnutt at its head. Thanking Brawley
for the "beautifully written and printed pamphlet," Chesnutt felt gratified
by "the very full reference to my own works" included in one of the first
published full-length books devoted to a consideration of African American literature.[15] With the publication of Brawley's book, which he would
expand and republish in 1918, Chesnutt would strike up a correspondence
about the current and future state of African American literature with the
young academic that would continue for a couple of decades.

About a week before turning fifty-two, on June 12, 1910, Chesnutt suffered a minor stroke while at work in his downtown office. He was rushed
to Huron Road Hospital after one of his employees found him collapsed
and unconscious on the sofa in his office. The incident was reported on the
following day under the headline RACE WRITER TAKEN ILL: "While working

in his office on the 11th floor of the Williamson building about 11 o'clock yesterday morning, Charles W. Chesnutt, fifty-two, court stenographer and the author of eight books dealing with various phases of the negro problem was stricken with an attack of what the doctors diagnose as pleurisy."[16] News of Chesnutt's illness led to phone calls and questions that Susan had to deal with. She was beside herself with worry. Susan had always told him he worked too much, and now she had been proven right. She would, at least for now, take charge of his affairs. He spent several weeks in the hospital recovering and then was ordered by his doctor to continue to rest at home, where Susan and his daughters Dorothy and Helen worried over him. By then, Edwin had accepted a job as a stenographer in Booker T. Washington's office at the Tuskegee Institute. Ethel was busy with her son and husband in DC. Susan insisted that they take him on a vacation in August to Sea Isle City in New Jersey, where he would not be tempted to go back to work too soon. By September, he found himself "at the end of it rejuvenated and ready for my fall business."[17]

For some time now, Chesnutt's business affairs had expanded; he had also become increasingly involved in politics. While working actively as a member of the Committee of Twelve, Chesnutt was also beginning to play a role in the emerging Niagara Movement. Somewhat larger and more publicly minded than the Committee of Twelve, the Niagara Movement was a national organization comprised mostly of Black men and women devoted to "manhood suffrage; the abolition of all caste distinctions based simply on race and color and freedom of speech." W. E. B. Du Bois served as general secretary of the movement and was central to the development of its policies. In late August of 1908, members of the movement convened in Oberlin, Ohio, inviting Chesnutt to deliver a welcome address on a topic that he felt was most appropriate for the occasion.

Chesnutt decided to speak on "The Courts and the Negro." Chesnutt's speech provided his listeners with a rigorous "history of our jurisprudence" particularly "in the matter of Negro rights."[18] He discussed a number of cases in detail, from the *Dred Scott* decision to the more recent *Plessy v. Ferguson* case, calling the latter "the most important and far reaching decision of the Supreme Court upon the question of civil rights." He concluded with a rousing defense of the Fifteenth Amendment and the right of all citizens to vote. But as Chesnutt spoke to the group, led by Du Bois, he was painfully aware of a growing factionalism. About a month later, he would address the Bethel Literary and Historical Association in Washington, DC, on a similar topic that he called "Rights and Duties." Here he would call his audience's attention to "two movements within the colored race [that] have been discovered and labeled. One is said to insist upon rights, the other upon duties and responsibilities. They are contrasted in such a way as to seem antagonistic." He would be one of the first to articulate explicitly and vocally the folly of viewing these movements, represented by Du Bois and Washington, as antagonistic. He became increasingly interested in moving beyond these factions; as he put it: "I am going to close my eyes to the obvious and insist that this is not true; that both of these movements are so absolutely necessary to the welfare and happiness and the progress of the Negro that a man is a fool who could see any antagonism between them."[19]

Strangely, Du Bois and Washington, for all their differences, were equally interested in Chesnutt's approach. They both reached out to Chesnutt, soliciting his help, his conversation, his opinions. He remained committed to solving the race problem. The solution Chesnutt proposed was simple: "Once you teach men to look upon other men and judge other men by some other standard than that of race or color, and all the other difficulties will vanish like mist before the sun." But in mid-November, as he was recovering from his stroke, Chesnutt could no longer close his eyes to the antagonism between them. Du Bois wrote to Chesnutt, enclosing a copy of a paper entitled "Race Relations in the United States," asking Chesnutt to sign his name in support of the written protest against Washington's leadership. Unsurprisingly, Chesnutt declined to "pitch into Mr. Washington." He concluded his response to Du Bois, which ran several typed pages, with his now conventional assertion: "There are many things yet to be done: some of them, of which Mr. Washington has fought shy, the NAACP seeks to accomplish. There is plenty of room and plenty of work for both."[20]

Du Bois was growing more than a little frustrated with Chesnutt's approach. Du Bois would succinctly explain his approach several years later in the pages of The Crisis, the magazine he'd started less than a year after writing to Chesnutt under the auspices of the National Association for the Advancement of Colored People. Under the title "Criteria of Negro Art," Du Bois insisted on the political standing of African American art, particularly literature. As he put it: "All art is propaganda and ever must be, despite the wailing of the purists."[21] Du Bois likely had Chesnutt's long letter from 1909 in mind when he decried "the wailing purists." As tensions between the Du Bois and Washington factions were heating up in late 1910, Chesnutt decided to take a step away from the political fray. On December 10, 1910, Chesnutt became an official member of Cleveland's most exclusive book club, the Rowfant Club. Founded in 1892 by a small group of Cleveland's wealthy "Book-Men" at the Hollenden Hotel in room 130 on the second floor, overlooking Bond Street, members of the Rowfant Club took pride in their "book-collecting abilities, discriminating taste, literary ability and gentlemanly breeding." Chesnutt had been associating with its members for well over a decade; but his racial status kept him on the outskirts of the club. It wasn't until Benjamin Bourland, a professor of modern languages at Western Reserve University who had been a member for less than a year, formally invited Chesnutt to join the club on December 8, 1910, that Chesnutt became its first colored member. Chesnutt was delighted by the invitation and wrote to thank Bourland for the "privilege which I appreciate very much" on December 10.

A few days later, he wrote to Frederick R. Moore, the new editor of *The New York Age*. Moore had written to Chesnutt requesting information about the political makeup of Cleveland's "colored population." His response revealed an underlying tone of impatience with the direction of race politics. "I haven't the remotest idea how many people in this vicinity voted the Democratic ticket, and would therefore be unable to state their reason for doing so." He continued the letter in an even harsher tone.

> Replying to your letter under another cover, requesting my opinion concerning the proper method for celebrating the fiftieth anniversary of the freedom of the Negro in 1913, I hope you will not think me indifferent in matters pertaining to the welfare of the race, but in this town the Emancipation Proclamation is celebrated by the colored people every year, and I have sometimes thought it might be well if they could forget they were slaves, or at least give the white people a chance to forget it. At any rate, there are gentlemen much better qualified than myself to make suggestions upon this matter.[22]

He closed this rather sharply worded letter cordially. "I read the *Age* every week with interest and pleasure. There is probably nothing in this letter that would be of public interest."

Two weeks later, on December 28, 1910, he wrote to Washington. This would be Chesnutt's last known letter to Washington. It is possible the two met in person again before Washington's death on November 15, 1915, but there is no record of it. Chesnutt thanked Washington warmly "for the handsome and characteristic calendar" that he received as a New Year's present "in excellent condition."[23] When Chesnutt wrote to Washington, Edwin had been working at Tuskegee for less than a year and seemed to be getting along well. The irony that Ethel, Helen, and Edwin, who'd all received classical training at elite New England colleges at great expense, ended up working for Washington at Tuskegee was not lost on their father. Chesnutt never spoke or wrote of his family affairs publicly. But he was always grateful to Washington for providing his children with jobs, even though he'd hoped that their college degrees would have given them access to careers more suited to their training.

Shortly before Chesnutt left for a second sunset tour of Europe in the summer of 1912, this time with Helen as his companion, Du Bois decided to publish Chesnutt's story called "The Doll." Rejected almost a decade earlier by Bliss Perry at *The Atlantic*, Chesnutt decided to retool the story slightly and submit it for publication in *The Crisis*. When Chesnutt had originally sent Perry the story back in 1904, he'd called it "A Close Shave" but had been playing with other titles for the story. He had considered, he told Perry, calling it "The Jointed Doll." Perry had rejected the story, as it dealt too much with the "eternal race question," preferring instead to publish "Baxter's Procrustes," a story about book men, rather than race men. Chesnutt was glad to have finally found a home for "The Doll." The story is written as a work of psychological realism in which the thoughts of a Black barber, father, and widower are slowly revealed as he shaves the face of the man who years before murdered his father without remorse or punishment. It is a penetrating story, written in the style of Herman Melville's much earlier novella *Benito Cereno*, regarding a similar exchange. Set about a half century later, in the post-Reconstruction South, Chesnutt's story is written almost entirely from the point of view of the Black barber who must steady his hand, quell his desire for revenge, and avoid slitting the throat of the former Confederate. It would be the first of four of Chesnutt's *new* stories Du Bois accepted for *The Crisis*. Published in its 1912 Easter issue, "The Doll" marked a new chapter in Chesnutt's literary career, one where he found himself again in New York City, which had now become the headquarters of the Harlem Renaissance. Led by Du Bois, James Weldon Johnson, and a group of New Negro writers he barely knew, Chesnutt had become a literary forefather of a movement that strayed far from the principles he'd spent a lifetime cultivating.

Fathering a Renaissance

I have always thought that the matter of race is too much emphasized in
this country; so much emphasized, that the far greater theme of humanity is often lost sight of.

—"Race Ideals and Examples," speech to the Literary
Societies at Wilberforce University, June 16, 1913

Chesnutt and his daughter Helen set sail for Europe in late June 1912
aboard a British ship called the SS *Marquette*. Both had been to Europe before but never together. The ostensible purpose of the trip was for
Chesnutt to rest, take time off work, and recuperate after his illness. Helen
"was chosen" by her mother to look after him because Susan did not enjoy
"strenuous sight-seeing trips," as she knew this was to be. As a student of
Latin with literary pretensions of her own, Helen was eager to go to Europe, to see the sights with her father, and to enjoy herself. Unlike his first
solo trip to Europe, Chesnutt did not keep a journal. He relied instead on
his letters to Susan to keep track of the journey, the places he visited with
Helen, and the names of some of the people he met along the way. Helen
was also writing frequently to her mother, so Chesnutt circumscribed his
accounts of their trip accordingly. "Helen has written you a 12-page letter
today, and has doubtless told you all about the trip," he wrote to Susan on
July 3, while still aboard the *Marquette*. His letters to Susan reveal the musings of a much older man, a father and husband, who is being held "rigidly
down" by his "skittish" daughter.[1] He managed to subvert her supervision
by finding ways to do his own thing, despite being constantly together.

During their two-week journey aboard the *Marquette,* Chesnutt made himself known to other passengers, of whom, he reported to Susan, there were about 125, "most of them teachers and college students, a great many of them Southerners." Chesnutt found himself in his element. Having happened to have a copy of his first and still most popular book, *The Conjure Woman,* with him, he "lent it to a passenger." The result of this encounter was that Chesnutt's name was added to the ship's entertainment program. He "was asked and had to read a story," which he did "with great success, receiving many compliments and developing into quite a character."[2] Chesnutt seemed to enjoy these moments of much-deserved celebrity, so different from that first solo trip to Europe more than a decade earlier when he had been an anonymous observer of the European cultural scene. Then he had published just a few short stories; "The Goophered Grapevine" had appeared in *The Atlantic,* but he had not yet made a name for himself as a literary artist. When he toured Europe alone in the summer of 1896, he had not yet published a book. Now he could count six books that bore his name. Why shouldn't he be recognized? People should know who he was. He took pride in his popularity as an American literary artist visiting the Continent with his poised and well-educated daughter as his companion.

This trip was all in all a much more *social* affair than his first European tour had been. Then, he had been alone, observing, writing, shopping, trying to capture the European literary spirit so that he could prove to himself that he had what it took to become an American author. This time, Chesnutt was almost never alone. He and Helen were always on the move, meeting people, participating in tour groups, visiting with new and old friends. Chesnutt provided Susan with detailed descriptions of their hotel rooms, their meals, and the people they encountered. They covered a great deal of territory during their two-month stay. Having sailed across the Atlantic, they arrived in Antwerp on July 4, raising a glass to America as they traveled by train to Bruges, Brussels, and the Hague. They went on to Rotterdam, stopping at Delft and Amsterdam as they made their way to Switzerland. This tour of Europe was nonstop, "chasing from city to city." Chesnutt bemoaned not being able to "stay long anywhere and cover our itinerary." It seemed that Helen had planned much of this trip, and she wanted to make the most of her time abroad. They took a delightful trip "down the Rhine from Cologne through Frankfurt," where they spent a day touring Goethe's home. Chesnutt offered few observations of its interior.

Italy and France seemed to bring Chesnutt the greatest joy. Helen's description of Chesnutt's mood and demeanor revealed a level of comfort and playfulness that seemed totally out of character, at least to her. Chesnutt was no longer the serious stenographer, preoccupied by the race problem, negotiating between factions, while staying up all night writing a story. Instead, as Helen described him on this trip, he "was as gay as a small boy and almost as irresponsible. He pretended that they were invisible, that no one could see or hear them, and said outrageous things about the people around them."[3] There is something slightly hilarious about Helen reporting on her father during their time in Europe. She seemed to be at once amused and embarrassed by Chesnutt's behavior. Mostly, she was surprised by how different he was in Europe. Chesnutt felt invisible and irresponsible in Europe, a singular state of being she rarely witnessed in her father back home. Father and daughter concluded their European tour in London, where they spent the afternoon with the classical music composer Samuel Coleridge-Taylor, his wife, Jessie, and their two children.

Chesnutt had first met the musician in 1904, when he and Susan attended two concerts conducted by him during Coleridge-Taylor's first tour of the United States. They met again at the home of his old friend, Ohio senator John Patterson Green, a couple of years later, when Coleridge-Taylor gave a recital in Cleveland in December 1906. Chesnutt had long admired the musician and his accomplishments. Helen's description of their visit with Coleridge-Taylor revealed an intimacy between the two men that indicates a shared vision of art and culture. "Coleridge-Taylor," as Helen described the scene, "was bubbling over with high spirits—he had just been invited to conduct his *Violin Concerto* in Berlin in the fall. This had been the dream of his life—to conduct an orchestra in Berlin, and now the dream was about to be fulfilled. So the atmosphere was very merry, and Chesnutt and Coleridge-Taylor told jokes and stories, and the room rang with laughter."[4] This would be the last time Chesnutt would see the young composer; when they returned to New York a few days later on September 1, 1912, "the first thing they saw was the announcement of the death of Coleridge-Taylor." Almost as soon as he was settled back in Cleveland, Chesnutt wrote to Jessie Coleridge-Taylor expressing his shock on hearing of her husband's death. In conveying his sympathy, Chesnutt declared "Mr. Coleridge-Taylor's death was a loss not only to his family, but to the world, and especially to the art which he practiced so beautifully."[5] For Chesnutt, Coleridge-Taylor, born the illegitimate son of a father who was the son of African slaves and a white British mother, who had risen to create some of the most popular pieces of classical music of the time, exemplified the possibility of putting art above race. Coleridge-Taylor was a "mulatto" in the racial parlance of the period. But his race made little difference in appreciating the music he composed. For Chesnutt, the composer, like the French writer Alexandre Dumas, born also of mixed-race parentage, represented the ideal. The kind of art they produced had the potential, Chesnutt felt, to solve the race problem in the United States. They were not alone and Chesnutt made a point of encouraging others like them.

Still recovering from the loss of Coleridge-Taylor's contribution to classical music, Chesnutt wrote to the well-known lyricist and diplomat James Weldon Johnson on January 18, 1913. Congratulating Johnson on the publication of his "magnificent Emancipation Anniversary poem 'Fifty Years,'" Chesnutt declared the poem to be "the finest thing I have ever read on the subject, which is saying a good deal, and the finest thing I have read from the pen of a colored writer for a long time." Chesnutt wrote to the younger "colored writer" to encourage him to write more such poems. He seemed to feel that as an older, experienced writer, he was able to offer Johnson some literary advice. "If you can find themes which will equally inspire you, why may you not become the poet for which the race is waiting? The deaths of Dunbar and Coleridge-Taylor have left a large gap in the ranks of men of color who have gained recognition in the world of creative thought and certainly no aspiring author could claim that the field was overwhelmed." It is curious that Chesnutt did not mention his own contribution to "the world of creative thought."[6] Perhaps this was too obvious. Johnson, like most "colored writers," was surely aware of Chesnutt's literary contributions.

But the avuncular tone of Chesnutt's letter was new. By this time,

Johnson had already achieved notoriety with the publication of his novel *The Autobiography of an Ex-Colored Man*. Chesnutt did not mention the novel, which had been published anonymously a few months earlier but had been rumored to have been authored by Johnson. He would allude to it explicitly in a later manuscript for a novel he tentatively called *Paul Marchand, F.M.C.* Johnson's novel, rather than his poem, would come to serve as a catalyst for the Harlem Renaissance, which would move into full swing almost a decade after the novel's first appearance. It would be republished in 1927 by Alfred A. Knopf, who had become increasingly interested in publishing Black writers, though the publisher rejected both Chesnutt's novelistic submissions during the decade. Johnson's unhappy story of racial passing seemed better suited to the well-known New York publisher. Its unnamed protagonist was a coward, forsaking his potential as a Black musician and collector of Negro spirituals to join the white race as a successful businessman. It was the novel's now-famous concluding line, in which the narrator bemoans having sold his "birthright for a mess of pottage" that Chesnutt attempted to overturn in his later novel. Written very much in the spirit of the French romance popularized by Dumas, he had thought of calling the novel *The Honor of the Family*, but since "Balzac wrote a story of that name," he had simply named the novel after its hero. "Perhaps 'The Family Honor' would be a better title than the one I have given it," he explained to the several publishers he sent it to.[7] Though Chesnutt knew the novel was flawed, in need of filling out and revision, he believed in its theme and character, thought it even urgent to offer readers an alternative to the growing number of novels featuring immoral or cowardly Black characters. Chesnutt's hero renounced the color line and its attendant restrictions of his native United States to live freely with his wife and children in France. Chesnutt's later novels, both written to combat the obsession with "race pride" that characterized the literature of the 1920s, were rejected repeatedly; he eventually gave up on novel writing altogether.

But for Chesnutt, it was Johnson's poem, prominently published in *The New York Times*, that made all the difference. He urged Johnson to continue writing such poems. This was a poem that celebrated the nation and the role former slaves played in its founding:

Just fifty years—a winter's day—
As runs the history of a race;
Yet, as we look back o'er the way,
How distant seems our starting place!

Look farther back! Three centuries!
To where a naked, shivering score,
Snatched from their haunts across the seas,
Stood, wild-eyed, on Virginia's shore.

For never let the thought arise
That we are here on sufferance bare;
Outcasts, asylumed 'neath these skies.
And aliens without part or share.[8]

Johnson's poem, like Coleridge-Taylor's compositions and Dumas's adventure novels, exemplified the power of art to diminish, if not entirely erase, racial divisions.

A few months later, Chesnutt learned "from the newspapers" that his own literary advisor and perhaps greatest advocate had been named by President Wilson as Ambassador to Great Britain. Walter Hines Page's move from the world of publishing to that of international diplomacy marked a major shift in the American literary scene, perhaps even the end of an era. Page was one of only a few editors at the time who believed in uniting the nation across regional and racial lines through literature.[9] Like Chesnutt, Page believed that "getting good literature into the hands and homes of the masses" was key to "instructing the whole American people in Literature." Page had believed in Chesnutt when no one else had. The publication of *The Colonel's Dream* by the firm Doubleday, Page & Company in 1905 was a testament to Page's commitment to Chesnutt's vision. Chesnutt's letter of congratulations to Page was the last he wrote to his friend and editor, concluding a fifteen-year relationship that had borne much literary fruit. "It is a signal honor, worthily bestowed." Chesnutt continued, "Considering the men who have filled the office, it calls for all there is in a real big man, and I feel that you can meet the requirements.

I hope you may have as successful and brilliant a career as a diplomat and statesman as you have had as editor and publisher."[10] Chesnutt's confidence in his former literary advisor was unwavering. Page's reply came quickly, full of his characteristic warmth and Southern charm:

Dear Mr. Chesnutt:

I wish you to know how heartily I appreciate your kind congratulations and good wishes. The President has great courage to entrust such a mission to a man out of the working ranks of our democratic life; and the confidence of my friends is now very helpful and, I assure you, very pleasant, too.[11]

Page served as ambassador to England for the duration of the First World War, from 1913 to 1918. Just before peace was declared on November 11, 1918, Page returned to his home in North Carolina, where he died a month later.

Shortly after hearing of Page's departure for England, Chesnutt accepted an invitation from William Sanders Scarborough, now serving as president of Wilberforce University, to speak at the nation's oldest, private Black college, situated just two hundred miles southwest of Cleveland. Chesnutt was slated to speak as part of the university's weeklong commencement exercises, when he would also be awarded an honorary doctor of laws, or LLD, the first and only college degree Chesnutt would possess. To have the degree conferred by one of the first and most renowned Black scholars of classical literature and languages, whose textbook on *First Lessons in Greek* Chesnutt had purchased and read diligently as a teenager back in Fayetteville, rendered the symbolic degree all the more meaningful. It was a great moment not only for Chesnutt personally but for American literature; its momentousness was surely not lost on all those gathered to witness the event as they listened to his speech outlining "Race Ideals and Examples" to the Literary Societies of Wilberforce University on June 16, 1913.

Chesnutt repeated the main points of his speech many times in many places over the next few years, most notably the following year at the

Rowfant Club in a talk he delivered on Alexandre Dumas. Chesnutt's Wilberforce speech would be published a few months later, in October 1913, in *The AME Church Review*, likely at the suggestion of Scarborough, who was an active member of the magazine's editorial board. With the delivery of the speech and its eventual publication, Chesnutt's literary career took a marked critical turn. Many of the themes and subjects he touched on were familiar; in fact, the tone of this speech resembled his earliest known speech delivered to the literary society decades earlier in 1881 while serving as principal of Fayetteville's normal school. But this speech was different in one major respect: it was that of a successful author, delivered from the point of view of someone with a great deal of experience and knowledge of the literary world that he was eager to share with those who were just setting out on the journey of independent adult life. Offering readers some context for the essay when it was published, the editor of the *AME Church Review* explained, "This address was delivered before the literary societies of Wilberforce University, commencement week, June, 1913. As a writer of fiction, Mr. Chesnutt stands at the head of American colored men of letters. We take pleasure in giving to our readers his views and ideals for Negro Youth."[12]

Chesnutt opened the essay in a conversational way, rather than in the style of a lecture or impassioned speech. He began, uncharacteristically, by employing the first-person singular pronoun, speaking to his audience intimately, revealing a few personal details that allowed his audience to get to know him. "When I rashly replied to your genial President's invitation to address the literary societies of your University, my first thought was to avoid the beaten path of addresses to colored audiences by speaking to you simply as men and women, interested, in the same way, in the same things in which other people are interested." Chesnutt would go on to explain his change of heart reflecting that "the matter of race will be a very vital thing in your lives." And yet, though he recognized the importance of race, he spoke to the students of other things: "Struggle is the law of life," "the most valuable attribute of a liberal education is the opportunity which it gives one to compare himself with others," and "Christian virtues—faith, hope and charity." Of course, all these subjects were inflected, to varying degrees, by "the deep-seated prejudice against your race." Going against the increasingly popular commitment to "race pride" as a solution to this race problem, Chesnutt asserted the principle of "race self-respect." He explained his departure from race pride this way: "You and your forbears have suffered so severely from race pride as to make it doubtful whether that particular quality is a virtue."[13]

He went on to suggest that the only way to counter caste prejudice and a racial hierarchy that puts "the Negro [at a] relatively low stage of development" is through "individual achievement." To support his unorthodox claim, Chesnutt concluded his "remarks by going somewhat into detail into the case of a colored family which for three generations shed the luster of intellect and achievement upon its own members, upon their nation and the two races from which their blood was drawn, one of which was the Negro race." Here Chesnutt launched into an excited, expanded account of his experience in Paris, dwelling on his favorite sites—the Luxembourg Museum, where "a striking canvas by Mr. Henry Ossawa Tanner" can be found, the Place de la Concorde, the Champs-Élysées, and the Louvre. Chesnutt took his readers on a tour of *his* Paris, the city that in some respects gave him the confidence to follow his dream of becoming an American author, and the city, as he found it on his most recent visit with his daughter, had only grown in cultural importance and beauty. But the purpose of Chesnutt recalling Paris was not just an exercise in nostalgia. It was to tell his audience the story of the Three Dumas. Chesnutt had been reading Dumas *père* for most of his life; it's safe to assume that Chesnutt had likely read everything the great romancer wrote in its original French, as he offered an almost complete descriptive bibliography of Dumas's works during his speech. Chesnutt believed and wanted those who might not have had the pleasure of reading Dumas to know that he was "assuredly one of the greatest masters of the art of narrative in all literature."[14]

But why would the story of the Three Dumas appeal to his young audience, recent Black graduates setting out to apply their newly acquired liberal educations? For Chesnutt, the story of the Three Dumas was something his young "colored" audience could take genuine pride in. As he explained, "I have selected this particular family to speak about for several reasons—primarily because of their blood, and the just pride which you may for that reason feel in their achievements." For Chesnutt, Dumas was the "Ideal and Example" because he went beyond his race, "thereby shown to be valuable to the world of intellect." Look beyond your race, Chesnutt urged his audience, "to contribute by the formation of right ideals for yourselves and their realization in your own individual lives to their realization for your race." Only by putting the individual over race will the race be served. It was a bold claim, and it is unclear how Wilberforce's students reacted to Chesnutt's words. They were a departure from the growing sentiment of race pride that would soon captivate, and eventually dominate, the literary scene that would come to be known as the Harlem Renaissance.

On August 16, 1916, Joel E. Spingarn, former professor of comparative literature at Columbia University and one of the key architects of *The New Criticism*, a theory of literary analysis that would dominate English departments for the next several decades, wrote to Chesnutt. When Spingarn left Columbia in 1911, he became involved in the work of the NAACP, having been elected chairman of the board of directors just as world war was breaking out in 1914. This would mark the beginning of a lifelong commitment to solving the "Negro Problem" in the United States. When he began organizing what would become the First Amenia Conference of 1916, it had been almost a year since Booker T. Washington's death, and there was a growing desire among intellectuals, Black and white, to unite the factions that had splintered the movement to secure civil rights for Black Americans promised by the Constitution. Although Spingarn hosted the conference at Troutbeck, his grand estate, W. E. B. Du Bois was its central organizer and provided the fullest account of the proceedings of the Amenia Conference. "The conference," Du Bois recalled, "as Mr. Spingarn conceived it, was to be 'under the auspices of the N.A.A.C.P.' but wholly independent of it, and the invitations definitely said this." Du Bois was not pleased with Spingarn's decision since he had "hoped that some central organization and preferably the N.A.A.C.P. would eventually represent this new united purpose."[15] But Du Bois held back his personal view on this occasion, given Spingarn's insistence and the fact that he was footing the bill for the entire proceeding. It was doubtless the conference's independent spirit that led Chesnutt to accept Spingarn's rather tardy invitation.

Chesnutt arrived in Amenia, New York, just days after receiving his invitation. He stepped off the train on the morning of Thursday, August 24, 1916, in time for luncheon on Spingarn's sprawling, picturesque estate. The following day, he was scheduled to chair the fifth, and last, session of the first full day of the conference. Chesnutt opened the session by delivering a short speech on "Social Discrimination," which, he declared, was "the last citadel to be assailed in the fight for equality, and the most difficult and delicate subject on the program."[16] Alongside Chesnutt sat Mary Church Terrell and Brown J. Smith, who took up the discussion following Chesnutt's opening remarks. Smith is listed as "lawyer" on the conference program and Terrell as "lecturer." Not much is known about Smith, but Terrell, who was married to Judge Robert H. Terrell, was likely known to Chesnutt. He had met the judge a few years earlier during a visit to Baltimore in 1908, where he lectured to a large audience at the Metropolitan African Methodist Episcopal Church on "Rights and Duties."

Terrell was from the South, the daughter of freed slaves who later went on to become highly successful in business. She would go on to major in classics at Oberlin College in Ohio, graduating in 1884. In many respects, Terrell exemplified the ideal of "individual achievement" that Chesnutt celebrated in his speech at Wilberforce University. Terrell began her career as a teacher of modern languages at Wilberforce, moving to DC to teach Latin at the M Street School. She would later become superintendent of the school, the first woman to hold this position in the school's illustrious history. Terrell was also, as literary critic Elizabeth McHenry recently discovered, a writer, too.[17] But much of her writing remained unpublished, as she was unable to find a publisher for her work. It is curious, given the similarities between them, that a friendship did not develop. The two likely talked during their session at the Amenia Conference, but not much seems to have come from this conversation.

Unfortunately, there is no transcript of the discussion, and since no reporters were permitted on the premises of Troutbeck during the conference, the event was not covered by any local or national newspaper. Chesnutt did keep his notes and the typed speech he delivered that day, which offers a good sense of his position, but there is no record of the conversation that followed among Chesnutt, Terrell, and Brown. Chesnutt wrote to Spingarn

shortly after his return to Cleveland, thanking him "for the generous entertainment of which I was the recipient at Amenia." He went on to express
how much he enjoyed his time at the conference, though he only mentioned
Spingarn's wife, Amy, and Roy Nash, secretary of the NAACP at the time,
by name. "It was a privilege and a pleasure to meet so many interesting and
worth-while people and to be associated with you and yours for a few days.
I am sure you were pleased, as I was, with the outcome of the Conference,
the real and valuable results of which will become apparent later."[18]

The Amenia Conference of 1916 marked Chesnutt's last foray into the
world of political activism. Though he would continue to monitor and
even write letters to prominent political figures concerning various political issues, he would not engage in the kind of political argument and essay
writing in which he had been engaged while Washington was alive. There
are many reasons for Chesnutt's decision to step back from the political
fray. The most obvious was probably his illness. Though Chesnutt had
recovered most of his physical and mental capacities after his stroke, he
was clearly changed after this event. A few years later, in 1920, Chesnutt
underwent an operation for appendicitis and required additional medical
treatment for peritonitis. Chesnutt spoke of his illness cheerfully, claim-
ing to have been "laid up for quite a while" but also boasting that he had
gotten "over it" despite being "an old man."[19] But it also became clear,
after Washington's death in 1915, that Du Bois and his singular vision
for a united "black folk" led by a "talented tenth" organized around the
NAACP, which he led either explicitly or implicitly, had become a foregone
conclusion. The kind of debate and conversation that precipitated coau-
thored books like *The Negro Problem*, published in 1903, in which readers
were presented with multiple, often opposing, viewpoints in a single volume had become increasingly hard to find on bookshelves.

In the summer of 1920, Chesnutt received a surprising, but welcome,
letter from the Micheaux Film and Book Company "with reference to
filming some of my stories."[20] The letter initiated a turn in Chesnutt's
literary career and an association with Oscar Micheaux, the elusive Black
filmmaker, that would cause considerable elation, disappointment, and

frustration in equal measure. Chesnutt was sixty-two, the proud father of "four children, all college graduates" and grandfather to Charlie Jr., named in honor of him by his eldest daughter, Ethel, and her husband, Edward, who by then had just bought a home in Washington, DC. Though he saw Edwin, his only son, less often than he did his three daughters, he took pride in Edwin's accomplishments, too. After earning a degree from Harvard College and working briefly as a stenographer for Booker T. Washington, Edwin went on to complete a degree in dentistry at Northwestern University in Chicago, eventually opening an office of his own there. By the time Micheaux contacted Chesnutt about adapting his published stories for the screen, Chesnutt had been enjoying success and prominence in his community. As he put it in a letter to an old acquaintance from Fayetteville: "I am a member of the Chamber of Commerce, the Cleveland Bar Association, the City Club, and other Clubs of lesser note, and also of the very exclusive Rowfant Club which belongs among the Clubs, membership in which is noted in *Who's Who in America*, which includes among its members half a dozen millionaires, a former United States Senator, a former ambassador to France, and three gentlemen who have been decorated by the French Government."[21] In enumerating this list of clubs to which he belonged, Chesnutt was signaling that he had mostly overcome the race problem still confronting many of the friends and family he'd left behind in Fayetteville. Chesnutt prided himself on belonging to clubs that were not defined by race but by other things—business, books, and the law. Nonetheless, he used his prominent position and associations within these clubs to do a good deal of political work on behalf of "his race."

As a member of the chamber of commerce, for instance, Chesnutt took it upon himself to rally its members to oppose the screening of the "moving picture film called *The Birth of a Nation*, because of its vicious anti-social character." Released amid the violence of the First World War, Chesnutt explained his opposition to the film's production with characteristic logic and eloquence. "The picture was made of course to make money, and to make it by stirring up race prejudice and race hatred, which it seems to me is a most unwise and most unpatriotic thing at this juncture in our national affairs." In continuing his argument against "the exhibition of this film," it became quite clear that Chesnutt had already viewed the film, "*The Birth of a Nation*, which, as a work of pictorial art is a superb and impressive thing, and all the more vicious for that reason, should not be permitted at this time, when all citizens should stand together to support the honor of the nation." It is not clear where or when Chesnutt saw the film, since it had been banned for several years from being shown in Cleveland. Chesnutt had taken a great interest in the emerging art of "moving pictures" long before he received a letter from Micheaux's film production company.[22]

Cleveland got its first movie theater in 1903, when *The Great Train Robbery* began showing at the American Theater on Superior Avenue, near East Sixth Street. By the time of the First World War, the city boasted several silent movie houses, many of which Chesnutt frequented. His favorite seemed to have been the Liberty Theater. By 1919, going to the movies had become one of Chesnutt's favorite pastimes. "One evening in the middle of May," Helen recounted in her biography, "Charles suggested that they go over to the Liberty Theater to see a movie. It was Friday night and the girls could spare the time, he said. They, however, were both too busy to go. Susan, who never really cared for movies, was not interested. They tried to persuade him to give up the idea and remain at home but he refused to be henpecked, and went off alone in the car."[23] Helen's anecdote revealed Chesnutt's fascination with the movies. Perhaps it was this fascination along with his desire to keep his stories in the public eye after they had gone out of print that allowed him to accept Micheaux's proposal to adapt his first novel, published over two decades earlier, for the screen.

In his response to the initial query, sent on behalf of the Micheaux Film and Book Company by George C. Anderson, Micheaux's assistant at the time, Chesnutt wrote that he would "be glad to talk to Mr. Micheaux." Though Chesnutt was planning to be on vacation at his summer home in Idlewild, Michigan, "for the greater part of the month of August," he explained that he would "not be far from Cleveland and if Mr. Micheaux can let me know what day he will pass through here, I will arrange to be at my office to meet him." Micheaux was eager to meet Chesnutt; he had admired Chesnutt's work and believed him to be "a mature gentleman with a keen sense of literary art." There is much speculation about what the literary artist and filmmaker discussed during their first meeting in Cleveland, which occurred most likely in late 1920. According to Micheaux's most recent biographer, when the director first met with Chesnutt, "it was to discuss Chesnutt's first book, a short story collection called *The Conjure Woman*."[24] Micheaux would eventually adapt *The Conjure Woman*, but we don't know much about this adaptation since there is nothing in Chesnutt's notes or letters about its adaptation. But there is good reason to believe that it was Chesnutt who suggested *The House Behind the Cedars*, which of all his books was his personal favorite and would make for a good film adaptation. No matter how the two decided to collaborate on a film version of Chesnutt's first novel, there can be little doubt that Chesnutt had been thinking about how to break into the emerging movie business for some time and that Micheaux's interest in his work presented him with an opportunity to do so.

On January 20, 1921, Chesnutt wrote to William B. Pratt, a relatively new member of the Houghton Mifflin Company whose job was to help its authors negotiate contracts with film producers under the auspices of the special sales department of the publisher's trade division. "Referring to our correspondence with reference to the motion picture production of my books, I beg to say that I have a letter from Micheaux Film corporation, 538 South Dearborn Street, Chicago, in which they make me a proposition to produce *The House Behind the Cedars*." Chesnutt laid out the terms of the proposition, the gist of which was that Micheaux would "pay for all screen rights" for the sum of "$500.00 payable, a portion down on acceptance say $25.00, $75.00 in thirty days thereafter or say March 1st, the balance June 15th, or on date of release should it be filmed and released before that time which is not likely." The film, according to this initial proposition, would be billed as "Oscar Micheaux presents *The House Behind the Cedars*, a story of the South by Charles W. Chesnutt, featuring Evelyn Preer." Chesnutt admitted to Pratt that he knew "nothing from experience about moving picture productions or authors' royalties in connection therewith," but based on his limited knowledge, he felt that "this does not seem like a very large remuneration." But he didn't seem to really care about the money, at least not when Micheaux made his initial proposal. He clearly liked the idea that his story would become a "moving picture" starring one of the most well-known Black actresses of the time. Preer had starred already in two of Micheaux's films, *The Homesteader* in 1919 and his more recent and well-known film *Within Our Gates*. She was also a stage actress and a blues singer. Though she would not end up playing the role of Rena, as Micheaux had promised, the possibility of her starring in the film would have surely enticed Chesnutt. Despite the low sum Micheaux was offering to purchase the rights to adapt the novel, Chesnutt was game. As he explained to Pratt, "If this proposition is agreeable to you I will write to Mr. Micheaux accepting it."[25]

Pratt wrote back a few days later, advising Chesnutt to proceed with greater caution. "As the price is so low," Pratt explained, "I think you could advantageously insist upon the full payment of the $500 on the signing of the contract." Making such a demand, Pratt felt, "would give you better protection than under the proposition as outlined by Mr. Micheaux."[26] He went on to ease Chesnutt's anxiety over the inevitable changes that would be made to the story when it was adapted for the screen. Pratt also wanted Chesnutt to cling fast to his, and by extension his publisher's, property rights over the story. "A rearrangement of the story to adapt it for motion picture use, would be essential, and most stories when screened have but slight resemblance to the original. This, if properly handled, should not be detrimental. On the other hand, there is always some advertising value to be gained from the screen presentation of the story, and it is important that in your contract it be stipulated that in advertising, and in the film itself, the statement be always made that the film is based on *The House Behind the Cedars* by Charles W. Chesnutt, by special arrangement with the publishers, Houghton Mifflin Company." Chesnutt conveyed all these stipulations by his publisher to Micheaux. He concluded his letter to Micheaux on January 27, 1921, with a mild injunction: "You ought to have this story on your list, because it is the most popular of my novels, which constitute a small body of literature which is in a way unique in its treatment of race questions."[27]

With this statement, Chesnutt was marking the distinction of his "small body of literature" from the ever-growing number of books that dealt with "race questions." Since Chesnutt was producing few new stories after 1920 for publication, he became increasingly interested in shoring up his legacy. Having Micheaux adapt his first novel for the screen was one way of introducing his old stories to a new generation of readers and writers. *The House Behind the Cedars* had been a tragedy, the story of a missed opportunity for love and happiness due to an overemphasis on racial origins and obsession with race pride on both sides of the color line. But in his adaptation of the story, Micheaux so altered the plot and premises of the original story, it was hardly recognizable to Chesnutt. He had transformed the tragic love affair into a happy racial romance. But there was nothing he could do about it. As he explained to Ethel years after the movie was released and his association with Micheaux had ended rather bitterly, "The young white lover reaches the house in time to see her coming down the steps of the house behind the cedars on the arm of Frank Fuller, evidently at the end of a wedding." In Micheaux's version of the story, Rena ditches her white lover, George, to marry the Black Frank, who had only ever loved her from afar in the novel. Micheaux ended up paying Chesnutt only "four of the five notes of $100.00" he had promised. The other remained unpaid, so Chesnutt had received only $400 for the rights to his "most popular novel." Despite this, as he explained to Ethel, he held no grudge against Micheaux. "When I saw it, I thought with you that it was very well done, but it was not my story."[28]

When the film was first released in 1924, it brought great attention to Micheaux but didn't do much for the novel on which it was based. *The Philadelphia Tribune* hailed *The House Behind the Cedars* as "a very faithful adaptation of the novel modernized in such a manner as not to destroy the story and at the same time making it a little more appealing." The film proved particularly popular in Harlem, where it was playing simultaneously "at three of Harlem's largest theaters."[29] The popularity of the film brought Chesnutt no joy, however. Micheaux had so changed the novel's plot from its original that it distorted Chesnutt's purpose and eviscerated the novel's message about the tragedy that ensues when race is used to judge character. Still, Micheaux's interest in Chesnutt's books reflected a wider critical interest in his work among Black and white readers long after their publication.

The same year *The House Behind the Cedars* was released as a silent film, the well-known literary critic and poet William Stanley Braithwaite published a review of "The Negro in Literature" in Du Bois's *Crisis*. Braithwaite held a very different view of the purpose of literature from that of the magazine's famous editor. Braithwaite had reached out to Chesnutt a couple of decades earlier, when he was just starting out on the path of poetry and literary editing, to appeal to "the very first writer of our race" for "assistance" with the "issuing of a magazine for the Negro in America." Braithwaite's idea was ambitious for someone so young with few resources: "There is a wealth of material among the colored writers in this country, and it is my aim that these, expressing their needs, ideals and art through a Race organ, shall create a backbone for a Negro school of writers in this country." Decades later, Braithwaite would recount his failed attempt to launch such a journal in the pages of *The Colored American Magazine*. "Chesnutt discouraged the idea, expressing his belief that the time was not ripe for such a venture." Despite Chesnutt's decision to rebuff Braithwaite's early request to contribute to a magazine that was no more than, as Braithwaite put it, an "embryo," his admiration of Chesnutt remained undaunted. Braithwaite believed then that Chesnutt possessed "a style quite exceptional, which as a rule is a rarity with us." He had asked Chesnutt "to give me your promise of a contribution," which he felt would "give weight and standard to the first number."[30] Though Braithwaite's plan was never executed, partially due to Chesnutt's reluctance to contribute, his appreciation of Chesnutt's body of work had only grown over the years.

By 1920, Braithwaite had become one of the preeminent critics of American Literature. He reviewed the work of contemporary writers for the *Boston Evening Transcript* and used his position to foster new literary talent, becoming known in Boston and New York City for reinvigorating poetic expression in the United States. He also became a much sought-after literary anthologist, compiling volumes of English and American poetry that would prove pivotal in determining an Anglo-American literary canon that included writers, like himself, of African descent.

Braithwaite's six-page review for *The Crisis* covered considerable literary territory. His purpose was to trace the origins of "Negro Literature" and opened with a couple of by now self-evident declarations. "True of his origin on this continent, the Negro was projected into literature by his neighbor. He was in American literature long before he was a part of it as a creator." He then offered a list of writers from the well-known Harriet Beecher Stowe and Thomas Dixon to that of more obscure writers like George Madden Martin and T. S. Stribling, who had made "the Negro" the focus of their fiction. When he turned his attention to "the Negro as a creator in American Literature," he began with Phillis Wheatley and went on to consider more recent creators like W. E. B. Du Bois and Paul Laurence Dunbar. But most of this section of Braithwaite's essay was devoted to Chesnutt, who, he claimed, "was to supply the conflict between the two worlds and establish with the precision of a true artist the fiction of the Color Line." For Braithwaite, Chesnutt was the "true artist"; the others he wrote about had "failed to awaken any general interest" among readers.[31]

Braithwaite's assessment of Chesnutt's work was unwaveringly positive. It quickly became clear that the sole purpose of Braithwaite's essay was to *celebrate* Chesnutt, to assert his importance as a writer to those readers of *The Crisis* who might doubt his value. As Braithwaite put it, "From first to last, he revealed himself as a fictional artist of a very high order. The two volumes of short stories, 'The Wife of His Youth and Other Stories of the Color Line,' and 'The Conjure Woman,' are exquisite examples of the short story form, equal to the best in American Literature." He concluded his review with the controversial claim that "from the publication of Chesnutt's last novel until the present year there has been no fiction by the Race of any importance." Braithwaite's celebration of Chesnutt was also a subtle critique of current trends circulating among Harlem Renaissance writers, a critique that Chesnutt would echo repeatedly in the last decade of his life.

Almost immediately after reading Braithwaite's essay in his copy of *The Crisis*, Chesnutt wrote to him. "My dear Mr. Braithwaite," he began. "Thank you very much for your fine appreciation of my literary work in the September *Crisis*. When I read something like that, it makes me regret that I stopped writing and resolve to start up again. However, it is not always easy to get the attention of publishers or of the public after one has stopped for so long a time." Chesnutt went on to explain that there were "several reasons" why he had stopped writing. The main reason was "psychological" and so "difficult to explain." It is hard to know what Chesnutt was referring to here. What "psychological" problems prevented Chesnutt from writing? Perhaps Chesnutt had lost confidence in his ability to write. More likely, as he explained in his own short essay for *The Crisis* published a couple of years later, he had grown weary, even disenchanted with New Negro writers who, he felt, were "too subjective." In his view, "the colored writer, generally speaking has not yet passed the point of thinking of himself first as a Negro, burdened with the responsibility of defending and uplifting his race. Such a frame of mind, however praiseworthy from a moral standpoint is bad for art."[32] For Chesnutt, Braithwaite's appreciation of his work, like that of other writers and critics like the novelist Carl Van Vechten and Spingarn, was "almost enough in itself for any writer, though he never did any more."[33]

In 1928, just four years before his death, Chesnutt was awarded the Spingarn Medal. The medal had been endowed by Joel E. Spingarn at the start of World War I, on June 29, 1914, well before the Amenia Conference. Spingarn wanted to award the medal each year to honor "the man or woman of African descent and American citizenship who shall have made the highest achievement during the preceding year or years to any honorable field."[34] Chesnutt was informed by a telegram from James Weldon Johnson that he had been named the recipient of the award for that year. Chesnutt was thrilled. His response to Johnson was muted, however. Chesnutt seemed to think that he didn't deserve the honor. As he put it: "I assure you and wish you to assure the committee that I appreciate very highly the honor conferred upon me. I was under the impression that the medal was awarded for current achievement, and am all the more pleased because the committee seems to have made it retro-active in my case."[35]

He and Susan flew to Los Angeles, where he accepted the award from Johnson and Spingarn's brother, Arthur. It was here that he delivered one of his last speeches, on July 3, 1928. It was in this speech that he spoke, perhaps for the first time, publicly about Susan, his wife of fifty years. "Mrs. Chesnutt—some of you have met her and others of you may have seen this quiet, unassuming little woman who leads me around and looks me up when I get lost—as I have been several times in this land of the wide open spaces—who tells me what to do, and when and how to do it—when she had opened and read my letter, she handed it to me and said, 'Of course you are going to Los Angeles. It would be beneath our dignity to receive this medal by proxy.'" Here Chesnutt presented his wife as a figure of authority, as the woman of the house who made the important decisions and upon whom he relied for direction. The Chesnutts spent a joyful week in Los Angeles, touring the city, meeting "many former friends and fellow townsmen, and some pupils of mine in the dim and distant past when I taught school, and they have all vied with one another to make our stay among you pleasant." Chesnutt was now content, with his wife by his side, surrounded by friends and admirers. He concluded his speech by surprising his audience with the claim that he was "writing another novel, dealing with present day conditions, and when it is published, as I confidently expect it will be, those of you who, for whatever reason, have read none of my other books, will have an opportunity to get acquainted with my work, and those of you who survived reading my other writings will have the opportunity to renew our acquaintance."[36] No such new novel ever appeared. However, a few months later, on February 2, 1929, Chesnutt received his "advance copy of *The Conjure Woman*" that had been reissued by his old firm Houghton Mifflin with a foreword by Spingarn. By this time, Chesnutt's novels had already become, as Spingarn put it in the opening sentences of his foreword, "history." Despite the decades that had elapsed since their first publication, Spingarn, like so many, believed that Chesnutt was "the first Negro novelist and still the best."[37]

A few years later, in 1931, Chesnutt would revise his speech slightly and publish it as an essay under the title "Post-Bellum—Pre-Harlem" in *The Colophon* magazine. *The Colophon* was a short-lived periodical that focused on the history of books. It was directed at "booklovers" of all kinds, without making any mention of race. In some respects, this essay has become Chesnutt's signature statement on his place in American literature. In it, he tells the story of the publication of his books, from *The Conjure Woman* to *The Colonel's Dream*. He recalls fondly his fellow writers and friends Albion W. Tourgée and George Washington Cable, as well as his publishers, paying particular attention to Walter Hines Page, who, he felt, "was of most assistance to me in publishing my first book." Chesnutt described himself as writing at a time, the postbellum period, during which "a literary work by an American of acknowledged color was a doubtful experiment, both for the writer and for the publisher, entirely apart from its intrinsic merit." He felt himself lucky to have broken into print at such a time and was grateful to those who had supported him along the way. He also observed the enormous changes in publishing that had taken place "after twenty years or more." Chesnutt was referring of course to the Harlem

Renaissance that has given "its large colored population in all shades . . . a new field for literary exploration which of recent years has been cultivated assiduously."[38] Though he was impressed by this flowering of "the Negro novel," he concluded the essay by pointing out that "to date, colored writers have felt restricted for subjects to their own particular group, but there is every reason to hope that in the future, with proper encouragement, they will make an increasingly valuable contribution to literature." Chesnutt was ready, even in the final year of his life, to offer New Negro writers the encouragement they needed to write beyond their particular group.

Chesnutt died on November 15, 1932. He held Susan's hand as his children watched him take his last breath. Helen described the funeral as a "simple Episcopal service" that was "held at the home in which he had spent so many happy years. He rested in his library surrounded by his beloved books."[39] Most of Chesnutt's savings had been wiped out by the stock market crash of 1929. At the time of his death, his 440 books were valued at sixty-six dollars, most of which were eventually donated to Fisk University by Helen. Though Susan had been named executrix of the estate, his daughter Helen was put in charge of Chesnutt's business and literary affairs. Less than a month after his death, Benjamin Brawley, who was now a professor of literature at Howard University and had long championed Chesnutt's fiction, wrote to Helen with a request. Brawley wanted to write a biography of Chesnutt to be included in a new biography series that he was editing. "As your father has so recently passed, however, it seemed to me as editor of the series that I should not want to do anything about the book whatsoever without consulting members of the family."[40] Helen declined Brawley's request. She was going to write a biography of her own, she explained, that would be published a couple of decades later with the help of the poet Arna Bontemps, who at the time was working as head librarian of Fisk University.

Helen's biography, as she put it in a letter to Bontemps on March 21, 1949, aimed to highlight that "Chesnutt's claim to fame rested not only on his literary career, but on the fact that he had brought up a family of four children as simple Americans in the truly American way." Helen's motive to write a biography of her father was poignant and has been an invaluable resource in understanding his life. But what if Brawley had written the *first* biography of Chesnutt? Brawley was a particularly close and sensitive reader of Chesnutt's fiction. He had corresponded frequently with Chesnutt, and in one of his last letters to Brawley, Chesnutt had written admiringly of his literary criticism:

> I am especially pleased to see that you were able to get away entirely from the race question in your subject and treatment of the English Drama. As some one else has remarked, it is extremely difficult for colored American writers to write about anything else, nor is this in the main to be deplored, since it is a vast field and has never been any too well written up from the Negro's viewpoint. However, the world is so wide, and life is such a vast complex, that it is well for the colored writer not to segregate himself intellectually.[41]

Though written for Brawley, this can be taken as Chesnutt's definitive statement on the purpose of literature. Though he was—and continues to be—called "the First Negro Novelist," writing novels and reading literature had always been about moving beyond race for Chesnutt. Brawley was one of Chesnutt's first readers to understand the distinction of his fiction. The time has come for all of us to know Chesnutt as he'd wanted to be known, through the books he wrote and read.

Acknowledgments

Without the meticulous attention of archivists, librarians, and editors, telling the story of Charles W. Chesnutt's life would have been impossible. I am so grateful to the librarians and archivists at Fisk University, whose painstaking labor I relied on to access Chesnutt's diaries, photographs, letters, manuscripts, scrapbooks, and various other sundry material that his daughter Helen bequeathed to Fisk's Special Collections Library following the publication of her biography in 1952. Arna Bontemps, the librarian at the time, was instrumental in making the connection with Helen and ensuring that Chesnutt's books and papers would be preserved in the vaults of the library. Subsequent librarians Ann Allen Shockley, DeLisa M. Harris, and Robert Spinelli have worked tirelessly maintaining Chesnutt's papers and working with scholars and editors like me to grant us the privilege of accessing them. I am similarly grateful to the librarians at Western Reserve Historical Society, particularly Ann K. Sindelar, for making available to me Chesnutt's papers held at the Society, particularly his European diary and correspondence with John Patterson Green and Oscar Micheaux, as well as talking with me about little known facts regarding Cleveland's history. Librarians at Fayetteville State University, Tulane University, and the Louis Round Wilson Special Collections Library at the University of North Carolina at Chapel Hill, as well as archivists at Smith and Harvard Colleges were so generous in answering queries regarding Chesnutt's association with both. I am particularly grateful to Zoe Hill, who walked me patiently through the labyrinthine records of the Houghton Mifflin Company in Harvard's Special Collections when I was ready to give up.

Anne Peale in the Chapin Library at my former home in Williamstown, Massachusetts, was also helpful in gathering material on Bliss Perry. It was the librarians closer to home in Brunswick, at the Hawthorne-Longfellow Library—Karen Jung, Guy Saldhana, and Marieke Van Der Steenhoven— who cheerfully put up with my constant requests for material, helping me to find microfilm and digital sources of historical newspapers and rare books, who proved indispensable. Bowdoin College provided funds to access all these collections and the time off from teaching to write.

Editors of Chesnutt's letters, fiction and nonfiction, whom I cite throughout the book, have made the task of accessing his work so much easier (and less expensive) over the years. I am particularly grateful to Stephanie Browner for sharing her collation of the multiple versions of "Rena" and "The House Behind the Cedars" and her development of the Charles W. Chesnutt Digital Archive for quick access to all things Chesnutt.

The historian John David Smith first suggested to me that I take on a biography of Chesnutt. Though the one I wrote was not the one we had first discussed, I thank him for introducing to me the art of historical biography; his own work has been instrumental in my thinking on Chesnutt.

Over the years, I have benefited from talking about Chesnutt with a great many friends, colleagues, students, and critics. It is an honor to list some of them now: William Andrews, Susanna Ashton, Ian Balfour, John Levi Barnard, Mia Bay, Tamara Berger, Sydney Bufkin, Dana Byrd, Jason Cahoon, Judith Casselberry, Elsy Chakkalakal, Jeff Clymer, Cecile Cottenet, Peter Coviello, Ella Crabtree, Sandy Darity, Theo Davis, Kathleen Diffley, Elizabeth Duquette, Mark Elliott, John Ernest, Bernadette Esposito, Yaya Jata Fanusie, Marieke Favrod, Grace Fenwick, Sally Ann Ferguson, James Finlay, Kevin Fleshman, Frances Smith Foster, Caroline Gephard, Timothy Griffiths, Frank Goodyear, Sandra Gustafson, Faye Halpern, Bill Hardwig, Marina Henke, Barbara Hochman, Terranicia Holmes, Coleman Hutchinson, Carolyn Karcher, Sean Keilen, Laura and Barry Korobkin, Greg Laski, Mary Loefelhoz, Gretchen Long, Stacy Margolis, Jason McBride, Barbara McKaskill, Fiona Mills, Ayaz Muratoglu, Jonathan Murphy, Steve Nadon, Marianne Noble, Sara Oommen, Lenore Peretto, Jason Potts, Ken Price, Brian Purnell, Sharon Raynor, Sarah Ruffing Robbins, Lucy Ryan, Francesca Sawaya, Ellery Sedgwick, Celinda Shannon, Claudia

Stokes, Dillon Stone, Andy Stoneman, Mark Sussman, Doug Taylor, Ken Warren, Franny Weed, Andrea Williams, and Sandy Zagarell.

Elizabeth Palmer, the unflappable Department Coordinator at Bowdoin, gave generously of her time to help with formatting in the final stages and Jennifer Edwards, as always, lent her expertise of all things visual in the book.

Just before I embarked on writing the book, I had the good fortune of taking a seminar at the Rare Book School with Michael Winship. It was working with Michael that helped me to understand the connections between Chesnutt's life and work and book history. Laura McCandlish's encouragement and unstinting support for the project was instrumental in helping me to secure a book contract. Laura led me to Wendy Strothman, who helped me to understand the book trade and led me to my editor, Michael Flamini, whose commitment to Chesnutt and his story were unwavering from the start. It is to Maria Giulia Fabi, coconspirator and fellow traveler, that I owe the most. She remains my most ardent supporter and collaborator. I am so grateful for her generosity and friendship.

My sons, Merrick and Edgar, who read to me aloud, asked questions and waited for dinner, helped out when I was steeped in a paragraph, and made writing a joy. Finally, thanks to my husband, Stephen Meardon, who made sure I had a room of my own to write and remains my best critic.

Notes

PROLOGUE

1. Houghton, Mifflin and Company to Charles W. Chesnutt, October 27, 1891, in the Charles W. Chesnutt Papers, 1864–1938, John Hope and Aurelia E. Franklin Library, Special Collections & Papers, Fisk University, Nashville, TN.

2. Charles W. Chesnutt, "Post-Bellum—Pre-Harlem," *Colophon*, February 1931.

3. Houghton to Chesnutt, October 27, 1891.

4. Walter Hines Page to Chesnutt, February 10, 1897, Walter Hines Page Papers, Houghton Library, Harvard University, Cambridge, MA.

5. Chesnutt to Page, May 20, 1898, in Chesnutt Papers.

6. Horace Elisha Scudder, "James, Crawford, and Howells," *Atlantic Monthly*, June 1886, 852.

7. Scudder, "James, Crawford, and Howells."

8. Joseph McElrath and Robert C. Leitz, eds. *"To Be An Author": Letters of Charles W. Chesnutt, 1889–1905*, Princeton: Princeton University Press, 1997, and Robert B. Stepto and Jennifer Rae Greeson, eds. *The Conjure Stories: Authoritative Texts, Contexts, Criticism*, New York: W.W. Norton & Co., 2012.

9. Chesnutt to Page, May 20, 1898, in Chesnutt Papers.

I. ANCESTRY

1. Charles W. Chesnutt, "The Free Colored People of North Carolina," *Southern Workman*, March 1902, 136.

2. Chesnutt, "The Free Colored People."

3. Chesnutt, "The Free Colored People."

4. Chesnutt, "The Free Colored People."

5. William Waller Hening, ed., *The Statutes at Large; Being a Collection of All the Laws of Virginia from the First Session of the Legislature, in the Year 1619*, vol. 3 (Philadelphia: R. & W. & G. Bartow, 1823), 454.

6. "Slaves and Free Persons of Color, an Act Concerning Slaves and Free Persons of Color," North Carolina General Assembly, 1830, c4 s3.

7. Chesnutt to Robert E. Park, December 19, 1908, in the Charles W. Chesnutt Papers, 1864–1938, John Hope and Aurelia E. Franklin Library, Special Collections & Papers, Fisk University, Nashville, TN.

8. Chesnutt to Nathan C. Newbold, May 24, 1922, in the Charles Waddell Chesnutt Papers, 1889–1932, Western Reserve Historical Society Library, Cleveland, OH.

9. Helen M. Chesnutt, *Charles Waddell Chesnutt: Pioneer of the Color Line* (Chapel Hill: University of North Carolina Press, 1952), 2.

10. Marriage license of parents in Chesnutt Papers, Box 16, Folder 4.

11. Cumberland County index of deeds, North Carolina Archives, Raleigh. See also Frances Richardson Keller, *An American Crusade* (Provo, UT: Brigham Young University Press, 1978), 179.

12. Charles W. Chesnutt, "Cicely's Dream," in *The Wife of His Youth and Other Stories of the Color Line* (Boston: Houghton, Mifflin, 1899).

13. Chesnutt, "Cicely's Dream."

14. "Our History," Fayetteville State University, J. H. Hood to S. S. Ashley, superintendent of public instruction and secretary of the board of education, state of North Carolina, November 2, 1860, North Carolina Department of Archives and History, Doc. No. 6; Keller, *An American Crusade*, 36.

15. Chesnutt, "Cicely's Dream."

16. Chesnutt, "Cicely's Dream."

17. Frenise A. Logan, *The Negro in North Carolina, 1876–1894* (Chapel Hill: University of North Carolina Press, 1964), 8–10.

18. Charles W. Chesnutt, "Why I Am a Republican," 1892, in Chesnutt Papers.

19. Chesnutt, "Why I Am a Republican."

20. Eric Foner, *Freedom's Lawmakers: A Directory of Black Officeholders During Reconstruction* (New York: Oxford University Press, 1993), 44–45.

2. THE TEACHER

1. Earle H. West, "The Harris Brothers: Black Northern Teachers in the Reconstruction South," *Journal of Negro Education* 48, no. 2 (Spring 1979): 126–38.

2. Earle H. West, "The Harris Brothers," August 26, 1864, AMA I11897, American Missionary Association Archives, Amistad Research Collection, Dillard University, New Orleans, LA.

3. A. M. Waddell to Examination Board, n.d., in John Edward Bruce Papers, 1856–1924, The New York Public Library, Schomburg Center for Research in Black Culture, New York, NY.

4. G. W. Jewett to Robert L. Harris, May 29, 1873, in Bruce Papers.

5. Adam Fairclough, *A Class of Their Own: Black Teachers in the Segregated South* (Cambridge: Harvard University Press, 2007), 4.

6. Stephen P. Andrews and Augustus F. Boyle, *The Complete Phonographic Class-book* (Boston: Phonographic Institution, 1846), 5.

7. Chesnutt, "Why I Am a Republican."

8. Chesnutt, "Address Before Ohio State Night School" reprinted in Joseph R. McElrath Jr., Robert C. Leitz III, Jesse S. Crisler, eds., *Charles W. Chesnutt: Essays and Speeches* (Redwood City, CA: Stanford University Press, 1999), 495.

3. READING ALONE

1. Charles W. Chesnutt, "Journals," in the Charles W. Chesnutt Papers, 1864–1938, Box 13. All subsequent reference will be to the manuscript version of the Journals from the Chesnutt Papers. For access to the edited version, please see *The Journals of Charles W. Chesnutt*, ed. Richard Brodhead (Durham: Duke University Press, 1993).

2. Ralph Waldo Emerson, "Self-Reliance," 1841.

3. William L. Royall, *A Reply to "A Fool's Errand, By One of the Fools"* (New York: E. J. Hale, 1881), 3.

4. Royall, *A Reply*, 5–6.

4. LEAVING FAYETTEVILLE

1. Charles W. Chesnutt, "Journals," in the Charles W. Chesnutt Papers, 1864–1938, John Hope and Aurelia E. Franklin Library, Special Collections & Papers, Fisk University, Nashville, TN.

2. *Catalogue of the North Carolina State Colored Normal School Fayetteville, N.C. For the Year 1880–81* (Fayetteville, NC: J. E. Garrett, 1881), 18–19.

3. Booker T. Washington, *Up from Slavery: An Autobiography* (New York: Doubleday, Page, 1902), 126.

4. Charles W. Chesnutt, "The Future of the Negro," speech delivered in Fayetteville, NC, c. 1882, in Chesnutt Papers.

5. Charles W. Chesnutt, "The Advantages of a Well-Conducted Literary Society," speech to the Normal Literary Society, Fayetteville, NC, October 1881, in Chesnutt Papers.

6. Charles W. Chesnutt, "Etiquette (Good Manners)," lecture to the Normal Literary Society, Fayetteville, NC, 1881, in Chesnutt Papers.

7. Chesnutt, "Etiquette (Good Manners)."

8. Washington, *Up from Slavery*, 122.

9. Chesnutt, "Well-Conducted Literary Society."

10. Chesnutt, "Well-Conducted Literary Society."

11. Charles W. Chesnutt, "Methods of Teaching," speech to the North Carolina State Teachers Educational Association, Raleigh, NC, November 23, 1882, in Chesnutt Papers.

12. John Patterson Green, *Fact Stranger Than Fiction: Seventy-Five Years of a Busy Life with Reminiscences of Many Great and Good Men and Women* (Cleveland, OH: Riehl Printing, 1920), 123–124.

13. The Charles W. Chesnutt Archive, http://chesnuttarchive.org.

5. ADVENTURE IN NEW YORK

1. The Charles W. Chesnutt Archive, http://chesnuttarchive.org. "Adventure in New York" refers to the title of one of two of Chesnutt's short stories that appeared in *The Fayetteville Educator* in 1875. The other is "Frisk's First Rat." Both are juvenile stories written during Chesnutt's teaching years. Though parts of "Adventure in New York" remain lost, the rest of Chesnutt's early stories have been digitized.

2. Helen M. Chesnutt, *Charles Waddell Chesnutt: Pioneer of the Color Line* (Chapel Hill: University of North Carolina Press, 1952), 34.

3. Henry Clews, *Twenty-Eight Years in Wall Street* (New York: J. S. Ogilvie Publishing Company, 1887).

4. Charles W. Chesnutt, "Race Prejudice; Its Causes and Its Cure: An Address Delivered Before the Boston Historical and Literary Association," *Alexander's Magazine*, 1905, 24.

5. Quoted by Leah Price, "The Death of Stenography," in *London Review of Books*, Vol. 30 No. 23: December 4, 2008.

6. Charles W. Chesnutt, *A Business Career*, ed. Matthew Wilson and Marjan A. Van Schaik (Jackson: University Press of Mississippi, 2005), 5.

7. Chesnutt, *Business Career*, 35.

8. Chesnutt, *Business Career*, 7.

9. Chesnutt, *Business Career*, 16.

10. Chesnutt, *Business Career*, 103.

11. Houghton, Mifflin and Company Reader Reports on Manuscripts Submitted for Publication, MS Am 2516, Box 28. Houghton Library, Harvard College Library, Cambridge, MA.

12. Helen Chesnutt, *Pioneer*, 36.

13. Helen Chesnutt, *Pioneer*, 36.

14. Charles W. Chesnutt, "The Wives," Charles W. Chesnutt Archive, https://chesnuttarchive.org/item/ccda.works00006.

6. A PROFESSIONAL WRITER IS BORN

1. S. S. McClure to Charles W. Chesnutt, November 14, 1886, in the Charles W. Chesnutt Papers, 1864–1938, John Hope and Aurelia E. Franklin Library, Special Collections & Papers, Fisk University, Nashville, TN.

2. McClure to Chesnutt, November 14, 1886, in Chesnutt Papers.

3. McClure to Chesnutt, December 8, 1886, in Chesnutt Papers.

4. William L. Andrews, *The Literary Career of Charles W. Chesnutt* (Baton Rouge: Louisiana State University Press, 1980), 18.

5. Charles W. Chesnutt, "Uncle Peter's House," Charles W. Chesnutt Archive, https://chesnuttarchive.org/item/ccda.works00004.

6. Chesnutt, "Uncle Peter's House."

7. Chesnutt, "Uncle Peter's House."

8. Chesnutt, "Uncle Peter's House."

9. S. S. McClure, *My Autobiography* (London: John Murray, 1914). See also Peter Lyon, *Success Story: The Life and Times of S .S. McClure* (New York: Scribner, 1964).

10. W. D. Howells, "Henry James, Jr.," *Century Illustrated Magazine*, November 1882, 26.

11. H. A. Byram to McClure, November 2, 1885, quoted in Charles A. Johanningsmeier, *Fiction and the American Literary Marketplace: The Role of Newspaper Syndicates in America, 1860–1900* (Cambridge, England: Cambridge University Press, 1997), 169.

12. Charles W. Chesnutt, "Literature in Its Relation to Life (The Relation of Literature to Life)," speech to the Bethel Literary and Historical Association, District

of Columbia, November 21, 1899, reprinted in Joseph R. McElrath Jr., Robert C. Leitz III, Jesse S. Crisler, eds., *Charles W. Chesnutt: Essays and Speeches* (Redwood City, CA: Stanford University Press, 1999), 114.

13. Chesnutt, "Literature in Its Relation to Life."

14. Chesnutt Archive, https://chesnuttarchive.org.

15. Helen M. Chesnutt, *Charles Waddell Chesnutt: Pioneer of the Color Line* (Chapel Hill: University of North Carolina Press, 1952), 37.

16. Helen Chesnutt, *Pioneer*, 61.

17. Charles W. Chesnutt, "Advice to Young Men," *Social Circle Journal*, November 1886, 18, reprinted in reprinted in McElrath et al., eds., *Chesnutt: Essays and Speeches*, 73–74.

18. Mark Twain and Charles Dudley Warner, *The Gilded Age: A Tale of Today* (Hartford, CT: American Publishing Company, 1874).

19. Charles W. Chesnutt, "Appreciation," *Puck*, April 20, 1887, 29.

20. See, for instance, Henry B. Wonham, *Playing the Races: Ethnic Caricature and American Literary Realism* (New York: Oxford University Press, 2004), 152, and William L. Andrews, *The Literary Career of Charles W. Chesnutt* (Baton Rouge: Louisiana State University Press, 1980), 19.

7. CONJURING *The Atlantic*

1. Samuel Roberts, *A Handbook for Home Improvement* (New York: Fowler & Wells, 1857), 17–18, cited in Richard H. Brodhead, ed., *The Journals of Charles W. Chesnutt* (Durham, NC: Duke University Press, 1993), 40.

2. Harriet A. Jacobs, *Incidents in the Life of a Slave Girl Written by Herself*, ed. Jean Fagan Yellin (Cambridge, MA: Harvard University Press, 2000).

3. Charles W. Chesnutt, "The Negro in Books," speech delivered in behalf of the National Buy-a-Book Campaign in the Interest of Negro Literature, Philadelphia, PA, December 5, 1916, reprinted in Joseph R. McElrath Jr., Robert C. Leitz III, Jesse S. Crisler, eds., *Charles W. Chesnutt: Essays and Speeches* (Redwood City, CA: Stanford University Press, 1999), 434.

4. Charles W. Chesnutt, "Post-Bellum—Pre-Harlem," *Colophon*, February 1931, 2.

5. Charles W. Chesnutt, "Journals," March 16, 1880, in the Charles W. Chesnutt Papers, 1864–1938, John Hope and Aurelia E. Franklin Library, Special Collections & Papers, Fisk University, Nashville, TN.

6. Chesnutt, "Journals."

7. Chesnutt, "Journals."

8. Charles W. Chesnutt, "The Goophered Grapevine," *Atlantic Monthly*, August 1887, 254.

9. Chesnutt, "Goophered Grapevine," 255.

10. Mark Twain, *Adventures of Huckleberry Finn* (New York: Charles I. Webster, 1885).

11. Chesnutt, "Goophered Grapevine," 260.

12. Max Bennett Thrasher, "Mr. Chesnutt at Work," *Boston Evening Transcript*, September 4, 1901, 13.

13. Chesnutt, "Post-Bellum—Pre-Harlem."

14. Thomas Bailey Aldrich, *The Story of a Bad Boy* (Boston: Fields, Osgood, 1869).

15. Chesnutt, "Goophered Grapevine," 254.

16. Charles W. Chesnutt, "Dave's Neckliss," *Atlantic Monthly*, October 1889, 501.

17. James Biddle Eustis, "Race Antagonism in the South," *Forum*, October 1888, 5.

18. Albion W. Tourgée, "The South as a Field for Fiction," *Forum*, December 1888, 6.

19. Tourgée, "The South as a Field for Fiction."

20. Tourgée to Chesnutt, December 8, 1888, in Chesnutt Papers.

21. Tourgée to Chesnutt, December 8, 1888.

22. George Washington Cable, *The Silent South Together with the Freedman's Case in Equity and the Convict Lease System* (New York: Scribner, 1885).

23. "Patriotic Societies," *Encyclopedia of Cleveland History*, Case Western Reserve University, https://case.edu/ech/articles/p/patriotic-societies.

24. George Washington Cable, "A Simpler Southern Question," *Forum*, December 1888, 392–403.

25. George Washington Cable Diary in George Washington Cable Papers, Tulane University, Special Collections, Howard-Tilton Memorial Library.

26. Cable to Chesnutt, January 30, 1889, in Chesnutt Papers.

27. Chesnutt to Cable, February 12, 1889, in George Washington Cable Papers, Howard-Tilton Memorial Library, Tulane University.

28. Cable to Chesnutt, May 30, 1889, in Chesnutt Papers.

29. Chesnutt to Cable, March 1, 1889, in George Washington Cable Papers.

30. Chesnutt to Cable, March 4, 1889, in George Washington Cable Papers.

31. Chesnutt to Cable, May 3, 1889, in George Washington Cable Papers.

8. THE NOVELIST AS COURT REPORTER

1. Walter Besant and Henry James, *The Art of Fiction* (Boston: De Wolfe Fiske, 1884).

2. Charles W. Chesnutt, "Some of the Uses and Abuses of Shorthand," speech to the Ohio Stenographers' Association, Cleveland, OH, August 28, 1889, *Proceedings of the Fifth, Sixth, and Seventh Annual Sessions of the Ohio Stenographers' Association* (Cincinnati: Wrightson Printing Company, 1890), reprinted in Joseph R. McElrath Jr., Robert C. Leitz III, Jesse S. Crisler, eds., *Charles W. Chesnutt: Essays and Speeches* (Redwood City, CA: Stanford University Press, 1999), 75.

3. W. H. Pritchard, "The Seventh Annual Meeting of the Ohio Stenographers' Association," *Phonographic Magazine*, 1889, 200.

4. Chesnutt to Albion W. Tourgée, April 18, 1893, in the Tourgée Papers, Chautauqua County Historical Society, Chautauqua, NY.

5. Chesnutt to Tourgée, November 27, 1893, in Tourgée Papers.

6. Chesnutt to Tourgée, November 27, 1893.

7. George Washington Cable to Chesnutt, June 12, 1889, in Chesnutt Papers.

8. Charles W. Chesnutt, "What Is a White Man?," *Independent* 41, no. 2113 (May 30, 1889): 5–6.

9. Cable to Chesnutt, June 12, 1889.

10. Chesnutt to Mary Adelene Moffat, September 2, 1889, in George Washington Cable Papers.

11. Charles W. Chesnutt, "A Multitude of Counselors," *Independent* 43, no. 2209 (April 2, 1891): 4–5.

12. Chesnutt, "A Multitude of Counselors."

13. Helen M. Chesnutt, *Charles Waddell Chesnutt: Pioneer of the Color Line* (Chapel Hill: University of North Carolina Press, 1952), 65.

14. Chesnutt, *Pioneer*, 65.

15. Besant and James, *The Art of Fiction*.

16. Charles W. Chesnutt, "Some Requisites of a Law Reporter," *Proceedings of the Eighth and Ninth Annual Conventions of the Ohio Stenographers' Association* (Cleveland: F. W. Roberts, 1891), reprinted in McElrath et al., eds., *Chesnutt: Essays and Speeches*, 84–87.

17. Chesnutt, "Some Requisites of a Law Reporter."

18. Chesnutt, "Some Requisites of a Law Reporter."

19. Chesnutt, "Some Requisites of a Law Reporter."

20. William Dean Howells, *An Imperative Duty: A Novel* (New York: Harper & Brothers, 1893), 86.

21. Howells, *Imperative Duty*, 144.

22. Charles W. Chesnutt, "The Negro in Books," reprinted in McElrath et al., eds., *Chesnutt: Essays and Speeches*, 433.

23. Howells, *Imperative Duty*, 17.

24. Charles W. Chesnutt, *Mandy Oxendine* (Urbana: University of Illinois Press, 1997), 112.

25. Chesnutt, *Mandy Oxendine*, 27.

26. Houghton, Mifflin and Company Reader Reports, bMS AM 2516 (6200)–(6254) MS. No. 6208, March 26, 1897.

9. STORIES OF THE COLOR LINE

1. Charles W. Chesnutt, "The Courts and the Negro," c. 1908, in the Charles W. Chesnutt Papers, 1864–1938, John Hope and Aurelia E. Franklin Library, Special Collections & Papers, Fisk University, Nashville, TN, reprinted in Joseph R. McElrath Jr., Robert C. Leitz III, Jesse S. Crisler, eds., *Charles W. Chesnutt: Essays and Speeches* (Redwood City, CA: Stanford University Press, 1999), 267.

2. Booker T. Washington, *Up from Slavery: An Autobiography* (New York: Doubleday, Page, 1902), 240.

3. Albion W. Tourgée, A Bystander's Notes, *Daily Inter Ocean*, Saturday, April 8, 1893, 4.

4. Chesnutt to Sarah Alice Haldeman, February 1, 1896, in Chesnutt Papers, reprinted in Joseph R. McElrath Jr. and Robert C. Leitz, eds., *"To Be an Author": Letters of Charles W. Chesnutt, 1889–1905* (Princeton, NJ: Princeton University Press, 1997), 89.

5. Chesnutt to Haldeman, February 1, 1896.

6. Chesnutt to Haldeman, February 1, 1896.

7. Chesnutt to Tourgée, April 25, 1896, Chautauqua County Historical Society, reprinted in McElrath and Leitz, eds., *"To Be an Author,"* 92.

8. Chesnutt to Tourgée, April 25, 1896.

9. Chesnutt to Tourgée, May 24, 1897, Chautauqua County Historical Society, reprinted in McElrath and Leitz, eds., *"To Be an Author,"* 99.

10. Charles W. Chesnutt, "European Diary," Western Reserve Historical Society, reprinted in Tess Chakkalakal, ed., "Charles Chesnutt's European Diary," *Anglo-Americana* 28, no. 169 (2018): 5–32.

11. Chesnutt, "Race Ideals and Examples," in Chesnutt Papers.

12. Chesnutt, "European Diary."

13. Chesnutt, "European Diary."

14. Richard Watson Gilder to George Washington Cable, March 13, 1889, GWC, reprinted in McElrath and Leitz, eds., *"To Be an Author,"* 38.

15. Houghton, Mifflin and Company to Chesnutt, October 27, 1891, in Chesnutt Papers.

16. Walter H. Page, "Study of an Old Southern Borough," *Atlantic Magazine*, May 1881, 648–58.

17. Page, "Study of an Old Southern Borough," 658.

18. Helen M. Chesnutt, *Charles Waddell Chesnutt: Pioneer of the Color Line* (Chapel Hill: University of North Carolina Press, 1952), 76.

19. Page to Chesnutt, February 10, 1897, Walter Hines Page Papers, Houghton Library, Harvard University, Cambridge, MA, MS Am 1090.3.

20. W. E. B. Du Bois, "Strivings of the Negro People," *Atlantic Magazine*, August 1897, 194.

21. Page to Chesnutt, October 2, 1897, Page Papers, MS Am 1090.3.

22. The phrase *Page's Protégé* in reference to Chesnutt is first used by the editors of his selected letters in *"To Be an Author"* and then is picked up by later critics such as Robert Stepto in the introduction to his edition of *The Conjure Woman*. See *The Conjure Stories: Authoritative Texts, Contexts, Criticism* (New York: Norton, 2012).

23. Page to Chesnutt, February 10, 1897.

24. Chesnutt to Cable, February 20, 1897, in Chesnutt Papers, reprinted in McElrath and Leitz, eds., *"To Be an Author,"* 98.

25. Quoted in Lawrence N. Powell, ed., *The New Orleans of George Washington Cable* (Baton Rouge: Louisiana State University Press, 2008), 29.

26. Helen Chesnutt, *Pioneer*, 75.

27. Cable to Chesnutt, April 14, 1897, in Chesnutt Papers, reprinted in Matthew Wilson and Marjan A. van Schaik, "The Letters of George Washington Cable to Charles W. Chesnutt," *Modern Language Studies* 36, no. 2 (Winter 2007): 8–41.

28. Cable to Chesnutt, August 19, 1897, in Chesnutt Papers, reprinted in Wilson and Schaik, "The Letters of George Washington Cable."

10. TAKES UP LITERATURE

1. William Dean Howells, "Mr. Charles W. Chesnutt's Stories," *Atlantic Monthly*, May 1900, 699.

2. James Lane Allen to Walter Hines Page, n.d., letter enclosed in Page to Chesnutt, June 28, 1898, in the Charles W. Chesnutt Papers, 1864–1938, John Hope and Aurelia E. Franklin Library, Special Collections & Papers, Fisk University, Nashville, TN, reprinted in Helen M. Chesnutt, *Charles Waddell Chesnutt: Pioneer of the Color Line* (Chapel Hill: University of North Carolina Press, 1952), 96.

3. Chesnutt to Page, June 29, 1898, in Chesnutt Papers, reprinted in Helen Chesnutt, *Pioneer*, 96.

4. Page to Chesnutt, July 6, 1898, in Chesnutt Papers, reprinted in Helen Chesnutt, *Pioneer*, 97.

5. Chesnutt to Page, December 7, 1897, reprinted in Joseph R. McElrath Jr. and Robert C. Leitz, eds., *"To Be an Author": Letters of Charles W. Chesnutt, 1889–1905* (Princeton, NJ: Princeton University Press, 1997), 102–103.

6. Page to Chesnutt, December 15, 1897, reprinted in Helen Chesnutt, *Pioneer*, 87.

7. Page to Chesnutt, March 30, 1898, in Chesnutt Papers.

8. Houghton, Mifflin and Company Reader Reports, Folder bMS AM 2516 (6547).

9. Page to Chesnutt, March 30, 1898.

10. Page to Chesnutt, September 6, 1898, in Chesnutt Papers, reprinted in Helen Chesnutt, *Pioneer*, 100.

11. Chesnutt to Houghton, Mifflin and Company, September 19, 1898, in Chesnutt Papers, reprinted in Helen Chesnutt, *Pioneer*, 101, and McElrath and Leitz, eds., *"To Be an Author,"* 113–12.

12. Chesnutt to Houghton, September 19, 1898.

13. Charles W. Chesnutt, "Post-Bellum—Pre-Harlem," *Colophon*, February 1931, 544.

14. Houghton, Mifflin and Company Reader Reports, Folder bMS AM 2516 (6547).

15. Page to Chesnutt, September 9, 1898, in Chesnutt Papers, reprinted in Helen Chesnutt, *Pioneer*, 100.

16. Chesnutt to Page, March 22, 1899, in Chesnutt Papers, reprinted in McElrath and Leitz, eds., *"To Be an Author,"* 122.

17. Susan Chesnutt to daughters Ethel and Helen Chesnutt, in Helen Chesnutt, *Pioneer*, 106.

18. Helen Chesnutt, *Pioneer*, 107.

11. PASSING ON RENA

1. Charles W. Chesnutt to Walter Hines Page, December 27, 1898, in the Charles W. Chesnutt Papers, 1864–1938, John Hope and Aurelia E. Franklin Library, Special Collections & Papers, Fisk University, Nashville, TN, reprinted in Joseph R. McElrath Jr. and Robert C. Leitz, eds., *"To Be an Author": Letters of Charles W. Chesnutt, 1889–1905* (Princeton, NJ: Princeton University Press, 1997), 118.

2. Chesnutt to Page, March 22, 1899, in Chesnutt Papers, reprinted in McElrath and Leitz, eds., *"To Be an Author,"* 122.

3. Chesnutt to Page, August 15, 1899, in Chesnutt Papers.

4. Chesnutt to Page, August 15, 1899.

5. Page to Chesnutt, January 24, 1900, in Chesnutt Papers, reprinted in Helen M. Chesnutt, *Charles Waddell Chesnutt: Pioneer of the Color Line* (Chapel Hill: University of North Carolina Press, 1952), 137–38.

6. Susan Chesnutt to daughters Ethel and Helen Chesnutt, January 26, 1900, in Helen Chesnutt, *Pioneer*, 139.

7. Page to Chesnutt, January 24, 1900, in Chesnutt Papers, reprinted in Helen Chesnutt, *Pioneer*, 138.

8. All references to manuscript versions of *Rena* are based on documents in Chesnutt Papers, Box 9.

9. Chesnutt to Susan, January 27, 1900, in Helen Chesnutt, *Pioneer*, 139–40.

10. Chesnutt to Susan, February 3, 1900, in Helen Chesnutt, *Pioneer*, 140.

11. Chesnutt to Edward Williams, May 12, 1900, in Helen Chesnutt, *Pioneer*, 148.

12. Francis J. Garrison to Chesnutt, March 24, 1900, in Helen Chesnutt, *Pioneer*, 146.

13. Page to Chesnutt, February 17, 1900, in Chesnutt Papers, reprinted in Helen Chesnutt, *Pioneer*, 140–41.

14. Chesnutt to daughters Ethel and Helen, March 24, 1900, reprinted in Helen Chesnutt, *Pioneer*, 146.

15. Chesnutt to Harry D. Robins, September 27, 1900, in Chesnutt Papers, reprinted in McElrath and Leitz, eds., *"To Be an Author,"* 149.

16. Chesnutt to Robins, November 19, 1900, in Chesnutt Papers, reprinted in McElrath and Leitz, eds., *"To Be an Author,"* 155.

17. Helen Chesnutt, *Pioneer*, 157.

18. Horace Elisha Scudder to Chesnutt, June 2, 1901, in Chesnutt Papers.

12. FUTURE AMERICANS

1. Booker T. Washington, *Up from Slavery: An Autobiography* (New York: Doubleday, Page, 1902), 222.

2. W. D. Howells, "An Exemplary Citizen," *North American Review* 173 (August 1901): 280.

3. Howells, "An Exemplary Citizen."

4. Chesnutt also sent "The Bouquet," along with "A Victim of Heredity" to Charles Scribner's Sons. See Charles W. Chesnutt Papers, 1864–1938, Box 4, John Hope and Aurelia E. Franklin Library, Special Collections & Papers, Fisk University, Nashville, TN.

5. Booker T. Washington, *The Story of My Life and Work* (Toronto: J. L. Nichols, 1901), 326.

6. Washington, *The Story of My Life and Work.*

7. Louis R. Harlan, ed., *The Booker T. Washington Papers* (Champaign, IL: University of Illinois Press, 1971).

8. Booker T. Washington, *The Future of the American Negro* (Boston: Small, Maynard & Company, 1900), 4.

9. Editors, preface to "A Plea for the American Negro," *Critic*, February 1900, 160.

10. Chesnutt to Edward Williams, quoted in *Pioneer*, 125.

11. Charles W. Chesnutt, "On the Future of His People," *Saturday Evening Post*, January 20, 1900, 646.

12. Chesnutt, "On the Future of His People."

13. Charles W. Chesnutt, "A Plea for the American Negro," *Critic*, February 1900, 160.

14. Chesnutt to Susan, March 14, 1900, reprinted in Helen M. Chesnutt, *Charles Waddell Chesnutt: Pioneer of the Color Line* (Chapel Hill: University of North Carolina Press, 1952), 145.

15. Joseph Edgar Chamberlin, *Nomads and Listeners of Joseph Edgar Chamberlin* (1937) Rpt. (Freeport, N.Y.: Books for Libraries Press, 1968), 23.

16. Chesnutt to Susan, March 14, 1900.

17. Charles W. Chesnutt, "The Future American: What the Race Is Likely to Become in the Process of Time," *Boston Evening Transcript*, August 18, 1900, 20.

18. Charles W. Chesnutt, "A Roman Antique," *Puck*, July 17, 1889, 351.

19. Charles W. Chesnutt, "A Matter of Principal," in *The Wife of His Youth, and Other Stories of the Color Line* (Boston: Houghton, Mifflin and Company, 1899), 98.

20. Chesnutt, "A Matter of Principal," 131.

21. Chesnutt, "The Future American: What the Race Is Likely to Become," 20.

22. Charles W. Chesnutt, "The Future American: A Stream of Dark Blood in the Veins of Southern Whites," *Boston Evening Transcript*, August 25, 1900, 15.

23. Charles W. Chesnutt, "The Future American: A Complete Race-Amalgamation Likely to Occur," *Boston Evening Transcript*, September 1, 1900, 24.

24. Joseph Edgar Chamberlin to Chesnutt, August 15, 1900, in Chesnutt Papers.

13. SOUTHBOUND

1. Chesnutt to Walter Hines Page, November 11, 1898, in Chesnutt Papers.

2. Literary Memoranda, September 1, 1900, in the Charles W. Chesnutt Papers, 1864–1938, Box 13, John Hope and Aurelia E. Franklin Library, Special Collections & Papers, Fisk University, Nashville, TN.

3. Literary Memoranda, in Chesnutt Papers.

4. Charles W. Chesnutt, *The Marrow of Tradition* (Boston: Houghton, Mifflin and Company, 1901), 1.

5. William Dean Howells, *A Hazard of New Fortunes* (New York: Harper & Brothers, 1890).

6. Howells, *Hazard of New Fortunes*.

7. Edward Williams to Chesnutt, March 4, 1900, in Helen Chesnutt, *Pioneer*, 143.

8. William Dean Howells, "Mr. Chesnutt's Stories," *Atlantic*, May 1900, 699.

9. Chesnutt to Howells, April 31, 1900, Autograph File, C. Box 38a, Houghton Library, Harvard University, Cambridge, MA, and Chesnutt to Booker T. Washington, October 29, 1900, quoted in Joseph R. McElrath Jr. and Robert C. Leitz, eds., *"To Be an Author": Letters of Charles W. Chesnutt, 1889–1905* (Princeton, NJ: Princeton University Press, 1997), 153. Original in Booker T. Washington Papers, Library of Congress.

10. Charles W. Chesnutt, "Charles W. Chesnutt's Own View of His New Story 'The Marrow of Tradition,'" *Cleveland World*, October 20, 1901, 5.

11. Chesnutt to Howells, April 31, 1900.

12. William Dean Howells, *Literary Friends and Acquaintance: A Personal Retrospect of American Authorship* (New York: Harper & Brothers, 1900).

13. Charles W. Chesnutt, "The White and the Black," *Boston Evening Transcript*, March 20, 1901, 13.

14. Chesnutt, "The White and the Black."

15. Charles W. Chesnutt, "A Visit to Tuskegee," *Cleveland Leader*, March 31, 1901, 19.

16. Chesnutt to Washington, March 13, 1901, reprinted in McElrath and Leitz, eds., *"To Be an Author,"* 158.

17. Chesnutt to George Mifflin, July 25, 1901, in Helen M. Chesnutt, *Charles Waddell Chesnutt: Pioneer of the Color Line* (Chapel Hill: University of North Carolina Press, 1952), 172.

18. "Marrow of Tradition Report," Houghton Mifflin Company Reader Reports on Manuscripts Submitted for Publication, Houghton Library, Harvard University.

19. Houghton, Mifflin and Company to Chesnutt, July 31, 1901, in Helen Chesnutt, *Pioneer*, 172–73.

20. Chesnutt to Ethel Chesnutt, October 29, 1901, in Helen Chesnutt, *Pioneer*, 175–76.

21. Anonymous, "Rev. of The Marrow of Tradition," *Literary World: A Monthly Review of Current Literature*, January–December 1902.

22. Chesnutt quoted from Fortune's letter in one he sent to Washington on November 16, 1901. The original seems to have been lost or misplaced.

23. William Dean Howells, "A Psychological Counter-Current in Recent Fiction," *North American Review*, December 1901, 872–88.

24. Howells, "A Psychological Counter-Current."

25. Chesnutt to Houghton, December 30, 1901, reprinted in McElrath and Leitz, eds., *"To Be an Author,"* 171.

14. THE NOVELIST AS PUBLIC INTELLECTUAL

1. William Hannibal Thomas, *The American Negro: What He Was, What He Is, And What He May Become* (New York: Macmillan, 1901), xv.

2. Joseph Edgar Chamberlin to Charles W. Chesnutt, February 1, 1901, in the Charles W. Chesnutt Papers, 1864–1938, John Hope and Aurelia E. Franklin Library, Special Collections & Papers, Fisk University, Nashville, TN.

3. Thomas, *The American Negro*, 117.

4. Chamberlin to Chesnutt, February 1, 1901.

5. Chesnutt, "In Re William Hannibal Thomas, Author of 'The American Negro,'" unpublished manuscript, 1901, and copies of Macmillan Company correspondence.

6. Booker T. Washington to Chesnutt, May 3, 1901, in Chesnutt Papers.

7. Charles W. Chesnutt, "The White and the Black," *Boston Evening Transcript*, March 20, 1901.

8. Chesnutt, "The White and the Black."

9. Charles W. Chesnutt, "A Defamer of His Race," *Critic*, April 1901, 350.

10. Chesnutt to James Pott & Company, June 16, 1901, in Chesnutt Papers.

11. James Pott, ed., *The Negro Problem* (New York: James Pott & Company, 1903), 79.

15. VICTIMS OF HEREDITY

1. Helen M. Chesnutt, *Charles Waddell Chesnutt: Pioneer of the Color Line* (Chapel Hill: University of North Carolina Press, 1952), 184.

2. Charles W. Chesnutt to Bliss Perry, July 1899, in the Charles W. Chesnutt Papers, 1864–1938, John Hope and Aurelia E. Franklin Library, Special Collections & Papers, Fisk University, Nashville, TN.

3. Chesnutt to Perry, July 1899.

4. Chesnutt to Perry, July 1899.

5. Bliss Perry, *The Plated City* (New York: Scribner, 1895), 55.

6. Perry to Chesnutt, August 30, 1899, in Chesnutt Papers.

7. William B. Parker to Chesnutt, September 24, 1900, in Chesnutt Papers.

8. Houghton, Mifflin and Company Reader Reports, Box 21.

9. Charles W. Chesnutt, *Evelyn's Husband*, ed. Matthew Wilson and Marjan van Schaik (Jackson: University Press of Mississippi, 2005), 7.

10. Matthew Wilson, introduction to *Evelyn's Husband*, vi.

11. Chesnutt, *Evelyn's Husband*, 49.

12. Witter Bynner to Chesnutt, November 6, 1903, in Chesnutt Papers.

13. Chesnutt to Perry, July 1899.

14. Bliss Perry to Chesnutt, March 19, 1904, in Chesnutt Papers.

15. Charles Chesnutt, "Baxter's Procrustes," *Atlantic Monthly*, June 1904, 823.

16. Charles Chesnutt, *The Colonel's Dream* (New York: Doubleday, Page, 1905), 4.

17. Houghton Reader Reports, Box 21.

18. Walter Hines Page to Chesnutt, June 24, 1904, in Chesnutt Papers.

19. Garrison to Chesnutt, May 12, 1904, in Chesnutt Papers.

20. Chesnutt to Page, June 29, 1904, in Chesnutt Papers.

21. Chesnutt to Isaac F. Marcosson, October 14, 1905, in Chesnutt Papers.

22. Chesnutt to Marcosson, October 14, 1905, in Chesnutt Papers.

23. Frank Norris, "The Novel with a Purpose," *World's Work* 4, no. 1 (May 1902): 2118.

24. Chesnutt, dedication in *The Colonel's Dream*.

25. Frank Norris, "The Responsibilities of the Novelist," in *The Responsibilities of the Novelist and Other Literary Essays* (London: Grant Richards, 1903), 11.

16. LITERARY CELEBRITY

1. William H. Trotter to Charles W. Chesnutt, April 3, 1905, in the Charles W. Chesnutt Papers, 1864–1938, John Hope and Aurelia E. Franklin Library, Special Collections & Papers, Fisk University, Nashville, TN.

2. Chesnutt to Trotter, December 28, 1901, in Chesnutt Papers.

3. Chesnutt to Hugh M. Browne, June 2, 1905, in Chesnutt Papers.

4. Chesnutt's "For Roosevelt" first appeared in *The New York Age* and was reprinted in *The Cleveland Gazette*, October 22, 1904, on its front page under the header "The following appeared in a recent issue of the Age and ought to, for an obvious reason, prove exceptionally interesting to The Gazette's readers in Cleveland and throughout Ohio."

5. "All the News from Boston," *New York Age*, Thursday, June 29, 1905, 1.

6. Charles William Eliot, "Inaugural Address as President of Harvard College," quoted in William Allan Neilson, *Charles W. Eliot: The Man and His Beliefs* (New York: Harper & Brothers, 1926), 2.

7. Harvard Commencement Program, HUC 6905 (1905), Harvard University Archives, Cambridge, MA.

8. "All the News from Boston."

9. "All the News from Boston."

10. Chesnutt to Alice E. Hanscom, September 22, 1905, in Chesnutt Papers.

11. Hanscom to Chesnutt, September 20, 1905, in Chesnutt Papers.

12. "Celebrate Mark Twain's Seventieth Birthday," *New York Times*, December 6, 1905.

13. Chesnutt to Leslie Pickney Hill, April 20, 1912, in Chesnutt Papers.

14. Benjamin Brawley, *The Negro in Literature and Art in the United States* (New York: Duffield, 1918), 45.

15. Chesnutt to Brawley, April 29, 1910.

16. "Race Writer Taken Ill," *Cleveland Plaindealer*, June 13, 1910.

17. Helen M. Chesnutt, *Charles Waddell Chesnutt: Pioneer of the Color Line* (Chapel Hill: University of North Carolina Press, 1952), 238.

18. Charles W. Chesnutt, "The Courts and the Negro," speech delivered c. 1908, in Chesnutt Papers, reprinted in Joseph R. McElrath Jr., Robert C. Leitz III, Jesse S. Crisler, eds., *Charles W. Chesnutt: Essays and Speeches* (Redwood City, CA: Stanford University Press, 1999), 262.

19. Charles W. Chesnutt, "Rights and Duties," speech to the Bethel Literary and Historical Association, District of Columbia, 6 October 1908, in Chesnutt Papers, reprinted in McElrath et al., eds., *Chesnutt: Essays and Speeches*, 255.

20. Chesnutt to W. E. B. Du Bois, November 21, 1910, in Helen Chesnutt, *Pioneer*, 244, reprinted in Joseph R. McElrath Jr. and Robert C. Leitz, eds., *"To Be an Author": Letters of Charles W. Chesnutt, 1889–1905* (Princeton, NJ: Princeton University Press, 1997), 84.

21. W. E. B. Du Bois, "Criteria of Negro Art," *Crisis*, October 26, 1926, 296.

22. Chesnutt to Frederick R. Moore, December 15, 1910, in Chesnutt Papers, reprinted in Jesse S. Crisler, Robert C. Leitz III, and Joseph R. McElrath Jr., eds., *An Exemplary Citizen: Letters of Charles W. Chesnutt, 1906–1932* (Redwood City, CA: Stanford University Press, 2002), 87.

23. Chesnutt to Booker T. Washington, December 28, 1910, Manuscripts Division, Library of Congress, reprinted in Crisler et al., eds., *Exemplary Citizen*, 88.

17. FATHERING A RENAISSANCE

1. Helen M. Chesnutt, *Charles Waddell Chesnutt: Pioneer of the Color Line* (Chapel Hill: University of North Carolina Press, 1952), 248.

2. Helen Chesnutt, *Pioneer*, 248.

3. Helen Chesnutt, *Pioneer*, 252.

4. Helen Chesnutt, *Pioneer*, 255.

5. Chesnutt to Jessie F. Coleridge-Taylor, September 14, 1912, in the Charles W. Chesnutt Papers, 1864–1938, John Hope and Aurelia E. Franklin Library, Special Collections & Papers, Fisk University, Nashville, TN, reprinted in Jesse S. Crisler, Robert C. Leitz III, and Joseph R. McElrath Jr., eds., *An Exemplary Citizen: Letters of Charles W. Chesnutt, 1906–1932* (Redwood City, CA: Stanford University Press, 2002), 98.

6. Chesnutt to James Weldon Johnson, January 18, 1913, in Chesnutt Papers.

7. Chesnutt to Houghton, Mifflin and Company, October 8, 1921, Houghton Library, Harvard University, Cambridge, MA, reprinted in Crisler et al., eds., *Exemplary Citizen*, 150.

8. James Weldon Johnson, "Fifty Years," *New York Times*, January 1, 1913, 16.

9. John Milton Cooper Jr., *Walter Hines Page: The Southerner as American, 1855–1918* (Chapel Hill: University of North Carolina Press, 1977).

10. Chesnutt to Walter Hines Page, April 3, 1913, in Chesnutt Papers, reprinted in Crisler et al., eds., *Exemplary Citizen*, 103.

11. Page to Chesnutt, April 9, 1913, in Helen Chesnutt, *Pioneer*, 259.

12. Charles W. Chesnutt, "Race Ideals and Examples," *AME Review* 30 (October 1913): 101, reprinted in Joseph R. McElrath Jr., Robert C. Leitz III, Jesse S. Crisler, eds., *Charles W. Chesnutt: Essays and Speeches* (Redwood City, CA: Stanford University Press, 1999), 331–45.

13. Chesnutt, "Race Ideals and Examples."

14. Chesnutt, "Race Ideals and Examples."

15. W. E. B. Du Bois, *The Amenia Conference: An Historic Negro Gathering*, Troutbeck Leaflets, No. 8 (Amenia, NY: Troutbeck Press, 1925), 9.

16. Charles W. Chesnutt, "Social Discrimination," speech delivered at the Amenia Conference, Amenia, NY, August 25, 1916, in Chesnutt Papers, reprinted in McElrath et al., eds., *Chesnutt: Essays and Speeches*, 423.

17. Elizabeth McHenry, "Toward a History of Access: The Case of Mary Church Terrell," *American Literary History* 19, no. 2 (Summer 2007): 381–401.

18. Chesnutt to Joel E. Spingarn, September 1, 1916, in *Exemplary Citizen*, 125.

19. Chesnutt to Annie Joyce Cassidy, May 12, 1923, Western Reserve Historical Society Library, reprinted in Crisler et al., eds., *Exemplary Citizen*, 187.

20. Chesnutt to the Micheaux Film and Book Company, August 2, 1920, Western Reserve Historical Society, reprinted in Crisler et al., eds., *Exemplary Citizen*, 139.

21. Chesnutt to E. J. Lilly, October 16, 1916, reprinted in Crisler et al., eds., *Exemplary Citizen*, 127.

22. Chesnutt to Munson A. Havens, April 3, 1917, in Chesnutt Papers, reprinted in Crisler et al., eds., *Exemplary Citizen*, 133–34.

23. Helen Chesnutt, *Pioneer*, 277.

24. Patrick McGilligan, *Oscar Micheaux: The Great and Only: The Life of American's First Black Filmmaker* (New York: HarperCollins, 2007), 160.

25. Chesnutt to William B. Pratt, January 20, 1921, Western Reserve Historical Society Library, reprinted in Crisler et al., eds., *Exemplary Citizen*, 141.

26. Pratt to Chesnutt, January 24, 1921, Western Reserve Historical Society Library, reprinted in Crisler et al., eds., *Exemplary Citizen*.

27. Chesnutt to Micheaux, January 27, 1921, Western Reserve Historical Society, reprinted in Crisler et al., eds., *Exemplary Citizen*, 143.

28. Chesnutt to Ethel Chesnutt Williams, May 16, 1932, Western Reserve Historical Society, reprinted in Crisler et al., eds., *Exemplary Citizen*, 301.

29. McGilligan, *Oscar Micheaux*, 208–209.

30. William Stanley Braithwaite to Chesnutt, November 29, 1902, in Philip Butcher, ed., *The William Stanley Braithwaite Reader* (Ann Arbor: University of Michigan Press, 1972), 240.

31. William Stanley Braithwaite, "The Negro in Literature," *Crisis*, September 1924, 204–10.

32. Chesnutt, "The Negro in Art," *The Crisis*, November 1926, 29.

33. Chesnutt to Braithwaite, September 8, 1924, Western Reserved Historical Society, reprinted in Crisler et al., eds., *Exemplary Citizen*, 203.

34. J. E. Spingarn, introduction to Charles W. Chesnutt, *The Conjure Woman* (Boston: Houghton Mifflin, 1928).

35. Chesnutt to James Weldon Johnson, June 11, 1928, in Helen Chesnutt, *Pioneer*, 303.

36. Charles W. Chesnutt, "Remarks of Charles Waddell Chesnutt, of Cleveland, in Accepting the Spingarn Medal at Los Angeles," July 3, 1928, in Chesnutt Papers, reprinted in McElrath et al., eds., *Chesnutt: Essays and Speeches*, 510.

37. Spingarn, introduction.

38. Charles W. Chesnutt, "Post-Bellum—Pre-Harlem," *Colophon*, February 1931.

39. Helen Chesnutt, *Pioneer*, 313.

40. Benjamin Brawley to Helen Chesnutt, December 3, 1932, in Chesnutt Papers.

41. Chesnutt to Brawley, March 24, 1922, Moorland-Spingarn Research Center, reprinted in Crisler et al., eds., *Exemplary Citizen*, 162.

Index

About the Author

Kristina O'Brien

Tess Chakkalakal teaches African American and American literature at Bowdoin College. Her writing has appeared in *The New England Quarterly*, *J19*, *American Literary History*, and many other publications. She is the author of *Novel Bondage: Slavery, Marriage, and Freedom in Nineteenth-Century America*, and has coedited both *Jim Crow, Literature, and the Legacy of Sutton E. Griggs* and *Imperium in Imperio: A Critical Edition*. She lives in Brunswick, Maine.